7-26.74

The Pacific in transition

To the memory of
Robert Ho
colleague and friend

The Pacific in transition

Geographical perspectives on adaptation and change

Edited by
Harold Brookfield

ST. MARTIN'S PRESS   NEW YORK

All Rights Reserved. For information, write:
St. Martin's Press, Inc., 175 Fifth Avenue, New York, N.Y. 10010
Printed in Great Britain
Library of Congress Catalog Card Number: 73-82818
First published in the United States of America in 1973

AFFILIATED PUBLISHERS: Macmillan Limited, London,
also at Bombay, Calcutta, Madras and Melbourne

Foreword

I am very glad indeed to have the opportunity of introducing *The Pacific in Transition*, for two reasons. One is personal: all its authors have had a substantial connection with the Department of Geography which I had the honour of initiating and leading for seventeen years. The other is public: the book contributes notably to the increasing and necessary questioning of the conventional wisdom—often more conventional than wise—of the 'development expert'; of which class *pars minima fui*.

To take the personal aspect first, it is a source of legitimate pride to see so well-rounded a book, so diverse and yet so coherent, springing from my own old department; a book which, to paraphrase Samuel Johnson, borrows rays of light from diverse origins and yet brings them to a focus. In the beginnings of the Department, so many were the untouched problems of Pacific geography that it seemed that, with limited resources, any definite programmatic or 'team research' approach would omit so much as to be distorting; since omission and distortion were inherent, one might as well take the opposite tack and proceed not by assignment of men or jobs, but to find really good men dedicated to their own projects and give them free rein. This was merely intuitive, following a hunch, but it seemed to pay off: as the book itself (and much else) demonstrates, we did get a remarkable group, though we could not call it a team—and after all, 'team work' has been defined as a device for a number of people to evade the responsibility for doing poorly what any one or two of them might have done well.

Nevertheless, it would be dishonest to disguise the fact that now and then I had my qualms: had we really done anything beyond piling up more or less empirical studies in an atomistic fashion, to produce an agglomeration rather than a structure? I rejoice that

THE PACIFIC IN TRANSITION

The Pacific in transition, as it seems to me, answers with a resounding No. Though the book is by no means tailored to a thesis, it does come together in a remarkable consensus. As in every consensus, each man's adherence differs in degree; but the total effect, the drift of the various arguments, is unmistakable. In the growth of the Department, my role was protective and avuncular rather than dynamic; the tough intellectual guidance—and I am sure that all the contributors would agree—was Brookfield's. To put it in a not inappropriate way, I was the *Roko Tui*, the representative in the corridors of power; Brookfield was the *Buli*, the field executive.

To turn to the public reason, the book seems to me to be important on several counts. First, simply as a matter of methodology, it marries very happily the particular and the general and approaches, by several techniques, what Brookfield terms 'the potential interrelation of selectivity and holism'. It demonstrates, with assurance, that there is no necessary antithesis between a microgeographical approach and the search for generality (but why, oh why, do we always think and speak of *micro* and *macro*, and disregard the infinite possibilities of the *meso*?). It seems to me that *The Pacific in transition* offers at least hints towards a new way in geographical thinking, and not just a tame middle road between 'traditional' and 'new' geography. It is balanced in its discussion of the question of rationality in choice; it insists, and this is surely wise, that rationality (always imperfect since human beings are imperfect) can be justly assessed only if the *total* context is taken into the reckoning—and that means including other satisfactions than those measured by GNP or net cash returns.

The Pacific in transition challenges (not, to be sure, for the first time) the usually unstated premise of 'development': that all mankind should and shall do the same things in the same way; and it faces up to that terrible First Law of Development: to him that hath much, shall much be given. In a bad sense, we do indeed live in one world—not one of harmonious diversity but, where its links are not those of conflict, of increasing uniformity. In this mindless conformity to 'values' which give no dignity, no lasting security, no peace of mind, what possibilities of richness, perhaps even of survival, are thrown away! And this is, implicitly at least, the moral of many of these studies.

It is fortunate that Brookfield's introduction absolves me from the responsibility of checking off each essay with some neat comment;

I should very soon be out of my depth. But I cannot refrain from mentioning two, those by Clarke and Lasaqa, since these raise most poignantly the dilemma just glanced at.

Clarke's is a most moving and powerful comment on this dilemma, and he does recognize the hard fact that the poor, deprived of the goodies which the affluent take for granted, do want the development which seems, as of now, the only road to these better material things. Faced with Illich's plea for voluntary poverty, his demonstration that these better material things are mere Dead Sea fruit, surely the natural retort of the Third World is: 'How convenient that the West is finding this out *now*, when we are at last stretching out our hands.' And it is noteworthy that both Clarke and Illich call the computer to the aid of the simpler life. . . . To have our cake and eat it too, that is what we all want, and—as Clarke makes amply clear—there is simply no easy way out of this dilemma.

Lasaqa's paper is a most appropriate coda to a collection in which every essay is concerned with the need to see the processes of change against the background of deeply-held values not our own, to understand the rationale of those values, to try to see things with the eyes of those who have to cope with the forces of modernization not by means of words on paper, of graphs and models, but in their daily lives. I would add but one rider: research results 'pertinent to the welfare of the local people' must include negative findings when these are firmly based on evidence. But a careful regard to Lasaqa's own evidence and argument would surely produce results most pertinent to the welfare of the researcher—to his intellectual welfare, by forcing him to examine his own assumptions, which is always good for one, though often disconcerting.

This is a book of good will, but not of easy optimism; but what honest student of human affairs, not blinded by the cults of bigness and newness, dare be optimistic in face of the follies and horrors of our age? Yet there remains to mankind an immense potential of resilience and, as their history shows, the peoples of the Pacific are far from the least endowed with this saving grace. If, however, we are to make good use of this potential, we must avoid the broad blind alleys of easy 'improvement', must get rid of illusions, and must seek, ardently and from both sides, an understanding of worlds not our own. To these ends this book makes a real and substantial contribution.

London, July 1973   O. H. K. SPATE

List of plates

The publishers' thanks are due to Harold Brookfield for permission to reproduce the photographs listed below.

Between pp. 76 and 77:

1   The village in transition
2   Intensive cultivation
3   Garden close-up
4   The traditional *koro*
5   The traditional food complex
6   The traditional *koro*
7   Modern village
8   Urban produce market
9   An old Pacific port-town
10 Cooking food with modern aids in a traditional setting
11 The continuing Pacific
12 Change and tradition in personal decoration
13 The traditional wealth

Between pp. 236 and 237:

14 The Pacific of dreams
15 The island Pacific
16 Change at sea
17 At the end of the line
18 Larger inter-island vessels
19 Island trader
20 The new Pacific
21 The new industrial economy
22 Village in the forest
23 The entry of international capital
24 Development basic
25 Dis-development
26 The new Pacific
27 Casualty of development
28 Modern port-city

Contents

ix

PERSPECTIVES ON CHANGE

xi

Notes on contributors

OSKAR SPATE: Professor of Pacific History, Australian National University. Ph.D. (Cantab.), 1936. At A.N.U. since 1951 as Professor of Geography, and from 1967 to 1972 as Director of the Research School of Pacific Studies.

HAROLD BROOKFIELD: Professor of Geography, McGill University, Montreal, Quebec. Ph.D. (London), 1950. At A.N.U. from 1957 to 1969, as Senior Research Fellow, and later Professorial Fellow in Geography.

ERIC WADDELL: Assistant Professor of Geography, McGill University, Montreal, Quebec. Ph.D. (A.N.U.), 1969. At A.N.U. 1963 to 1968, as Research Assistant in the New Guinea Research Unit, later as Scholar.

DAVID LEA: Professor of Geography, University of Papua and New Guinea. Ph D. (A.N.U.), 1964. At A.N.U. 1960 to 1963, as Scholar.

ROGER FRAZER: Reader in Geography, University of Waikato, New Zealand. Ph.D. (A.N.U.), 1962. At A.N.U. 1958 to 1961, as Scholar.

ALARIC MAUDE: Senior Lecturer in Geography, Flinders University of South Australia. Ph.D. (A.N.U.), 1965. At A.N.U. 1961 to 1964, as Scholar.

RICHARD BEDFORD: Lecturer in Geography, University of Canterbury, New Zealand. Ph.D. (A.N.U.), 1971. At A.N.U. 1968 to 1971, as Scholar.

IAN HUGHES: Research Fellow, New Guinea Research Unit. Ph.D. (A.N.U.), 1971. At A.N.U. since 1967, as Scholar until 1971.

ALASTAIR COUPER: Professor of Maritime Studies, Univesity of Wales Institute of Science and Technology. Ph.D. (A.N.U.), 1967. At A.N.U. 1964 to 1966, as Scholar.

DIANA HOWLETT: Research Fellow in Geography, Australian National University. Ph.D. (A.N.U.), 1962. At A.N.U. 1959 to 1962, as Scholar, then as Research Assistant, New Guinea Research Unit.

WILLIAM CLARKE: Senior Research Fellow in Geography, Australian National University. Ph.D. (California), 1968. Joined A.N.U. as Research Fellow in 1969.

ISIRELI LASAQA: Permanent Secretary, Ministry for Fijian Affairs and Rural Development, Government of Fiji. Ph.D. (A.N.U.), 1968. At A.N.U. 1965 to 1968, as Scholar.

Editor's introduction

This is a book by a group of geographers united by a common environment. All of us have at some time been members of the Department of Geography (since 1968 the Department of Human Geography, following the separation of our inhuman colleagues) in the Research School of Pacific Studies in the Australian National University. All of us have also worked in the Pacific islands on problems involving prolonged field-work either in rural areas or on the sea. All of us have felt a certain unity of spirit arising from our common experience, and this common bond was enhanced both by separation from like-minded geographers far away in other continents and, more particularly, by a substantial gulf that during the 1960s came to separate us not only from traditionalists, but also from innovative geographers of very different persuasion. One could almost say that this book was born of irritation, for while our urban and economic colleagues could point to a large stream of literature progressively colonizing the major journals, we seemed for several years to be hoeing our own row in the wilderness.

We felt the need to present ourselves more coherently as a group, and about 1968 two or three of us began to talk about a book of this kind. In 1969, just before my departure from Canberra, a rather more serious discussion took place over beer at the A.N.U. Staff Club, leading to a firm base of agreement. Later that year, as dark winter began to close in around University Park, Pennsylvania, I wrote off a series of letters which led to the proposal that I took to the publishers in London, in January 1970. All but one of those approached agreed to write, and though it has been touch and go at times, all but one who agreed have in the end come through with their contributions. My apologies go to certain contributors for the deviousness that I have used in order to speed their writing. There have been inevitable delays as individuals became over-committed, and some eighteen months have elapsed between receipt of the first essay and the last. To the eleven substantive essays I have added an introductory piece which tries to extract the collective meaning of the whole.

Despite the diversity of our subject-matter, the years separating our major field-work and the fact that we have never all met as one group, we are united in believing that a 'school of thought', however small, can arise within a discipline in the presence of common experience. In our case the common environment has two main elements, the one no less important than the other. First was our base in a very unusual research school, where academics of different generations, disciplines and persuasions came together and were free to work on the problems of a corner of the earth. Second was the field, the islands themselves, where all of us have spent much time. Our meetings have been there as well as in Canberra, and our 'seminars' were not only formal discussions but also meetings by some airstrip, or in a 'haus kunai' by the light of a hissing pressure lamp. This experience more than anything else has helped to forge a common outlook, a 'view from within' a region undergoing the revolutionary experience of colonial change and decolonization.

This emerges in what we have written. As I indicate in Chapter 1, our initial purpose was somewhat different from the book now collected. When I saw that this was happening, I asked Isireli Lasaqa, the only Pacific islander among us, if he would agree to write on the work of the rest of us as he saw it, rather than on his own substantive material. This he has done, very handsomely, and I build a large part of my introductory chapter on what he has to say. Change and adaptation have become our main themes, calling into question our contribution as geographers to the study of the profound transformation taking place in the Pacific, as elsewhere in the Third World. We believe that our common method has given us a distinctive outlook in this task.

Somewhat arbitrarily, the essays have been divided into two groups, the one concerned primarily with adaptation, the other with change. There is inevitable overlap in approach, but a distinction does seem to emerge that is perhaps more obvious at each end than in the middle. The essays cover a wide range, in territory, in subject-matter and in approach and methodology. Some will

xvi

seem to range quite far outside the 'normal' ambit of geography; but perhaps the widening of this ambit, and demonstration of the fascinating research frontiers indicated and developed on the interdisciplinary periphery in the context of this island world, constitute our main claim to notice.

All the essays have been standardized, some edited quite substantially, and my thanks go first to a group of authors who have endured such treatment and yet remained friends. The maps and diagrams are an important part of the whole, and to our pleasure it has been possible for Ian Heyward, who has drawn so many other maps for many of us, to draw these in the map room of the Canberra department. His talented work is greatly appreciated by us all. Several of us have thanks to individuals, but this is the place in which to offer our collective thanks to the Australian National University, which supported almost all our field-work and gave us such excellent support in other ways. A wisely tolerant policy of research funding by the Australian government, administered through the A.N.U., was based on the individual rather than on the cramping research proposal formulated in advance, and permitted us the flexibility of approach which made experiment possible. We would like to think of this book as our united appreciation of that confidence.

In Canberra, we must also offer thanks to Sir John Crawford, Director of the Research School of Pacific Studies from 1959 until 1967, who created an environment so conducive to productive work. And more particularly we must also thank his successor as Director, and the head of our Department until 1967, Oskar Spate. Some of us, including myself, have had invaluable guidance from him at different stages in our work, and to all of us his warm support was never failing—if at times tempered a little by alarm at the size of our demands. He is contributing a Foreword to this book.

It would be unseemly of me not to thank also another University. McGill has given me a freedom as great as I enjoyed in Canberra, to complete a job which impinges only indirectly on my present work. My colleagues and students here include several of like mind to our Canberra group, and I hope they will accept this book as a contribution to their ongoing and innovative work among the people of developing countries. Though the historical and cultural contexts of the Caribbean, Latin America, maritime eastern Canada and the Arctic are unlike those of the Pacific in many ways, many of the problems are strikingly parallel, and I hope our mutual exchanges have been as profitable to my friends here as they have been to me. Much of the work done from this Department has a great deal in common with our work from Canberra. Unfortunately we lack any comparable institutional and national encouragement, but perhaps this renders the contribution made in McGill to forging this kind of geography all the more notable.

Here in Montreal I offer particular thanks to my former secretary, Mary Thomson, who retyped many manuscripts, and helped me correspond with the authors, with cheerful enthusiasm and interest. Judy Liske has retyped the rest with equal cheer. John Brookfield and Christian Girault helped me with the job of ordering and cross-checking the bibliography. And last of all, but not least, my thanks go to a publishing house already renowned for its encouragement toward experiment in geography, with whom it has been at all times a pleasure to deal. Particular thanks are due to John Davey for suggesting the title of this collection.

Department of Geography,   HAROLD BROOKFIELD
  McGill University, Montreal
Autumn 1972

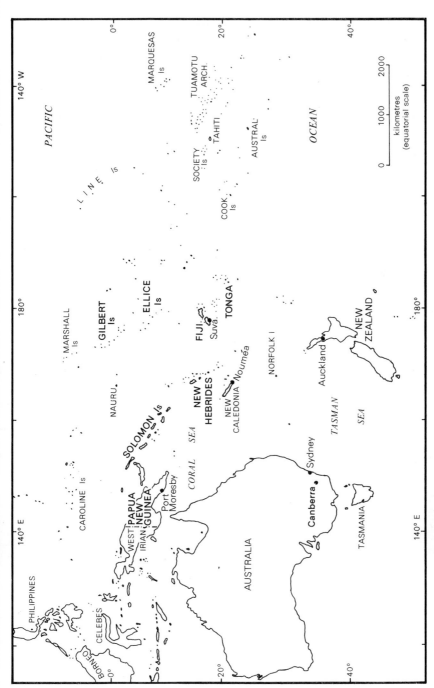

Fig. 0.1 The South Pacific: areas mentioned in the text

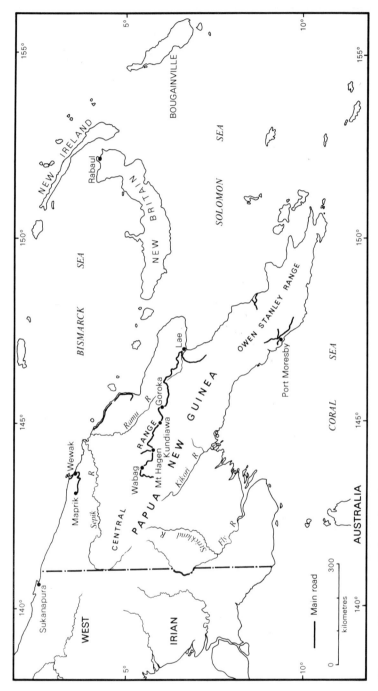

Fig. 1.1 Papua New Guinea: location map

Perspectives on adaptation

1 Explaining or understanding?

The study of adaptation and change

Harold Brookfield

The purpose of this general essay is to introduce the twelve specific essays that follow it. Like almost all collections of this nature, the present book has worked out in a way different from the original plan. Our initial objective was to show the interrelation of changing methodology in geography with changing subject-matter in a region passing from colonialism to independence during the fifteen years covered by our work. Little of this ambitious if rather *recherché* objective remains, for almost all of us have found ourselves carried directly into the problems themselves, and our methodology has synthesized our experience through time, rather than demonstrated its evolution. Change, and adaptation to change, dominate the collection: in writing we have found ourselves within the problem and looking outward toward method and generalization. What we collectively have to say thus seems to arise directly from this immersion in the problems of a region and its people; yet there is a wider message, and it seems to have three parts. First is the nature of our methodology and its relation to the so-called 'new geography'; second is the particular contribution offered by micro-geographic method as followed by us all; third is the role of the geographer in studying a region undergoing revolutionary change.

NOT-NEW-GEOGRAPHY?

Is the real world really necessary?

The upheaval which created the quantitative revolution and the 'new geography' arose from cumulative dissatisfaction with an emphasis on description bequeathed to the subject by Vidal de la Blache and reformulated, under the sobriquet of 'differentiation',

3

by Hartshorne, following Hettner. But quantification was not the only element in that revolution, nor in the long run is it the most important. More universally significant has been a new emphasis on rigour in the formulation of hypotheses or questions, and in the search for explanations or answers. Inevitably, this rigour has led us to shift our emphasis from differentiation to process, so that we have advanced from a direct concern with man/environment relationships to the more complex problem of seeking interrelationship between temporal process and spatial pattern (Harvey, 1969).

Adoption of this higher-level paradigm has both made geography more challenging as a discipline and also brought it into much closer relationship with other social sciences. But whereas the new paradigm logically builds on the old and incorporates it, the practice has rather often been to disregard the old and proceed via abstraction in order more swiftly to advance to theory. When the physical environment has been nailed down flat and featureless, then the real work can begin. By extension, the human environment can also be nailed down in the same form, and with the same advantages. We can thus have a geography that is environment-free and value-free or, if this distresses us too much, we can allow selected elements to peep up one at a time in order that their distorting effect may be examined.

The result is something rather close to spatial economics, yet much more catholic and fertile than that somewhat arid discipline. The environment of the new geographers has contained a great many more practical souls who have encouraged them never to lose sight of the real world on which the discipline has traditionally rested. Much of immense value has emerged from two decades of rising insistence on theory. In particular, we have learned to seek universals first and particularities second. We have been provided with a valuable armoury of statistical and mathematical tools to enable us to do this. We have found that many basic principles are both cross-cultural and scale-free. And we continue to do so, as the rise of general systems theory greatly widens our ability to deal with diverse phenomena in parallel formats. The emergence of a new 'general geography' based on theoretical principles—an idea widely derided when Bunge proposed it only a decade ago—can already be seen in outline.

But a fundamental question of direction and purpose arises, and is being faced more and more insistently since the publication of

4

Harvey's prolegomena to a theoretical geography, in 1969.* Is the core of the discipline to be its structure of theory, converting the rest of the field into an 'applied' geography, or is it to lie in the spatial patterns of the real world, in whose explanation formal theory is but the most powerful aid? One suspects that the decision has been taken in favour of the latter, but that the implications have not fully been faced. Before considering a collection of essays such as the present, it is important that we examine this question a little more closely.

Noise and triviality

If we are concerned with theory, then a great deal of local or cultural particularity becomes noise of various hues. If I am desirous (as the Australians would say) of explaining the land-use patterns of Chimbu in terms of general theory, then I would proceed, as I do in Chapter 5, to test various hypotheses statistically and go further in this direction than I have done, and I would end by being very disappointed at the low values for explained variance. I might modify the raw data, sample within my samples, introduce correction factors and other devices to eliminate the level of noise, and probably still remain disappointed. Or I might find my poor results sufficiently consistent as to be 'not discouraging' and thus end in a position rather parallel with the testers of central place theory.

If, on the other hand, my objective is to understand the totality of the spatial pattern, I find that my hypothesis-testing helps me by showing that there is an underlying regularity, but that there is a great deal left that I must explain in other ways. I might find that all that I have 'explained' is the obvious, though it may be important to establish the obvious in order to avoid the sin of cultural particularism. Bedford (1971) had a similar experience, though he does not report it in Chapter 8. As a stage in his studies of New Hebridean internal migration, he performed a most comprehensive series of tests of the gravity model, and other hypotheses involving curve-fitting. He found limited results which explained the obvious, leaving him the greater part of the work still to do, and it is this that he reports here. In work still in preparation, Lesley Key of McGill has had an even more chastening experience. Hypothesiz-

* Especially in a number of articles published in the *Canadian Geographer*. Those by Guelke (1971) and Harris (1971) are perhaps the most noteworthy.

5

ing that Indians released from plantation servitude in nineteenth-century Guyana would migrate more and more freely away from the plantation as time passed, she fitted curves to painstakingly-re-searched data on destinations at selected dates, and found no significant difference through time. Yet the nature of the destinations had changed, and her job of explanation remained before her. In none of these instances was the quantitative hypothesis-testing without real value, but in each the researcher had to conclude that the particularities—or seeming particularities—constituted the greater part of 'explanation'.

Particularities, or seeming particularities—this is the nub of the problem. The poor or trival results of much testing of general theory at its present stage do not indicate that general explanation is impossible. Most certainly they do not indicate that we should return to some form of Vidalian concern with the unique. But they do indicate that our efforts in the direction of general explanation are as yet so young that we need an immensely greater quantity of hard data, analysed through rigorous use of comparative method, before we can even begin to talk in terms of satisfactory explanation through general theory. And this is nowhere so true as in dealing with the developing, or 'third' world.

Theories for the Third World

Social science, with the economists in the van, burst on the developing countries after World War II with only a slight discordance between the Keynesian and neo-classical trumpeters. All problems would be solved and the walls of underdevelopment would quickly tumble. A crescendo was reached in the early 1960s, with the opening of the First Development Decade, the aerodynamic fantasies* of W. W. Rostow's (1960) 'non-communist manifesto', and the confident elaboration of modernization theory by sociologists, political scientists and later by some geographers. The result of all this is well known; unsought consequences of simple remedies are legion, and the literature is becoming spattered with *post mortem* inquiries. The world has never witnessed so enthusiastic an application of formal theory to practical problems. Hypotheses were tested by experiment on a massive scale, but the 'level of explained variance' was unfortunately rather low—with consequences that have to be reaped by the succeeding generation.

* This apt phrase belongs to my student, Mr. K. Wachiira.

6

In the shadow of these developments another debate has been more quietly evolving on the issue of appropriate methods and theories for the study of and dealings with non-Western societies. It began among anthropologists, and has spread massively into economics in the last few years. The argument is in fact a very old one, and can be traced back to the origins of colonialism by those so minded: it has been latent in much writing in modern times, in geography as in other disciplines.

The problem has many dimensions, but several of these resolve into a set of fundamental issues most clearly delineated in a recent exchange between I. C. Jarvie and Peter Winch (*in* Borger and Cioffi, 1970, 231–69). The questions are how we should attempt to analyse an alien society and, by implication, how we should compare one society against another. Can we avoid imposition of any values and view a society and its institutions and beliefs simply in their own right by their own standards of truth and falsity? Alternatively, should we quite openly use our own society or some other, and its collective wisdom, as a 'sounding board' or standard of measure, and determine truth and falsity by these 'objective' standards?* This is not simply an ethical and philosophical issue, for it has important corollaries. If we take the two alternatives at the extreme positions, the first implies the denial of any rational comparison or general theory, while the second implies the necessity of comparison in all instances and over all phenomena. And if we weaken the alternatives to bring them closer together, we admit of some comparison in the one position, and deny the possibility of universal theory in the other.

All the evidence suggests that only some such intermediate position can be justified on present knowledge, except that we can sustain the concept of universals over a limited and essentially physical range of human phenomena.† But behaviour, economic or otherwise, is not among these, and this is crucial for the social sciences. Rather different attempts to deal with the difficulty are being evolved. Almost wholly within Western societies, the behavi-

* Paradoxically, it is the latter approach that is usually termed 'value-free'!
† If neuroscientists in fact succeed in establishing that all basic causal connections of the brain and nervous system can be explained in neurophysiological terms, then the *potential* range of universal theory will be enormously expanded. But this is not likely to be of much help in the practical problems facing social scientists of our generation.

oural movement, which has burgeoned since 1955, has attempted to take account of variations in human behaviour and cognitive perception; but it does not prove easy to translate the methods and concepts of this school into a developing country context. The so-called 'structural' school of economics has arisen about the same time, mainly among Latin American economists, giving weight not so much to perception as to the structures of economies and the institutions of society. Geographers of developing countries have made variable direct use of these innovations; but independently of the economists many of us have given considerable weight to the structures and institutions of societies and economies; similar trends are also apparent in the work of social urban geographers, in developed and developing countries alike.

These latter approaches have in common an attempt to blend use of deductive theory and standardized comparison with a vision of internal perception and cognition, and with an understanding of the structures and institutions of society. The method is strongly empirical, and while it does not entail any rejection of the search for universal principles and laws, it does require that theorizing over the larger body of phenomena lying beyond established laws proceed inductively, from the ground up, and from within outward. Our appeal to our colleagues is comparable with that made by Polly Hill (1966) when she pleaded for an 'indigenous economics' which would take account of differing values, emphases and institutions; Lasaqa here echoes her plea in Chapter 12. We must compare, but by standards that require empirical justification, that are not unthinking implementation. In particular, we must reject the idea of any simple continuum of progress along a histori-cally-determined course. As Djilas (1969, 78–9) argues, 'higher' and 'lower' forms are categories based on human knowledge and conceptions of time. There is nothing absolute about them. We are able to comprehend because man has enormous powers of cognition, but 'we can never gain final understanding because of the measureless dimensions and innumerable aspects of the real world'. It is by such humility, and striving—rather than prematurely 'by our theories' (Harvey, 1969, 486)—that this group of geographers hopes to be known.*

* This reference to David Harvey's slogan for geographers in the 1970s—'By our theories you shall know us'—perhaps sums up a difference which is more of emphasis than of kind. Harvey visited Canberra in 1968, and several of us then

SEARCH FOR UNDERSTANDING

The 'inner workings of systems'

Explanation and understanding have closely-related meanings in common parlance, and even in scientific writing they are sometimes used almost interchangeably. But there is also a strict scientific meaning of 'explanation', implying the specification or imputation of causal relationships and, more particularly, a process of logical deduction. Understanding, or making sense of, is a more catholic process; it may incorporate reasons and expectations and is far more diffuse. Explanation proceeds from defined premises to defined *explicanda*; in relation to explanation, the role of understanding is to ensure that the premises and *explicanda* themselves have meaning.

Many of us here are concerned with adaptation, whether to on-going variables or to secular change. Using a variety of methods, but particularly through conceptual systems, elaborated to varying degrees, we attempt to explain adaptation. But in doing so we find we have to deal with behaviour that by 'objective' standards seems irrational: Lea's discussion in Chapter 3 is a striking illustration. To deal with such behaviour we have to detach explanation from the world of objective or material phenomena, and move into the world of cognitive perception within a particular social and economic system. Couper faces a similar problem in Chapter 9; he shifts from material explanation partly to preferences between perceived alternatives, and partly to the contrasted structures of a dual economy. None of us who face this problem discards the assumption that behaviour is intentionally rational; but in essence we assume also that it is imperfectly rational, being based on less-than-complete search procedure and incomplete evaluation of possible outcomes. It is not easy, or even feasible, to apply the logic of decision theory to such behaviour, but understanding makes it possible to arrive at a structured 'explanation'.

It is often remarked that idiosyncratic variations can be subsumed within a set of assumptions in dealing with large aggregates. But when it becomes necessary to explore such variations in

---

there derived great benefit from his trenchant advice and are still thinking over our discussions with him. But we found his advocacy of logical positivism hard to relate to our own problems. Harvey has since found his own involvement in reality, but we fear we cannot claim credit: his own common sense, and deep humanity, have led to a result surely predictable on *a priori* grounds. . . .

9

order to establish assumptions, it follows conversely that the scale of analysis must be magnified. All attempts to establish a valid intermediate standpoint between the unique and the universal demand that we study the nature of variations in a cautiously comparative manner. Basically, this requirement is the reason for the abrupt liberalization of scale in human geographical inquiry of which our work has formed a part. We sought to explore the inner workings of systems in order better to establish generalities.

Microgeographic method

We thus became microgeographers in order that we might be better macrogeographers. We were not seeking examples, or samples, of regions or societies or economies. We left regional description to the field of pedagogic writing, while regional analysis became deeply infused by the newer methods of regional science. We felt it more productive to know a lot about a little than to know a little about a lot. We sought intrinsic connections between phenomena by research in depth, as a first stage leading through comparison and abstraction to the generation of theory.

In this effort there has been continuing experimentation with scale and combination of scales. Much of the variation in area and population that has been covered is exhibited here. Thus among the earlier field workers Frazer (Chapter 4) covered a whole Province of Fiji; I dealt (Chapter 6) with an area of only a few square kilometres, but one that included parts of the territory of several social groups and the whole of only two; Howlett (Chapter 10) worked in three village communities and their lands, chosen to exemplify different ecological conditions, population densities and distance from the town. Lea (Chapter 3) also worked in two communities, contrasted initially in population density, later in many other respects also. Later, Waddell (Chapter 2) based his inquiries on a single community, and gathered most of his data from only a few families within it.

Insofar as there has been a trend, however, it has been towards a clearer definition of the meaning of a microstudy. My topographically-defined area would have been improved for some purposes by shedding its outlying pieces of 'foreign' group territory, but its selection led to an emphasis on inter-group relations that has been of importance in subsequent theorizing. Maude and Bedford (Chapters 7 and 8) used microgeographic method in order to obtain data

10

that could not be had within the wider territorial frame given to their whole inquiries. Hughes and Couper (Chapters 5 and 9) did not base their research in a single community at all; they were concerned with the networks linking communities, whether in the traditional or modern economy, and their populations were the traders and the crews of ships. In what sense can we call work of this scale a 'microstudy'?

The terms 'micro' and 'macro' have rather different meanings in different disciplines. Except in the minds of scale-bound geographers, however, the distinction is essentially functional. Thus microeconomics is concerned with the firm; macroeconomics with larger organized aggregates. The size of the firm is not directly relevant, nor does it immediately affect analysis to know whether the firm has only a single plant, or a dispersed group of plants. There is a similar unity with us. Our microgeographic work is concerned with some particular, isolable and meaningful element, whether this is a community or the linkages between communities. Macrogeographic work, by contrast, is concerned with aggregates. Data of rather different kinds are accessible at one level, but not at the other. Larger problems such as population distribution, migration and the production of some particular crop can be analysed effectively only at the macro level. But questions concerning the reasons for migration and its effects can be answered best at the micro level, where it is possible to examine the connections between migration and other activities and phenomena. Coffee production in central New Guinea is a macro-level problem, but the effects of the coffee innovation, and the reasons for variable response to economic incentives are micro-level inquiries. Production of goods for indigenous trade is best approached first by macrogeographic examination; examination of the trading networks calls for specialized inquiry; to go beyond this and investigate the interconnections between trade, production and consumption at the community level would require a broadening of the subject matter, but a sharp narrowing of the areal coverage.

Our experimentation thus encourages a completely flexible attitude towards the question of scale, and an awareness of the complementary relationships, not just of microgeographic and macrogeographic research, but also of different forms and scales of inquiry within each. The essential criterion is quite simply the nature of the question. Where our problem has called for an areal overview we

THE PACIFIC IN TRANSITION

have worked at this level; where it has required sampling and we have had the means to do this, we have sampled; where it has called for investigation of interconnections in depth, we have not hesitated to narrow the focus to a single village, an areally-dispersed population of individual traders, or only a few families or farms. But our admitted preference has been for the last of these approaches, for it is in this way that we have been able most readily to approach understanding.

The problems of understanding

But if the central quality of microgeographic method is the gain in access to understanding, we run up against a rather serious question: how far have we succeeded? In Chapter 12, Lasaqa tells us very clearly that the interpretative powers of expatriates are limited, and that in their beleaguered state of mind under colonialism, islanders take pleasure in the inability of outsiders to comprehend the rich nuances of their culture and society. We can all confirm this and in particular recount the extreme difficulty often experienced in overcoming reluctance to offer information of any complexity. Lea was studying yam cultivation, but it took him some months to get information on named varieties within the basic classes; the Abelam told him that they had wished to save him work.* In Chimbu, Paula Brown and I did not get beyond the conceptualization of Chimbu social structure as enshrined in the government record until the last days of our first field season. And while I have known the significance of some symbolic designs in woodwork for many years, I am still likely to be told by Chimbu informants that they are mere idle decoration. To overcome these reticences demands patience and persistence, and especially a willingness to listen tirelessly to the garrulous from whom the breakthrough frequently comes, if it comes at all.

The nub of the problem arises where our understanding of social structure and cognitive perception either governs our interpretation, or permits an interpretation alternative to one derived by

* Lea had other credibility problems. Abelam ceremonial yams may not be grown or approached by anyone having sexual intercourse. When he was alone in the field he was allowed into the gardens freely, but after his wife arrived was permitted to view them only over the fence. One long yam had been planted in his name while he was unaccompanied, and he did not doubt that it would continue to grow well after the arrival of his wife. He was wrong, however: the yam died.

12

objective consideration. There are three possible paths, and all are exhibited in this collection. We may rest wholly or mainly on our understanding of internal structures and perceptions; we may note a total or partial conflict; we may impose an objective structure of explanation which rationalizes conscious responses and assumes unconscious adaptations.

In this book, Frazer in Chapter 4 and Couper in Chapter 9 rely most heavily on internal structures and perceptions. Frazer 'explains' the persistence of the Fijian village through change by its continuing value as a social institution to the Fijians themselves; Couper argues that the main reasons for the failure of Pacific islanders in commercial marine enterprises is the conflict between the demands of commercial success and the qualities of the island social systems as perceived by the islanders. Bedford, in Chapter 8, finds an essentially parallel reason for the persistence of circular migration based on the village in the New Hebrides; though he couches this in theoretical terms, the observation preceded the use of theory.

Bedford, like Maude in Chapter 7, also sought evidence to link migration from particular areas with perceived land shortage. In work not reported here, he made a serious attempt to examine land availability in selected islands, but he found so little evidence to support any perceived connection with migratory behaviour that he tacitly deleted the hypothesis from his research. Maude finds very definite objective evidence that land shortage in parts of Tonga is impoverishing both the resource base and the freedom of individual action. However, he is unable to find any clear indication that this condition is either consciously linked with migratory behaviour, or is generating an awareness of need for agricultural intensification. In making this test of Mrs Boserup's theory of agricultural change, he reaches a verdict of 'not proven'.

In sharpest contrast to this approach we have Waddell's in Chapter 2, consisting of the imposition of a total structure on the whole man/environment system, involving automatic switches and regulatory mechanisms to determine class of response, and very definitely linking behaviour with ecosystem maintenance and population balance. This develops the approach pioneered by Rappaport (1967) and by other advocates of systems modelling. Waddell's abstraction incorporates his understanding of the Raiapu Enga, but he nowhere suggests that these elaborate interconnections form part of their cognized system. He is therefore assuming a set of

13

unconscious responses. Like the work of our McGill colleague, W. B. Kemp,* whose help he acknowledges, this systemization is in some measure parallel to the efforts of neuroscientists to establish wholly causal relationships in the brain and nervous system, referred to above: understanding of society in great depth is fundamental to its construction, but the necessary assumption of automatic response patterns will not appeal to all.

Waddell's interpretation is cyclic but also closed: he does not incorporate the effects of external change. Lea, whose use of systems modelling in Chapter 3 is far less elaborated, concerns himself very specifically with change during colonial time, and runs into an acute difficulty. Initially, he recognized 'perceived stress' in the Wosera and found it to be isomorphic with 'objective stress'. Later, he saw that while the objective conditions had deteriorated, the perceived state of affairs had improved. He relies heavily on stated reasons in his rationalization of this conflict. Lea and Waddell are methodologically in substantial agreement in dealing with the biological subsystem: however, Lea's insistence on the need to 'understand a community's changing values and aspirations' may be interpreted to cast doubt on the tenacity of a cultural subsystem when its analysis is projected through a period of change.

This was also my problem, partly reviewed in Chapter 6 and partly in earlier writing. Without formalizing a systemic diagram I also find a fairly tightly-constructed cyclic system, characterized by expansion and retreat and locational bipolarity.† But into and over this have come changes of a more far-reaching kind than those described by Lea, and unlike the other writers I have been able to observe these changes frequently through much of their history. I have been aware of very substantial differences through time in aspiration levels, and of several of the swings between optimism and

* Kemp's work exceeds in depth anything reported here, being based on a population of only 27 Eskimo at Lake Harbour, Baffin Land, studied and known as individuals over a period of nine years. Kemp's (1971) attempt to present the man/environment system of these people in systemic terms is notable both for its pioneering quantification of energetics in this context, and also as by far the most profound effort to date in the use of systems theory in human ecology.

† However, I part company with Waddell and other writers to some degree by arguing that the Chimbu pig cycle is socially determined, in that numbers of livestock are not permitted to rise to a level at which stress becomes evident until the organizing of a new pig-killing ceremony becomes desirable for other reasons. This removes a major material determinant from my parallel 'system'.

14

pessimism such as have been caught at two poles by Lea. Yet when I come to analyse my data I find these ephemeral changes less clearly reflected, and the tenacity of the underlying system more apparent than I had supposed.

Lasaqa is entirely right that it is very difficult to achieve understanding, and especially so for an expatriate who is unfamiliar with the internal workings of even a closely comparable society. The very thought patterns are different, in that they relate to an unfamiliar set of objects and concepts, and to a set of values which vary somewhat from those of the researcher. Whether or not one proceeds to the formality of a constructed system, one is seeking from the outset to find order and meaning in the disorderly and trivial. Aware of the need to understand, one listens and selectively accepts—as Lasaqa did to the Tadhimboko, who in their turn saw him as representative of a society whose colonial experience *they* conceived as parallel to their own. In my own experience I was for long too ready to seek orthomorphism between objective comprehension and perceived understanding: I first organized Chimbu perception of land into categories meaningful in terms of my own geographical training; I later structured Chimbu responses to innovation in terms that related to at least one view of development theory. Finally came the crunch; with my predictions thrown awry I looked anew at my assembled data and saw in them underlying systemic regularities that I could discern only at a level beyond the perception of the people I was studying. I thus fell back on explanation rather than understanding, but on an explanation enormously enriched by my efforts to understand. The very questions I asked had changed, and as I sought answers I mentally ticked off what was reasonable or unreasonable in terms of my understanding.

I think that we must therefore accept these different weightings given to external theory, internal 'understanding' and synthesized system as a set of partial contributions towards comprehension of the whole truth. Djilas, cited above, remarks rightly that complete understanding is beyond us, notwithstanding the limitless powers of cognition of the human mind. But each individual finds a new piece of the whole truth, and so understanding grows collectively, and explanation—that partial aid to complete understanding—improves with time. And even if we have only partly succeeded, there is another solid benefit from trying. We do not emerge from the experience of living among and depending on a host group, trying to see the world through their eyes, without becoming different people ourselves. We have absorbed something of the outlooks and perceptions of people whose whole world is radically different from our own. This much at least we carry away with us and, if we are thoughtful and concerned, it colours all that we write, say and do for the rest of our lives.

SOCIAL RELEVANCE AND DEVELOPMENT

A digression on unnecessary originality

To judge from some recent developments in the United States, it would seem that the great new geographical discovery of the early 1970s is the challenge presented by real public issues in the real world.* We herald the emergence of a new 'radical geography' and of a group termed Socially and Ecologically Responsible Geographers under the leadership of Wilbur Zelinsky. We are invited to consider a new 'revolution of social responsibility' in the discipline. It is good to see this, and to hope that some dignity may now be afforded the pioneer efforts of Bunge and his associates in the geographical study of urban poverty in American cities; but one must respectfully submit that it is new only within the context of the United States. And the United States is not the world, contrary to rumours widely disseminated.

For at least a generation geographers concerned with developing countries (including many Americans) have been intimately involved with problems of poverty and underdevelopment. Many of the much-derided regional geographers have had things to say on the subject. Some who have worked in the Third World have been writing a 'radical geography', in various places that would publish them, for many years before 1971. But perhaps we who work outside the heartlands have one advantage to compensate for our otherwise peripheral status: we read what the others write, but they do not always see the same necessity.

Without listing all our relevant writings, this group of geographers could fairly claim to have found a necessity for involvement in public issues many years ago. Not all of us have accepted it with equal enthusiasm, for many still adhere to the belief that academic study

---

* See, for example, the reviews of the 1971 meeting of the Association of American Geographers in *Area* (Prince and Smith, 1971), or the new publication *Antipode*, issued from Clark University.

16

should be divorced from value judgments and try to live this belief. But in developing-area studies it is less and less easy to separate private beliefs from professional writing, and for most of us it is now several years since we passed the threshold of discontent which forced us to abandon the distinction.*

View from the periphery

Our private beliefs are not necessarily radical in the political sense, but they do flow from a concern for people disadvantaged by public and private policies that show scant concern for people in the periphery, and whose economies are organized in ways that do not satisfy the criteria of a 'modernized society'. This is inevitably our view of development, for we have worked away from the growth-poles or 'centres'; in Myrdalian terms we are more aware of 'backwash' than of 'spread'; by our whole experience we find the macro-economic approaches of most development writings unsatisfactory and even dangerous.

Several of these essays reveal this outlook. With the exception of Waddell and Hughes, whose subject-matter in this instance excludes any consideration of development, we all are concerned with modern change to greater or lesser degree. The gentlest in their expression of views are Bedford, Frazer and Maude. Bedford argues for an understanding of the real nature of urbanization in the New Hebrides before scarce resources are committed to urban housing designed for a great body of permanent migrants.† This is not to discount the need for a new urban housing policy, as his own context makes clear, but to ask for an understanding of New Hebridean habits before unsuitable developments are undertaken. Frazer's message is similar, and closely reflects that of Lasaqa's closing essay: the shape of the future should reflect the continuing desires of the Fijians themselves. Maude, writing of an independent Kingdom, avoids the delicate issue of land redistribution in Chap-

* Certain of my colleagues in this book would not go along with this statement. The content of their writings would suggest that they are a minority, but they have my apologies: I do not pretend to speak for all.

† It would seem he has little to fear. The need for low-cost housing in Vila was first pointed out by the survey in which I participated in 1965. Several committees have since sat on the matter, land has been acquired, and in 1969 a plan was prepared closely resembling a suburb of an English new town. But nothing had been done up to 1972.

ter 7, but warns that cash cropping is creating potentially serious problems of access to land.

Lea is concerned that the government of Papua New Guinea take advantage of an improved outlook in a depressed area, and suggests that policies based on development *in situ* are unlikely to be successful; he calls for the greater integration of a peripheral area in which local efforts have met with small return. I am both less constructive and less optimistic. In Chapter 6, I argue that the best opportunity to effect real transformation in Chimbu has been squandered in the 1960s; that the attempt to graft coffee cultivation on to a subsistence base has succeeded in a material sense only, but that it has offered no satisfaction and led to the loss of many of the most innovative from the area. A large total investment by the Chimbu people has been wasted, yielding minimal continuing gains. I see my field area degenerating into a 'dependent rural slum' if present trends continue, and my earlier optimism (Brookfield, 1968b) has evaporated.

I also suggest that the changes I have witnessed may be widely replicated, and in this I reflect the argument of the more directly 'developmental' essays of Couper and Howlett. Couper traces the inexorable story of failure in 'modern' Pacific maritime enterprise, leading to the substantial exclusion of the islanders from trade and resource exploitation in the seas which they once controlled with skill and managerial competence. Howlett tells a similar story on land. She explores the manner in which the sort of man/land adaptation delineated by Waddell in another part of the highlands has been penetrated but not transformed by expatriate-dominated enterprise; how initial co-operation has been followed by an essentially dualistic separation; how 'progress' has gone sour as attempts to capitalize its early gains have been diffused into small-scale enterprise offering limited gains and blocked in access to the means of further growth. She concludes that this sort of development is 'terminal', leading only to an 'infinite pause' in the supposed transition to something higher.

Blame it on sex

These are widespread phenomena, by no means confined to the changing Pacific. However, many writers would argue that the real problem is with the rate of population growth, which soaks up the benefit of rising incomes, and creates its own problems of land short-

18

age and deteriorating resources. Several of us, myself included, note that growing pressure of population on resources is accentuating forms of stress already present, and aggravating the difficulties due to conversion of land from impermanent subsistence crops to cash crops which remain a generation or more in the ground. Maude addresses himself to this problem more directly, but—with the exception of Lea—none of us finds that there is much perception of acute land shortage. This is not to deny that there is a problem: we find it unmistakably clear that growth in numbers of people are in danger of converting a tolerably-adjusted 'subsistence affluence' into a condition with which we are abundantly familiar from the literature on south-east Asia.

None of us sees this as a problem incapable of short- and middle-term easement by other means. We see the issue as also one of commitment to a particular pattern of resource exploitation and allocation; Waddell especially notes that pressure of numbers in a difficult environment has already stimulated very considerable inventiveness in adaptation; Maude finds some reason to suppose that intensification *à la* Boserup—rather than noxious involution *au* Geertz—will be found possible in Tonga, though he sees only limited evidence of it in the here and now. All of us who turn to this problem see the changes resulting from 'development' as of greater magnitude in their immediate effect on local man/environment systems. While it is possible that in doing so we are unconsciously adopting the short-term view of change held by our informants in the field, we adduce solid empirical evidence that the major problem is the failure of the development effort to reach these people in ways that do not destroy their capacity for independent action. We thus agree that there are more immediate—if more costly—things to be done than simply persuading the islanders of the virtues of contraception.

Road to nowhere?

Collectively, we are pessimists who see little early prospect of improvement in the lot of the rural Pacific islander. We recognize that island governments—whether still colonial or newly independent—are concerned mainly with growth and with increasing the mass of revenue for redistribution from the centre; but we also see that these policies favour larger-scale enterprise and urban growth,

19

and that limited benefits tend to get thinly spread by the time they reach the periphery.

But, as the temper of Lasaqa's concluding essay reflects, there is a growing feeling within developing countries that some fundamental new thinking is needed. Shortly before these pages were written, the Third United Nations Conference on Trade and Development, meeting in Santiago, Chile, had revealed starkly the depths of self-interest among developed and developing alike inspired by growth-orientated policies. While the acrimony was perhaps inevitable in view of the numerous failures of the 'First Development Decade', the sudden setback to the principle of international redistribution was not widely anticipated. While one party hopes that the gap will be filled by private international investment, another party views this as uncomfortably like a new and very powerful form of colonialism, and sees the need to rethink the underlying philosophy of development if accentuated dependence is to be avoided.

Most of us in this book subscribe to the idea of development as a 'good thing', though our viewpoint prevents us from equating this with 'growth' at the national level. But we are implicitly critical of policies which yield such growth without bringing benefit to the periphery, and in this context, Clarke's Chapter 11 is less discordant than it might be in other collections. Clarke strikes at the fundamental question which the rest of us—even Lasaqa—avoid: is the aim to go forward and upward, accepting progress as 'good' and change as 'good', really justifiable? Or is the burden of all our arguments rather that this aim itself is questionable? We are at great pains to demonstrate the complexities of Pacific man/environment systems as we have been able to understand them: we see most change as having penetrated these systems harmfully, and as having deprived them of control not only over their freedom of action but also over some of their resources. We are impressed by the choice made by Pacific islanders to retain the securities of their own systems, but at the same time critical of outside forces which have blocked efforts of individuals and groups to escape from these systems. Are we being, like the people we have studied, hopelessly ambivalent on this matter? We appreciate the qualities of the old Pacific, but we want full and active participation in the new for the islanders. Lasaqa asks that we take account of what the islanders want to achieve, and I think that most of us try, however inadequately, to do this: but in complaining, as the islanders also do, about the present dilemma, have we really any positive solutions to offer? Clarke has. He makes an impassioned and wholly-committed plea against the existing philosophy of development. Perhaps without realizing that he does so, he invokes the 'law of opposites' of the Marx–Engels dialectic more than once, thus reminding the rest of us that this is what we also are doing when we implicitly say that tribalism becomes peasantry in opposition to more commercial forms of development, or that 'primitive affluence' becomes underdevelopment in opposition to the greater 'development' of Village X, or of the expatriates. Periphery only becomes periphery because there is also a centre. And Clarke tells us also that all production means the destruction of something; all development means the destruction of what was developed; greater consumption creates greater excretion; unrestricted growth may create disaster. He demands consideration for ecology, for the stability of ecosystems, and for education that will include ecosystem management. He argues that economic theory and its remedies are of value only insofar as they aid the proper management of man's ecosystem. He has little hope that his views will be accepted in the 'developing' Pacific —we have all met his unworried economist, and not always in a white skin—but he offers an approach to the future which lifts the spirit, and not merely the potential levels of consumption, destruction and pollution.

More than any of us, Clarke links this small corner of the earth to the whole earth. But in so doing he comes back to the beginning, to Waddell's elaboration of a complex and finely-balanced human ecosystem, for his appeal is for an intensification of the search for more exact knowledge of man/environment interaction through inquiries in depth—such as his own sensitive inquiry in north-central New Guinea, which he hardly mentions (Clarke, 1971). It is through the popularization of inquiries of this sort that he hopes to increase mutual understanding, and stimulate co-operative effort in the task of redesigning the earth as a lastingly tolerable home for man.

CONCLUSION

For its editor, this is an uncomfortable collection of essays. They force reconsideration of some very basic faiths; the success of the microgeographic method in gaining understanding; the underlying philosophy toward change. Methodologically, I am uncertain how successful we have been in making a link between the time-free study of man and his environment at a particular place, and the dynamic study of change advancing through time and sweeping across area. But I hope that we have at least indicated an approach to the problem of explaining spatial pattern through understanding temporal process, utilizing work at different scales and different time-dimensions comparatively and in conjunction. The potential interrelation of selectivity and holism are also exhibited.

At the same time, I think we have more surely demonstrated the virtues of a sense of involvement, whether or not this leads also to the conscious acceptance of a set of values in research. Our 'view from within' does offer a different sort of geography, one imbued with conscience and social relevance which emerge necessarily from our method. This much at least we commend to our colleagues in developed as well as developing countries. For the widespread 'revolution of social responsibility' in academic work—perhaps better put simply as a wider acceptance of social responsibility among a privileged class than has been apparent in recent years—demands that we seek to understand as well as to explain.

Acknowledgement

This essay has not been submitted to my colleagues for their criticism, and I seek their forgiveness where I have misinterpreted them, and their tolerance where they disagree. Hoping that they will consent, I therefore acknowledge their forbearance in advance.

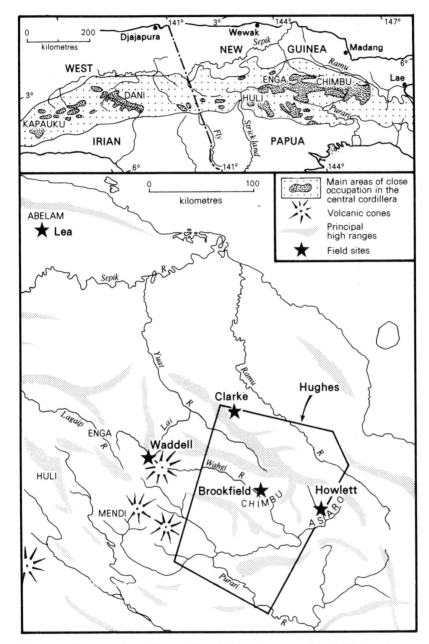

Fig. 1.2 The central cordillera of New Guinea: location of the field sites of some authors

2 Raiapu Enga adaptive strategies

Structure and general implications

Eric Waddell

Over the past decade or so the study of man/environment relationships has been radically transformed. Geographers have witnessed the abandonment of a possibilist philosophy, promoting an exceptionalistic view of man and research directed towards purely idiographic goals, in favour of an ecological approach that ostensibly offered their discipline a 'unifying conceptual framework' and a distinct unit of analysis—the ecosystem. The origins of this innovation can be traced back to Sorre (1947); however, the real stimulus was undoubtedly provided by the 1961 Honolulu symposium on 'Man's role in the island ecosystem' chaired by Fosberg (1965b). This symposium saw a convergence of geographical and anthropological interests, founded on a common concern with cultural adaptation and a shared interest in biological ecology as a framework for elaborating this concern. Significantly attention was directed at the conference to small, comparatively simple and clearly delimited units (or ecosystems)—with considerable effect.

There followed in the latter part of the 1960s both enthusiastic programmatic statements at the methodological (Stoddart, 1967) and theoretical (Harris, 1968, Ch. 23) levels, and a number of highly successful studies directed towards the investigation of man/environment relationships among small, isolated populations. Notable among these latter are Rappaport (1967), Brookfield (1968b), Lee (1969) and Kemp (1971). All utilize the ecosystem as their research model and hence aim at synthesis in their concern to establish linkages (functional relationships) between the various components of their respective systems. Thus directly or indirectly there is a preoccupation with the flow of energy, and similarly all are more or less concerned with the cycles or trends that characterize

25

their systems. Little attempt is made, however, to present meaningful generalizations or to proceed to comparative analysis in any systematic way.

For the social scientist of the 1970s, it is precisely at this level that the seeming deception of the ecological approach is located. Empirical research has so far failed to legitimize the earlier programmatic statements, and increasingly charges are being levelled to the effect that these ecological methods are only useful in the analysis of so-called 'static' or primitive societies, or in Rappaport's own words (1971, 131), 'small, autonomous ecological systems'. In effect it is argued that traditional ethnography is being cast in a new mould, where the research model espouses the same shadowy aims of synthesis and thus, to guarantee success, demands an extremely high degree of competence and intuitive ability on the part of the practitioners.*

The basis of this essay is a concern to demonstrate the much broader utility and potential of the ecological approach, founded on the analysis of individual systems. The immediate stimulus, however, derives from an independent source, the publication of a seminal paper by Watson (1970) which postulates an extremely attractive hypothesis for explaining the nature of individual New Guinea highland social systems in terms of the dynamics of inter-group relationships. The author's basic assumption is that a social system is concerned to organize a flow of personnel in space and time. While the purpose of his exercise is strictly anthropological—to put into an entirely different perspective the whole issue of organization of central highland societies that has plagued social anthropologists for two decades now—it is its considerable ecological potential which strikes this writer. Specifically, the paper stimulates thought as to how adaptation may be interpreted at a much larger scale in a situation where populations are nevertheless locally organized (and locally studied!). It has thus led to a reinterpretation of some of my own material, and to a consideration of the appropriate highlands literature in the light of it, since evaluation of the hypothesis demands consideration of the interrelationships among local and regional systems.

In order to demonstrate the facility with which one can proceed

---

* It is interesting to note that human ecology, like traditional regional geography, has been characterized as reflecting an 'attitude of mind' rather than a discipline in its concern to investigate associations between phenomena rather than the phenomena *per se* (Shepard, 1969).

26

from the study of a local ecosystem to the identification of variations in adaptive strategies and generalization at the regional level, a major diagnostic variable is identified—*technology*. This is conceived as the mechanism by which a human *population* exploits a given set of culturally-defined *resources*. Since these two latter are the key components in the adaptive equation, and the former reflects the principal point of interaction between them, it is suggested that variations in technology may reasonably indicate changes in either the biophysical environment or in demography. Thus, in addition to providing the point of departure for the analysis of individual ecosystems, it can also provide a critical parameter for effecting regional comparison both in terms of variation in pattern and in transformation through time. At the same time the focusing on an explicit set of data renders cultural ecology a methodologically more precise subject for the would-be practitioner, dissipating some of the intellectual vagueness inherent in synthesis. It is intended that the present exercise illustrate the validity of some of these propositions.

The regional context

Highland New Guinea provides an excellent experimental situation for conducting a research exercise of this nature on account of the general isolation of its population, local variations in specific ecological variables that are set against a perspective of generalized uniformity, and a distinctive political organization which facilitates both local study and regional comparison (and therefore generalization). The mountains form a central spine to the island some 1,100km long, and rise abruptly from the coastal plain and lowland valleys to altitudes of 3,000–4,000m. Wholly enclosed within them are a series of wide valleys ranging in altitude from about 1,350 to 2,000m, supporting a population of about 750,000 people—virtually all sedentary subsistence farmers—that is subdivided into small, autonomous territorial groups of 200–400 persons, each occupying an area of about 3–25km². The region is characterized by a high degree of uniformity in terms of population, resources and environment. Thus patrilineality everywhere provides the basic referent for social organization, and a similar set of strategies are used by all populations for conflict resolution and to regulate social relations (warfare, ceremonial exchange). In addition subsistence is achieved primarily

27

through the cultivation of a sweet potato staple along with pig husbandry, utilizing a tool kit centred on the hand axe and digging stick. Finally, settlement is effectively restricted to the lower parts of the valleys within an altitudinal range whose absolute limits are located at about 1,500m and 2,700m respectively. Within this context of generalized uniformity of adaptive strategy two major variables are identifiable, one of population density and the other of agricultural intensity. Thus densities range from as little as 1/km² on the periphery up to between 40 and 185/km² in a series of 'core' concentrations. Furthermore these latter generally coincide with large pig populations and agricultural systems involving a high degree of technical elaboration designed to increase soil fertility, regulate moisture availability and minimize erosion. Two additional variables, presumed to be dependent on the above, are also identifiable—a varying emphasis on the actual degree to which social groups are structured in terms of agnatic descent and patrilocality, and a range from stable-nucleated through 'pulsating' to stable-dispersed patterns of settlement.

In sum, the highlands context satisfies the dictates of the conventional ecological method and provides an appropriate framework for controlled comparison. Thus each territorial group can be viewed as a local ecological system, in the sense that each population subsists almost entirely on the resources of its particular territory and has, equally, exclusive access to them. Further, the general uniformities shared by these local groups make it possible to 'control' one's variables in a fairly precise way—a rare opportunity in the study of human populations. Finally, the distinctive agricultural methods of the highlanders bring ecological relationships more clearly into focus, encouraging a research strategy that focuses initially on technology or, more generally, the agronomic techniques used to exploit a specific set of biological resources. It is with reference to this 'adaptive core' that the characteristics of the larger ecological system are elaborated.

The relationships between the different sets of variables are identified principally with reference to one local group (or ecosystem), this providing a basis for discussing variations in adaptive strategy among the entire cultural group. Finally the ecological significance of certain of them is considered in the context of the highlands as a whole; and it is at this level that some indication of the methodological significance and theoretical import of the study is provided.

The study group: a Raiapu Enga clan territory

The Raiapu Enga number some 30,000 and form a component subculture of the Enga, who are about 150,000 strong and hence the largest cultural and linguistic group in the highlands of Australian New Guinea. They distinguish themselves from the majority by dress, dialect and agricultural practices. Geographically they are concentrated in and around the Tchak and middle and lower Lai valleys centring on Wapenamanda patrol post and within the altitudinal range of 1,650–1,950m, but extending occasionally up to about 2,450m. The autonomous territorial groups into which they are subdivided comprise on average 270 individuals supported on a territory of 2·6km². Resultant densities range between 42 and 140/km². Territories are contiguous, distributed along both sides of the valleys and extending from riverside to ridge-top. What follows is an analysis of the internal structure linking a population with its territory in one such group in the middle Lai, in which a population of 460 persons is supported on a territory of 6·5km², giving a density of 71/km².

The adaptive core: technology and biological resources

The population of this territory subsists exclusively on agriculture and pig husbandry, 99·9 per cent of the dietary intake, by weight, being derived from these two sources.* Agriculturally they are concerned primarily with sweet potato (*Ipomoea batatas*) cultivation (71 per cent of total production), secondly with yam (*Dioscorea* spp.), sugarcane (*Saccharum officinarum*) and pit pit (*Setaria palmaefolia*) (15 per cent), thirdly with temperate vegetables produced for sale (5 per cent), and fourthly with a highly-varied range of minor subsistence crops. In addition to directly supporting the human population, these cultivated foods are fed in significant proportions to the pigs. This is necessitated by the fact that the animals are kept in large numbers (at times they may exceed the human population by a ratio as great as 3·3 : 1) but can derive little of their sustenance from foraging. In effect they consume on average 50 per cent of the total production

---

* These and following data pertaining to the local group are derived from an intensive study of the residents of one locality within the territory, comprising in most cases a survey of ten households. For detailed information see Waddell (1972a).

of food crops, including almost two-thirds of the sweet potatoes and over half of the *S. palmaefolia*. The pigs, in turn, are of considerable nutritional and social significance to the populations that support them in that, in the form of meat, they provide an important source of protein, while feeding them highly perishable subsistence foods creates an effective, if inefficient, means of storing readily available energy 'on the hoof', thus serving as insurance against the periodic risk of crop loss from frost and other environmental hazards. Finally, in a sociological sense, they are a major prestige food and thus basic to all ceremonial exchanges that are used to negotiate alliances and cement social relationships at the inter-group level, and to assert individual political power within the group.

The exploitation of these domesticated resources is organized in a very distinctive manner in relation to terrain. As has been noted, each territory typically comprises a strip of land extending from valley bottom to ridge-top. Three distinct terrain units are identifiable within each such strip, the main range slopes, fragmented terrace sections, and dissected gorge slopes (Fig. 2.1). The first is characterized by moderately steep slopes (generally 10–30°) and largely supports *Miscanthus* and *Imperata* grassland plus some surviving forest near the summit; the second comprises a level or gently-sloping surface (1–10°) and is mostly under intensive cultivation but includes some 'economic' trees; the third covers the steep slopes which form the banks of the river Lai and its tributaries separating the segments of terrace from each other. This latter is largely covered by secondary growth, both spontaneous and controlled, plus scattered food gardens, and slopes are steep (c. 20–50°).

The Raiapu possess a precise taxonomy of garden types, which draws a basic distinction between sweet potato gardens (*mapú eé*)—the staple food—and yam gardens (*amú eé*)—comprising, in effect, the subsidiary crops—and further subdivides the former on the basis of mode of tillage into large mounds (*modó*) and small mounds (*yukúsi*) (Fig. 2.2). Each subsystem in fact accords with a basic operational distinction between what are here termed open fields and mixed gardens, where fundamentally different ecological characteristics are attributable to each. In effect the contrast is between, in the case of the latter, an agricultural order which 'is integrated into and, when genuinely adaptive, maintains the general structure of the pre-existing natural ecological system into which it is projected' as compared to the former, which involves

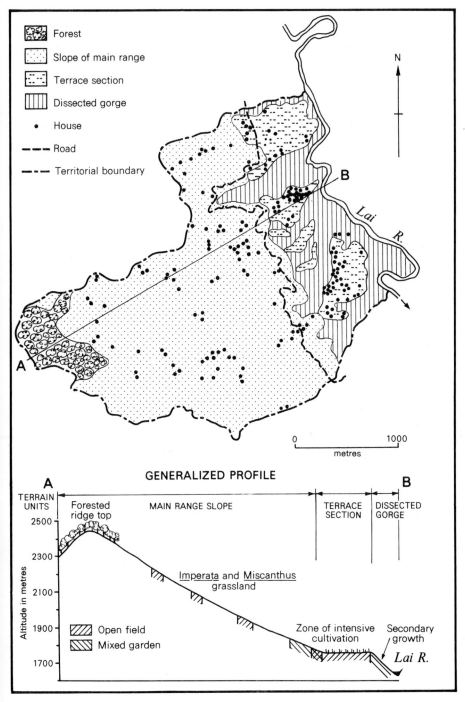

Fig. 2.1 Terrain, land use and settlement within a selected Raiapu group territory

'creating or sustaining one organized along novel lines and display-
ing novel "dynamics" ' (Geertz, 1963, 16).

A strict association between garden-type and terrain exists at the
subsystem level, in which open fields are restricted almost exclusively
to the terrace sections and mixed gardens to the dissected gorge
slopes, leaving the main range slopes virtually unutilized. Thus the
open fields are devoted exclusively to the cultivation of the staple,
primarily in large mulched mounds (c. 3·8m in diameter and 0·6m
high) that form extensive improved areas covering entire terrace
sections. This technique permits continuous cultivation of the soil.
Bordering on these, particularly on the upslope sides, are areas
under small unmulched mounds which, in a dynamic sense, highlight

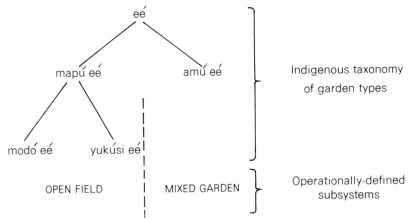

Fig. 2.2 The Raiapu agricultural system: cognized and operationally-defined
units

the process adopted for bringing enclosed land into a condition
suitable for continuous cultivation. Such a process involves tillage
of the soil to progressively greater depths over a period of four to five
years. Finally each open field area is bounded by a continuous
fence-line, to prevent intrusions from the domestic pigs, and the
farmsteads are scattered along it.

Since the open fields are under what is effectively continuous
cultivation, involving complete tillage of the soil, intensive weeding,
etc., and there is a sustained demand, both to support people and
pigs, for their sole crop, regular uninterrupted work on a daily
basis is demanded.

The mixed gardens by contrast are managed on a system of casual, shifting cultivation operating on a 10- to 15-year cycle with a single planting in each cycle. Holdings are restricted largely to the dissected gorge slopes, although a few are located at the foot of the main range up to a maximum altitude of about 1,830m. Individual enclosures are about 0·1–0·2ha in size, although they vary considerably, in relation to the number of individuals cultivating distinct sections within a single boundary fence. Pigs forage among the regrowth between these holdings, returning in the evening to the farmstead to sleep, and eat the sweet potatoes and other food wastes on which they largely subsist. As many as 20 or 30 different *genera* of food-plants are intercultivated in these gardens in a largely random manner. However, since gardens are established strictly on a seasonal basis, labour inputs are highly irregular and little maintenance is required once planting is completed. In effect continuous, high-level labour inputs are required for clearing and planting, extending over a period of six to eight weeks. Thereafter the gardens are visited only infrequently, largely in order to harvest the various crops as and when they mature.

To summarize, in descriptive terms the Raiapu Enga adaptation can be characterized as an exclusively agricultural one which nevertheless serves to sustain a pig population that, at most times, exceeds the size of the human. The livestock are housed with the women in the farmsteads located adjacent to the sweet potato gardens. Further, from the point of view of adaptive strategy, a precise internal structure is recognizable where each of the two major agricultural subsystems is associated with a specific terrain unit or microenvironment—the open field with the terrace section and the mixed garden with the dissected gorge slopes—each being exploited in a particular manner. Thus the one is utilized for intensive monoculture of the staple, and the other for extensive inter-cultivation of the subsidiary crops.

These, then, emerge as the key associations between population, resources and environment. An interpretation of the pattern can be readily achieved through an identification of the properties associated with each set of variables.

The relationship between the adaptive core and the physical subsystem

The most obvious fact emerging from the internal organization of agricultural activity is that the staple food is cultivated on the soil

33

with the highest natural fertility and the greatest potential for intensive cultivation. The terrace sections have well-drained and deep, productive soils with a strongly developed upper (A_1) horizon that is generally 0·4m or more deep, is friable, well-structured, and has a significantly higher organic matter content than any of the other soils within the group territories. Elsewhere greenish or reddish-brown clays are largely exposed at the surface, and the upper horizon is poorly developed. Hence their fertility status is substantially lower (C/N ratios of the order of 4 to 8 instead of 12), and they are also less stable and harder to work. The reason for this direct association between the terrain unit supporting the best soils and intensive, and almost exclusive, cultivation of the staple, is obvious—it best ensures the high yields necessary to meet the large and sustained demand for sweet potato.

These same considerations account, in part, for the distinctive practice of mulch-mounding. Following completion of harvesting the mound is broken open and the earth piled in a ridge at the perimeter. Some 20kg of vegetable matter (sweet potato vines, various ruderals and forbs, and food waste) are then introduced to the centre and, once decomposition has commenced, the mound is closed. This practice, repeated every one to two years at re-cultivation, effectively serves to maintain soil fertility at a continuously high level, while actually improving the texture of the soil. Thus a survey of a single cultivation cycle in ten mounds indicated a rise in the C/N ratio from 11·8 prior to mulching to 12·7 40 weeks after closure, the pH from 5·4 to 6·0 and electrical conductivity from 0·053 to 0·069 (millimho/cm³ at 25°C).

For the Raiapu mulching demonstrably facilitates the continuous cultivation of the soil. Yet this does not satisfactorily account for the associated phenomenon of the mound, for a diversity of techniques of fertility maintenance are practised in the central highlands.* Thus mulching may simply be associated with various forms of complete tillage or grid-iron ditching, as sometimes among the Chimbu. Elsewhere the fertility status of the soil is maintained through the use of such techniques as planting *Casuarina* fallows and various systems of field drainage. The distinctive microtopography of the open field can only satisfactorily be interpreted in terms of climatic variables, more specifically the frost hazard. Effectively the lower limit of mounding among the Enga coincides roughly with the

* See Brookfield (1962).

elevation at which the risk of frost is considered to commence, about 1,520m. Below this altitude the Raiapu practise only casual mixed gardening in which the staple is intercultivated with the subsidiary crops. Above it mounding is utilized for the cultivation of the staple regardless of variations in population density. Finally, as altitude increases so does the tendency for mounding to become the sole medium of cultivation for all annuals.

A particular feature of the food complex of the Raiapu and other highland populations is that it is a humid tropical lowland crop association with limited tolerance of low night temperatures and none of frost. However, the latter is a significant environmental hazard at higher altitudes. It is generally the product of nocturnal temperature inversion under clear, calm conditions when outgoing radiation is excessive. Observation indicated that with screen temperatures of 5·5–4·4°C there is a slight risk of ground frost, while below the latter figure it is highly likely. An investigation of minimum temperature readings at Wabag (2,001m) for the period 1957–66 indicate an average of 2·1 days per annum with readings below 5·5°C and 0·6 days below 4·4°C. Thus ground frost emerges as a significant agricultural hazard for the Enga, although naturally one which varies in degree with altitude, being a relatively infrequent occurrence for most of the Raiapu who, as noted above, are concentrated mostly between 1,650 and 1,950m.*

In functional terms the shape of the mound serves to modify the microclimatic regime close to the ground where the extreme temperature fluctuations associated with inversion are experienced. An experiment conducted at about 2,650m (close to the upper limit of settlement) indicated that regular inverted temperature gradients develop near the ground, exceeding 3·3°C when the screen minimum temperature fell below 5·5°C, with temperatures being consistently lowest on the surface of cleared, unmounded ground, and of the order of 2°C below those registered on the top of an 84cm-high mound. Thus the mound was demonstrated both to

1817798

* From an adaptational point of view, infrequency must not of course be equated with insignificance. As Vayda, Leeds and Smith (1961, 70) have pointed out, one of the most firmly-established ecological generalizations is Liebig's law of the minimum which 'states that biological reactions are controlled not so much by the *average* amounts of essential factors in the environment as by *extremes* in the presence of these factors'. Hence an adaptive strategy can only be properly understood by reference to events that may occur only very rarely.

35

elevate the sweet potato plant above the zone of lowest temperature and to promote the drainage of dense air away from the vines. Further to facilitate air drainage, mounds are generally distributed orthogonally up and downslope in open fields at high altitudes, and clean-weeding the sides and intervening channels also aids the process.

Finally, a generalized relationship was observed through the Enga culture area between increasing altitude, mound dimensions and minimum height on the mound surface at which sweet potato vines are established. Towards the upper limits of settlement the mounds are significantly higher (0·85m compared with 0·55m) and wider (3·9m compared with 3·1m) and the sweet potato plants are increasingly concentrated on the top (at a minimum of 0·64m) above the ground surface compared with 0·24m).

Thus the generalized mound topography serves as a critical mechanism by means of which an ecologically vulnerable crop is cultivated in a marginal environment. The process of mulching also serves incidentally to minimize the risks inherent in sweet potato cultivation at this altitude, in that its decomposition raises soil temperatures by the order of 1·2°C.

It may be concluded, then, that insofar as Raiapu group territories are concerned, the selection of the best soils, on the level or gently sloping terrace sections, for intensive cultivation of the sweet potato dictates practices which involve mulching, to maintain fertility, and mounding, to eliminate or minimize the risk of frost which is present at these altitudes and occurs most frequently on this topographical segment of the territory.

Conditions governing the selection of land and cultivation method are very different with the subsidiary crops. Since almost two-thirds of Raiapu food intake consists of sweet potatoes, these crops have only a supplementary role in diet. The range is wide, including tubers, cereals, vegetables and fruits, and the utilities are also diverse. Several are considered luxuries, consumed largely at feasts or distributed in ceremonial exchanges. A crop is designated a luxury both by its scarcity value and also by its nutritional importance (high protein and essential nutrients value) in a context of comparatively low productivity. As a class these crops have a poorer tolerance of low temperatures than the sweet potato, and hence are effectively restricted to altitudes below about 1,950m. This constraint applies most importantly to taro and yam, two alternative sources of bulk carbohydrate, as well as to several nutritionally important greens. Altitude for altitude, taro and yam are also lower yielding than the sweet potato in the montane environment, and for this collective set of reasons they are not grown on the best soils, but cultivated on an extensive basis in mixed gardens. These slash-and-burn type gardens are made on the steep dissected gorge slopes, where gradient and low altitude together eliminate any risk of frost. There remains, however, a persistent risk of crop loss through slope failure in this terrain unit, but this does not pose critical problems in the adaptive sense due to the limited demand for the crops, and the fact that protein requirements can, if need arise, be met from the pigs.

These same considerations also serve to explain the avoidance of the higher slopes on the main range, where both poor soils and the prevalent risk of frost militate against any systematic exploitation of food crops.

The cultural subsystem: towards an interpretation of the adaptation

The food complex of the Raiapu emerges as having a specific set of nutritional properties and ecological tolerances, and the strategy for their exploitation within Raiapu group territories clearly reflects these controls—the demands generated by demographic pressure and the constraints imposed by climatic marginality and suitability of soils and slopes for cultivation. This distinctive strategy in turn demands that the population organize itself in a particular way in order that it may operate effectively. Two particular dimensions emerge as being significant: first, the organization of population over space and second, the recruitment of members to the locality group.

While in a very general sense the pattern of settlement within group territories may be categorized as dispersed, a quantitative expression of the pattern, using the technique of nearest neighbour analysis, indicates a marked and highly significant tendency towards agglomeration, this concentration being observed to occur on the terrace sections around the periphery of the open field areas. This emergent pattern can be conceptualized as being a 'distorted lattice' in which departure from a uniform distribution of settlement (or 'triangular lattice') occurs in response to the presence of a major resource which assumes a distinctly zonal form, namely the open fields.* The actual pattern of the farmstead organization emerges

* See Haggett (1965, 94–5).

then, in an idealized sense, as one in which each is located adjacent to the appropriate portion of open field area in the terrace section, but a widely scattered, and annually changing, group of mixed gardens is also exploited on the dissected gorge slopes (Fig. 2.3). The distribution of settlement is thus based on the division of agricultural activity into two subsystems, the arrangement of each over space, and their comparative productivity. A rational interpretation of this pattern is readily forthcoming in terms of the general

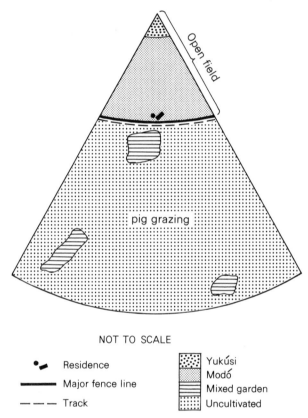

NOT TO SCALE

•‿ Residence	▦	Yukúsi
▬▬ Major fence line		Modó
	▤	Mixed garden
─ ─ ─ Track	▦	Uncultivated

Fig. 2.3 Schematic representation of a Raiapu farmstead

principles of location theory which state, basically, that the intensity of utilization, and therefore level of production, declines with distance from a central location. In a subsistence economy, such as is the

Raiapu's, individual farmsteads clearly function as central places. A formal analysis of the internal arrangement of each farm, based on the differing requirements of each agricultural subsystem and the location of the farmstead in relation to these, can be provided by reference to a basic mechanical problem, that of the resolution of parallel forces: that is, in spatial terms, each subsystem is conceived as exerting a force (in the form of area under cultivation, labour input, yield, frequency of journeys), the open-field force being significantly the stronger. A systematic analysis of ten farmsteads and their holdings, more fully reported in Waddell (1972a, 178–9), shows that the farmstead locations offer a reasonably close approximation to an optimal location, at the point of minimum energy where the forces exerted by the open fields and the more scattered and less frequently-used mixed gardens cancel out. The essential point to emerge from this survey is that the distinctive spatial-economic characteristics of Raiapu agriculture generate a specific response in the location of residences with respect to the two types of agricultural holding.

Adaptation at the territorial level brings us to a higher order of generalization within the system. The agricultural system as a whole is involved in parallel with the structure of political organization and social interaction between groups. We have seen that the Raiapu practise an intensive, partially permanent form of agriculture with a limited tool-kit, involving a large 'investment' in permanent 'improvements' to land. This investment involves the preparation, through tillage, of terrace section soils over a period of several years prior to intensive cultivation. Environmental constraints applied to the crop complex employed explain this in part, but equally important in requiring intensification is the high level of population pressure on limited resources of improvable land. This population pressure also affects the political and territorial system in ways that must now be examined.

Intensification has arisen and persists in a context of extreme political instability. Highland societies in general, and the Raiapu in particular, are acephalous, leadership of local groups being achieved and constantly reasserted because of challenges from other contenders. Between each of these political units there exist continually fluctuating arrangements of alliance and opposition, arising from the fact that pressure on resources may vary significantly through time and space from one group to another. It is thus frequently necessary

39

to modify the allocation of land between groups, and this in a behavioural context where inter-group disputes of all kinds are normally settled by warfare and territorial conquest.

Thus in functional terms there exists an evident and fundamental incompatibility between an unstable political system, characterized by small, belligerent populations, and a stable agricultural system involving a high level of intensification. The political instability must be viewed as a cultural fact for which no explanation can readily be provided;* the intensification, however, is clearly necessitated by factors of environmental marginality and high population density. The point is that, from an adaptive point of view, a potentially dangerous situation exists in which the agriculturalist is continually confronted with the risk that the improvements he has effected to the land over the years will be destroyed through warfare, or that territorial conquest will result in others reaping the benefits of his labours.

This potential dilemma is in fact resolved among the Raiapu, and seemingly elsewhere in Enga country also (Meggitt, 1958; 1965), by the formulation of a very rigid and much-vaunted agnatic ideology. Membership of each local group is considered to be restricted exclusively to those claiming direct descent from an eponymous ancestor through the male line. In a system of patrivirilocal residence this rule is designed to ensure that rights to land cannot be transmitted to individuals resident in other group territories. Thus the residential rule and agnatic ideology together serve to guarantee that each territory remains physically intact, to define allegiance with respect to that territory, and to give that allegiance continuity through time.

However, in spite of rigid ideological statements, some flexibility over admission to agnatic status is permitted, and indeed actively encouraged at times, while at other times the agnatic principle is systematically applied. Thus mechanisms exist whereby immigrants

---

* General relations are, of course, considered to exist between societal level, population size and density where, in the case of the New Guinea highlands, densities are in excess of those normally associated with a 'tribal' level of societal evolution (see Sanders and Price, 1968, especially Chs. 1 and 4 and Fig. 4). The observed stress may derive directly from this fact. Watson (1965) and Heider (1967), following in some respects a similar line of thought, have suggested that certain of the structural and ideological characteristics of highland societies can best be understood as 'archaic elements' more appropriate to small, mobile. hunting and gathering populations.

40

are periodically invited and progressively become assimilated to full membership of the group (i.e. they become agnates). The process is a slow one, taking at least one generation. Following the change of residence it involves the male migrants relinquishing all rights in their natal territory. Only after this is done can they acquire unqualified land rights in their adopted local group, and hence effectively assume agnatic status. Thus the process in turn results in migrants becoming unequivocally committed to their host group.

Defining group loyalties in terms of an explicit territory which remains intact through time is of considerable significance in a situation in which grounds for solidarity are few, owing to the dispersed pattern of settlement which serves to minimize interaction among group members, the low level of co-operation in agricultural work, the individualization of tenure on improved land, and the constantly fluctuating pattern of leadership based on considerations of prestige and influence. In the final analysis it is this agnatic ideology which assures defence of territory in the collective good by guaranteeing solidarity at the intra-group level. However, the organized and variable flow of migrants from one group to another can only be understood in terms of the dynamics of inter-group relationships. As noted above, population size and density of individual group territories vary over space and through time, and it is these variations which largely account for the varying patterns of alliance and opposition, aggression and defence. Thus it is intergroup variations in the relative scarcity and abundance of land (and therefore resources) in relation to population size which stimulates the flow of migrants from one to another. This flow functions as an equilibrium-seeking mechanism designed to equalize population densities among the Raiapu generally, so minimizing the grounds for territorial expansion and therefore the risk of warfare, and more overtly allowing group populations to be maintained at an adequate level for the effective defence of their territories.

Following this interpretation, the agnatic ideology no longer appears as one which seriously restricts rights to land in a group territory. Rather it serves as a flexible mechanism which regulates the admission of individuals to the status of group membership as a function of the collective need, and which defines their loyalties with reference to a territory which must remain intact at all cost. Thus the status, whether inherited or acquired, carries with it clear sets of obligations. This mechanism makes agricultural intensifica-

41

tion among the Raiapu possible and maximizes the possibility that those who intensify can reap the benefits of their labours. Without such an agnatic ideology this could scarcely be achieved, given the basic political instability and the low level of integration achieved prior to contact; and hence it is in turn unlikely that such large population densities could have been sustained in this environment without such an ideology.*

The system conceptualized

Fig. 2.4 represents an attempt to identify the structure of an individual Raiapu ecological system based on the preceding discussion of its principal components. For the purpose of the exercise the physical subsystem is disregarded, in the sense that the particular organization of the biological subsystem is viewed as being in itself an adjustment to environmental variables. Thus the adaptation is represented as being characterized by a fundamental duality between largely autonomous biological and cultural realms. In the first, very substantial demands for resources are created by large pig and human populations, and this demand is met by a particular organization of agricultural activity involving a clear division into intensive exploitation of open fields and extensive exploitation of mixed gardens. Pigs are viewed as being both part of the problem and part of the solution, in that they impose pressure on resources and provide essential animal protein and energy storage. Thus they are managed in close association with the open fields. It is the resultant spatial arrangement of activity which generates the dispersed pattern of settlement—as a means of reducing to a minimum human energy inputs. The structure of the cultural realm is viewed as imposing potentially serious restrictions on the effective management of the total system, in the sense that a lack of clear social stratification and hereditary leadership plus a potentially restrictive system of recruitment to group membership are hardly compatible with the very substantial demands for food energy and a scattered population distribution. It is the big man who is ascribed the critical role of manipulating the two to arrive at adequate population maintenance. This is achieved through managing the growth in pressure and equalizing its distribution through space.† In effect he seeks to

* See also Lea (this volume).

† The role is, of course, an extremely delicate one in that the big man must manipulate the system in order to assert himself, while at the same time his very

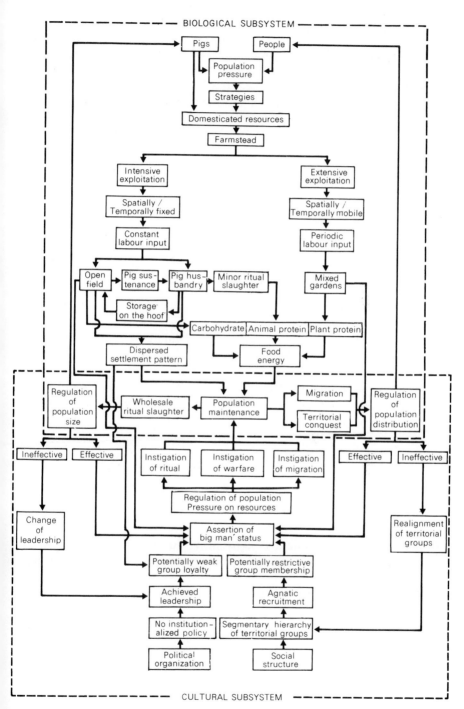

Fig. 2.4 The Raiapu adaptation conceptualized

control the *size* of the pig population (while at the same time getting maximum political capital from it) and to *regulate* the *distribution* of the human population. Where this is achieved the system functions efficiently, where it is not major transformations occur involving a change in leadership and a realignment of groups in both a spatial (boundary) and hierarchical sense. These perturbations have the effect of restoring stability, but at the risk of interfering with the flow of foodstuffs to the population that is producing them.

While the model indicates both the stresses and ultimate validity of the Raiapu adaptive strategy, it also points to the fact that no constraints are applied to the growth of human population. This is

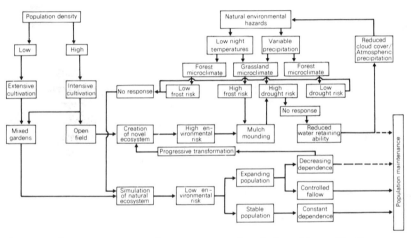

Fig. 2.5 Cause, processes and consequences of agricultural intensification

simply being redistributed constantly through space in order to maintain a uniform relationship between population and resources. The adaptive strategy must therefore be modified constantly to accommodate this uncontrolled variable. The cultural management

position requires that he regulate it. To achieve the first end he must stimulate the growth of the pig population in the short run, and to assure his second aim he must control its size in the long run. This task involves both extracting pigs from his supporters and guaranteeing their overall system of production, and demands fine judgment.

44

and environmental consequences of the basic evolutionary process as they may be presumed to operate in the case of the Raiapu are illustrated in Fig. 2.5.

As is widely appreciated, the development of an intensive agricultural subsystem is viewed as a direct response to increasing population pressure. By definition its main purpose is to increase productivity per unit area and this demands maintenance of soil fertility, here achieved through tillage and mulching. As densities increase so the relative significance of extensive cultivation decreases; or alternatively it may become stabilized through the introduction of controlled fallowing techniques to the mixed gardens. To the Raiapu, the elimination of forest vegetation that accompanies agricultural intensification aggravates the incidence of certain natural environmental hazards at the local, or terrain, level. The two that are particularly pertinent are low night temperatures, resulting in periodic frost, and variable precipitation, giving rise to periods of soil-moisture deficit and hence drought. The two constraints are related in the sense that both are highly seasonal, being associated with the clear, calm climatic conditions characteristic of dry periods. They are nevertheless of limited significance under forest conditions (and therefore in a system of extensive cultivation) since transpiration from the vegetation itself is presumed both to contribute to atmospheric moisture directly and also to reduce the effect of seasonality. Removal of the forest vegetation (consequent upon intensification), however, reduces the magnitude of changes at the surface, increasing run-off and surface evaporation and reducing transpiration. This serves to increase the effect of seasonality by reducing cloud cover and, most significantly, the persistent mists that cling to forests in these mountains, and consequently reducing atmospheric precipitation and increasing the risk of frost. Mulch mounding is, as has been shown, an effective agronomic adjustment to inverted temperature conditions close to the ground. What is striking in the case of the Raiapu, however, is that no adjustment is made to the drought hazard. In effect the system appears to have a 'weak link' that can result in major crop losses and hence endanger population maintenance.

Interestingly, calculations of moisture balance in the soil in the Enga area fail to support the observation that drought is a serious hazard. Thus Fitzpatrick (1965, 66–8), in estimating mean evapotranspiration for Wabag, concludes that in only four months over

45

the years 1954–60 did precipitation fall below assumed need. Further:

Assuming that up to 4·00in. (101·6mm) of available water in soil storage could be drawn upon over those intervals when rainfall failed to meet evapotranspiration, it seems unlikely that there would ever have been a case with soil moisture reserves so low as to inhibit growth.

However, there is sufficient evidence available in the literature to show that any estimates of both evapotranspiration and soil moisture-storage capacities are likely to be of doubtful validity. Thus, on the one hand, actual evapotranspiration rates obtained in the tropics are invariably far in excess of calculated Thornthwaite values, while on the other retention capacities vary considerably from soil to soil and tend to be particularly low under tilled conditions where any excess precipitation is likely to be lost through run-off (Chang, 1968, Chs. 13 and 19).

Measurements of soil-moisture tension close to the surface in the sample group territory demonstrated unequivocally that, while both forms of tillage (*yukúsi* and *modó*) lead to improved drainage conditions during the wet season, they also result in a rapid drying out of the soil when abnormally dry conditions prevail, even if only for a few days. Hence while the risk of saturation is minimized, that of drought is greatly increased, and the mulch has no regulating effect on these extreme fluctuations in the soil-moisture regime, presumably because it is located at a depth below that at which most evaporation occurs. It is this side-effect of tillage, and more particularly of mounding, that accounts for the periodic droughts and attendant crop losses that are known to have occurred among the Raiapu; yet such losses could scarcely be avoided, given the premise that complete tillage is demanded by the significant population pressure on resources, and mulch mounding by a concern to maintain the fertility status of agricultural soils and minimize the risk of frost damage to food crops.

Whether it is mounding itself which precludes the Raiapu from coping with the drought hazard or whether they fail adequately to recognize the hazard itself is unclear. What is certain is that population maintenance is thereby periodically endangered, and the only alternative sources of food energy within the ecological system are the products of the mixed gardens, where the drought risk is low, or the pigs, which serve as a mechanisms for 'on the hoof' storage of open field production.

Overall the models demonstrate in an explicit sense how individual Raiapu ecosystems are structured and how they are modified through time in response to a progressive growth in human population. Their capacity to support high population densities adequately is described, while the nature of such critical factors as leadership by big men and periodic risks of drought are also indicated.

The diagnostic value of the models

It was stated at the outset of this paper that an evaluation of the role of a particular technological complex in the operation of a single adaptive system can greatly facilitate the search for explanation and generalization at a wider level. In the case of the broad relationships between agronomic practices and environmental constraints, this proposition has been ably demonstrated in Brookfield's comparative analyses of agricultural methods both within the highlands (Brookfield, 1962) and in Melanesia generally (Brookfield with Hart, 1971, Ch. 4). In the context of the present exercise its validity can be readily illustrated with reference to two phenomena: drought consequent upon tillage, and the spatial relationship between agricultural mounding and frost.

It has been observed that, in the case of the Raiapu, complete tillage of the soil leads to a significant reduction in moisture storage capacity and hence virtual drought under a rainfall regime that would not normally be expected to produce such a condition. In effect the system itself generates a hazard which in turn serves to threaten its very viability. Instances of drought affecting agricultural production have been reported elsewhere in the highlands in association with various forms of complete tillage—cases among the Dani and Korofeigu being reported in Brookfield (1962, 24)— but always in a general climatic context characterized by only slight seasonality. As has been suggested this practice, and the transformations in the natural vegetation that precede it, invariably increase the magnitude of fluctuations in soil-moisture regimes, which may in turn critically affect agricultural practices. This proposition is clearly substantiated in Moss (1969) in a discussion of water balance and microclimate in tropical rainforest soil-systems. He demonstrates that a forest plant/soil system is much more strongly buffered against changes in atmospheric conditions than other

47

vegetation associations on account of extensive rooting systems and the very important contribution transpiration makes to atmospheric precipitation. It is argued that once this system is ruptured the *effect* of seasonality increases significantly (*ibid.*, 201–3). This is probably significant in all highlands agricultural ecosystems characterized by deep tillage, continuous cultivation, and monoculture of shallow-rooting, low biomass food plants. Responses are rare, but it is likely that the major ditching systems of the Kapauku and Dani may be so interpreted in that they are conceived for the dual purpose of drainage and irrigation. W. Clarke (*pers. comm.*) advises that the Dani ditches do have this dual function.

With regard to adaptation to frost hazard, it has been argued that the practice of transforming the soil surface of open fields into a patterned surface of plano-convex mounds is a direct response to the incidence of frost. Further it was noted that mound dimensions vary with the gravity of this hazard, the practice ceasing below the approximate altitude at which the risk of frost is considered to commence (c. 1,525m). Below this level, Enga populations practise the simple bush fallowing of most of lowland New Guinea.

While not exclusive to the Enga, this cultural practice is restricted to a series of contiguous groups, including the Kakoli, Huli and Mendi, among which the Enga are numerically predominant. Other major highland populations utilize variants of complete tillage that are unlikely to modify to any significant degree temperature regimes close to the surface of cultivated land. It may be assumed from this that, whereas population pressure on resources emerges as a generalized highland phenomenon, in response to which intensification occurs, the nature of environmental constraints varies, and hence the particular character that intensification assumes also varies. A glance at the altitudinal zones and types of terrain occupied by the principal populations confirms this proposition. If the central Enga and northern Chimbu are disregarded, the general altitudinal range of highland settlement lies between about 1,500 and 1,750m, with only limited areas cultivated above this altitude. As noted above, a risk of frost is only considered to commence around 1,520m, and reports indicate it to be neither a frequent nor serious hazard for such populations. Instead their principal environmental preoccupations are with water control and fertility maintenance. In those areas where dense populations reach altitudes comparable with the Enga—notably in the northern

Chimbu where settlement extends up to 2,600m—dissected terrain effectively promotes the drainage of cold air. Hence for them too frost does not emerge as a significant agricultural hazard. By contrast much of the main zone of Enga settlement and of such adjacent groups as the Kakoli, Mendi and Huli, as well as lying within a zone of persistent frost risk, is much more open in character. Here the association of large extents of unbroken country and broad valley flats or terraces with a relative absence of cloud actively encourages the development and concentration of cold air on agricultural land. In the circumstances an active concern to modify the microclimatic regime around the cultigens becomes critical.*

In addition to being able to elaborate on the functional relationships between agronomic techniques and environmental constraints at the pan-highland level, it is equally possible to proceed from an appreciation of the significance of specific cultural variables within the framework of a single system to an interpretation of regional variations in the same variables. This can be readily demonstrated with reference both to variations in settlement pattern and to stress on agnation as the basis for recruitment of group members.

With regard to settlement pattern, it was noted that the Raiapu farms are closely 'tied' in a locational sense to the open fields and that, by virtue of the relative permanency of these latter, they remain on the same site through time. Elsewhere in highland and lowland New Guinea, settlement forms diverge radically from this pattern, being sometimes permanently nucleated, sometimes alternatively nucleated and dispersed, and sometimes partly agglomerated with great locational mobility. Controlled comparison would indicate that the variations are related to the degree of intensification in an agricultural economy, this latter being defined as the extent to which emphasis in production is placed on a single staple food and the degree to which this is segregated from the subsidiary crops to create the open field/mixed garden distinction so characteristic of the Raiapu.

Where population densities are comparatively low but people rely essentially on food gardening for subsistence, as among the lowland Orokaiva where densities range from 3 to over 23/km², simple bush fallowing is practised, involving the intercultivation of a wide range of food plants. The soil is not tilled, there is only casual weeding

* For an elaboration of some of these points regarding the upper limits of settlement see Brookfield (1964, 29–31).

and a single planting prior to abandonment. Here there is no differentiation in labour requirements and inputs are irregular. The associated settlement form is one of stable villages with populations of about 150 persons that are completely relocated at intervals of 10 to 20 years, presumably in response to the agricultural cycles (Waddell and Krinks, 1968).

Where densities are higher, as among the Siane where they average 30/km², and these are compounded by large pig populations, greater reliance is placed on a single staple (sweet potato) which is however still cultivated within the framework of an undifferentiated mixed garden. However productivity (and labour inputs) are increased by partially tilling the soil into small mounds, and inputs are more regularly distributed throughout the year. Here the village form survives with populations averaging 250 persons, but individuals become highly mobile, with at any one time 30 per cent being resident in isolated homesteads adjacent to the food gardens where the pigs are quartered (Salisbury, 1962; 1964).

An analogous situation occurs among the Maring, where human population densities are of the order of 25–35/km² and moderately large domestic pig populations are maintained (the pig : human ratio rising on occasion to 0·8 : 1). The latter are largely dependent on cultivated foods which are produced by casual mixed gardening. Rather than there being a persistent flux in population between village and isolated homestead, as among the Siane, stress is resolved by means of a pattern of settlement that 'pulsates' through time. When pigs are scarce the population concentrates into villages (because of infrequent inputs into agricultural activities and a low level of demand for the products), but as their numbers increase the population disperses progressively through the group territory.* The fragmentation process is only arrested by the periodic massive slaughtering of livestock which restores equilibrium within the system and hence permits the return to nucleation of population (Rappaport, 1967; Clarke, 1971). In the case of both the Siane and the Maring, dispersal can be accounted for by the additional pressures pigs impose on the system owing to the need to increase agricultural production, attend to the livestock, at at the same time minimize the environmental degradation and liability to infection that follow from their excessive concentration. At the same time dispersal of the

* See also Brookfield (this volume) for a rather similar relationship of settlement pattern to the pig cycle.

population is not stabilized because the agricultural system itself remains an extensive one, characterized by irregular labour inputs and the frequent relocation of fields.

Among the Raiapu, overall pressures on resources are not only substantially higher (in terms of both pigs and people) but they have also resulted in major transformations in agricultural practices. Specifically there is a greatly increased concentration of activity in certain, geographically distinct, gardens within the system involving the application of more refined agronomic techniques to the staple crop. Associated with them is a much more continuous level of labour imputs. Thus it is this combination of a segregation of crops and the selective application of a different work routine which leads to the stabilization of dispersal, thereby placing the Raiapu at the end of a clear developmental sequence whose other extremity is now principally characterized by lowlands agricultural populations.

Finally, this consideration of a single ecosystem helps illuminate the whole problem of patrilineality as the organizing principle for populations. Among the Raiapu, agnation clearly serves as a model for group membership, that is an ideal state to which reality only in part conforms. At the same time it serves as a device for recruitment by assimilation in a situation where it is the sole referent for political groups which are in turn land-holding corporations. Highland populations generally possess an agnatic ideology, yet at the same time they are also characterized by what is evidently considerable mobility between groups, facilitated by the fluctuating political alliances and the web of affinal ties that are erected through clan exogamy. The key point to emerge from this observation is not whether some local groups are in practice more agnatic than others in terms of real membership, for indeed, as the literature would suggest, such a controversy can hardly be resolved satisfactorily, but why some place greater stress on the model than others and seek to hasten assimilation.* Here agricultural intensification again provides the key. It is suggested that it is precisely those societies that effect substantial improvements to agricultural land through tillage that place the greatest emphasis on agnatic status, for it is those that are likely to suffer the most materially from fluidity of group member-

---

* An appreciation of the importance of this fact is, fortunately, now gaining wider currency in the literature: see particularly Watson (1970). For an elaboration of this somewhat sterile controversy as it concerns the Enga, see for instance Meggitt (1965, Ch. 9) and McArthur (1967).

51

ship and loyalty. In order to effect improvement and reap the benefits, maximum solidarity among members of the land-holding corporation is required; at the same time maximal flexibility must be retained in order to sustain the numerical strength of the population. Elsewhere more casual forms of cultivation enable migrants to move more freely between local groups and reduce both the appeal of territorial conquest and the need firmly to define loyalties. Thus it is not population pressure on resources *per se* which leads to stress on agnation, but rather this pressure as expressed in more intensive forms of agriculture. Similarly it is not the degree of agnation *per se* which varies, but rather the measures which are taken to encourage immigrants to acquire agnatic status—that is, the extent to which the local population are pressed to conform to the model.

What is being postulated, on the basis of the Raiapu material, is that Meggitt's (1965, 279) general ranking of highlands societies, according to 'stress on agnation' in relation to population density, stands. Namely it is the higher-density populations such as the Enga and the Chimbu that place the greatest emphasis on agnatic status. However, the interpretation of this ideological attribute is modified to the extent that it is considered to be directly correlated with the dictates of agricultural intensification. More important, though it is suggested that mobility ('organized flow') between local groups operates independently of generalized variations in population density. Rather this latter is determined by the degree of local rather than regional variations in density. Migration may thus be equally significant under high as under low densities. That which varies according to agricultural intensity (and thus indirectly population density) is the way in which these migrants are treated. Systematic assimilation is characteristic under conditions of intensive agriculture, whereas retention of immigrant status is more freely tolerated under extensive conditions.*

* In terms of this argument a comparison of the Enga and the Chimbu is pertinent. The most recent statement illuminating the differences is in Brookfield with Hart (1971, 238–9), and it has generated a rather prolonged dispute centred around a contrast between Enga 'fixity' and Chimbu 'flexibility', both populations being characterized by high density and evident pressure on resources. Although Chimbu agriculture also contains some semi-permanent elements (Brookfield, this volume), there is no sharp distinction in technology between temporary and semi-permanent plots; nothing comparable to the 'improvements' contained in an Enga mulched-mound open field is encountered. The Chimbu responses to varying population pressure between groups include both easier transfer of

Such generalizations as these about highlands adaptations which derive from the Raiapu case study are of course highly tentative, being based on a review of the literature rather than empirical testing. However this is not the issue. It is rather that a functional analysis of a single adaptation aids in highlighting the properties of many others, through the identification of those elements that are common to all and those that vary. And it is in exploring the nature and patterns of variations that valuable observations about adaptive strategies at a regional level can be made.

Conclusion

An explanation of variations in pattern through space can in turn lead inquiry into an entirely new domain, that of speculation about processes of change through time using a synchronic approach. This has been attempted elsewhere with the aim of advancing our understanding of the controversial problems of agricultural evolution in the New Guinea highlands.* The prospects are appealing. No longer can the cultural geographer justifiably bemoan 'the lack of applicable concepts for dealing with such variables as economic organization, technical apparatus, livelihood strategies, and spatial integration.' (Wagner, 1965). And in turn, no longer will he be denied the opportunity of elaborating viable theory generated by his own substantive research, so long as identifying the regularities that characterize individual ecosystems does not become an end in itself and the search for diagnostic criteria is not rejected in favour of total synthesis.

Acknowledgements

The field research on which this chapter is based was carried out in 1966-7. W. B. Kemp provided crucial assistance in the preparation of Figs. 2.4 and 2.5.

---

persons between groups, and also rearrangement of territorial boundaries. The agnatic ideology is the same, the recourse to warfare is the same, and the notion that groups and their land are indivisible is the same. However, in a less severely-constrained environment, there is no similar attachment to improvements in land, and no comparable scarcity of improvable ground within group territories (Brookfield, *pers. comm.*). The regulation of flexibility mechanisms is thus much more relaxed.

* See Waddell (1972a, Ch. 8; 1972b).

53

POSTSCRIPT—JULY 1973

During June–October 1972 highland New Guinea experienced a severe drought accompanied by widespread frosts at higher altitudes; only one-quarter to one-half the mean precipitation was recorded. There were significant food shortages, and the agricultural cycle was retarded several months. At one stage Administration officials feared they would be obliged to provide relief food supplies for one million people.

The vulnerability of the system to drought was starkly confirmed, but from the present point of view the failure of the mounding system to cope with low temperatures is the more revealing consequence. Above about 2,300m, frosts were of such severity and frequency that almost all cultivated foods were destroyed. This has happened twice before in the lifetime of living men, and such periodic but unpredictable disasters require adaptation at another level. Local intragroup adaptation is ineffective, and its place is taken by a regional, extra-group migration, the possibility of which is assured largely by the maintenance of agnatic and affinal kinship ties. Temporary residence elsewhere, and the establishment of food gardens on lower ground mainly in the territories of other groups, are the elements of this emergency strategy.

The Raiapu Enga were only marginally affected, but a return visit to high-montane Enga areas indicated that mounding serves as an effective adjustment only to the minor, perennial frosts. The periodic, intense frosts experienced at higher altitudes call for a radically different adaptive strategy. But to develop this question would require another paper!

3 Stress and adaptation to change

An example from the East Sepik District, New Guinea

David Lea

Human geographers working in the tropics have for long been concerned with areas that appear to be under some form of population pressure (e.g. Gourou, 1969; Steel, 1970). There has, however, been an overriding concern with the environment and its ecological degeneration rather than with the people who live in these areas. This discussion is concerned with how one group of people in the East Sepik District of New Guinea have reacted to various pressures at different times, and it emphasizes that in the study of rural 'problem areas' perceptual factors are just as significant as ecological facts.

Societies usually have mechanisms to cope with intra- and inter-group tensions and environmental problems. Where one society comes into contact with another which has a vastly superior technology and political organization, many of the abating or adapting mechanisms—for example rival exchanges, infanticide, distribution of surpluses or warfare—are no longer acceptable or feasible. New mechanisms must be devised or introduced to cope with new or changing pressures. No attempt is made to predict future changes or to explain the causes of the present situation, or even the cause of the initial high population density in the study area. What is presented is a discussion of the methods used to describe areas under population pressure and a descriptive model of the changes that have taken place in one particular problem area over the last forty years or so. Some suggestions are made about what factors are important in the adaptation process.

For a meaningful discussion of population and resource problems, much attention must be given to the interaction between environment and society; the idea of stress is particularly useful in this context.

55

In plant ecology, 'stress' can lead to changes in the physiology of the plant and either temporary wilting or extinction will take place. Such a concept can be applied in a wider ecological and social framework, for we can look at all the external and internal forces exerting pressure on or affecting an organism (i.e. man) or a complex or organisms (i.e. society) resulting in a sense of strain. Stresses may be felt at many different levels. In this essay I am not concerned with those felt by individuals but rather with stresses felt by groups. These stresses may be caused by a whole range of biological, environmental and cultural factors: biological stresses may be caused by insect and weed infestations, plant and human diseases, hunger and malnutrition; environmental stresses may be caused by drought, flood, erosion, cyclones, declining fertility of soils and destruction of plant habitat; cultural stresses may be caused by war, social tensions, land and labour shortages, poor and wasteful gardening techniques, uneven distribution of land and external pressures exerted by another cultural group. All these stresses, and many others, may be endemic, periodic or epidemic. Some may be harmful and lead to poverty, real social distress, ill health or death; some may provide a stimulus to change and adaptation.

As Vickers (1968, 358) points out, all societies are subject to pressures or stresses in some form, for conflict within societies is endemic but in itself is not 'noxious'. Some stresses are indeed desirable for 'there are ill-effects of having too little stress in that comfortable monotony is not only boring, but may lead to mental disorders' (Rosenberg, 1968, 427). There is no doubt that in some situations population pressures and other stresses may aid the modernization process in that 'stress acting on traditional systems causes a breakdown in ethnocentricism and indigenes are unable to accept their way of doing things as natural and best' (Lea, 1972). Wolpert (1966, 95) suggests 'that some stresses may be conducive to relatively higher performance levels and innovative behaviour'. This is similar to the Toynbee theory of 'challenge and response' or Hirschman's inducement mechanism (1958, 181). Such theories, however, do not help to explain the vast number of hungry people in the world or those countries that cannot 'take off'.

Boserup (1965) argues that great changes could occur within primitive agricultural communities exposed to the pressure of population growth. Assuming that the land has inherent qualities which allow continued improvement and intensification, she argues that

56

the stresses resulting from population increases bring about changes in society and economy which force intensification of agriculture bring about agrarian changes. However, intensification of agriculture will nearly always mean greater labour inputs without proportional increments in output (see for example, Clarke, 1966; 1969); and a spiralling intensification of land use seems to offer little scope for any future development (Geertz, 1963; Gourou, 1969, 16). Agrarian change in itself does not necessarily result in a better way of life, nor does it necessarily alleviate noxious or potentially noxious rural stresses (see Wolpert, 1966, 93).

Some obvious examples of human societies subjected to serious stresses are mining towns with a rapidly-diminishing resource base, non-immune communities subjected to introduced lethal diseases, areas of urban blight, and villages caught in a no-man's-land between two warring parties. To understand the causes of these particular stresses is not difficult, and any intelligent person can see how they are felt by the residents of an area. Other areas or societies are subjected to severe but more subtle stresses, and it is extremely difficult to see whether they will adapt or wither. Two problems therefore exist: how to identify areas of stress and how to measure the intensity of the stress (Berry, 1965, 24).

Berry (1965, 25) claims that the combination of factor and dimensional analysis solves these problems, and D. M. Smith (1968) uses a multivariate approach to identify areas of economic distress in England. Both authors are, I think, rendering the problem of identification unnecessarily complex. I see no problem in subjectively recognizing areas of severe stress. Land shortage, malnutrition, discontent and other symptoms of stress are usually obvious to the most transient visitor, and inhabitants are acutely aware of them. Berry is too optimistic over problems of measurement, for he excludes the most significant factors such as sensory overload (crowding), conception of standard of living and sociocultural needs, just because they are difficult to number objectively.

A cruder measure most commonly adopted to indicate pressure or stress in man/land relationships has been population density. Among animals it has been found experimentally that mortality is dependent on population density (Hoagland, 1966, 358) and it is obvious that gross overcrowding produces social stresses and tensions that are capable of shattering community organizations (Morris, 1968, 155). However, such measurements are inadequate for our purposes because they do not consider ecological or social relationships, nor do they make sufficient allowance for varying agricultural practice and environments, external sources of food and money, variety in soil fertility or changes through time. It is axiomatic but necessary to emphasize that there is no simple correlation between high population density and rural problem areas: pressure of population on land and resources is but one factor among many in the emergence of a problem area, and its impact obviously varies according to culture and environment. Some densely-populated areas produce an agricultural surplus and have great potential for economic progress and social stability, while some sparsely-populated areas are subjected to great pressures due to poor relative location, environmental, political or economic factors.

Some workers such as Allan (1949; 1965, 20–65) and Carniero (1960) have made some interesting attempts to assess carrying capacity.* This is generally defined as the number of people and other organisms which may be supported within a given area without inducing degradation of the environment (Rappaport, 1967, 88). Variables such as total area of arable land, length of fallow period, length of cropping period and the area of cultivated land required by an individual in any one year are considered. The concept originally introduced by Allan (1949, 71) has been refined by Brookfield and Brown (1963, 108ff.) to categorize land into various types of varying value; Rappaport (1967, 95ff. and 87ff.) has considered changing pig population in his estimates and Porter (1969, 191; 1970, 201) divides yields by a standard diet (*per capita*/annum food requirements). Allan's aim was to calculate an absolute carrying capacity for a given piece of land, and the concept so used does assume technological and gastromonic stagnation (Street, 1969, 104). It also ignores non-food requirements such as building materials, fuel and sociocultural needs. Brookfield and Brown surround their use of Allan's technique with many *caveats*, stating that their purpose is 'to evaluate the adequacy of group territories in terms of present . . . utilization of land' (1965, 108) and 'to identify quantitatively those group territories that are approaching conges-

* Hunter (1966) compares population densities with migration tendencies (as indicated by sex ratios) and where sex ratios fall below 98 he assumes net migration indicates an agricultural system which is inadequate for that population density. Such an assumption is patently invalid in Melanesia, if, indeed, it is valid anywhere.

58

tion and those with abundant capacity' (1965, 120). Brookfield and Brown maintained that they were not concerned with the long-term capacity of the land; however, there seems some lapse from this position in their use of the resulting statistics. There is no theoretical reason why the concept of carrying capacity should not be viewed more dynamically than it has been to date. Allowance could be made for changing crops, distance from settlement sites, increasing intensity of land use, changing perception and evaluation of the environment, technological innovation, changing land-tenure systems and socio-economic change. However, few if any informed field-workers with intimate knowledge of even a small area would be brave or foolish enough to attempt it. More important objections to the use of such methods in the present context are that they are mechanistic and concerned only with the environment and agricultural techniques. Also, where stress obviously exists there seemed little point in estimating a theoretical carrying capacity when it was apparent that with existing land-use technologies the land was 'over capacity'.

By selection of significant environmental relations, and by treating man in most cases as the dominant part of the ecological complex, Moss has outlined a method which attempts to relate morphological limiting factors to land-use and vegetation systems. Moss views plants and soil as a continuously-varying, interacting system, rather than as sets of partially-correlated features (Moss, 1969, 18); and, although his approach is more dynamic than the carrying capacity concept, he is still interested in obtaining 'a picture of . . . relative stability under present economic and social pressures' (Moss, 1938, 124) and his basic interest is in assessing agricultural-potential rather than stress.

Systems analysis, especially along the lines of the energy system model suggested by Foote and Greer-Wootten (Foote, 1967; Foote and Greer-Wootten, 1966; 1968) offers a promising method of isolating the causes of stress. To some extent they do this in explaining the cause of a seasonal decrease in a fish catch in a Northern Alaskan community. Briefly their method was to use a team of geographers to collect

standard meteorological observations and river water temperatures, level and current speed, three times daily; it weighed and measured sample lots of various fish species; tape-recorded stories

59

related to past land use patterns, and obtained detailed information on demography, housing, diet and village economy. (Foote and Greer-Wootten, 1968, 87)

With data collected by these methods they made calculations on energy expenditures and receipts throughout the physical, biological and cultural subsystems, using the common 'currency' of kilocalories. It seems to me that the returns of this method hardly justify the effort required, and often they express quantitatively what is usually subjectively obvious. Further, when making studies of subsistence societies, teams of even partly-trained geographers are not usually available, and when finance and time are at a premium it is necessary to eliminate irrelevant data or excessively time-consuming tasks.

What I attempted initially in a study of some village communities in 1961–3 seemed to combine (with the advantage of hindsight) many of the approaches just discussed. Generally it was an analysis of the man/environment system. With insights obtained by greater precision of expression of some parts of the man/environment system I hoped to be able to see, and perhaps predict, the points of strain within the system. However, such systems are extremely complicated and many components and linkages do not lend themselves to mensuration. If just one aspect of a man/environment system, the garden subsystem (see Fig. 3.1), is envisaged we can see at a glance some of the objects which make up the system and the most important relationships between the objects. With a model such as Fig. 3.1 (adapted from Foote and Greer-Wootten, 1966) it is easy both to visualize the factors affecting the growth of garden crops and to isolate and measure, if necessary, the causes of ecological stress produced by a whole range of biological and environmental factors.

The objects in the system which show the end results of these stresses are food (mainly garden produce) and diet (the physiological needs). Of these, human nutrition is the most important, because produce is often wasted or fed to pigs or fulfils non-nutritional functions (Lea, 1969). In my early work a systems approach much simpler than that shown in Fig. 3.1 was the conceptual framework, but only production and diet were studied in any detail. Several other objects in the system, their attributes and relationships, were studied if they seemed significant and if they were

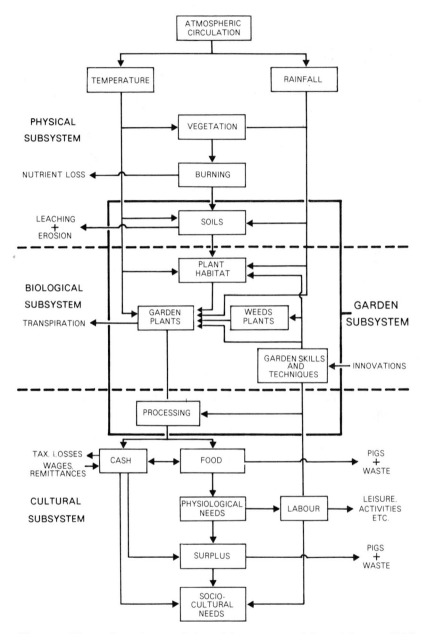

Fig. 3.1 The garden subsystem (adapted from Foote and Greer-Wootten, 1965)

amenable to quantification. Examples of these objects included soil composition and quality, vegetation conditions, population characteristics, land availability and land disputes.

It is true that these data merely supported the obvious—ecological stress existed—but they also indicated the causes of some stresses and allowed quantitative statements to be made about the degree of stress. More important, in the course of this work it became apparent that other stresses were being exerted by outside influences such as government and mission, and these stresses were quite different from 'internal' stresses and much harder to measure. Some examples of these external pressures were inter-mission tensions, forceful and often indiscriminate opposition to traditional values, land and labour being used for road construction and maintenance and for cash cropping, and a rapid increase in populations caused basically by the availability of effective medical facilities provided by missions and Administration.*

A return to the study area in 1970 and 1971 made me realize that a further set of stresses—perceived stresses—were acting and had previously aggravated both the internal and external stresses studied. In earlier periods of field-work these perceived stresses were used as evidence that internal and external stresses existed: in 1970 it seemed that in the process of adapting to these perceived or psychological stresses, both internal and external stresses had been relieved with very little expenditure by concentrating on relieving the perceived stresses. Whether this is only a temporary respite is another question. The period could be the precursor of a new period of development in which the people accept new ideas, intensification, emigration and new techniques. If nothing is done to exploit the respite, the people of the area could well sink back into a great slough of despair.

THE WOSERA

Background to the problem

The Territory of Papua New Guinea has an overall population density of 6·2km², and there are only a few areas that appear to be

* Population increase was also caused by other factors such as abandonment of parturition taboos and the taboos on sexual intercourse during the yam-growing season, which had ensured that most males over the age of 30 remained celibate for at least six months of every year. The growth rate in the period 1956–68 was 2·9 per annum.

under any form of stress induced by great population pressure. The exceptional areas are the Gazelle Peninsula and the Chimbu, Enga and Maprik areas. The Gazelle Peninsula's problems are associated with excessive land alienation before 1914 and with urbanization, and are not particularly relevant to this study. The Chimbu and Enga areas, both in the New Guinea Highlands, have been studied by Brookfield and Brown (1963) and Meggitt (1958; 1965) and both investigations were concerned *inter alia* with the different mechanisms that the Chimbu and Enga people had for coping with land pressures. Meggitt considers that the greater the population pressure, the more rigidly rules of land tenure would be applied and interpreted (Meggitt, 1965, 263). The Enga, who use patrilineality and patrilocality as the principal norms in organizing social activities, rarely make land available to non-agnatic kin and affines. Brookfield and Brown (1963, 176–7), in contrast, found that the Chimbu were prepared to accommodate fellow-tribesmen by rearrangement of group territories and by allowing individual negotiation in land matters between non-agnatic kin: 'for the individual short of suitable land, ties with clansmen, kin, and affines are vital to survival' (Brookfield and Brown, 1963, 129). Kelly presents a hypothesis that the more a people see problems of land shortage as a group concern, the more it will be handled in terms of descent, while the more they see it as an individual problem, the more will reciprocity between all kin be emphasized (Kelly, 1968, 60–6).*

At the time my research began in 1960 a basic anthropological study (Kalberry, 1941; 1942; 1965) had been made of the Abelam people living in the Maprik area of the East Sepik District, but little else was known about the area, its land or land use, or how the people felt or reacted to an unusually high population density by lowland shifting cultivation norms. The Abelam are a tribe of some 35,000 people and their land is more densely populated than any other lowland area of equal or greater size in New Guinea; in places population densities approach $200/km^2$. It is true that higher densities occur in the New Guinea Highlands (Brookfield, 1960; Ward, 1970), on the Gazelle Peninsula, and far higher densities are encountered in the Indonesian and Philippine Archipelagos and on some Micronesian islands to the north. However, all these areas have either significant cash cropping or other cash income, access

* See also Waddell, (this volume.)

to marine resources, some technology of land use that permits more permanent cultivation of the soil, or land of relatively high initial fertility. The distinctive characteristics of Abelam land use, by contrast, are little cash cropping (particularly in the early stages of this study), soils of low initial fertility, shifting cultivation techniques and agricultural practices that are in the main lacking in elaboration.

In the Abelam area a clear areal differentiation was observed between the North Abelam, east of Maprik, and the Wosera living in the south-west of the area. (Fig. 3.2). In the Wosera, population densities vary between 60 and 200/km² as contrasted with densities

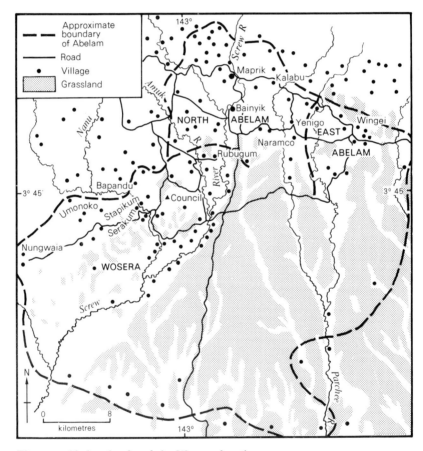

Fig. 3.2 Abelam land and the Wosera: location map

64

of between 30 and 150/km² elsewhere in Abelam land. More important, in the Wosera land shortage was the rule; discontent, hunger
and land disputes were rife and there was palpable ecological stress.

Nearly all the Wosera live in the North and South Wosera Census
Divisions. Here we are concerned mainly with the more densely-
populated North Wosera Census Division containing 15,138 people
in June 1971; these people lived in an area of approximately 144 km²
(which includes about 18 km² of low *Themeda-Ischaemum* grasslands
rarely used for gardening). Excluding the grasslands, the population
density within the Census Division is 120/km². Land, however, is
unevenly distributed. Some villages, particularly to the west, are
sparsely occupied, while much higher densities are found in the
central Wosera near the Nanu River. For example, Stapikum and
Serakum villages in this area have a total population of 1,052 (1971)
and have only 5·18 km² of potential gardening land—a physiological population density of about 200/km². Thus within the Wosera
population densities are exceptionally high for shifting cultivators,
and they have probably been high for many generations.

The Wosera—before European contact

The first known contact of the Wosera with Europeans was in 1914,
when Richard Thurnwald made three traverses between the Sepik
River and the north coast of New Guinea: one of these traverses was
through the eastern part of Wosera territory on the eastern side of
the Screw River (Thurnwald, 1914). It seems that no further contact
was made until the 1930s when administrative patrols and the
Townsend-Eve mapping expeditions (Townsend, 1968) entered
and quickly passed through the area. In 1937 the Administration
established a patrol post at Maprik, and a Roman Catholic mission
station was established at what is now Kunjingini. Although these
events marked the first permanent European contact, trade goods,
particularly steel axes, had long been traded in from the coast and
Sepik River, and the people were well aware of the presence of
Europeans because miners and labour recruiters were operating in
the general area throughout the 1930s.

There is no doubt that the Wosera was densely populated before
the 1930s and its inhabitants acutely aware of land shortage. Thurnwald reported dense population in the area, and from his descriptions of fortified villages, and oral tradition, it is obvious that warfare
was endemic. Territorial aggrandizement provided the means where-

65

by a village could protect the land it had or increase the holdings it had at the expense of its neighbours. There was also active expansion of Wosera territory into the sparsely-populated Gawanga areas to the west (Lea 1964, 42) but densely-populated Abelam and Arapesh areas to the north, grasslands to the east, and swamp to the south, prevented expansion in these directions.*

As a result of warfare being associated with territorial conquest, village and clan boundaries were very unstable and badly defined and this later led to many problems when the Administration fixed boundaries and forbade warfare. However, in a pre-contact situation the very flexibility of boundaries had its advantages, for the people had a set of responses which gave at least some of them relief from stress and others permanent freedom from worry (for casualties were often very high in Wosera fights).†

The Wosera—the early 1960s

When the Administration fixed boundaries, it created or accentuated problems of maldistribution of land and population by freezing what was formerly a fairly fluid situation. Some villages such as Rubugum and Umonoko, which were powerful and expanding groups when inter-village fighting was stopped just before the Second World War, have plenty of land, whereas other groups such as Bapundu and Stapikum, which were weak at that time, are desperately short of land. However, maldistribution of land relative to population was only one of the problems in the early 1960s.

In a previously published work (Lea, 1965) based on field-work carried out between 1961 and 1963, I attempted to show that because of severe land shortage and traumatic culture contacts, severe ecological and social stresses existed in the Wosera which were not as significant elsewhere in Abelam land. In that paper it was shown that in comparison with North Abelam areas, soils and vegetation provided a poorer garden habitat, population density was much higher, yields lower, fallow period much shorter, 'cargo cult' thinking‡

* Population pressures may have induced a technological innovation along the lines suggested by Boserup (1965) in the period before European contact. Cultivation techniques, and a special variety of yam (*Dioscorea esculenta*), were developed which allowed frequently-inundated floodplains to be cultivated.

† Usually in New Guinea fighting stopped when one or two men had been killed or wounded. In the Wosera often 10–20 men were killed, and in one fight between Serakum and Jambitanga 50 men were killed.

‡ See note on p. 74.

ubiquitous and land and sago disputes much more frequent.* Land disputes seemed to be an obsession with the Wosera, dominating their restricted relationship with the Administration and leading to apparently insoluble disputes and hostile relationships between individuals, subclans, clans and villages.

However, in the early 1960s the evidence of stress was not only a conclusion derived from comparative studies. In absolute terms the situation was serious. Mortality rates were extremely high in the 0–15 age group, as were stillbirth rates and maternal mortality rates.† Using the method discussed earlier (see Fig. 3.1), emphasis was placed on those objects in the system which seemed to be directly responsible for physiological stress—food production and diet. The quantitative data on yields was only of value in the comparative study between the two study areas, but the dietary studies (Lea, 1965, 201–4; Bailey, 1963) indicated that in the Wosera there was 'an apparent chronic total food shortage of some severity' (Bailey, 1963, 8) and that protein intakes were low. Bailey (personal communication) also found that there were significant seasonal fluctuations in the body weight of both males and females which indicated severe seasonal food shortage.

In addition to morbidity, population pressure and dietary stresses, the Wosera were subject to real sociocultural stresses. Generally they received only the authoritarian aspects of Administration control until the late 1959s. During the Second World War the region was largely neglected by the Japanese who occupied the Maprik area, and there was some reversion to tribal fighting. Shortages of staff and lack of economic opportunity in the area explain in part Administration neglect, but also the Wosera was (and to a large extent still is) an unpleasant area to patrol: the water was bad; food was difficult to obtain; the people were obsessed with land disputes and talked to Europeans of little else; access was often difficult because there are no bridges over the Screw or Nanu Rivers; and there was incipient 'cargo cult' thinking throughout the area.

* During a 28-month period from June 1960 to October 1962 there was one land or sago dispute per 423 people in the Wosera and only one per 7,319 people in the rest of the subdistrict (Commonwealth Bureau of Census and Statistics). It is likely that many other disputes existed then but were not brought to the notice of the Administration—especially in the Wosera.

† Dr. F. Schofield (1963) found child mortality rates of 620 per 1,000 live births, maternal mortality rates of 32 deaths per 1,000 total births and 96 still births per 1,000 total births.

67

The net result was that no schools or hospitals were established west of the Screw River and there was little cash cropping, for land was either diputed or needed for subsistence crops.

The Roman Catholic missionaries were the first Europeans to show any real interest in the people, and until about 1960 their influence was considerably greater than that of the Administration. However, some of the early missionaries were insensitive and heavy-handed, and one encouraged the wholesale destruction of the elegant ceremonial cult houses and sacred objects. These attitudes, combined with the fact that plantations would not accept labourers from the Wosera (as they had acquired a reputation for thieving and deserting), led to a sullen withdrawal. It seemed that the mechanisms for settling even the most minor disputes within the village had lapsed, as had mechanisms conducive to the emergence of leaders: traditional culture had been undermined, cargo cults flourished and the people were ill-fed, bemused and demoralized.

In 1964 I wrote: 'they would respond to energetic leadership from someone who is interested in them. . . . Obviously leadership in the present pass must come from the Government but first the more positive aspects of Government influence such as schools and hospitals have to be established. All this would be very difficult unless . . . the isolation of the Wosera is ended' (Lea, 1964, 168). But even at that time I was able to write that 'the establishment of the Wosera Local Government Council had created a beneficial outlet for the people and had given them a new self-respect' (Lea, 1964, 166).

The Wosera—the early 1970s

By 1970 it appeared that agriculture and diet had not changed (*contra* Boserup, 1965) in any way even although the population continued to increase at a rate of just under 3 per cent and emigration had not significantly increased. By the criteria of the factors measured in the early 1960s it seemed that the Wosera was much worse off than before: the crime rate was still high, and as there is a strong correlation between crime and land disputes one can assume that land disputes continued unabated,* land shortage still limited the

* In the time available in 1970 it was not possible to obtain data on the cause of crimes, but during a 15-month period from November 1968 to February 1970 the Wosera had one crime per 63 people while the rest of the Sub-district had one crime per 216 people (Subdistrict office, Maprik, Court Register).

opportunity to obtain cash from coffee and rice (Lea and Weinand, 1971); and although no quantitative data were collected one can assume that diet had not improved greatly, for agricultural practices had not changed not had the opportunity to earn cash for buying tradestore foods increased.

However, in 1970 the Wosera did seem to be a happier place than before. Some local leaders were beginning to emerge, people had plans for the future (still tempered by some cargo cult thinking*) and they were not so obsessed with land disputes. It seemed that the Wosera had a new outlook and were learning to adapt to a situation which had formerly subjected them to excessive stress. In the main these adaptations were psychological, and were induced at little expense by four administrative actions:

(1) Some excellent young patrol officers were posted to a newly-created patrol post near Kaugia in the centre of the North Wosera Census Division. They were generally liked by the people and were 'concerned' with the problems of the area.

(2) The Wosera Local Government Council was established in 1963.

(3) Government schools teaching in English were established at Serangwantu and near the Nanu crossing.

(4) A resettlement scheme was established 26km west of the Nanu River in the territory of the Gawanga people. Believing the situation was critical, the Administration acquired 1,844 hectares of land and made it available for settlement to the people from the central part of the Wosera. While the psychological impact of this scheme has been beneficial and some 186 families have registered blocks, only about five have actually moved into the resettlement area and these can only be considered intermittent settlers. All Wosera complain that the resettlement area is too isolated and unhealthy, that medical and school facilities are non-existent and that there is little chance of earning a cash income in the area.

Although these actions made no great difference to the physical well-being of the Wosera, they 'felt' that they were no longer rejected and despised. They perceived a situation which had improved even although the real situation had perhaps worsened. In the early 1960s the 'real' and the 'perceived' situations were essentially isomorphic: by 1970 the perceived situation had improved. To exploit this

* It is, however, very significant that very few Wosera west of the Screw River became financial members of the 1971 Yangoru Cargo Cult.

situation and allow real improvements to follow such a promising start needs tact and planning. New Guinea cannot afford changes such as resettlement and irrigation schemes in densely-populated areas (see Fisk, 1962) and these and intensification are probably only temporary palliatives. Any form of birth control is unlikely to succeed, and even if it were immediately successful it would have no great effect on growth rates for some decades. Two alternatives are therefore available. The Administration can attempt to use the Friedmann (1966) model to attack the Wosera's problems. Friedmann suggests that certain measures can be taken inside and outside a downward transitional area (DTA). External measures are to create an identity of interests between core regions and DTAs, to encourage a flow of capital from core regions to DTAs, to enlarge the absorptive capacity of potential core regions along the perimeter of DTAs through carefully staged programmes of investment, and finally to undertake large-scale rural resettlement along the edges of DTAs (Friedmann, 1966, 89–93). These external measures must be accompanied by internal measures that focus primarily on structural changes within the DTA. These internal measures include planning the location of growth points and bringing service to these points, expanding and improving road networks and transport services and focusing them on the growth points; developing light processing and labour-intensive industries and encouraging a changeover from subsistence to commercial farming (Friedmann, 1966, 93–8). This strategy would be difficult to implement because the Wosera is a small area which must remain low in national priorities, and there is no core area to assist its growth. Also the area has poor resources and is badly located.

Perhaps the second alternative is more realistic, and it is best to concentrate on relieving perceived stresses and inducing depopulation because the hope of rural rebirth in such areas 'is a hoax and a delusion' (Morrill, 1969, 118). The Wosera Resettlement Scheme failed because it was neither traditionally orientated nor capable of offering a way for the Wosera to better themselves, or to escape from most of the external stresses. Even if it were successful it would have helped only a small proportion of the total population in the Wosera. A more effective method of coping with excess population would be to break down the isolation of the area, and improve access to the outside world by building bridges across the Screw (nearly completed in July 1971) and Nanu Rivers, and improving road access: this

70

would provide a route in for technological innovations and a way out for people, cash crops and occasional surpluses. The long-term solutions to most of the Wosera's problems are not, therefore, to be found locally, but in migration and in the industrialization and urbanization of the Papua New Guinea economy as a whole.

DISCUSSION

Types of stresses

While undertaking this study of the Wosera area it has become apparent that many different types of interrelated stresses are operating simultaneously. Some of these stresses act as stimuli resulting in changes that alter the environment. techniques or beliefs; but other stresses are harmful and individuals and groups suffer. It is only by looking at all the stressors, especially the 'noxious' ones and their relationships, that we can really understand a community or area. Once this is done it would be possible to devise a list of priorities which would allow economic and feasible action to be taken. For convenience we could classify harmful stresses as follows:

A   Internal stresses   (i) Personal stresses   —substantive
                                                      —perceived
                          (ii) Group stresses   —substantive
                                                      —perceived
                          (iii) Ecological stresses   —substantive
                                                      —perceived
                          (iv) Psychological stresses

B   External stresses   (i) Personal stresses   —substantive
                                                      —perceived
                          (ii) Group stresses   —substantive
                                                      —perceived
                          (iii) Ecological stresses   —substantive
                                                      —perceived

Interpersonal and inter-group stresses are well outside my field of competence and, except for obvious manifestations, I do not intend to discuss them in any more detail here. With reference to Fig. 3.3, however, the other stresses could be briefly discussed.

The internal stresses, particularly the physiological ones, are the easiest to recognize and to measure. With the aid of models such as that shown in Fig. 3.1 we can isolate those objects in a system which

71

affect diet, garden habitat, land availability, labour and yields and we can study them and their interrelationships. To know how far to go into these topics and where to stop is a test of the field-worker's judgment, but the essential criterion is to find the pressure points in a system and to be able to suggest ways of alleviating them.

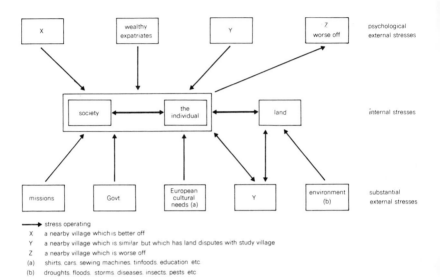

Fig. 3.3   Internal and external stresses

However, with the personal (inter-individual), group (inter-group), and ecological stresses it will always be difficult to separate the real or substantive stresses from the perceived stresses, for as Brookfield says, 'decision makers . . . base their decisions on the environment as they perceive it, not as it is' (1969, 53) and the perceived environment may of course result in land being lost by litigation or conquest or land being taken out of production. Probably more important, land disputes lead to hostile relations between individuals, social groups or residential groups (e.g. villages).

Contact with Europeans creates stresses by imposing new belief systems, destroying or denigrating traditional, agricultural, political and social systems which allow man to live in some sort of equilibrium with his environment. With new demands on time to be spent in new activities such as road-building and cash cropping come new

72

needs for experiences and goods which cannot be obtained. The internal and external stresses are all inter-related. In 1965, in the article comparing a Wosera community with a North Abelam community, I wrote:

It seems that the effect of greater ecological stress . . . deriving from greater population pressure on land resources, aggravates the impact of forces upon society. In turn these external forces aggravate the ecological situation. It appears that forces of both local and external origin interact to produce this observable fact: that one community is worse off, more short of land, less well-fed, more slovenly in its agricultural practices, more depressed and demoralized, than the other. (Lea, 1965, 192.)

However, 'perceived' stresses are also acting. They can be illustrated by village X (a nearby village which is more prosperous in terms of land, food and money) and the expatriate community at Maprik, Bainyik and on some mission stations who enjoy a rich, varied and— as seen from the village—a carefree existence. The presence of these communities kindles ambitions which have little hope of realization and creates conscious or unconscious feelings of jealously, inadequacy or inferiority. Rural as well as urban poverty normally appears so much worse to both the dispassionate observer and the inhabitants when it is compared with better-off areas, even if we acknowledge that 'one group's slum is another's sensory enriched environment' (Hall, 1968, 84). I heard Wosera men in the early 'sixties say that they were 'rubbish men'. They described themselves thus not only because they were hungry and poor but also because they felt that they were short of land and that they were despised by other Abelam, the police and many Europeans. These stresses are largely the result of widening contact because the people are more mobile, and they have seen with their own eyes their comparative poverty. They have learnt to consider themselves poorer and inferior to the people in surrounding areas. It was the easing of these stresses that resulted in an improved situation in 1970.

The perceived stresses of comparison are not unique to depressed areas, for they can be seen in well-off suburban areas where individuals try to keep up with the Joneses or are persuaded to buy goods they cannot afford. Stresses arising from considerations of status, pride and shame are just as likely to lead to sickness, emigration, technological and socio-economic change as substantive stresses such

73

as hunger and drought (see Saarinen, 1966, 40). As there is a close relationship between internal and external forces acting on a community, so there is an extremely close relationship between perceived and substantive stresses. To understand this relationship we must also understand a community's changing values and aspirations.

EDITOR'S NOTE

Lea's essay touches on a question that is worthy of a little expansion: the role of the so-called 'cargo cult'. These movements which, though known elsewhere, are especially identified with Melanesia, take the form of attempts to find means of access to power and wealth within the comprehension of the environment as perceived. Commonly, a mystical solution is envisaged, and also it is often alleged that the greater wealth of the Europeans is intended for the Melanesians, but is being intercepted by the outsiders—who have the secret of the 'road *bilong* cargo'. 'Incipient cargo-cult thinking', such as Lea describes, is far more widespread than elaborated cults; it imples a rationalization of the otherwise incomprehensible or unacceptable gap in access to wealth and power between colonizer and colonized. As such, this element in total perception is a major and widespread force in the whole man/environment system of many people described in this book, whether or not full-blown 'cargo cults' have ever been recognized. For a fuller discussion, see Lawrence (1964).

4 The Fijian village and the independent farmer

Roger Frazer

The Fijian village has traditionally been the focus of Fijian life.* Events of the last fifty years have shown an accelerating trend away from the village. This essay seeks to examine certain aspects of this change and in particular to focus upon variation through time in the functions and attributes of the village. Most examples are drawn from

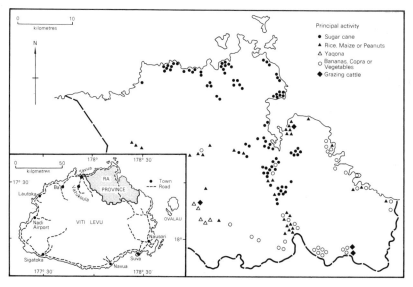

Fig. 4.1 Villages of Ra Province, Fiji: principal economic activities (*inset:* location of Ra Province in Viti Levu, Fiji)

* 'Fijian' here means the people of autocthonous origin, and excludes persons of Indian or other overseas descent.

75

Ra Province in northern Viti Levu where field-work was carried out in 1958–60 among some 7,000 Fijians, most of whom were resident in 78 separate village communities (Fig. 4.1).

The village may be conceptualized as a set of interconnected systems, social, political, and economic, and of physical structures, which Ra Fijians have evolved to obtain what they perceive to be the most satisfactory solution to problems encountered in the occupation of the area. If one subscribes to the view of McLoughlin (1969, 37), *'that optimizing action taken by an individual or group at a particular time has repercussions which alter the context for decisions to act by other individual or groups at subsequent times'*, then to understand the contemporary role of the village it is necessary to understand the village of the past as well as the decision-making systems of the present. It is further postulated that because elements of the system are continually changing no equilibrium situation is ever reached. In the case of Ra the time-gap between action and reaction is increased not only by what might be described as normal time-lag due to dissemination of the effects and inertia, but also by the actions of those who would seek to prevent any change in the village. While neither knowledge of the Ra area nor knowledge of systems analysis as applied in this field have reached a level where a thoroughgoing study in systems terms is appropriate, this is a tentative essay in that direction, an attempt to indicate those elements which in changing have interacted with other parts of the system and of connected systems to produce further change. Attention is specifically focused on the reason for the continued existence of the village, particularly in view of the growth of the *galala* (independent farmer) movement.

Three time-periods are selected in Table 4.1, at each of which the significant functions and attributes are analysed. The first is in the period prior to European contact, which in Ra meant no later than the very early nineteenth century, and which for lack of specific knowledge is difficult to treat with great confidence. Much which is imputed to the village system of that time must necessarily remain conjectural. The second period chosen is in the time following Cession in 1874, and the third that of the early 1960s which saw many of the colonial policies in their final stages.

The pre-contact village

Legend states that Fijian occupation of Ra can be traced back

Plate 1   The village in transition: small village with banana groves and gardens behind on the upper Rewa river in Fiji. Bananas have been a major cash crop for two generations, but have undergone severe decline in recent years from marketing problems and disease.

Plate 2 . Intensive cultivation: newly planted ditched sweet-potato field with house by fence, and a background of *casuarina* thicket, Chimbu, 1963.

Plate 3 (below) Garden close-up: a newly prepared part of a clearing in New Georgia, Solomon Islands, 1969. Young taro at left; stakes to provide trellis for yams planted in loosened earth.

Plate 4 The traditional *koro* in Ra Province, Fiji. This photograph was taken in 1963; by 1969 all these houses had been replaced by modern structures (see Plate 7).

Plate 5 (*below*) The traditional food complex of much of the Pacific: taro, yams, with vines on a trellis and banana, all in a rather badly overgrown garden prepared by simple swidden methods, New Georgia, Solomon Islands, 1969.

Plate 6   Another view of the traditional *koro* shown in Plate 4.

Plate 7 (below)   Modern village: Nacamaki, Koro island, Fiji, June 1973. No houses i
the traditional style now remain in this village, as in many others. The new styles are hardl
pleasing to the eye, and they both heat and cool more rapidly than their predecessors. Bu
they are more durable, less readily infested with vermin, and much better suited to the housin
of furniture and other possessions of the modern villager.

Plate 8　　Urban produce market: a corner of the market at Suva, Fiji, June 1973, with a large variety of vegetables on sale, principally taro (*dalo*). Rapid urbanization has led to many of these markets being seriously under-supplied.

Plate 9　　An old Pacific port-town: Levuka, Fiji. In the nineteenth century this was one of the principal trading centres of the western Pacific, and Levuka remained a major port for copra until recent years. Little business now remains, and the town serves only a local clientele.

Plate 10   Cooking food with modern aids in a traditional setting: the preparations for a feast in the New Guinea highlands.

Plate 11   The continuing Pacific: a group of men around the *yaqona* (kava)
bowl at a meeting with the District Commissioner in a new school building under
construction, Koro Island, Fiji, June 1973.

Plate 12 Change and tradition in personal decoration in the New Guinea highlands: two Enga men on a road in the western highlands, October 1959. The breastplate shell worn by the man on the right is a larger baler shell (*Melo* spp.), valuable but comparatively rare until the 1930s. Hughes (1971: 326) notes that large shells such as this have mostly been introduced by European traders. The knapsack is also a modern introduction, but the bark and bamboo belts and the woven cloth pieces and carrying bag are traditional.

Plate 13 The traditional wealth: two traditionally attired men carrying a display frame bearing shell and bird plumes to a wedding. The main highway through the Wahgi valley, New Guinea highlands, 1959.

through some fourteen generations to the legendary Lutunaso-basoba and Degei, though archaeological evidence points to an even longer period of occupancy (Frazer, 1968a). Fighting broke out among the various groups, and by the time of first European contacts the situation had reached a stage where the Native Lands Commission reported:

Ra at one time seems to have carried a large population; but . . . intertribal wars were carried on within its borders, with but little interruption, up to the brink of Cession—wars in which tribes split up and took different sides. The consequent migratory movements of the population left large tracts of the country unoccupied—country in which it was not safe to settle—which remained unsettled at Cession. (Native Lands Commission, 1927)

At this stage it is clear that the critical function of the village was the defence of its inhabitants. Banding together and living in fortified villages (*koro ni valu*) was absolutely essential to the pre-servation of life. Whatever other social or economic goals the in-dividuals of a community may have had, they were almost certainly subordinate to the demands of survival. These would have included the preservation of the social unit with its hierarchical system of leadership and mutual obligations, together with the protection of clan lands on which much of the social superstructure was founded. The economic goals of society included the normal essentials of food, clothing and shelter, which in general could not be pre-served or accumulated beyond immediate needs. Where production of durable goods did take place, it was almost certainly in the form of mats, *masi* ('tapa' cloth), *vaqona tabua* (whale's teeth), which, together with 'surplus' food, would be used in ceremonial exchanges with other social groups for the promotion of social and political solidarity.

The locational pattern of village communities was a product of the need to find a defensible site, which was usually a craggy hill-top but sometimes a moated coastal situation, with access to food and water, and preferably in proximity to such other villages as might offer mutual aid. It appears that in some cases the desire to locate in a safe remote area led to abandonment of lands and taking up residence in different areas with the acquiescence of the land-owning group. Little is known of the size of villages at this time,

77

Table 4.1 Summary of attributes of Fijian villages in three time periods.

Attributes	Pre-contact village	Post-Cession village	Village of the 1960s
Major goals	Survival in war Food and shelter Preservation of social unit Protection of lands	Food and shelter Preservation of social unit Retention of lands European goods	Continuance of social unit (diminishing) Personal freedom and status European possessions and foods European style houses Capital goods (ploughs, etc.) Health services and education Good communications with urban areas
Economic base	Swidden agriculture Hunting, fishing, gathering Static stone-age technology Minimal specialization	Swidden agriculture Hunting, fishing, gathering Contract labour wages Tax garden surpluses Minimal specialization	Swidden agriculture (declining) Limited hunting, fishing, gathering Commercial crops Wages Incipient entrepreneurial activities Incipient specialization
Location regulators	Defence Access to food Political groupings	Access to food Administration Health	Health Communications Commercial opportunities or access to food Education and social services Ownership of land
Size regulators	Minimum viable defence force Maximum which food supply would support	Minimum viable production group Maximum which food supply would support	Virtually no minimum Maximum which total local economy would support

Population regulators	Balance of high birth and death rate Battle casualties Migration to safety	Balance of low birth rate and high death rate Migration to work	Balance of high birth rate and low death rate Migration to work (largely in urban areas) Independent farming
Decision-making	Hereditary chiefs and community councils	Hereditary chiefs and community councils Appointed chiefs Government officers and magistrates	Hereditary chiefs (declining) Community councils Government officers and magistrates Individuals and groups
Agency enforcing decisions	Life or death power of chief Community attitudes	Community attitudes Native police (jail and fines)	Community attitudes (declining) Police and Fijian Provincial constables (jail and fines)
Centripetal forces	Safety Leadership Tradition Group organization—reciprocal assistance	Leadership Security Tradition Group organization—reciprocal assistance	Tradition Security (diminishing) Sense of identification Limited reciprocal assistance Official restraints on out-migration
Centrifugal forces	Nil	Desire for cash income—labour contracts Incipient desire for freedom from community obligations and restrictions	Strong desire for freedom from community obligations and restrictions Attraction of urban life Opportunities for higher incomes Desire for higher status Education

but it is assumed that the lower limit would be set by the minimum number of able-bodied males required to defend the site, a number clearly related to such variables as the nature of the site and the expected opposition. Upper limits were probably imposed by the food supply available within the 'safe' area. Some must have attained considerable size if one accepts the reports of Miss Gordon Cumming (1885, 257) that 450 people were massacred in one incident in Ra in 1873, or of Derrick (1950, 225) that Cakobau's Christian troops killed or wounded 157 people in another. Seemann (1862, 222–3) recorded on one of the two Nananu islands that 'there may be about one hundred inhabitants, who lived in a town defended by a deep ditch and high earthern mounds'.

Little can be said with certainty of the manner in which decisions were made and implemented in pre-contact times. France (1968, 12) claims that it was the habit of Fijians 'to discuss matters in council at a village level, or even at the level of a local group of villages in time of war'; but Derrick and others have also stressed that powerful hereditary chiefs had life or death powers over individuals who transgressed the accepted rules of the group; and to what extent the advice and counsel of non-chiefly persons was admitted is unknown. There is reason to believe that a chief had to be a strong man, whether to attain and/or retain his position of leadership. The range of matters in which a commoner could make and carry out personal decisions was probably extremely limited, particularly if he was for any reason (such as being a refugee) not a member of a land-owning group.

Classification of forces acting upon village inhabitants in terms of whether they were centripetal, and therefore contributing to the cohesion and continuance of the village system, or centrifugal and thus causing the reverse, leads to the conclusion that in the pre-contact period virtually all forces were centripetal. For the individuals there was virtually no possibility of an alternative combined with survival, other than removal to another friendly village, where he at once became subject to the same constraints. Within the village lay safety, an assured and probably prescribed and unchangeable position in a homeostatic social and economic system. The social unit might rise or fall, strengthen or weaken (C. S. Belshaw, quoted in Spate, 1959, 10), but it is unlikely that an individual's position within it would change significantly relative to that of others. From birth, the pre-contact Fijian was conditioned to accept that his village was the centre of his world and that there was no alternative.

To suggest that the pre-contact society was completely static and unchanging would be naïve, but within the lifetimes of individuals it must have seemed so, and for the purposes of this study it can probably be treated as such. More rapid change eventually came through a progression of beach-combers, traders, missionaries, planters, and the like until the ceding of Fiji to Britain as a colony in 1874.

The post-Cession village

Upon taking up his appointment as first permanent governor in the new Crown Colony of Fiji, Sir Arthur Gordon (later Lord Stanmore) wasted no time in setting up a form of administration which in its central policy aims remained quite remarkably intact almost until independence in 1970. His major organizational constraint was that his administration had to be self-supporting financially, while his major policy constraint, a self-imposed one, was that Fijian rights, customs, and institutions were to be preserved and overlaid with, but not restructured by, the benefits of education, law, medicine, and economic progress. To overcome the financial problem he taxed Fijians on a provincial basis, Ra taxes varying between £750 and £850 annually, which called for a contribution of about five shillings per taxpayer (Frazer, 1968a, 101). Seeing that this might force Fijians into becoming contract labourers on European-owned plantations, thus negating the policy constraint, Gordon demanded that tax gardens be set up by communities to grow assigned commercial crops. However, in the case of Ra, then considered to be one of the poorest provinces, a high proportion was accepted in cash originating from contract labour. There was also a complete prohibition on the further sale of Fijian land.

To minimize administrative costs the system operated with only a small number of European officers, acting through and in conjunction with Fijian chiefs who were appointed to official positions. The provincial Fijian administration was headed by a *Roko Tui*, beneath whom the administration of each district was carried out by a *Buli* assisted by native constables. Fijian magistrates and medical practitioners were in due course added to the class of appointed officials.

In this new environment the functions and attributes of villages

81

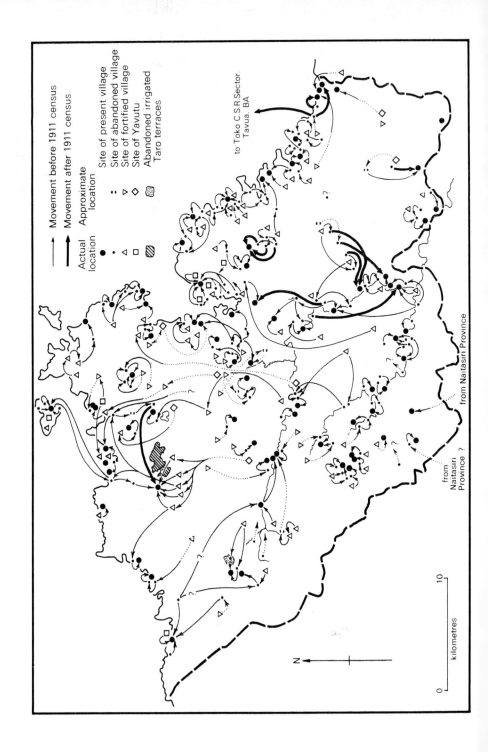

Movement before 1911 census

Movement after 1911 census

Approximate location

Actual location

Site of present village
Site of abandoned village
Site of fortified village
Site of Yavutu
Abandoned irrigated Taro terraces

to Toko C.S.R.Sector. Tavua, BA

from Naitasiri Province

from Naitasiri Province ?

kilometres

0   10

N

quickly underwent marked changes. First in importance was the new peace, which removed many of the constraints that war had hitherto placed on the location, organization and character of villages. Survival quickly fell away as the predominant social and economic goal—though at times such as the great measles epidemic of 1875 it may still have seemed that survival was in question. The maintenance of land now became first in order, and the battle for the protection of clan lands was fought before the Native Lands Commission. Continuance of the social unit central to the Fijian concept of desirable life was heavily dependent upon the security of titles to land, and many a sharp legal skirmish resulted. New goals had also by then been established. There was a demand for at least some European possessions such as tools and boats, while adoption of Christianity also called for at least some extra efforts. Education and taxes were also demanding increased productivity.

A new set of locational factors became operational. Defensible positions were abandoned for more convenient sites close to the sea or to garden land (Frazer, 1961, 31).* Initially, these shifts were sometimes accompanied by the splitting of the village into several smaller hamlets. Many of the new sites were found to be damp and unhealthy and a large number were subsequently moved on orders from the provincial medical officer (Frazer, 1968a, 99). Administrative convenience seems to have led to other villages being re-sited closer to the newly-constructed government tracks or amalgamated once again into larger units. Such measures caused the average population per village to rise from 66 in 1891 to 80 in 1901, despite a drop in population.

One may deduce that upper and lower population limits for a village were also set by new criteria. The lower limit was presumably set by the minimum viable production group. Fijian society habitually relied on collective groups to carry out such tasks as house building, the maintenance of tracks, for the district and province, and the growing of food and production of mats and *masi* for communal hospitality. The minimum size may well have been quite low, as the 31 villages of the Saivou and Tokaimalo districts together in 1891 had a range of populations from 18 to 134 with a

* Fig. 4.2 represents the locations of previous villages and movements reported by the villagers to the author, with additional material from sources such as Native Lands Commission maps, and evidence supporting claims to the Lands Commission after Cession.

median of 52. Thus, the minimum viable size was almost certainly very much lower than during previous troubled periods when defence was a paramount consideration. The possible upper limit had almost certainly grown with the relocation of villages in the midst of productive agricultural lands; however, because of population decline this limit was probably nowhere reached.

The structure of decision-making in the village had also changed. With government backing the hereditary chief no longer found it necessary to be a charismatic leader to achieve or retain the rank to which he was heir. A weak leader could be endured in peacetime, and indeed could hardly be got rid of in the post-Cession situation. But the range of decisions open to a hereditary leader had narrowed because of changed circumstances. Government officers, both European and Fijian, were able to make and enforce decisions in areas which had previously been the sole prerogative of the hereditary chief. Village location, health measures, laws, punishment, and many other decisions were now made in the Queen's name. Spiritual leadership had fallen into the hands of the missionaries and their native catechists. The untitled commoner was also becoming aware of alternatives to the acceptance of chiefly or group wishes. A man who flouted traditional authority was no longer in danger of his life, but satisfactory life in the village remained virtually impossible. Increasingly however it became feasible to opt out of the system for shorter or longer periods, by accepting a labour contract at some distance or by going to live in another village where conditions were more acceptable.

Nevertheless, the village remained a close-knit community. Most who left the village did so with the acquiescence of the community, in the expectation that they would return and share out their accumulated wages. Missionaries and administrators deferred to chiefly status wherever possible, and many chiefs who accepted official appointments as *Buli* or *Roko* were able to strengthen and entrench their own position by utilizing the power of the state to back up their own remaining authority. Some took on the role of economic leadership and were able to use their traditional powers to organize community activities, or to raise money for such purchases as community boats.

The post-Cession village was one in which the interest of the group remained paramount; the interest of the individual was still subjugated to the collective will. No man might rise above his

84

station and remain in the community, and the hereditary chief still had the function of decision-maker over a wide range of social and economic matters. His position still embodied the status and pride of the clan, and it was his obligation to ensure the continuance of accepted custom. Centripetal forces leading individuals to remain within villages included the security of a place in a carefully-ordered society, a sense of mutual obligation, and the economic right to reciprocal assistance from the clan in house-building, hunting, fishing, and other activities which were better carried out by larger groups. Centrifugal forces were still minimally effective, being largely limited to the attraction of a small number of government positions and plantation contracts for those who were ambitious, or who wanted freedom from the obligations and restrictions of the village.*

It is clear that villages had changed in location, size, and organizational structure, but many of the essential features of pre-contact times remained virtually intact.

The village of the 1960s

Visually the Ra village of the early 1960s had probably changed little since the beginning of the century. Over 90 per cent of the houses were of traditional thatched construction, and in some villages all were of this type. Chiefs' houses were probably somewhat smaller than formerly, and there is some likelihood that the houses occupied by the ordinary villagers were also smaller. But while there was thus physical continuity, very great changes had taken place in the function and attributes of villages.

Fiji had moved through a further period of change in its economic, political, and social systems. As the village is a subsystem of these systems, changes in the wider system provoked compensating changes in the local system. Many of the reasons for the existence of villages had been undermined, but at the same time the policies originally formulated by Gordon had been continued by subsequent administrations until they had reached the status of an 'orthodoxy' (France, 1968). Many measures were designed specifically to con-

---

* It is not possible to say how many Ra Fijians were living outside villages in post-Cession times. Of the Fijians enumerated in Ra in 1891, only 1·4 per cent lived outside villages, but many of these would have been officials and labourers from other provinces. No estimate is possible of the fairly considerable number of Ra Fijians who were working in other provinces for government or on contract.

tinue the existence of village communities in the belief that positive benefits would be realised. In the forefront of these policies was the reorganized Fijian Administration set up in 1945, and described by Spate (1959, 31) as a state within a state. This tiered system of administration began in the village with the official elected headman (*turaga-ni-koro*), and on up through the appointed district and provincial heads to the Secretary for Fijian Affairs. Paralleling it at each level was an elected committee or council which acted in an advisory capacity. A system of Fijian courts presided over by special Fijian magistrates attempted to ensure that the Fijian Regulations (which applied only to indigenous Fijians) were carried out, while the whole structure was financed by a head tax on all adult Fijian males. As Spate indicated (1959, 35–6), virtually all the effort of the system went into maintaining itself, to preserving supposed Fijian custom and sponsoring the 'communal way of life'—even to the extent of preventing other government departments carrying out work among Fijians which might conceivably run counter to the central policy, which was a remarkable effort at social conservation.

Even if it had ever been true, the Fijian population could no longer be looked upon as a homogeneous group with similar goals and outlooks. Particularly among the younger Fijians aspirations were changing and individuals were taking personal optimizing action which often ran counter to the wishes of the conservative older generation, which were supported by the Fijian Administration. To these younger people the village was no longer the centre of the world but part of the periphery. The possessions and experiences which they coveted did not originate in the village, but in the outside world, particularly in the urban places such as Suva. Most did not appear to be ready completely to abandon the values and goals of the village, but rather to accommodate the new ones within the system. The compromise was often an uneasy one.

While pre-contact Fijians had little choice as to where they lived, what they ate, how they allocated their time, or to what material possessions they could aspire, Fijians of the 1960s had a greatly-increased range of choice. For the most part they still desired continuance of membership in the social unit and were generally prepared to give time, effort and cash or produce to satisfy its demands, but to a lesser extent than in the past. Being a landowner or *taukei* was no longer simply to be one of a secure, landed group. The role had become differentiated economically, depending upon the amount of land available, its commercial value, and the number who shared access to it. Socially, most men put at least some value on the status land conferred, but by 1960 the exercise of rights as a landowner no longer depended exclusively upon residence within the village and full participation in all the activities of the social group. Moreover, the economic goals of individuals (the building of European-style houses, the possession of European furniture, and the acquisition of capital goods such as ploughs, tractors and trucks) were difficult to satisfy in association with full participation in a traditional village pattern of life.

The general locational pattern of villages had not changed substantially since the nineteenth century in Ra, but those changes which had taken place, when seen in conjunction with population changes, indicated that the regulators of village size and spacing were no longer what they had once been. Amalgamations had reduced the number of villages from 97 in 1901 to 78 in 1960, while the average village population had at first fallen and then risen to just over 80. The size-range of the villages had widened, with more villages in the upper and lower size groups.

Improvement of communications seems to have been the major reason for village shifts during this century; most new sites were either on or closer to the roads. Not many more such changes are likely to take place, as most of those villages still located at off-road locations have no land adjacent to the road on which they can resite. A few Ra villages have been able to beg land informally on which to relocate, but a growing awareness of the commercial value of land and uneasiness that occupation might confer more permanent rights makes it likely that only formal leasing will be feasible in the future.

Despite the obvious social and commercial advantages of roadside locations, it is clear that off-road locations still remained viable for a large number of inhabitants. Analysis of populations of villages since 1911 (Frazer, 1961, 68–73) showed that while the isolated interior hill-country villages lost population overall, individual villages showed substantial gains. Even these interior villages offered educational and medical facilities at an acceptable level, plentiful land for subsistence crops, and a minimal level of cash income from growing *yaqona*.

While to a very considerable extent the village had become fixed in its location, the individual was much less bound to the village than ever before. The longstanding habit of Ra Fijians working away from the province, either permanently or temporarily, had gained momentum (Frazer, 1969), while the amount of internal migration had also increased. Through marriage, blood relationship, or ties of friendship many Fijians had been able to shift to villages which offered a more acceptable way of life. The significance of these shifts does not lie in their spatial pattern, which cannot easily be analysed, but rather in the greater freedom of choice now available. For a person who was in any way dissatisfied with his own village there were three basic alternatives: migration out of the province (probably to an urban area), migration to a non-village location within Ra, or migration to another village.

Favourably-located villages could now grow to much greater size than in earlier times. The upper size limit was no longer set by the local food supply and by considerations of 'tolerable distance' to the gardens, but by the economic opportunities available. In contrast, the minimum size of a village seems also to have fallen. Some had fallen to only a few households but continued to function at least as living places. A large body of able-bodied men seemed no longer to be essential for the maintenance of a community.

Hereditary chiefs were still persons of consequence, though the importance varied with the individual. With the growth of bodies such as elected village councils, and with more contact with government officers, the areas of life in which the chief could make and enforce decisions had declined further. The individual villager could make decisions over a wider range, and if his wishes ran counter to those of the chief or the community then there were more opportunities for him to move elsewhere. Men of initiative were making use of economic opportunities which gave them goals outside traditional community values and became ends in themselves. In their pursuit of these goals they were now able to set themselves outside the traditional framework of village decision-making, further eroding the effective powers of the chief.

The independent farmer

In many ways the greatest local challenge to the village system came from the *galala* or independent farmers. In 1959 there were some 180 *galala* in Ra, representing almost 14 per cent of Fijian males actually engaged in agriculture (Frazer, 1961, 224–36; 1964). These were men who wished to be free of the statutory obligation to perform communal tasks at the behest of the *Turaga-ni-koro*, to be allowed to work their own land commercially, and to shift their residence away from the village if they so wished. To become a *galala* a man had to make formal application through the official district headman (*Buli*) to the provincial headman (*Roko*), giving evidence of his ability to support himself and his family with an annual cash income of £100, and to pay an additional Commutationa Rate of £1 per year to compensate the village for the loss of his services. Spate (1959, 87) has indicated how much difficulty some men had in gaining the necessary permission from a system which was dedicated to the promotion of village life. Many who applied were rejected, and a number who were successful in gaining exemption later had their permission revoked in the course of annual inspections by the *Buli*, required during the first five years of independence. A few, finding that the life was not to their taste, had voluntarily returned to the village or abandoned their holdings and migrated to an urban area.

Interviews with a high proportion of these men revealed a great deal about the nature of village life, and of the kind of men who found it unsatisfactory. The most frequently given reasons were that communal tasks left no time for the planting of commercial crops, which were essential if a satisfactory cash income were to be attained. However, it is clear that the objection was less to the actual amount of time taken by communal tasks as to the twin frustrations of the inefficiency with which they were carried out (Spate, 1959) and the timing, which often led to demands being made just when some pressing farm duties required attention. Other personal reasons for leaving the village were less often mentioned but undoubtedly applied to some men. Quarrels, jealousy, and often a desire not to be given orders by a *Turaga-ni-koro* who was over-zealous, undoubtedly motivated some. Nevertheless, in some of the smaller villages, men were already able to order their affairs in such a way that exemption merely to satisfy the economic motive was irrelevant.

As a group the independent farmers had more business acumen, energy, and strength of character than the average villager. They also tended to be better off in terms of experience though not in formal education. Only about five percent had been trained at agricultural schools or training centres, but over a half had served in the police force or army; most of the latter had served overseas either in World War II or during the Malayan Emergency. Almost all

89

had followed the normal village pattern of working away from the province at some time, and a number had been employed at skilled or semi-skilled jobs. Their number included ex-teachers, three ex-*Buli*, tradesmen, and non-commissioned officers. At least four had hereditary titles of a level which allowed them use of the honorific of *Ratu*. Most were men of mature years, and among 134 men whose ages were recorded only 25 were under 30 and 100 were between the ages of 30 and 50. Nearly all were married and had children.

Less than one-third of the *galala* lived within their own villages, though few had moved more than 1·6km away. A few had shifted several kilometres, but usually they were then close to, and in a few cases actually resident in, other villages, so that it was unusual to find a *galala* more than a few minutes walk from a village; none was more than 5km from a village. In many cases the shift was undoubtedly symbolic rather than dictated by considerations of time saved in travelling to other fields. The cost and effort of building a house only a hundred metres or less from the village and abandoning a perfectly good (and sometimes better) house could not have been justified on purely economic grounds. Rather, the action was a mark of independence from the village, and of desire to be free of such time-consuming activities as the entertainment of casual visitors and the drinking of *yaqona* during working hours.

The agricultural activities of the *galala* varied according to the area in which they farmed. The most successful economically were sugarcane producers, eight of whom had annual production in excess of 100 tons with the most efficient producing almost 200 tons. Many supplemented their cane income with vegetables and root crops, and some with rice. In other areas the principal crops included copra, rice, maize, bananas, and *yaqona*, and a number gained additional income by grazing cattle. Many were unfamiliar with the techniques of growing and marketing field crops and their profits suffered accordingly. Fertilizers and insecticides were almost unknown and few sought information from the Field Assistants of the Department of Agriculture, even though they often showed considerable initiative in experimenting with new crops or enterprises.

Despite these inadequacies the mean *per capita* output of the independent farmers was much higher than that of the villagers. Their cane output per head was twice that of the non-exempted Fijian growers, and though accurate comparison of the output of other crops was not possible their performance was visibly superior. Inevitably, some *galala* had shown no increase in production since becoming independent, and the villagers were quick to point to such cases even though in general they considered the exempted men better off; the *galala* unanimously considered themselves to be better off.

The success of the enterprise as revealed by living standards was not so easy to judge. The proportion of *galala* with iron-roofed houses was about the same as for villagers; but while many of the village houses were paid for by communal contributions, such as pooled lease monies, or by money sent home by absentees, all the *galala* had paid for their own. Some had had their houses built by the community in the traditional manner in which the workers, who were generally members of the independent farmers' clan, were supplied with food and *yaqona* and rewarded by a feast. However, an increasing number lived in houses that they had built either by themselves or with the aid of close relatives, or which they had paid for as a purely commercial contract, leaving themselves free to continue with their farming operations. Possession of furniture, radios, sewing machines, pressure lamps, and kerosene stoves were the mark of established *galala* rather than of the newly independent, who, in the manner of most pioneers, preferred to give higher priority to the acquisition of capital goods. Here the *galala* were clearly superior to villagers, with a high proportion of exempted men owning ploughs and other implements with which to grow field crops—such items being rare in the villages.

The pattern of business enterprise displayed some reverses, following attempts to move into a larger scale of business after initial success within a familiar round of activity. Some men invested their accumulated capital in such ventures as lorries, tractors and launches, but failed to operate them at a profit. Comparatively few were able to make this major jump from the level of peasant farmer to that of entrepreneur.

In the early 1960s most village Fijians seemed to regard *galala* ambivalently. As individuals they often envied their freedom to lead a life free of petty exactions, and their consequent ability to make more money. As members of a community, however, they looked askance on a member contracting out and leaving the village poorer economically by the loss of his productive capacity and, possibly more important, poorer and weaker in spirit by the loss of his personality. Each such defection represented one more stage in the destruction of the way of life in which the villager had been brought up, and which gave him a security which he probably could not find in the outside world. Undoubtedly many looked upon the *galala* as being mean and 'un-Fijian', particularly in that, having made more money, they did not share it freely with their less fortunate brothers.

It must not be inferred that the exempted man was in any way an outcast from Fijian society. Most visited their villages regularly and took part, sometimes prominently, in activities such as church services, entertainment of important visitors, and the raising of funds for church or community purposes. Many had become substantial benefactors to their villages, supplying cows for weddings and funerals, making donations for schools or water supplies, and loaning implements and bullocks to plant village gardens. Such men were looked upon as bringing honour to their villages and as examples of what Fijians were capable of doing.

The relation between the *galala* and the villager illuminates very clearly a great many of the strengths and weaknesses of the Fijian village. Of the cohesive factors, the sense of belonging to a related group with a code of behaviour which includes love and generosity to fellow members, assistance for the aged, and security for the young, is probably now the most potent. While some of the benefits in social security and group assistance may have been showing signs of relative diminution, they were still very real in the eyes of most residents and *galala* alike. Compared with this central factor, the more formal official restraints on men leaving the village, and the imposition of an added tax burden on those who did, were probably of much lesser significance in holding the village together.

But centrifugal forces leading to pressures for the abandonment or restructuring of the village were also becoming more apparent. The freedom from the 'burden of obligations' (Spate, 1959, 22–6) conferred by exemption seems to be chief among the advantages gained by leaving the village. These obligations were interlinked with community attitudes regarding custom, behaviour, and status, many of which the young or less conformist found irksome if not intolerable. There were also the growing 'pull' factors relating to the excitement of urban places in contrast with the sometimes dull and uneventful life of the village. Education was also proving to be a disruptive factor. A few men left isolated villages to improve the educational opportunities of their children, but more significant was the effect of secondary education on those fortunate enough to obtain it. The proportion of these returning to village life was small, and with those who did, their personal ambition to achieve higher status generally led to activities such as independent farming, entrepreneurial activities or group leadership in projects which tended to upset the traditional hierarchical status structure of the village. In a very few villages, those which had grown larger, emergent difficulties in obtaining access to land were also contributing to out-migration.

It would be misleading to suggest that all villages reacted similarly to the changing circumstances. Watters (1969) has suggested that there is a considerable spectrum of reaction to the invasion of the commercial world, from the traditional village, with little apparent commercial motivation or achievement and with many of its traditional attitudes and customs more or less intact, to the village where commercial goals have become more central and where institutions have been modified to allow their achievement. If anything, the range and variety of reactions in the Ra villages was even wider than Watters has suggested. All generalizations regarding them must therefore be seen in this context.

Conclusion and prognosis

Since pre-contact times the village has been in a constant state of change. From being a highly cohesive entity bonded together by the necessity of survival and with a highly centralized decision-making and enforcing system, it has evolved to a situation where it is far less cohesive, with diversity of individual goals, and where the making of decisions affecting both the individual and the community are dispersed among people at all levels both within and outside the community. One might well pose the questions: What is a contemporary Fijian village? How should we assess its place in the present fabric of Fiji society? Does it have a continuing function, or is it now an anachronism?

Physically the village consists of a group of Fijians living in houses of a distinctive style clustered in close proximity, together with their land. Socially the group is welded together by the majority having membership in clans with a common eponymous ancestor, and with others related by ties of marriage or friendship to the clan members. Residence in a village normally carries both rights and obligations in social and, to a lessening extent, economic matters. But individuals have found it increasingly possible to replace the services offered by the village with others, often without losing too many of the benefits. Alternative styles of life are available and are being chosen, but a substantial number still find that within the village system they are able to satisfy their social and economic aspirations without having to undergo the mental and physical dislocation which such a basic change in life entails.

When judged from a social point of view, the worth of the village system is that for a large number of Fijians it provides a stable way of life, entailing a large number of positive social benefits. It also provides a number of less tangible but still highly important social benefits to members who do not choose to live there, particularly in the emotional sense of a place of belonging; few *galala* want the village to disappear. Economically it is much less attractive. Spate (1959) and others have shown how the traditional ability to organize and carry out productive enterprises within the village has been stifled by the imposed system, and have traced the manner in which individual enterprise has been curbed. Other systems of settlement would almost certainly prove more productive from a purely economic point of view, as does dispersed Indian settlement in Ra (Frazer, 1968b). Now that many of the artificial restrictions placed upon the individual by the Fijian Regulations have been removed or relaxed (Brookfield with Hart, 1971, 242), the village is free to evolve further. One possibility is that as present houses reach the end of their economic life more residents will choose a dispersed pattern which will improve the economic solution to the settlement problem, while retaining the social benefits of community membership in a manner similar to the *galala* of the fifties and sixties.

The location, form and functions of Fijian villages result from decisions taken both within the villages and by government. At each level, decisions have been taken in reasonable expectation of a satisfactory outcome, and in relation to a particular set of conditions which required decision. Within the village, the principal decisions include whether to remain or to leave, whether to disperse or aggregate the settlement, whether to support the leadership or to oppose it. Village leaders have found their freedom of action restricted, whether by the circumstance of war and land quarrels in former times, or by the growing role of Government in modern times.

Government actions, seeking to conserve a 'way of life', have often been restrictive of others, but have permitted growing individual freedom in recent years. The combined effect has been to slow down and even obscure changes that have taken place, for while the village has remained as a physical institution, its *raison d'être* and function are very different from what they were. An understanding of the present forces, and of their evolution, is essential if there is to be adequate social and economic planning for the future.

APPENDIX: GLOSSARY OF FIJIAN TERMS

Buli   A salaried government official in charge of Fijians and Fijian affairs in a district. Responsible to the *Roko Tui* of the province.

koro ni valu   Fortified village(s) of pre-contact times.

masi   'Tapa' cloth of the south Pacific, made from the bark of the *Broussonetia papyrifera*.

Ratu   The usual title of a man of chiefly status.

Roko Tui   A salaried government official in charge of Fijians and Fijian affairs in a province.

tabua   A sperm whale's tooth used for ceremonial presentation on important occasions.

Turaga-ni-koro   Unpaid, elected village headman. Responsible to the *Buli* and *Roko*.

taukei   The indigenous owners of the land.

yaqona   Refers to both the *Piper methysticum* shrub, and to the ceremonial drink made from its roots when dried, pounded and mixed with water.

EDITOR'S NOTE

There have been a number of changes in the Fijian village system since the middle 1960s; the *Buli* has been eliminated and with him an important element of control; communal obligations have also been abolished, so far as the law is concerned. There has been a rapid increase in the proportion of *village* houses built of frame, composition board and iron—requiring more capital, but of longer life. At the same time it has become possible for at least some men to enclose portions of clan land without becoming *galala*, and without removing themselves from the villages. These changes have perhaps reduced the 'centrifugal' forces described by Frazer. But at the same time the rate of emigration to Suva and other towns has increased very greatly, and Ra Province is as much affected by this emigration as any part of Fiji.

5 Stone-age trade in the New Guinea inland

Historical geography without history

Ian Hughes

In all the world, only inland New Guinea provides an opportunity for understanding an extensive system of neolithic trade in all its complexity—its ecological basis, its physiographic constraints, and the cultural adaptations of those that took part. Elsewhere the neolithic traders are dead and have left no records other than a handful of durable artefacts. Most of the area of this study remained prehistoric until the 1930s, some of it until the 1950s. In some parts, a few worn steel axes preceded the first literate visitors by a year or two, but during the years of data collection, 1967–8, there were everywhere men who had been mature adults during truly stone-age times and remembered them well.

Some of the problems of working at the interface between geography as human ecology and anthropology, history and pre-history, the way in which concepts and methods drawn from those disciplines affected the study, and the techniques used to satisfy the methodological requirements of oral history are discussed elsewhere by the writer (Hughes, 1971). That work also examines documentary sources for the New Guinea coast and the periphery of the study area to put beyond doubt the pristine nature of the neolithic economy in the central area of interest, to delineate the moving frontier of exploration, and to provide comparative material on the nature of traditional trade and the processes of diffusion of foreign introductions. There, too, the data and analysis are presented at length. Here it is possible only to state briefly the methods, to outline the distribution of resources and the environmental and cultural diversity that underlies the rationale of indigenous trade, and to present some of the general findings.

Data were collected in structured but informal interviews in a

97

Table 5.1 Classification of trade goods: a framework

Sets of needs	Geographical and ecological	
	Inter-regional emphasis	Intra-regional emphasis
General attributes	Goods that expose the problems of distance and access by being of very restricted natural distribution or manufacture and very wide demand	Goods that highlight smaller differences in resource bases including those of forest and farm by being of restricted distribution or manufacture and wide demand
Particular attributes and categories of goods	Localized minerals, for inland areas—marine products, goods dependent on very specialized and localized skills for which a demand exists elsewhere	Minerals of discontinuous distribution but general demand, animals and plants of restricted habitat, goods dependent on special local skills for which a demand exists elsewhere
Goods	Stone of implement quality, stone tools, pottery, salt, selected pigments, sea-shells	Stone tools, pottery, stone of implement quality, potting clay, salt, pigments, mineral oil, sea-shells, wild animals and birds, animal and bird products, forest plant products, vegetable oils, crops, domestic animals, medicaments, stimulants
Aspects peculiar to the study areas	No stone raw material traded inter-regionally	Stone raw material trade only very local in one region, no trade in potting clay, only stimulant trade was lime in one region

series of traverses working outwards from the central highlands and extending north–south from Astrolabe Bay to the Papuan Gulf and east–west from the Asaro Valley to the upper Wahgi Valley. More than 30 languages are spoken in the area. Observations were made of surviving trade objects and practices, and supplementary information was gained from the sparse ethnographical notes of early white visitors. A little comparative material has been unearthed by archaeologists, but there is an effective gap of some hundreds of years between their most recent dates and the oldest oral traditions, which, on the evidence, are reasonably reliable only to about 1900.

Economic	Historical
Goods that are important because of high unit value or large quantity which are transferred between groups	Goods that reflect technological and cultural change by the possession of traits shown here and elsewhere to be distinctive
Valuables, luxuries, subsistence essentials	Artefacts, especially pottery, tools, weapons and ornaments; domestic animals, crop plants, pigments
Ceremonial stone tools and weapons, other valuable stone tools, bulk salt, valuable ornaments of shell, teeth, and feathers, pigs, dogs, cassowaries, marsupials, special pigments, skins, fur, feathers, vegetable oil, pottery, small containers of salt, minor pigments, mineral oil, specialized luxury crops, forest timber and fibre products, medicaments, stimulants, seasonal staple crops	Pottery, stone tools, stone weapons, tools and weapons of wood and fibre, ornaments and tools of shell and bone, pigs, dogs, crops, pigments
No trade in seasonal staple foods (unlike sago elsewhere)—only stimulant trade was lime in one region	Historical research largely dependent on the methodology and techniques of archaeology; therefore durable products most useful; no trade in staple crops

Because closing this gap and demonstrating older cultural continuities over time and space depends on archaeological prehistorians, special attention was paid to trade goods which had been shown to survive well in New Guinea excavation sites, which were likely to be diagnostic of particular traditions, and which were specially suitable for testing the hypothesized ecological basis of trade and delineating inter-regional, intra-regional and local trade. The scheme of the selection criteria is shown in Table 5.1. In addition to the key items (stone tools, pottery, sea-shells and mineral pigments) salt proved to be important as a valuable in its own right, and as a consumption good it was found to demonstrate a significant cultural adaptation, small trade areas of potassium salts being embedded in large trade areas of sodium salts.

The regional distribution of resources

The 18,000km² of the study area has an altitude range of 4,500m from near sea-level to the summit of Mt Wilhelm, and nearly all of it is exploited. While geological structure often controls the location of trade routes and determines (through altitude, aspect and internal relief) the diversity of habitats, the main flows of trade goods conspicuously move across the strike of the central cordillera between areas of the greatest environmental contrasts, emphasizing the importance of two factors on the resources used for trade— proximity to the sea and the vertical zonation of altitude. The third vital factor is the presence in the central ranges of hard, fine-grained metasediments suited to the manufacture of stone tools. Annual rainfall varies from 2000mm in the Asaro Valley to more than 5000 in the southern lowlands, and population densities vary from over 200 per km² in some of the high valleys to less than one person per km² in parts of the southern lowlands.

These areas represent extremes of man/environment relationships, for in the high valleys man has been the dominant species for thousands of years while in the southern lowlands he is still comparatively unimportant. In the former, the forest has been destroyed, there is no hunting for food, the agricultural system is labour-intensive and pig husbandry is developed. In the latter, there is much primary forest where hunting supplies important protein, sago forms the staple of many, gardens are small swiddens and pigs are only semi-domesticated.

Access to the specialized resources of the sea-coast, soil, forest, grassland and farmland tends to coincide with the regions, largely physiographic, each with its own production and trading advantages. These are the northern subcoastal hills, the Ramu plain, the northeast fall of the Bismarcks, the Jimi, Asaro and Wahgi Valleys, the southern slopes of the Kubors, the Poru Plateau near Mt Ialibu, the volcanic plateau around Mts Au and Karimui, and the low Erave River/Lake Tebera karstland.

The main trade goods and their distribution

The special product of the subcoastal hills was clay pots which,

100

together with sea-shells received from the north coast, were traded south to the Ramu plain. The scattered people of the plain benefited most from their role as middlemen, passing shells on to the south and stone axes to the north, but they also exported forest and grass-land products, mainly to the south, and produced carved wooden dishes. They were rich in such useful trade items as the lesser bird of paradise, crowned pigeon, cassowary, hornbills, brightly-coloured parrots and pigeons, wild pigs, and in such valuable woods and fibres as black-palm and rattans. The people of the Bismarck Fall also had access to many of these products and added to the shells received from the Ramu, trading them over the mountains into the densely-populated upland valleys, largely in return for stone axes and pigs. Those living in the Simbai Valley produced sodium salt as their main export south to the Jimi Valley (Fig. 5.1). In the central part of the Fall the Gende made sodium salt and traded it south and also produced pigments and a medicine for pigs. Their principal advantage, however, was their location near the main pass into the Chimbu Valley, for through their hands passed most of the shells from the north coast on their way to the huge population of the Wahgi Valley.

The highlanders produced polished stone axe blades and used domestic pigs as a means of converting garden staples into valuables. Axes and pigs were their main exports. The trade areas of the main quarries are shown on Fig. 5.2 but the products are known to have reached as far north as the lower Ramu and the Adelbert Divide, west to Lake Kopiago and south to the deltas of the Papuan Gulf. To the east, they met competition from the eastern highlands but there was some overlap. The highlands and adjacent regions had a vigorous salt trade, dominated in this area, as Fig. 5.1 shows, by a 'factory' in the Wahgi Valley. However, many highland groups made potassium salt from plant ash and exchanged it locally. The most important imports were shell ornaments, which, with axes, bird-plumes, pigs and cassowaries, formed the main store of wealth. Figs. 5.3 and 5.4 show the distribution of the main shell types. In addition to bird-of-paradise skins from their own valleys and mountains, those of other varieties were imported from lower altitudes, together with cassowary chicks, marsupials and their skins, and parrot feathers. Pottery from the hills region penetrated as far as the north side of the Wahgi Valley. A valuable tree oil reached the upper Wahgi from the south-west, and lowland woods

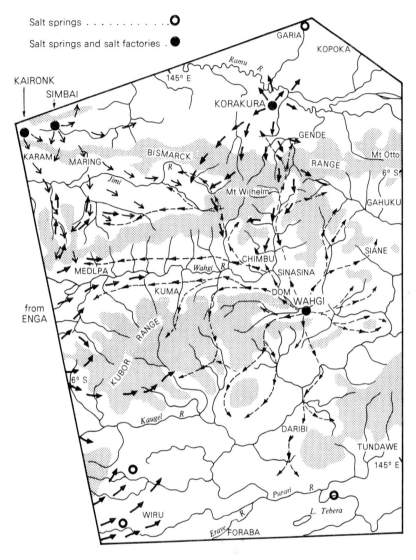

Salt springs . . . . ⭘

Salt springs and salt factories . ●

GARIA

KOPOKA

KAIRONK

SIMBAI

145° E

Ramu R

KORAKURA

KARAM

MARING

BISMARCK

Jimi

R

GENDE

RANGE

Mt Otto

6° S

Mt Wilhelm

GAHUKU

MEDLPA

Wahgi R

CHIMBU

SINASINA

SIANE

KUMA

DOM

WAHGI

from
ENGA

RANGE

KUBOR

6° S

Kaugel R

DARIBI

TUNDAWE

145° E

Purari R

L. Tebera

WIRU

R

Erave FORABA

Fig. 5.1 Central New Guinea: the salt trade (for location see Fig. 1.2, p. 23)

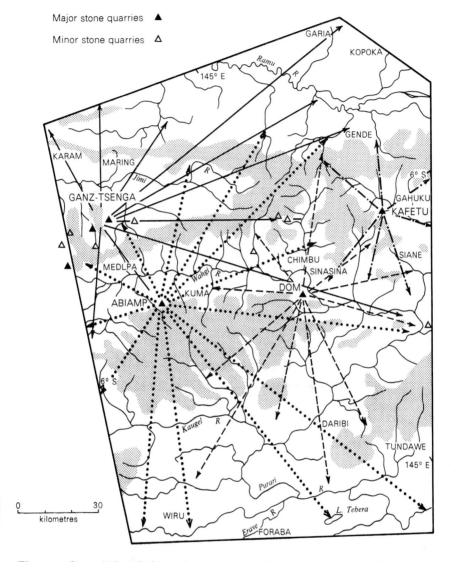

Fig. 5.2 Central New Guinea: the stone-axe trade—main quarries and known distribution within the study area

and fibres entered the highlands periphery from both north and south. Within the highlands, mainly intra-regionally, there was an important trade in coloured pigments.

The southern Kubor region depended on forest products and re-exported to the Poru region stone axes received from the Wahgi. The Tua region, too, depended on forest products to pay for the axes, shells, salt and young pigs received from the Wahgi. In this region, within memory, an earlier small shell trade from the south coast has been completely overshadowed by the expansion of trade with the north, consequent upon the migratory contact of both Wahgi and Tua peoples. The inhabitants of the Poru region also had no specialized exports of their own and depended mainly on re-exports, passing on shells from the south and west for the small supplies of stone axes that they got from the north, and in turn re-exporting some of these. Their two salt springs were not developed into manufactures. The sparse population of the Tebera region also failed to make salt from their spring. Here trade was minimal, though a few shells and stone axes passed right through the region.

General findings

The general findings of the research may be summarized briefly before we turn to discuss the basis and conduct of trade.

(1) The evidence suggests that within their own territories people had thoroughly explored their environment and that all salt springs, exposures of earth pigments and outcrops of superior axe stone were known.

(2) All informants said that, unless goods were produced by neighbours, they had not been aware of the origin of the products they received in trade, only that they came from a particular direction.

(3) The trade in pigments reflected the overriding influence of fashion.

(4) The trade in potassium salt within the sodium salt trade area showed that, even with a substance usually regarded as a basic item of diet, physiological need was overruled by custom.

(5) Most of the variation in style of finished axe blades was not due to differences in raw materials or function, but to the evolution of aesthetic styles characteristic of each factory.

(6) Shell ornaments were the trade goods which most frequently performed the functions of money, some being of high individual

value and others being finely divisible. Only salt shared both of these characteristics, although axe blades, plumes and pigs were matched against other commodities by size and quality.

(7) Shell ornaments nevertheless clearly showed the strength of local tradition, for those that occupied the highest place in some areas were valueless in others.

(8) The shell trade grew greatly during the first 30 years of this century and was probably in effect a diffusion wave of traditional wealth objects made possible by pacification on the coast and in part due to the devaluation of old wealth forms there by new forms introduced by whites.

The traders

Men dominated the production of trade goods, their transfer between individuals and between groups, and their consumption. Women were not involved in the production of important goods like stone axes, nor in the collection of the best pigments or oils, bird plumes and animal skins, cassowaries and wild animals, nor (within the study area) shell ornaments. The luxury crops like pandanus nuts and fruit which in some parts figured in exchanges, usually ceremonial, were men's crops. But women quarried and prepared clay for the potters, helped to collect grasses for salt making, produced most of the string and fibre products made from garden and semi-cultivated plants and some of those made from wild plants, made net bags and some clothing, and were on special occasions important users of pigments, oils and ornaments. They wore minor shell ornaments and, by permission, major shell ornaments during dances. When goods were being transferred in the context of ceremonial exchange, women were often involved in prominent but minor roles which varied from place to place; they were the public mourners of the pigs they had reared, the wearers of shell ornaments received in bride-wealth payments or of dowry-shells being given by the bride's group, and the formal receivers of 'women's things' (net bags, bark cloth and clothing) being presented to the women of the groom's group at weddings. Barter was the province of men; women's roles in producing the goods were formally recognized only in some places and usually only in the case of transactions involving pigs, where it was not unusual for part of the goods received to be demonstratively presented to her to ease her sorrow at the animal's loss. In the case of valuables, however, she was normally only the custodian.

105

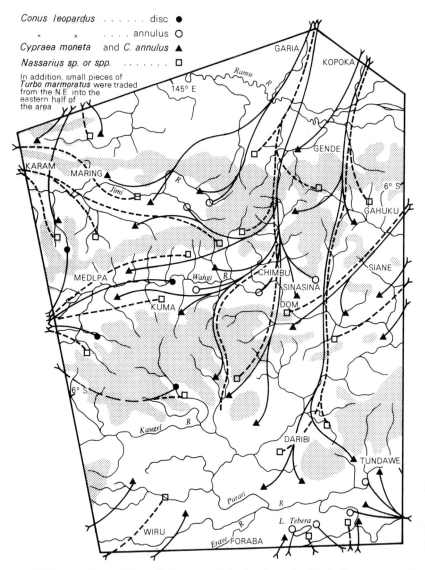

Fig. 5.3 Central New Guinea: trade in the less valuable shells

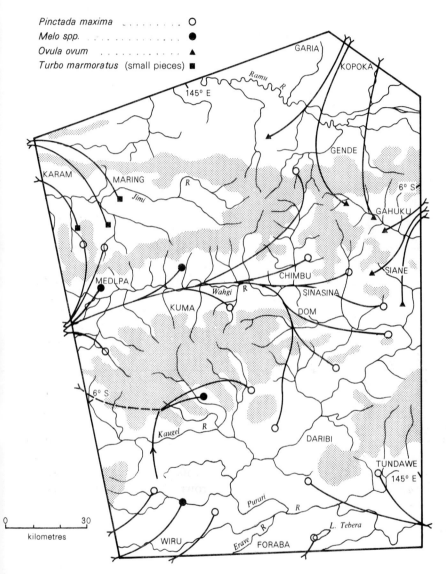

Fig. 5.4 Central New Guinea: trade in the more valuable shells

Every man took part in ceremonial gift exchange and bartered on his own account when opportunity offered; there were no professional traders, no merchants, no itinerant pedlars. The trade delegations that travel so widely since pacification are a new phenomenon in this area; formerly, armed parties rarely moved more than 8 to 10 miles in closely settled parts, and even among the scattered hamlets of the southern lowlands travel rarely exceeded 12 to 15 miles. The longest described individual trade links were those between northern Poru settlements and the west Kambia people around Kegu, and between the north-eastern Poru and the Daribi of the lower Kaugel area. Even here, the distance between the last kinsmen and the first trade friends was little more than 15 miles and was covered in the course of dual purpose trading and hunting expeditions. In general, the closer the density of settlement, the more restricted was individual movement, showing that the presence of enemies rather than physical distance was the principal obstacle. Only one case was cited where a particular group of men were privileged to travel further than usual among potential enemies—that of Gende speakers from the Bismarck Fall visiting trade friends in the middle Chimbu Valley. Gende living in the upper valleys of the central Bismarck Fall had marriage ties with the people of the upper Chimbu Valley but in former times these did not extend to the middle part of the valley.* Nevertheless, from time to time they moved beyond the normal limits of affinal connections to establish trade friends further away—still only a total of about fifteen miles, but in this populous region that was a very long way. Kokia and his brother Kondiagl of Duglpagl recounted a tradition illustrating that the chief protection for the people from the Bismarck Fall was their reputation as sorcerers. Once, long ago, a Gende man had been killed just south of Duglpagl and that very same night a great land-slip had blocked the Chimbu river near its junction with the Kwinigl and a number of men had been drowned in the resulting flood. Ever since then Chimbu men have invited Gende visitors to their homes and take care to establish trade friends among them.† Of course, the people of the Chimbu Valley were dependent upon the Gende for shell valuables and lowlands products.

Fear of their powers of sorcery also helped to protect the Daribi in their contacts with Gumine and Nomane dialect speakers in the

* Nowadays they extend to the Wahgi Valley.
† How this was done has been described by Aufenanger (1966).

south-eastern Wahgi region, though the risk of violence may have been less than to the Gende, since the highlands population here was low. They had no shell valuables to offer, only feathers and skins and other forest products, but they safely visited the southern fringes of highland settlement. In general, there was a marked tendency for men involved in trade to move uphill: the men of lowland communities tended to travel up to the settlements of those living at intermediate altitudes more often and further than men from the intermediate levels travelled down to them. The same was true of the trading relations between men of intermediate altitudes and the highlanders. This was brought about by three things, an extension of the patterns of movement of daily life, a desire for those important 'production goods', superior stone axes, and comparative fear.

Since they lacked the trappings of 'primitive affluence' that so impressed the first white visitors to the highlands, one tends to assume that the people of the highlands fringe and lowands had a greater economic need than did the highlanders and that for this reason they could be expected to show more initiative in trade. Despite the axe trade, I do not believe that this was so. The thousands of highlanders had needs which, though they could have been met from local products, could better be met with fibres and woods from the lowlands. Those living on the outer limits of highlands settlements wanted the luxury of lowlands fruits, in particular oil pandanus, as well as vegetable oil. More importantly, they had unsatisfied and growing wants for ornaments and valuables, feathers and skins of lowland birds and animals, the live creatures themselves, and in particular sea-shells. They were more numerous and competitive, and their trading initiatives were probably greater than those of the people around them. This is supported by the remarkable expansion of trade, and in particular *travel* for trade, which developed in the highlands immediately some safety was assured. It began with carriers accompanying the first patrols and has extended ever since. Expeditions to the lowlands did not begin until the 1950s, but within ten years Chimbu traders, especially plume-buyers, had been reported as visiting the far western highlands, the far eastern highlands, the interior of the Finisterre Ranges and the Rai Coast. Differences in trading initiative was not a reason for the predominance of inland and upward movements in trade journeys.

Extensions of the patterns of movement used in subsistence was a contributing factor. In the normal course of getting a living the men

109

of the sparsely settled lower altitudes moved much further than did the highlanders, partly because of their pattern of garden use, partly because of their pattern of forest use, and partly because of the wider movement required to maintain social relationships. Unlike the intensive social and economic domain of the highlanders, that of the fringe population was extensive and that of the lowlanders was more extensive still.

However the main reason was the highlanders' fear of the lowlanders' powers of sorcery. It is true that sorcery by strangers and enemies was always to be feared, and that in some places such fears marginally increased when former enemies were prevented by the administration from expressing aggression by physical violence; but the phenomenon being stressed here was different to and separate from the sorcery accusations made about fellow tribesmen or others seen as belonging to the same general cultural tradition, and it is a phenomenon that men said had always existed. It was independent of the highlanders' association of malignant spirits with lowlying swampy places, though the reinforcing mechanism of disease was the same. When most highlanders travelled beyond the limits of their own security circle, to borrow Lawrence's term (1964, 24), they feared mainly spears and arrows, but those living on the highland limits were inhibited in their movement away from co-linguists by fear of sorcery. Because it was impalpable it was much more to be feared. There was a regional gradient of fear of sorcery by strangers, running from high country to low country and probably quite independent of local differences in sorcery practice and belief. It was expressed first by helpers and carriers recruited in each region and later affirmed by strong, positive statements by older informants in every group visited, always in reference to the people of the region below them, never about their upland neighbours. The Chimbu feared the Gende and the Gende feared the Ramu people; the southern Dom dialect speakers feared the Daribi of the Tua region and the Daribi feared the Tundawe and Foraba of the Lake Tebera region.* With the sorcery charges went accusations of cannibalism, unintentionally ironic from the Daribi. As pacification was extended and highland traders began to visit the lowlands their fears were

* I know nothing of these people's own claims of proficiency as sorcerers. If there is a gradient close to the coast which overrides varied parochial reputations, it may be the reverse of the inland one as far as the sub-coastal hills (cf. Harding, 1967, 63; Lawrence and Meggitt, 1965, 16, 19).

greatly reinforced, for many became ill and some died. The extension of medical services, especially the malaria eradication programme, has diminished the incidence of infection and death but so far has not diminished the fear of lowland sorcerers.* While now travelling widely, no highlander travelling south of the Wahgi region at low altitudes will casually discard worn-out personal belongings, even deposit them without care, sleep with unfastened doors or windows or go outside at night without a companion if he can help it.† In former times, the strictures imposed by their *orientation* of fear restricted the options of highlanders and extended some initiatives available to the fringe people; they more often had the choice of trade partners and this strengthened their position as the suppliers of valuables and as 'middlemen'.

Risk of life and limb was the one meaningful transport cost—no price was put on time. Nowadays men will talk of the arduousness of past travel and the obstacles of some routes; but the goods which travelled over the most hazardous course were exchanged at the same rates as goods which travelled easy routes and short distances.

I have used the term 'middlemen'. In most cases it is appropriate only in the sense that trade goods everywhere travelled in a series of chainlike steps, and except for the producers and consumers, the other traders were acting as middlemen at stages along the trade route. In fact durable goods were used and circulated locally by intermediaries, and while they had them they continued to circulate. This was the case with implements, ornaments and pots; most of the goods which travelled fairly rapidly through intermediate hands were semi-perishable consumer goods and only in the case of these are the concepts of true 'middlemen' and 'end-users' applicable. Examples of goods handled in the manner of true middlemen (the nearest approach to a short-haul carrying trade) were salt, pigments, bows and fibre products, live cassowary chicks, parrots, cockatoos and lowland animals. Except for cassowaries, which grow into

* Cf. J. L. Taylor's observation that malaria had placed a cordon around the highlands. Having lost their tolerance to malaria, the highlanders fear of lowlands sorcerers was an effective measure of preventive medicine. It was fortunate that, like trade goods, *Plasmodium* 8pp. had to travel slowly from group to group over routes inhibited by natural and manmade barriers.

† On more than one occasion I was saved from the consequences of my own ignorance by the attentive care of companions: my colour and culture was inadequate protection. For others, my presence was a safeguard and it was implied 'if anything should happen to you where would we be?'

111

dangerous adults, live birds and animals would sometimes remain in intermediate hands for a time before being passed on. Traffic in pigs and dogs occasionally followed this pattern but this was rare. The longest examples of middleman through-trade were from the Ramu region to the highland valleys via the Bismarck Fall. Salt travelled almost as far within the study area but, like pigments, it tended to be stored in the houses of intermediaries for varying periods, large quantities being divided and some used. Goods which travelled as transit traffic through the highlands fringe did not normally continue to do so in the highlands: they either stopped or began to circulate.

Trade routes and flows of goods

The maps show the flows of the principal goods as linear but, except where these movements were channelled into single paths by the constraints of physiography or lack of population, the flows are simply the sum effect of myriad transfers of goods taking place in many different directions. In regions of light and moderate population the total pattern or routes on the ground is in no way remarkable, consisting of the expected network of varying density stretching from coast to coast. All the physiographic constraints result from high or steep relief or from rivers, sometimes in combination, and portions of the communication net near these barriers have the usual dendritic patterns focusing on nodes on each side of the obstacle. Where the channelling of flow is due to low population, the web retains a cell-like structure. Notably, within the study area, neither these nodes nor any other intersections had developed market characteristics before contact: barter transactions occurred every-where. Nevertheless the people living near these nodes were better placed for developing trading activity, and flows tended to funnel into their hands before again spreading out. The largest quantities of goods per kilometre of route, the heaviest unit loads and the most frequent traffic occurred where path density was restricted by natural barriers. In most parts of the highlands regions the web is so dense and structurally so simple that in spite of physical obstacles and the fact that it has not evolved in response to marketing prin-ciples, it represents as close an approach in nature to the simplest communication landscape models of Christaller and Lösch as can be found in any region of the world. Settlement hierarchy is undeve-loped, consisting in the main of two levels in the west, garden houses

112

and hamlets, and three levels in the east, garden houses, hamlets and villages, the last being in effect agglomerations of hamlets with a minimal development of central place functions. It is true that where more men were gathered together more transactions occurred, but in general in this area it was a one-to-one relationship, not generative of another order of exchange transactions. Where a particularly important manufacturing activity was carried on, such as near a stone quarry or salt spring, the increased nodal importance of the surrounding hamlets was shown by the more frequent movement of persons, more rapid flow of goods, and increased quantities of goods being transported and exchanged, not by an increase in the density of the network of paths. Within the areas of close settlement and minimum natural barriers, not all paths were of equal importance, but most linkages had a multiplicity of alternative routes and in general there was no development of trunk routes. Where a path gained minor importance it was usually because it was orientated toward a physical feature, bridge site, ridge saddle or gentle spur, or away from a cliff or swamp.

The economic decision-making that went on in men's club houses and on the plazas beside them affected trade, and there, too, transfers of goods by both ceremonial exchange and barter sometimes took place. The only other nucleation that concentrated the incidence of economic transitions and increased the quantities changing hands was the periodic use of clan ceremonial grounds for prestations. Where this was for functions associated with the preparation and carrying out of the large pig-killing ceremonies held every few years or for lesser events, dyadic barter transactions between individuals often preceded or followed the main business. It would be placing an incorrect commercial emphasis on those ceremonial occasions and overstating the importance of the associated trading to see them as proto-markets, for the continual trading activity in hamlets and elsewhere had much more quantitative importance. Nilles has described a genuine proto-market held near the R.C. Mission in the upper Chimbu Valley in the late 1930s (1944, 12) but by that time the pattern of trade had already been changed by pacification, as he himself noted (*ibid.*, 11 : 1943, 105) and informants' statements suggest that by then the peace of the marketplace had begun to follow the peace of the government and mission.

The discovery of new resources and changed avenues of access to old ones brought about considerable long-term changes in the

113

importance of alternative trade routes, new links growing at the expense of old ones. Trade in the Tua Region, for example, was completely reorientated from a southward-facing system to a north-ward-facing one after the northward-moving Daribi contacted the southward-moving Chimbu, perhaps no more than 100 years ago. The incidence of this type of change since contact and a number of instances described during the course of field-work suggest that it has been a constant process for thousands of years.

The isolated people of central Kambia provided a precise example of post-contact route loss and new route establishment which illust-rates the point. Formerly, they had a difficult but direct connection with the people at the head of the Tuman River not far from the Abiamp axe quarry. In those days their connections with the people of the Minj River over the 3,200m Kinkainku Pass were unimportant. The Tuman headwaters link continued to be maintained during the 1930s, but as soon as steel had replaced stone it was allowed to lapse into disuse and by the 1950s was overgrown. In contrast, the track to the Minj headwaters had become what for Kambia was a major highway leading to the steel tools and shells being distributed by European establishments in the middle Wahgi Valley.

Temporary route alterations were brought about in a number of ways. Some choices were made on the basis of seasonal hunting needs, sometimes whole sections of routes were closed by agreement to aid the trapping and hunting of pigs for an approaching festival. Mountain passes were used in all weathers but the choice of lowland routes was affected by the seasons, spells of wet weather and floods, nocturnal rains and flash-floods and the state of repair of bridges. Some were changed by politics. All were affected by current states of enmity and alliance and in many cases the signals of hostility were clearly shown on the tracks, bridges being cut down and warn-ing signs posted. This happened in every region but the patterns of response varied, largely because of contrasting settlement patterns.

In former times, in both densely-populated highlands and sparsely-populated lowlands, marriage ties rarely extended beyond immediate neighbours. One's consanguinal kin, relatives by marriage, and enemies, habitual and temporary, were all neighbours. In isolated settlements, once enmity broke contact with a neighbouring group, all trade in that direction ceased until peace was made. In closely-settled parts alternative strategies were possible, for enemy territory could be avoided and contact with more distant groups made

114

through the land of allies or through uninhabited mountains, all without much interruption to the dominant directional flows of goods. The demand for particular goods and ease of access to them was a powerful incentive to re-establish peace—salt-makers and axe-makers enjoyed more peaceable relations than most—but alternative paths were frequently used because of hostility.

Journeys around the main block of the Bismarck Range exemplify the phenomenon. Established popular routes over the lowest cols joined the surrounding valleys, the Jimi headwaters to the Mambu and Marum tributaries of the Ramu, other Ramu tributaries in Gende territory to the Chimbu, the Chimbu to the Koronigl and the Koronigl to the Jimi headwaters. When fighting made the use of a regular low-altitude route hazardous, secondary and tertiary paths were used. Typical of these are the multiplicity of routes over the Iwam pass between the head of the Chimbu Valley and the Bismarck Fall, and the routes from the middle Chimbu Valley via the Singganigl and Mainigl Valleys to the Koronigl. Higher still, hunting paths criss-crossed the alpine grasslands and scrub: in former times these were not through routes but men sometimes met trade friends from other valleys in the hunting shelters. The mountain-tops themselves, here generally above 3,750m, were carefully avoided* for they were the haunt of spirits. Since pacification these tracks have occasionally been used for through traffic. As informants in highlands regions said, it was not just that safety was achieved by avoiding settled areas but that the danger came from neighbours, not distant friends, and that by using circuitous routes in times of danger it was possible to pass behind one's neighbours to meet people with whom one had never come into conflict and among whom men of enterprise had trade friends. The flexibility of strategies open to highlanders helps to explain their evident success in promoting transactions of all types, ceremonial exchanges and trade.

Something should be said of the ingenuity with which physical obstacles were overcome; New Guinea terrain has a notorious reputation among people dependent upon the wheel. Mountain passes which carried significant traffic varied in altitude from 1,800m in the western Bismarck Range to 3,500m in the Kubor Range. Most were easy to use, the paths climbing gradually by spurs and ridges to the saddles, the only difficulties being long, relatively level tracts inside the high mountain forest which remained quagmires

* In marked contrast to Medlpa and Enga traffic near the summit of Mt Hagen.

115

of tangled roots, and the occasional necessity to use a steep water-course as an avenue of access to a summit ridge. Most passes could be crossed in a day, though one in the Bismarck Range and both of the principal Kubor Range routes required nights on the track. In the Kubors these had to be spent at altitudes above 2,750m, always cold, usually windy and wet,* and the people did not wear clothes. Yet not only men travelling for trade used these routes: as elsewhere, most roads were used by families, including heavily-laden women and small children. The longest routes had named shelter sites where low huts of pandanus leaves were built and maintained by passing travellers. In middle altitudes and in the lowlands rock shelters were used, and in the lowlands, lean-tos of sago fronds.

In all regions the precise location of a route was often dictated by the position of cliffs and river gorges. Large rivers forced paths to converge on canoe and raft crossings and bridge sites, the latter dictated by engineering problems and the former by the need for stretches of quiet water. New Guinea paths may have more bridges per mile than anywhere else in the world. They vary from the flimsiest branches over garden drains to logs half a metre in diameter over deep gorges. Rivers in level terrain may have arch-bridges supported on posts fanned out from each bank, where high banks and tall trees are lacking, or suspension bridges ingeniously set on pylons. Where large timber is scarce, bundles of laths are lashed together to form a beam. The main paths over the plateaus of the Tua region often ran for long distances along fallen logs, through garden and forest alike. There, many gullies were bridged simply for convenience, to avoid a short steep descent and ascent, for timber was in prolific supply. Where cliffs, giant boulders or tall trees provided suitable sites, suspension bridges were constructed of every size, some spanning distances of 100m, the lowest point sometimes 20m above the surface of the water.

The context of exchange

This study has been concerned with the overall flow of trade goods and its underlying economic rationale, irrespective of the context of exchange itself. A detailed discussion of the relationship between

* Everywhere in the central highlands silence is enjoined while passing through alpine forest; if men have to talk they should do so in low tones. A variety of calamities can result from loud violation of the realm of mountain spirits, the most frequent being rainstorms.

transfers of goods which were manifestly prestations and those which were manifestly barter is to be made in another place, but some aspects can be mentioned here. Most of the goods which appeared in one form of transaction also appeared in the other, even if, in the case of minor trade items like forest fibres, they were first treated, combined and transformed into ornaments or clothing. However, the context of exchange of some times differed according to whether it took place in exporting regions or importing regions. Within the study area as a whole, only one type of product ceremonially exchanged failed to be mentioned anywhere in trade, and that was staple root crops and common green vegetables. Only one product mentioned in trade failed to be mentioned as being used in some prestation, and that was the bark of a large lowland forest tree (*Cinnamomum* sp.) used as a medicine and aromatic. Doubtless there are others, but they are minor forest products.

The staple food prestation of the Wahgi and Asaro regions has elements of the potlatch and is a fiercely competitive redistributive transaction with a long delay before the gift is reciprocated.* It has elements in common with the longer-cycle competitive pig slaughter and pork distribution and the two forms combined resemble the other examples of competitive feasting of rival groups and aggressive food distributions with which the anthropological literature abounds. However, in terms of the total traffic in goods within the study area the transactions involving staples were unique: other goods used in prestations, including pigs, pork and luxury vegetable foods, were also traded—staples were not.

In general, goods which brought the highest economic reward usually brought the greatest sociopolitical reward, and while valuables as a class tended to appear more often in prestations, utilitarian goods tended to appear more often in trade. Transactions elsewhere in tribal societies are sometimes described in terms of a model based on separate spheres of exchange derived from the restricted convertibility of categories of goods. This model will not fit any region in the study area. Although values had to be matched in both trade

---

* A check of the recorded occasions of pig festivals and staple food distributions throughout the Chimbu area over a period of 20 years suggested that while clansmen could not give staples when their own pig festival was approaching, they did not receive staples at only these times. The two prestations did not appear to be an example of what Schwartz called 'the co-ordination of different ecological and ceremonial calendars' (1963, 79).

117

and prestations, and ornaments, axes, salt and animals or cassowaries of certain minimum value were needed for important ceremonial exchanges, different items were favoured in different regions and were often accompanied by items of lesser value, including such mundane things as cooked food. Pigs were the means of converting cheap carbohydrate into expensive protein and were the principal means of changing the most ubiquitous garden produce into valuables. Varying quality and size in the most valuable items, together with the divisibility of cooked pork, minor shell, tooth and feather ornaments, salt, pigments, oil and luxury crops, and at lower altitudes, tobacco, meant that somewhere in the process of production and manufacture and the network of distribution, complete interchangeability could be achieved.

Trading was aided by the institutionalizing of certain aspects: the commercial use of kinsmen, the establishment and maintenance of trade friends, the ritualizing of behaviour appropriate to trade, the extending of credit (not always by choice) by the acceptance of delayed payments, the recognized use of minor shell valuables as a medium of exchange for many transactions, the appropriate use of pigs and pork in certain exchange contexts, and in some parts the use of special stone axes as stores of negotiable wealth.

Because I have been concerned with total traffic in goods I have used the word 'trade' loosely, in places using it to refer to all movements of a particular product, elsewhere using it only for simple interpersonal transfers of goods unaccompanied by ceremony. The data show that 'pure trade' and 'pure ceremonial exchange'* are only idealizations, the poles at the ends of a continuum of occasions when goods change hands.

In contrasting what he called 'market', 'trade partnership' and 'affinal exchange' transaction in the Admiralty Islands, Schwartz (1963, 78) found that the following terms described important differentiating criteria: ceremonial/non-ceremonial, among kin/ among non-kin, intra-ecological/cross-ecological, immediate/ delayed, symmetrical/asymmetrical (as to persons and goods). On an earlier occasion (1969) I listed the characteristics of the polar extremes as they appeared on the evidence of the present study. As amended they are as follows:

* 'Pure gift' seems to have little utility even as an idealization, as Mauss (1967) suggested more than 40 years ago when criticizing Malinowski's use of the term, and as M. Panoff recently reminded us (1970).

Trade	*Prestations*
Goods always differ	Goods often the same
Goods always the product of specialized resources and/or labour	Goods sometimes not the product of specialized resources and/or labour; usually not the specialized product of givers or receivers
Return 'gift' usually immediate	Return gift usually delayed
Transaction often between non-relatives	Transaction nearly always between relatives
Transaction usually between individuals independent of any group exchange	Transaction usually between individuals but usually as part of a group exchange, usually initiated by a leader and sometimes channelled through him
Transfer itself rarely involves prestige or status	Transfer itself always involves prestige and status
Transfer usually private and unceremonial	Transfer nearly always public and ceremonial
Magic in support of a successful transaction rarely used	Magic to ensure a successful outcome and return of wealth often used
Traders usually stress material benefit more than socio-political benefit	Giver often stresses socio-political benefit more than material benefit

The barter end of the continuum is well exemplified by planned journeys to get stone axes or salt, specific goods for payment being prepared in advance, perhaps plumes, shells or a pig, and an armed party setting off to the limits of the security circle of the most important man. The prestation end is best shown by a transaction involving no material return, such as the payment of blood-money without which neither trade nor peaceful social relations can resume.

The overall trade system

This investigation drew an arbitrary boundary around a large section of the central highlands and adjacent lowlands of eastern New Guinea to enclose an area of contrasting resources, habitats and cultures. It was found to be covered by a network of trade routes which the presence of marine shells showed extended from coast to coast. The network itself was created by and built up of the interlocking and overlapping personal trading networks of individual men. For the purpose of this study they formed the smallest

119

components. An analysis of the way in which the activity of individuals created their personal trade nets might usefully break them down on the basis of a number of separate criteria—linkages established primarily for subsistence ends, for luxuries or to acquire valuables and to participate in wider political relationships: or it could examine the portions of the net which were dependent upon consanguinity, affinity or friendship, and the basic dyadic connections that comprise them.

Each personal network and every larger unit of which it was a part was found to be an open system. Although the individual links of personal trading nets were not strictly coterminous with those of personal communication nets, when the trading connections were combined with connections for prestation they covered the entire personal communication net. A study of the total flow of goods therefore could ignore the differences between these webs of interaction and treat each man's personal communication network as the basic unit. Each was nested in a hierarchy of open systems in which trade took place. If the relationship of prestations to barter were to be further analysed, note would have to be taken that they belonged to two different but overlapping hierarchies. The most notable manifestation of this was that the great ceremonial exchange cycles tended to take place within regions of similar resources whereas trade was most vigorous between regions of great contrast. Orders of magnitude in both of these hierarchies increased with the size of the social or areal units examined, family, men's house group, clan, relatives, trade friends, or hamlet, village, clan territory, tribal territory and region. With each step the order of complexity of the growing web was multiplied by an unknown large factor.

Aspects of the totality of trade other than the network were also nested in rank order, and this characteristic explains some aspects of the flow-pattern of goods. For example, the main determinant on the supply side, access to resources, on which all trading ultimately depended in an area lacking merchants, can be abstracted in this way. It then appears as a hierarchy of production and supply systems, one inside the other, each order of magnitude being a resource access region of increasing ubiquity. Thus, access regions for minor mineral products were nested inside those for major mineral products which in turn were set inside large ecological zones determining plant and animal resources, each producing characteristic flow-patterns. Comparative advantages in supply and regional and local

120

differences in demand resulted in a pattern of trade areas for individual goods which were nested in another way, those for minor products, irrespective of the type, being encircled by those for valuable items like stone axes and shells.

The study has shown that the linkages that made up the basic network as well as the flows of goods which passed through them not only extended across physiographic, ecological and cultural divisions* but were most vigorous there, for that was where the potential for trade was greatest. The origins and destinations of the flows of goods traced by observation and interview supported the initial hypothesis that, in inland New Guinea as elsewhere, resource differences made it possible for trade to develop. Only areally specialized products were traded.

It is not correct to describe a segment of the wider trading network as 'a trading system' if it is distinguished by area alone. A trading system must have unique systemic characteristics. Where specialized merchants exist, such as coastal canoe traders, it is meaningful to describe their set of delimited movements as a system within a system, as Harding (1967) has done with the Siassi of the Vitiaz Strait. If a portion of the inland trade is exceptionally highly developed and active, as the early references suggest the Kikori–Samberigi–Kewa–Kakoli section was, it might usefully be studied and described as a separate system. However, within the area which has been examined here, no such dominant system exists. Within the overall pattern of flow of goods, however, there were individual regional and inter-regional product-distribution systems for localized mineral resources, pottery, salt, pigments, stone axes, and identifiable regional ceremonial exchange systems. There were no Chimbu, Wahgi-region or central-highlands trade systems as separate entities. Trade within the study area was one large segment of a web of trade that covered every part of the mainland of New Guinea, extended to the Bismarck Archipelago as Harding has shown, to all the offshore islands, to Australia and to Asia. Individual goods travelled far beyond the horizons of individual traders, and the network itself far exceeded the trade area of the most widely-distributed good.

As a result of his analysis of the trade of the Vitiaz Strait, Harding was of the opinion that special mechanisms of regional integration had developed in Melanesia which were not seen elsewhere, and he

* Whether these are regarded as boundaries or as gradients depends on the degree of abstraction.

121

suggested that this may have been 'related to' the greater scale of trading, especially the existence of a long-distance canoe trade (1967, 241, 242). He was referring to the Kula-type valuable exchange system to which he likened the Vitiaz Strait trade in pigs' tusks and dogs on the one hand, and pigs and dogs' teeth on the other (*ibid.*, 244). Schwartz likened the Kula to the Te and Moka chains of the highlands and characterized them as an integrative system based on a 'horizontally structured network' in opposition to the 'dispersed network' typical of the Admiralty Islands (1963, 89), which appears to be the most common form in New Guinea.

The existence of this form of integrative system in the highlands shows that it was not dependent on long-distance canoe trade. Nor was it the result of a greater scale of trading, though more goods obtained by trade permitted more to be invested in prestation and the scale of the ceremonial cycle to grow. It in turn stimulated trade by raising the demand for valuables to even higher levels. Whether the scale of trade is measured by distance travelled by particular goods, by quantities or by the number of traders participating, that which took place in and around the central highlands was very great, and it was not restricted by seasons as was the canoe trade. It developed and continued without the need for specialized traders.*

Nor was the Wahgi-region cyclic pig festival a parallel system purposively keeping trade connections and obligations open, though where it occurred this was one of its effects. We have already noted its restriction to a region sharing what were essentially similar resources. Although within this region shell valuables, stone axes, pigs and pork circulated and moved to and fro along the strike of the central cordillera, the dominant trade flows were between the regions of contrasting resources, the highlands, the lowlands and the coast.

The phenomenon of delayed exchange has been seen by some as a purposive Melanesian mechanism sustaining social relations and trade (Harding, 1967, 243). Statements by informants in the present study showed that prolonged obligation and credit certainly facilitated all traffic in goods, just as it does in Western society, but that in the context of barter it was largely making a virtue of necessity.

* In contrast to inland trade, it seems likely that the development of a hazardous canoe trade resulted largely from necessity, commenced for subsistence and continued for wealth and social success; for many islanders it may have been the best economic option; some may have had no option.

Alternating feasting and redistribution was a desired end in the large cyclic prestations, and although delay was due to the need to accumulate wealth, grow food and raise pigs before commencing the exchange transaction, the cyclic nature was co-ordinated and each group's festivals planned not to coincide with another's. In trade, however, delay resulted mainly from the inability to co-ordinate planning between regions and was due to lack of telecommunications.

On an earlier occasion (1969, 14) I said that I believed Rappaport (1967, 105–9) to be correct in his suggestion that among the Maring and their neighbours the unlimited demand for valuables allowed unmatched demands for utilitarian goods to be met;* utilitarian goods and valuables could be exchanged for each other, they were not in separate 'spheres of exchange'. This hypothesis and the relevant data will be briefly reviewed.

Rappaport noted that the Tsembaga Maring of the Simbai Valley produced salt which they traded through a chain of intermediaries to the Tsenga and Ganz River axe-makers of the southern Jimi Valley for work axes. Each was dependent on the other, he said, but, these were utilitarian goods and the demand for utilitarian goods was limited: should either suffer an oversupply of the imported good they would cease production of their own speciality. Moral pressure to continue to supply without reward would be ineffective because of the distance and other groups intervening.† Because shell and plume ornaments and 'bridal axes' were always in demand, especially for 'bride price', and could be exchanged for utilitarian goods, they 'provided a mechanism for articulating the production' of the two specialized utilitarian items.

The fact that there was no firm division between work axes and 'bridal axes', and that elsewhere salt was used as a true valuable, does not invalidate Rappaport's hypothesis. No ordered data were collected on the effectiveness of transmitted requests for goods, but

* Rappaport also suggested (*ibid.*) that valuables enabled population distribution and rates of population growth to be equalized by causing women to flow to the group which was slowest growing and hence had the smallest demand for utilitarian goods (cf. Salisbury, 1956). This subject is far too large to be considered here, but it should be pointed out that the ramifications in the directional flow of both valuables and utilitarian goods revealed in the course of the present study suggest that the asymmetry of marriages will show a pattern equally as complex—perhaps, because of the role of marriages in access to land and in political alliance, more complex.

† Within the area of this study no one supplied goods without some reward.

123

the general statements of informants suggest that they were rarely effective when more than one mutual trade partner was the medium. Rappaport suggested that they may be effective when the trader or group was the centre of a trading *web* rather than a trading *chain*. This was unnecessary, for in the Simbai and Jimi Valleys and through-out the study area the webs were constructed of chains; the path of a product through the web was a series of links in a chain of exchange forming part of the web. Utilities tended to take shorter paths than valuables but goods of both categories moved in the same basic steps, sometimes across one link, sometimes another, but tending in a general direction.

To derive his hypothesis Rappaport regarded the set of transac-tions as a closed system, which it patently was not. Pigs played a vital part in the total traffic, as he himself went on to show. The Maring could have made less effective but adequate work axes from river boulders as others did when good imported axes were scarce. The Maring were well off for axes and they had some choice; while most came to them from the Tsenga factory some came via different intermediaries from the Ganz River factory. Maring demand for work axes was not limited by the number they could work with, for some were traded north; similarly some salt was passed on by the axe makers. They, in turn, were not dependent on the Maring for salt for they also got it from the Karam of the Kaironk Valley and they received Enga salt from the west; the people of Tsenga and Ganz River actually exchanged Maring and Enga salt. They also made potassium salts. A cessation of Maring demand for axes would not have stopped axe production, for they were exported in many directions, and conversely, not only the axe-makers ate Maring salt and in most places the demand for salt exceeded the supply.

A serious objection is that the model underrates the importance of the intermediate links in the chain. In former times, neither party knew of the existence of the other. Simbai Valley Maring knew only that axes could be got from their Jimi Valley Maring neighbours to the south and vaguely that they came from across the Jimi River. The axe-makers knew only that salt came to them from over the river to the north. For each, their political and commercial worlds were circumscribed by the demands expressed by their neighbours and the goods which they had to offer. Each node in the many-stranded web that stretched between the Simbai and Tsenga-Ganz River areas had a different set of demands and a different set of goods to offer, all affected by their location in reference to east–west as well as north–south flows of goods, and by past, present and planned trading and ceremonial activity. Money cowries, for instance, came down the valley from the east, and dog whelks and green snail shells came up from the west. A host of minor ornaments and utilitarian goods were exchanged in a multiplicity of directions, mediating between transfers of larger items and often masking for a time the dominant directions of flow.

Rappaport's limiting assumption may have helped to derive his hypothesis; but his main argument is sustained even when the assumption is relaxed. My own evidence shows that valuables were not the only media of exchange and that the transfer of utilitarian goods would have proceeded without the circulation of special axes and shells and plumes, that subsistence needs would have been met and luxuries like better work axes and more and better salt would have been exchanged. Nevertheless, valuables stimulated the production of utilitarian goods, increased the quantities and rates of flow through the network and assisted their transfer by acting as supplementary and better media of exchange, better because their relative values changed less spatially and temporally than those of specialized utilitarian goods. In addition, shell valuables were almost as durable as stone axes and the small shells could be combined or divided almost as freely as the small denominations of other currencies. They gave flexibility to trade and added a new quality to the practice of politicking with gifts. This usefulness added value to beautiful ornaments and axes, and it is reasonable to suppose that it played a part in the evolution of valuables as a class of goods, but I cannot show that it did.

Traffic in goods reached its greatest elaboration in the highlands regions, well founded on a basis of mineral resources, benign agricultural environment, intensive and highly productive agriculture, intensive pig husbandry and a salubrious climate. In the context of New Guinea these regions had developed a series of high-consumption affluent societies. But whether the region was rich or poor, subsistence needs, luxury wants and the desire for wealth and sociopolitical success all caused men to initiate and continue trade.

We can see neolithic New Guinea trade as part of the process of human adaptation to a number of contrasting environments, see the resulting pattern of intersecting paths as a structure connecting

125

regions of great ecological and cultural diversity, and see the long flows of goods as integrating the products of discrete localities into the economies of others, the paths and the flows transcending physical barriers and the dangerous boundaries of conflicting political hegemonies. As an abstract construct we may even refer to the trading network as an 'integrating system', though it seems to me to imply more than the evidence will bear. To the participants it would be quite unreal; for them, integration was tenuous in the extreme and for most of them it extended no further than the horizon.

6 Full circle in Chimbu

A study of trends and cycles

Harold Brookfield

This is a study concerning an unusually long time-span of data, extending over a period of some 13 years from 1958 to 1970; it arises in part from the basic data-collection programme of the continuing Chimbu inquiry, and in part from an attempt to review earlier interpretations both of cultural ecology and of the development path in Chimbu. To do the two in one place is not easy, for while I have solid data on land use and related phenomena of agrarian adaptation, my questions came to include the nature of development only as the research evolved, and after the major periods of field-work were over; I thus lack essential data on incomes, time budgets and cash production, except in fragmentary form. However, it is necessary to my argument to deal with both aspects, both because my conclusion is that modern trends are closely related to internal cycles and *vice versa*, and also because it seems to me possible to invert the 'normal' (Harvey, 1969) order of geographical explanation, and to utilize change in spatial pattern in order to obtain light on temporal process. And it is temporal process that is my main *explicandum*.

I argue that the sort of 'development' that has taken place in Chimbu since the early 1950s has taken the form simply of the partial acceptance of 'modern' innovations into a continuing system whose 'essential variables' have not been transformed. Despite some evidence that they might became transformed in the middle period of my inquiry (Brookfield, 1968b), this has not happened. The innovation of a major cash crop (coffee) has thus been absorbed, and has not effected any structural transformation. But at the same time it has led to modifications in the use of land, consumption patterns and perception of total environment, and has

127

had the effect of partially integrating the Chimbu economy into the national New Guinea economy in the role of deprived periphery. The traditional system has been in some measure impoverished; the newer quasi-system has not provided adequate satisfactions in its place.

With the advantages of hindsight, I can see how a very different research programme could have shed much more light on these questions than has the inquiry which Paula Brown and I began in 1958. We were anthropologist and geographer, and our research questions stemmed from these disciplines as they then stood. By combining our questions, we were able to produce something that in its day was perhaps innovative in cultural ecology. As our disciplines changed, the questions also changed. Yet the problem that came to assume dominance is not readily amenable to the tools of either discipline; the study of change demands a more eclectic borrowing of concepts and methods widely across the social sciences. For example, we could hardly see in 1958 that the key to a behavioural interpretation of change might lie in Chayanov's (1966) trade-off between 'family' satisfaction levels and the drudgery of self-exploitation in peasant economy. Hindsight is unhelpful in research, and however vital in subsequent explanation it can never yield the data that should have been collected. This is not an uncommon problem, but it is one that becomes especially severe when it is necessary to disentangle internal cycles from externally-induced trends, or to judge how far the revealed pattern is peculiar to one area, or reflects little-considered forces of wide domain in their effect on the process called 'modernization'.

In what follows, I begin with the area and my data, then turn to some discussion of the course of events. Then I analyse the spatial data much as any geographer might do: the results are not greatly illuminating, except on one or two points of critical interest. However they are truly critical, for it was they that enabled me to reach the essentially qualitative, and tentative, interpretation that follows.

ELEMENTS AND EVENTS: A DESCRIPTION AND REVIEW

Chimbu farming

The content of the Chimbu production system has already been described in detail in numerous publications by Paula Brown and myself. Only the briefest of restatements is offered here. Chimbu of the Naregu tribe, within our study area, farm a steepland terrain developed on limestone, shales and greywackes at altitudes ranging from 1,500m to 2,250m, under an annual rainfall between 2,200mm and 2,800mm in normal years, exhibiting only a weak seasonality though characterized by prolonged spells of wet and dry weather. There is great micro-environmental variety, and an understanding of this variety is exhibited not only in the responses of informants, but also in the selection of land and in cropping patterns. The base of the system is the production of sweet potatoes and the rearing of pigs. Sweet potatoes of four or five main varieties, and many more lesser varieties, are grown in 'open fields' devoted wholly or mainly to the one crop. They provide some four-fifths of the human diet by weight, and a comparable but unmeasured proportion of the diet of pigs. Pigs browse and root by day in open, uncultivated areas, separated from cultivation and enclosed fallow by stout wooden fences constructed of *Casuarina* stakes. *Casuarinas* are grown in both enclosed and unenclosed fallow to yield wood for fencing, house-building and firewood, and also to aid recovery of the structure and humus content of the soil in this long-deforested region. Pigs live mostly in houses located along the fences, and entered from either side. They are fed cultivated sweet potatoes by women whe some-times live in the same houses, sometimes elsewhere within the enclosed blocks, sometimes with their husbands.* Men traditionally occupy communal men's houses located on higher ground in the heart of the enclosed areas, and linked together by a network of permanent walking tracks. Individual land holdings are dispersed, and 75 per cent of food-crop land lay in both 1958 and 1965 within 1,370m of the dispersed houses of a quasi-random sample of men and their wives: the furthest gardens lay within 4,500m. Regression analysis of the moves of the same sample, and the movement of their

* Settlement pattern is dispersed, and a plot of all house sites used during the years 1958–65, sampled at a ten per cent fraction by random methods without stratification, yielded a nearest-neighbour statistic of R= 0·70 (more aggregated than random). Drawing another sample from the small quadrats of the grid system employed in all transformation of these data, the distribution was then found to be accurately described at the 95 per cent level by the negative binominal distribution. However, this distribution failed using larger quadrats. Further, the distribution of wives by distance from their husbands is found to be accurately described at the 95 per cent level by an exponential distribution. Unfortunately, these interesting statistics are of little help in explaining the patterns.

gardening activities, suggests that when the central point of garden distribution becomes separated by more than 1,400m from the residence, a residential move will tend to follow in order to shorten this separation.

Subsidiary crops are usually intercultivated in 'mixed gardens'. They include several types of banana, sugar cane consumed by chewing, a range of beans and leafy vegetables, some taro and yam, and a very little cassava. There is a number of fruit trees, and two species of pandanus are grown as long-term crops. There are also a few semi-domesticates of considerable interest to those who would speculate on the origins of agriculture.

With the exception of the tree crops, all these varieties are cultivated in ground prepared by the same methods, and in contrast to practices among the Enga (Waddell, 1972a) and some other highland peoples, there is no difference in the basic mode of preparation of open fields and of mixed gardens. Land is wholly or substantially cleared, with or without use of fire, and is then ditched in a gridiron pattern, except on some areas of very friable soil and some steep slopes, where the whole surface is instead lightly tilled with spades or digging sticks. In the gridiron system, ditches are about three metres apart and about 10—15cm deep; in normally waterlogged areas, ditches are much deeper and closer together, and commonly feed into a localized drainage system. Spoil from the ditches is spread over the beds, then worked into small hills to receive crops. Some farmers dig in vegetable trash; others do not. All work is done with spade, bush knife, axe and digging stick. The evidence of early photographs shows that there has been no change in methods since 1933, following the replacement of stone, wood and bamboo tools by steel.

When a sweet potato field grows old, and ceases to yield worthwhile crops from digging at intervals among the growing plants, pigs are commonly brought into the field and tethered. By rooting, they effectively harvest the balance of the crop and at the same time till the soil to the depth of their snouts. After a short rest, such land is then commonly reditched and replanted. Unfortunately, hungry pigs frequently break through old fences at weak points to invade productive gardens. This is a major source of damage and loss, and of dispute between pig-owner and garden-owner. The Papuan pig has a well-developed directional sense, and its depredations are commonly held to be malicious rather than random.

130

The land-use data

A first task in understanding Chimbu use and occupation of land in 1958 was to map land holdings and their use. In the absence of any base map, or of usable air photographs,* and of the resources to permit anything better, the first map was prepared by compass and pacing methods, supported by compass triangulation. This same map was used again in 1959, amended as necessary, and again in 1962. By this time, the pattern had changed so much that a new base map was needed; the inaccuracies of the earlier map had become very patent. In 1963 an attempt was made to fly uncontrolled air cover, using a 127mm war-surplus camera suspended from the open door of a light aircraft flying at 2,500–2,600m. This experience did not yield a base for a new map, but demonstrated abundantly the value of low-altitude photography. With a grant from the Reserve Bank of Australia, new professional cover was flown in 1964 using high-resolution film and lens, at 3,600m. Coupled with some tellurometer triangulation kindly performed by the Department of Lands, and a contour map prepared for a road survey and adapted to control elevations, it became possible to construct a new and accurate base map on to which all previous data were transferred. The photographs themselves, of quality sufficient to permit counting of individual sweet potato hillocks in new open fields, were used as a base for field mapping in 1965 and again in 1967, for which date some additional new photography also became available. Unfortunately, the time demanded for frequent resurvey ceased to be available after 1967, and the run of data ends at this year.

Problems of mapping were severe. Plot boundaries are at best marked by a ditch, or a sight-line between stones or trees, and *Casuarinas*, or a rank growth of tall *Miscanthus* grass or *Phragmites*, obscure all detail over large areas—on the ground as much as from the air. An individual's holding is notionally fixed in size and location, but there is in fact a large measure of amendment and adjustment, sometimes giving rise to dispute but more often agreed or tolerated. This flexible element in land holding would create problems even if survey were precise at all dates; given the addition of a considerable measure of survey error we have a situation in

* Photographs taken in 1955 from 7,600m had insufficient resolution to be useful at this scale of work. They did, however, provide a basic drainage and track network for mapping.

131

Fig. 6.1 A portion of the 1965 field-survey map, redrawn, showing a part of the Chimbu study area

Legend:

- Open field
- Mixed garden
- Coffee
- ■ Men's house
- ● Other house
- ▬ Fence
- Enclosed fallow under trees
- Enclosed fallow under grass
- Unenclosed fallow
- ▬ ▬ Subclan territorial boundary
- Form lines at 15·24 m (50ft) intervals
- Individual holdings (in use)

N

0 ___ 100
metres

which accurate plot-by-plot comparison through time is unattainable. In terms of accuracy, the best survey is that of 1965 and a portion of the 1965 map is illustrated in Fig. 6.1. Comparable detail, including name of operator and type of crop for every cultivated field or garden, was collected in 1958 and 1965, but at the other dates only land-use data were comprehensively recorded, information on operators being only partial.

The 1965 data and the transferred 1963 data were first plotted on a scale of 1 : 3,600, and later reduced without information on operators to 1 : 10,800. 1958, 1959 and 1962 data were plotted on a map scale about 1 : 5,600, later transferred to 1 : 10,800; the 1967 data were plotted only on the latter scale. Final data on group territories, altitude by 15·2m contours (50ft), on surface lithology, soil-moisture condition and liability to recent land-slipping were all plotted initially on 1 : 10,800, in 1965. A mean slope map was derived from the contour map. Data on residence of individuals were plotted on the 1 : 3,600 scale at all dates to 1965.

In order to generalize the error, and obtain comparability between dates, a 4mm grid was laid over the 1 : 10,800 map and data were transferred in code into the resulting grid squares, each representing an area of 0·185 ha. All subsequent measurements, replacing measurements published up to 1966, rest on a count of grid squares, and hence on decisions to allocate a particular category to each square. Individual cultivated plots may on occasion be as small as 0·05 ha, and decision rested on a visual estimate as to whether or not 50 per cent of the area of each square was occupied by a particular category. A number of very small plots, and small uncultivated patches, are thus generalized out of existence, It is hardly feasible to place confidence limits on the plot, but the order of accuracy is reasonable given the limited resources and the methods employed.

Cycles, periodicities and trends

These data were collected with a view to quantifying the Chimbu agricultural system, and in particular to test the presence of two types of cycle in the system and to quantify long-term trends. The two cycles were respectively the land rotation often crudely called 'shifting cultivation', and the longer-term 'pig cycle' which is demonstrably a major event in Chimbu land use, as in society as a whole. The initial longer-term trend was the supposition of growing overpopulation in this densely occupied area; the establishment

133

and rapid expansion of coffee as a cash crop soon came to eclipse this in importance, and with its associated changes seemed for a time to be eclipsing all else that we came to Chimbu to study.

The presence of cycles was important in any interpretation of land and society. It seemed that the shifting pattern of dispersed settlement, and with it the shifting territorial pattern, and hence the local grouping of people, might be directly related to the need to move activity over the surface of the land in order to sustain production. We were told by informants that territorial stability of groups was a post-contact phenomenon; that earlier there was much mobility of people and fluidity of boundaries. Observing that settlement was shifting, we initially proposed an explanation depending directly on the shifting cultivation model. Eighteen months later it was obvious that this would not do, for there was far more continuity than we had supposed, and the impression of stability grew as time went on, disposing me to look for stable central points in the settlement and circulation pattern, and to examine distance decay from these centres. It seemed possible to dispose of the idea of an ecologically-determined cultivation cycle in this system.

The pig cycle was still more important. Pig herds are individually owned and raised, but their main use is in periodic group prestations involving whole tribes numbering from 1,000 to 10,000 persons, generally in association with other tribes which kill pigs at about the same time. Each few years, a 'pig ceremony' (*bugla gende*) is held at temporary village-like aggregations of houses built on a ceremonial ground; each tribal territory may have from two to a dozen such sites, and while some are semi-permanent and are marked by specially-planted decorative trees of mature age, others may be shifted in place from time to time. The ceremonial activities have a religious aspect (Reay, 1959), but their dominant worldly function is the massive giving of prestations. These 'gifts' are made ultimately by individual to individual, but in such a way that they are also shown to be given by tribal segment, and by tribe, to parallel groups in the surrounding population. Several months of intermittent dancing and festivity precede the climax in which almost all grown pigs are assembled, slaughtered, butchered and cooked: in ceremonies held in 1960 in neighbouring tribes we saw as many as 800 pigs slaughtered in a single morning. Carcasses are displayed by constituent segments of the tribe around a central *bolum*, or shrine, and the occasion is one of demonstration of group wealth

134

and power. Butchering and cooking are then done by small groups, and the conclusion is a *mêlée* of individual prestations of pieces of cooked pork by individuals to individuals. Reciprocal relationships are thus established or continued, debts are repaid or recognized. At the same time tribes and segments signalize their identity and interrelationship, while individuals, who may often move between groups, also record their primary affiliation.

These ceremonies require planning and co-ordination of a higher order than is demanded by any other Chimbu activity. The activities of related tribes must be planning in some association, and two or more years of preparation are required during which sites are prepared, pig herds are built up, additional gardens are planted, and ceremonial accoutrements are acquired or made. Immediately before a ceremony, the pig population may number from 1 to 1·5 per head and even more of the human population of a tribe, whereas immediately after the ceremony the number is minimal and scarcely any adult pigs survive.

Remarkably little is known about the ecology, nutrition and demography of pigs in central New Guinea, notwithstanding their demonstrated importance in society. Because of the dispersal of pigs, and the unpleasantness and sometimes danger of close observation, no one has yet subjected them to systematic investigation under conditions of normal pig husbandry. Isolated studies in the western highlands (Rappaport, 1967; Waddell, 1972a) indicate that around the peak of a cycle as much as 60 per cent of sweet potatoes harvested is fed to pigs; the total pressure on resources is more than doubled between the peak and trough of a cycle. Since pig diet is obtained both from intensive sweet potato cultivation and from very extensive use of land for grazing, browsing and rooting for worms, it follows that in space-using terms a large pre-ceremony herd is most efficiently accommodated by increasing cultivation. However, since this makes heavy demands on labour at a time when people have other unusual demands on time, the extensively used unenclosed land is normally allowed to be overgrazed, notwithstanding the practice of seeking agistment on the land of neighbouring groups who will receive pork, and are themselves at a lower point in their own cycle. Over-use of the unenclosed land, and some reduction in its area by additional enclosures, leads to increase in the vigour with which pigs attack the fences in order to gain access to the producing fields. As Rappaport (1967) also

135

notes, the pre-ceremonial period is one of considerable stress on human patience and vigilance, as well as on resources.

It would help if we knew something of the net reproduction rate of pigs, given no slaughter at intermediate dates. We know that pigs, especially young pigs, are liable to rather severe mortality from disease, and that the incidence of disease rises sharply when pigs are concentrated. Dispersal of herds among many houses, and extensive roaming in the unenclosed tracts, are known by Chimbu to be valuable devices in limiting mortality. Very tentatively, we might suggest that a full population of pigs might be rebuilt in as little as four years after a major ceremonial slaughter. But the interceremonial period is normally much longer than this. The scale of organization needed to mount a ceremony is alone hard to achieve under the uncentralized conditions of social authority in Chimbu, where a time-lag of several years between intention and achievement is a matter of normal observation in the simplest matters. It is thus tenable that the periodicity of the ceremonial cycle is related to pressure of social needs, as it becomes necessary to repay obligations, and to make the call on group allegiance that a ceremony constitutes. It does not seem likely in Chimbu, nor perhaps in most other central highland societies, that the cycle is determined by the demography and ecological conditions of pig production.

The pig cycle is also very germane to the question of overpopulation, which was seriously raised concerning Chimbu in the middle of 1950s, following identification of some nutritional diseases in this area. Population densities in this area approach 150/km², and many observers have claimed to see evidence of soil erosion and other indications of progressive environmental deterioration. Our earliest quantitative employment of the land-use data was an attempt to measure population pressure, making use of the approach of Allan (1949). We concluded that while certain segments of Naregu tribe were approaching 'capacity' by such objective standards, there remained adequate space in the tribal territory, and in Chimbu, as a whole (Brookfield and Brown, 1963, 105-24). But this was a static exercise in which the pig cycle was largely disregarded. Because of this cycle the demand on land varies enormously; there may be severe pressure at the peak, but none at all once the pigs have been slaughtered. Short periods of pressure can be tolerated, even though there is damage, and no Chimbu group seems yet unable to hold a ceremony for want of land on which to build up its herds. However, the trend of population is currently sharply upward, and it seems probable from sundry evidence that pressure is more severe in the current cycle than in the last. But there have also been secular changes which make it impracticable to isolate population trends as a causal factor in generating ecological stress.

The course of events

Naregu held a major pig ceremony in 1956, the climax being in December, a year and a half before our first field-work in the area. In 1955, Government had introduced coffee as a cash crop to selected Chimbu leaders and a small number of 'communal' coffee blocks had been laid out and planted. These blocks, together with individual nurseries, provided the seedling material for a massive and entirely spontaneous expansion of the coffee area that began in 1957, after the ceremony, and continued until the mid-1960s. By 1962 almost every farmer in our study area had some coffee.

In 1959, the first Local Government Council in the highlands was set up in central Chimbu, and was seen as a vehicle of progress along a self-controlled road to wealth and equality with the Europeans. Directions of Councillors, which were readily obeyed, included work reorganization, road building, the enclosure of large new areas for planned cash crops which never materialized, accelerated completion of a pig ceremony in some neighbouring tribes within the Council area, and the abandonment of many spare-time pleasures which were held to interfere with progress. By 1962, increasing dissatisfaction with returns which failed even to approach earlier expectations was exhibited in growing resistance to Council and government exhortation, leading to a major confrontation in 1963. It was then first proposed to mount a new pig ceremony in Naregu, in 1964 or 1965. Improvement in the price of coffee, and a new series of innovations in the field of coffee processing and marketing, together with increased availability of new goods through a growing number of retail outlets, led to a new surge of enthusiasm which continued through 1966, then evaporated again following new disappointments and a temporary breakdown of coffee-buying arrangements through mismanagement of a co-operative marketing and processing organization. After 1967 a sort of plateau was attained; increasing numbers of men and some women left Chimbu to work in the coastal towns; there was renewed urging to organize a ceremony. The coffee-processing innovations fell into disuse, and

137

the supply of coffee began to fall off; by 1970 it could not even be stimulated by a new price peak, which proved to be only temporary. By this year organization of a new ceremony was in full swing, especially in the study area; pig pressure was evidently onerous, and severe damage was being done especially to coffee, which was being killed through trampling of the soil and its drains by invading pigs. The ceremony was completed in January 1972, and meanwhile a new innovation was combining fortuitously with the resurgence of old ways; tourist parties were visiting the area frequently to see 'native dances' performed, at a price which offered a far better return for inputs of time than growing coffee. Thus ended a decade and a half of 'progress' and 'modernization'.

A perplexing contrast between sudden change in some respects and immense time-lags in others appears throughout this course of events. Initial enthusiasm for coffee, the Council, the processing innovations and the co-operative Kundiawa Coffee Society, and for numbers of lesser innovations, was very great. While there was always a falling-off in enchantment, some of the new ways were only reluctantly relinquished, and the doctrine of progress through toil continued to be preached late into the 1960s, notwithstanding repeated failures. Difficulties within the production system which resulted from the innovations were at first shrugged off, later accepted, and only very slowly indeed were attempts made to come to terms with these problems. Thus one product of the early changes was an immense increase in the enclosed area, reducing the unenclosed 'waste' in the hope of bringing it into productive use, and thereby throwing a heavy strain on women who had to look after a growing number of pigs at a greater distance. In 1962 and 1963 there were major breaches in the fences and large areas were devastated by pigs, yet it was 1965 before new fence lines, more than 1,000m back in some places, were firmly established.

The basic conflict has seemed to lie between pigs and coffee, respectively peripheral and central users of land and labour. Both steadily increased their demand on total resources. But the conflict ran much more deeply than the simple competition for space and labour. Pig production offers rewards in the securities and satisfactions of the closely-meshed network of interpersonal and group relations; coffee production, on the other hand, is seen as rewarded by access to the envied and desired wealth and power of the invaders. Ever seeking stable equilibria, this observer once supposed that a

138

balance was emerging in which the pig cycle would be levelled out through the innovation of more frequent, but smaller and less demanding ceremonies, thus permitting coffee a continued but less dramatic rate of growth (Brookfield, 1968b). But a new major ceremony has in fact been held, to be followed by a new period of low demand from pigs, and new opportunities for innovation and change. But whether or not a fresh surge of coffee planting is likely to ensue cannot be predicted from the local scene alone. Larger disequilibriating forces are also at work, and the conflict and complementarity of internal and external systems is assuming new and wider dimensions.

Changes through time

The set of open-ended questions thrown up by the course of events must now be explored through closer examination of actual changes on the ground. The questions are temporal, rather than spatial, but Harvey's order of explanation, mentioned in the introductory paragraph, may usefully be inverted to seek light on temporal process through variations in the spatial pattern.

Table 6.1 demonstrates a very clear set of aggregate changes through the 1958–67 period in the study area. Total area under cultivation, and under cultivation per head of population, increased substantially. Both open field and coffee area increased, while mixed gardens declined greatly. These same trends are presented diagrammatically in Figure 6.2, where the central areas are distinguished from the northern and southern tracts which were little used in 1958. Almost all coffee is in the central block, while the net increase in food-crop area is almost wholly in the outlying tracts.

A spatial differentiation of significance is thus immediately introduced. The central areas, as bounded here, comprise just over half the 8·816km² contained in the total study area. At most dates they have housed over 85 per cent of the population, and at the beginning of the period of survey also contained almost all the cultivation. Progressively over the years more and more of these outlying areas have been enclosed, and brought into food-crop cultivation. The initial impression is that food crops have been displaced toward the periphery by coffee. However, a sample of 13·3 ha that has gone under coffee since 1958 includes only 5 ha that were under food crops before being put down to the new tree crop; the balance of 8·3 ha was uncultivated before being planted. Further-

139

Table 6.1 Distribution of land by use-classes at each survey date, Chimbu (hectares).

	1958	1959	1962	1963	1965	1967
A Northern mountain area						
Open field	9·1	17·9	—	25·1	36·9	29·5
Mixed garden	3·0	3·6	—	1·1	1·5	0·4
Coffee	0·0	0·2	—	0·2	0·0	0·6
Enclosed uncultivated	4·2	2·1	—	16·4	13·7	16·0
Total enclosed	16·3	23·8	30·0	42·8	52·1	46·4
Forest	68·2	68·2	68·2	68·2	68·2	68·2
Total unenclosed	186·6	179·2	173·0	160·2	150·9	156·6
Total area (less (forest)	202·9	202·9	202·9	202·9	202·9	202·9
B Central block						
Open field	83·6	111·9	108·9	95·6	83·6	108·9
Mixed garden	54·9	50·2	21·3	17·7	23·0	12·7
Coffee	6·7	12·2	27·9	44·7	55·5	62·3
Enclosed uncultivated	151·4	119·1	227·6	198·7	145·5	135·1
Total enclosed	296·6	293·4	385·7	356·6	307·6	319·0
Total unenclosed	177·7	180·9	88·5	117·6	166·6	155·2
Total area	474·2	474·2	474·2	474·2	474·2	474·2
C Southern lowland area						
Open field	6·1	5·7	—	20·0	26·8	28·5
Mixed garden	0·0	0·8	—	0·6	0·8	0·2
Coffee	0·4	0·4	—	0·8	1·5	1·3
Enclosed uncultivated	0·0	3·8	—	23·8	15·2	29·8
Total enclosed	6·5	10·6	27·0	45·0	44·3	59·9
Total unenclosed	129·8	125·6	109·2	91·2	92·0	76·4
Total area	136·2	136·2	136·2	136·2	136·2	136·2
TOTAL STUDY AREA						
Open field	98·8	135·5	c138	140·6	147·3	166·8
Mixed garden	58·0	54·5	c 22	19·4	25·3	13·3
Coffee	7·0	12·7	c 28	45·6	57·0	64·2
Enclosed uncultivated	155·6	125·0	c255	238·8	174·4	180·9
Total enclosed	319·4	327·8	442·7	444·4	403·9	425·2
Forest	68·2	68·2	68·2	68·2	68·2	68·2
Total unenclosed	494·0	485·6	370·7	369·0	409·5	388·2
Total area	881·6	881·6	881·6	881·6	881·6	881·6
(Percentages of non-forested area, 813·4ha)						
	%	%	%	%	%	%
Open field	12·1	16·7	—	17·3	18·1	20·5
Mixed garden	7·1	6·7	—	2·4	3·1	1·6
Coffee	0·9	1·6	—	5·6	7·0	7·9
Enclosed uncultivated	19·1	15·4	—	29·4	21·4	22·2
Unenclosed	60·7	59·7	—	45·5	50·3	47·4

c—estimates. Totals for 1962 reliable for central block only. Because of rounding, additions do not always equal totals.

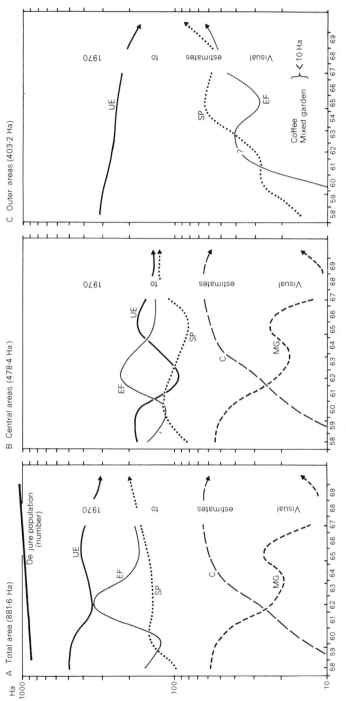

Fig. 6.2 Chimbu study area: curves showing the progression of land in use in certain main classes through the survey period. A—total study area; B—central areas; C—northern and southern areas together UE—unenclosed; EF—enclosed follow; SP —sweet potato open field; C—coffee; MG—mixed garden.

more, there has in fact been no reduction in the open field area in the central block from its 1958 level. Disregarding the coincidental equivalence of values, there is an interesting suggestion here of a cyclic fluctuation in open field area, with an 8–10-year wavelength.

The evidence of cultivation cycles

Transition probability matrices drawn up for two independent samples are summarized in Table 6.2. Despite difference in areal extent and time-interval, the revealed pattern is rather similar. Mixed gardens show the least stability; the stability of coffee is rather variable between the two samples, but seems to increase through time. Except around 1962, unenclosed land remains fairly stable, while transition probabilities for enclosed but uncultivated land, and for open field, both move within a comparable range so that any plot in either of these classes has between a one-third and two-thirds probability of being found in the same use at the next survey date. There are no absorbing states. Most interesting, however, is the fluctuation in the transition probabilities for stable continuity in sweet potato-growing open fields. Initially below 0·5, they tend to decline toward the middle of the survey period, then rise in the later years to reach almost two-thirds. It seems that as the pig cycle advances, and with it the demand for sweet potatoes, the probability rises that an open field will be retained in production; the probability of a transition to non-cultivation declines steadily from 1959 onward.

In the first sample, covering the central areas, 82 squares were in cultivation in 1958. Of these four remained throughout in cultivation, 45 underwent only a single change to non-cultivation, and the balance switched from cultivation to non-cultivation from two to five times, or went into coffee at some date. Among the 297 squares included in this whole sample, 75 underwent only one change of land use as between food-crop cultivation and fallow, while 68 underwent only two changes. There is thus some evidence of a cultivation cycle, very variable over the area, but it is a cycle of long duration, longer than the period of survey: at least half the land once cultivated remains in use from three to eight years, some longer; it is then uncultivated for a comparable, or slightly longer period. Other land goes regularly in and out of cultivation on a much

142

Table 6.2 Land-use transition probability matrices (Chimbu); (**A**) Grid sample of 297 squares (54.0ha), in the Central Block only; (**B**) Stratified sample of 225 squares 41.6ha) over the whole area. (Rows total to P = 1.00.)
OF—Open field, mainly sweet potatoes; MG—Mixed gardens, many crops; Cf—Coffee; E/N—Enclosed, uncultivated (Sample A); UnE—Unenclosed, uncultivated (Sample A); N/C—Not cultivated (Sample B: includes categories E/N and UnE of Sample A). *Notes*: (1) Principal diagonal values are asterisked. (2) All values are probabilities. (3) Squares in Forest or Pandanus all have P = 1.00. and are not included in the matrices.

	OF	MG	Cf	E/N	UnE
1958–9					
OF	0·43*	0·16	0·02	0·27	0·12
MG	0·29	0·33*	0·03	0·25	0·10
Cf	0·33	—	0·67*	—	—
E/N	0·32	0·13	0·04	0·40*	0·11
UnE	0·08	0·04	—	0·06	0·82*
1959–62					
OF	0·43*	0·06	0·07	0·44	—
MG	0·23	0·06*	0·12	0·59	—
Cf	0·14	—	0·43*	0·43	—
E/N	0·23	0·12	0·10	0·52*	0·03
UnE	0·13	0·03	0·01	0·38	0·45*
1962–3					
OF	0·35	0·13	0·09	0·39	0·04
MG	0·29	0·18*	0·06	0·47	—
Cf	0·20	—	0·65*	0·15	—
E/N	0·23	0·03	0·07	0·69*	0·07
UnE	0·04	0·02	0·02	0·04	0·88*
1963–5					
OF	0·50*	0·08	0·06	0·22	0·14
MG	0·35	0·23*	0·06	0·18	0·18
Cf	—	0·03	0·84*	0·10	0·03
E/N	0·13	0·03	0·06	0·50*	0·28
UnE	0·03	—	—	0·06	0·91*
1965–7					
OF	0·60*	0·02	0·03	0·28	0·07
MG	0·43	0·07*	0·14	0·22	0·14
Cf	0·03	—	0·87*	0·05	0·05
E/N	0·27	0·04	0·08	0·56*	0·05
UnE	0·08	0·03	0·02	0·13	0·74*

(**A**)

	OF	MG	Cf	N/C
1958–62				
OF	0·42*	0·03	0·12	0·42
MG	0·40	—*	0·20	0·40
Cf	—	—	—*	—
N/C	0·17	0·03	0·02	0·79*
1962–5				
OF	0·34*	0·04	0·07	0·53
MG	0·17	—*	0·17	0·66
Cf	—	—	1·00*	—
N/C	0·18	0·03	0·07	0·73*
1965–7				
OF	0·63*	0·02	0·09	0·26
MG	0·17	0·17*	—	0·67
Cf	—	0·04	0·96*	—
N/C	0·10	0·01	0·04	0·85*

(**B**)

shorter cycle: there is no regular regional variation in the incidence of the two patterns.

Spatial variation in the frequency of cultivation

The weak evidence for the presence of cultivation cycles is thus of limited aid in explaining the revealed trends. However, it is clear that the total increase in cultivated land is not to be explained only by a physical spread of cultivation of constant frequency. Some land is used much more frequently than other land, and it may be hypothesized that preferred tracts are cultivated more continuously, while other land is brought into cultivation only as demanded, and for shorter periods. Land of lower value is thus the 'reserve' land which is brought into use at the peak of the pig cycle, and which is also being used more often as total demand increases under the impact of rising population, and the intrusion of coffee.

Earlier work had suggested that both ecological and distance variables were important in distinguishing preferred from other land. Because of the wide dispersal of settlement, and the finding that distances more than 1,000m from residence are within a 'tolerable' range, it was not easy to disentangle the effect of these two main classes of factor. However, the pattern of circulation, and the distribution of men's houses, show much more centrality than the settlement pattern as a whole (Brown and Brookfield, 1967; Brookfield, 1968b); and various exercises in centrographic analysis have demonstrated a cluster of central points of house, garden, coffee and population distribution, all occupying a limited area around and below the point called Giglmuno, where the main axial walking path crosses the modern road. An additional measure was produced for this research, based unlike the earlier measures on a fully random sample of people. From a numbered card index of 720 persons adequately recorded, 60 individuals were selected using random numbers and were located from information on their residences at three dates, 1958, 1962 and 1965. The sample included 31 males and 29 females, fortuitously representing all but one of the subclan segments in the population. Following Bachi's method (Berry and Marble, 1968, 101–9), co-ordinate means were obtained for the whole sample, and for males and females separately. All were found to lie within a range of 100m, and to be within the cluster of points determined earlier for non-random samples.

144

Table 6.3 Summary of 2n-factorial analysis (Chimbu)

(A) Factor combinations	Mean sample values (rounded)		
	% time cult.	% time encl.	% time coffee

					% time cult.	% time encl.	% time coffee
a	ab	abc	abcd		40	44	3
			abc		51	54	2
		ab	abd		61	84	11
			ab		81	90	—
	a	ac	acd		25	38	—
			ac		29	41	—
		a	ad		28	68	4
			a		14	40	—
l	b	bc	bcd		44	68	12
			bc		17	27	—
		b	bd		34	44	15
			b		14	33	6
	l	c	cd		45	76	11
			c		17	35	4
		l	d		37	70	14
			l		16	30	4

a—altitude
  Yes—above 1,829m = a
  No —below 1,829m = 1

b—slope
  Yes—0–19% = b
  No —20–99%

c—soil drainage
  Yes—well-drained = c
  No —often waterlogged

d—accessibility
  Yes—within 183m of
    main path = d
  No —more than 183m
    from main path

(Original measurements in ft or yds)

(B) Summary of scores by main factors

	% time cult.		% time encl.		% time coffee	
a—altitude	Yes—43	No—27	Yes—46	No—48	Yes—2	No—8
b—slope	—43	—28	—46	—48	—6	—5
c—soil drainage	—35	—36	—46	—47	—4	—7
d—accessibility	—39	—31	—61	—32	—9	—2

(C) Summary of results
Significant factor combinations in rank order. Negative relation *italicized*.
(1) % of time under cultivation:

Significance level			
99·9%	a, ab, b,		
99·0%		*ad,*	
95·0%			bc, abc, d

(2) % of time within enclosure:

99·9%	d, *acd,*		
99·0%		*abcd,*	
95·0%			ac, cd

(3) % of time under coffee:

99·9%	*d,*
99·0%	*a*

Standard distances were 1,138m for the whole sample, 1,032m for males and 1,240m for females, the male/female difference just failing to reach significance at the 95 per cent level.

A number of experiments were carried out to explore the distribution of cultivation frequency. Input was obtained by converting data on uses of land at unequally-spaced survey dates into a percentage of time spent in cultivation, including coffee. It was assumed that change, if any, between surveys took place at the midpoint of time between survey dates, in 1958, 1959, 1962, 1963, 1965 and 1967. Periods of 25, 24, 16 and 21 months were thus assigned to the 1959, 1962, 1963 and 1965 surveys. Extending this assumption, a notional time equal to half the 1958–9 intersurvey period was added before the 1958 survey, and similarly a time equal to half the 1965–7 intersurvey period was added after the 1967 survey. In this way, periods of 15 and 19 months respectively were assigned to the 1965 and 1967 data so that the whole time span was extended to a total of 120. Data for each survey were then assigned a weight equal to the percentage which the allotted period formed of this total span. Generally, only the percentage of time spent in all cultivation was used as dependent variable, but in a first exercise with 2n-factorial analysis the percentage of time spent in coffee, and within enclosure, was also examined.

The 2n-factorial analysis was designed to parallel the method used by Haggett (1964) as closely as possible. In practice it became necessary to follow Bailey (1959) rather than Yates (in Davies, 1956), because of some problems with the latter; results are not therefore comparable with Haggett's. However, his sampling design was exactly paralleled. Factors were dichotomized and combined into 16 combinations; a random sample (with replacement) of 16 grid squares was then drawn for each stratum. Factors used were altitude, slope, soil-moisture condition and distance from a walking track. Results are summarized in Table 6.3.

Notwithstanding the enormous loss of information suffered by dichotomizing the variables, some very interesting results do emerge. Except with coffee, soil-moisture condition is surprisingly weak in explanation; but altitude, slope and accessibility are all clearly effective. Period under all cultivation is responsive to higher altitude, gentler slope and good accessibility; period within enclosure to accessibility alone. Tests of significance confirmed these findings. With coffee, the lower input values affected results seriously, but lower altitude, poorer soil drainage and accessibility were all effective, though less significant. Factors affecting coffee distribution are thus somewhat different from those affecting cultivation frequency as a whole, reinforcing our finding that much of the present coffee represents a net addition to cultivated land within the survey period, and that the displacement effect on other crops, and especially open-field crops, is less than might appear at first sight.

Accessibility was alone in being significant at the 95 per cent level in all three experiments, but with time under cultivation it is weaker than the ecological variables of altitude and slope. Other attempts were made to obtain a more conclusive result, but a multiple regression analysis achieved only 20·1 per cent of explained variance. In a step-down programme, the last variable to be eliminated, and hence the most effective, was distance, in this case measured from a central point.* It was also intended to use an agglomerative polythetic system to approach the relative significance of ecological and distance variables through measures of association. However, a sample of only 80 squares was possible, and this proved inadequate in view of the highly uneven distribution of attributes.

At this stage it became apparent that interpretation of the factorial approach raised such problems that diminishing returns had set in rather early. Thus gentle slope and good soil drainage affect settlement location and circulation, as well as cultivation; altitude, slope and soil drainage are all interrelated. Even if we could establish that distance is the most effective factor in 'explaining' cultivation frequency, it is quite possible that we would be concealing ecological variables that themselves mark out a favoured central area, so that centrality would be the combined effect of the ecological factors that we were testing only individually.

Accordingly, a final measure sought only to describe the generalized distribution of cultivation frequency. After a test for randomness, trend surfaces were fitted to cultivation frequency data for a grid-sample of 297 squares originated at random, and covering the central areas alone. Since variation between the central and outer areas in frequency of cultivation is visually obvious (see also Fig. 6.2), inclusion of the outer areas might impose a regularity on the central areas that did not in fact exist. The quadratic and cubic surfaces, together with the plot of deviations, are shown in Fig. 6.3.

* The validity of this exercise is in any case doubtful, since variables were quantified by different forms of scaling.

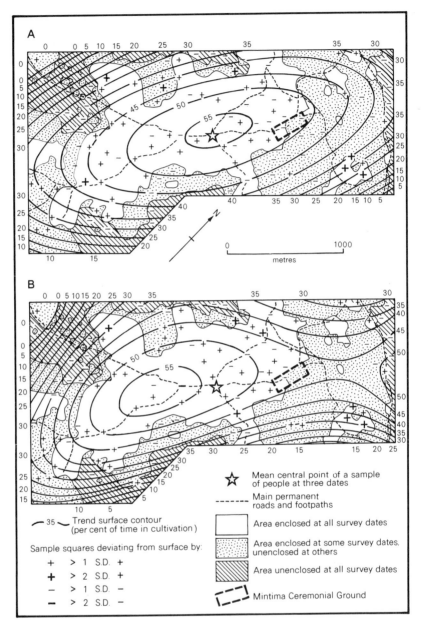

Fig. 6.3 Quadratic (**A**) and cubic (**B**) trend surfaces showing the frequency of land use through the survey period, against a background indicating the variation of enclosure between survey dates, the principal permanent tracks, and central points

The level of explanation of the surfaces is low. The coefficient of determination is only 0·179 and 0·224 for the quadratic and cubic surfaces respectively, and the coefficient of correlation rises only to 0·474 for the latter.

However, it is remarkable to note that the 'crest' of the quadratic surface coincides almost exactly with the independently-determined central point of population distribution, and that the axis of both surfaces corresponds closely with the axial path. The hypothesis of greater frequency in the core areas is well sustained. The slope of the surfaces is initially gentle, but falls away steeply at the edges. Expansion of cultivation through the pig cycle around a constant core, which continues in use at high frequency, underlies this pattern. We thus gain support for supposing that the pig cycle is the most important determinant of the pattern of farming activity.

This represents the effective limit of our ability to generalize statistically without transforming the data, but it does offer probable confirmation of what we have suspected. To explore the interrelation of spatial with temporal variables further we must now turn to the non-linear methods of mental argument. However imprecisely, these methods can yet make more effective use of a wide range of very mixed data than any quantitative method currently available.

PEOPLE, PIGS AND COFFEE: A LOCAL SYNTHESIS

We have established the concentration of coffee, and the partial displacement of food crops to the periphery. A high use-frequency in the central areas has also been established, falling away toward the edges of the occupied area. Furthermore, we have seen that there have been fluctuations through time in the area under open field, while mixed gardens have declined and the area under coffee has increased. To these limited data we must now add interpretation derived from observation in detail over space and through time, in order to try to understand the interrelation of these several trends.

People and pigs

A distance range of 1,000–1,500m crops up rather frequently in Chimbu. Within it lie the range from residence within which lie 75 per cent of gardens, the range from husbands within which live 75

149

per cent of wives, the critical distance where residential shifts and shifts in the central point of garden distribution begin to show correlation, and the standard distances of male and female population distribution around the mean centre. In Chimbu, as in many other societies, there is a strong suggestion of a 'tolerable distance' limited somewhere within this range, and beyond which the separation of everyday activities becomes onerous and unusual.

A Chimbu farm consists of a number of plots of land scattered over the enclosed areas, and use of the unenclosed land which is the common of all who have rights in enclosed land bounding it. Usually, it has three or more 'central' points, the residences of the man, his wife or wives, and other dependent women, and the family pigs. Chimbu houses are short-lived, with a mean life expectation at construction of 46 months (Brown and Brookfield, 1967); mobility is thus quite readily accommodated into the system. The evidence indicates very considerable mobility of persons during the survey period, both within and between group territories. Within the farm itself, median distances separating occupied houses at first increased, then decreased sharply. It seems reasonable to suppose that families have more freedom in the location of their activities during the early phases of the pig cycle, but that distance constraints become more and more oppressive as the cycle advances, and the burden of the pig herd increases. Expansion of enclosure is thus offset by deep interpenetration of the common into the enclosed land, so that more land can be brought into use without sacrificing the advantages of central grouping of the population.

But while the high use-frequency of the central areas is thus sustained, the weight of human activity is also very unevenly distributed on the land. The extremely onerous demands of the final stages of the cycle, and the ceremony itself, would press very heavily on resources in those areas, such as Naregu, where the clusterings of people forming local groups run to several hundreds. Thus an arrangement quite common in this part of central New Guinea, where the ceremonial ground is asymmetrically located in relation to its tributary population, has great convenience.

Mintima ceremonial ground lies some 1,250m upslope from the mean centre of population in the study area (Fig. 6.4). Since oral evidence suggests that all present men's house sites were occupied at the time of European discovery in 1933, and that Mintima itself has been used as a ceremonial site for several generations, we may

150

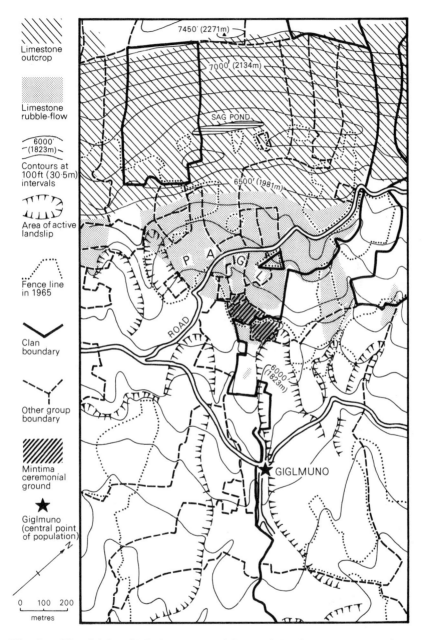

Limestone outcrop

Limestone rubble-flow

6000' (1823m)
Contours at 100ft (30·5m) intervals

Area of active landslip

Fence line in 1965

Clan boundary

Other group boundary

Mintima ceremonial ground

★
Giglmuno (central point of population)

N

0   100   200
metres

7450' (2271m)

7000' (2134m)

SAG POND

6500' (1981m)

P   A   G
L

ROAD

6000' (1823m)

★ GIGLMUNO

Fig. 6.4 The vicinity of Mintima ceremonial ground: land types, group territory and enclosure

suppose that this relationship between population and ceremonial ground has endured for some time. There may, however, have been a second clustering of house sites about 1,000m further upslope beyond the ceremonial ground, and on the crest of the mountain, in a period about 40–50 years ago: Mintima would thus have lain about midway between two central points. A residuum of this pattern remains, and some trace of its effects may possibly be revealed in the cubic trend surface of cultivation frequency (Fig. 6.3).

Immediately upslope of Mintima lies a minutely subdivided area known as Pagl (Fig. 6.4), of friable soil offering easy tillage and yielding fast-maturing crops, albeit of rather small tubers. Ten hectares of land on a limestone-enriched rubble flow descending from the mountain face are here divided among members of nine subclans, all of which also hold plots on the Mintima ground. In 1958 most of this area was in cultivation, and report was unanimous that it was highly-valued land (Brookfield and Brown, 1963, 30). Since 1962, however, most of it has lain waste, becoming common land outside the fences. It has been thoroughly rooted over by pigs, and only small sections have remained enclosed, almost continuously cultivated by a few individuals.

The abandonment of Pagl puzzled me greatly for a long time. It seemed to indicate failure of the whole ecological interpretation of the territorial system which we had earlier advanced. Later interpreting it as a downhill shift of activity following the coffee innovation, I was more readily led to believe in a definitive shift toward a new static equilibrium in the production system. But a far simpler explanation is now available, one which might not have eluded me had I earlier been more prepared to accept oral evidence covering the period before surveys began.

During the pig ceremony, the pattern of settlement is for a brief space radically transformed. The dispersed houses are largely vacated, and people live in a temporary village on the ceremonial ground together, during a few days of the climax, with at least an equal number of visitors. The catchment of the Mintima ceremonial ground, which is larger than the study area, had a population of some 1,400 in the late 1950s. We may assume that at least 1,000 of these moved to Mintima during the 1956 ceremony, and that great numbers of visitors and pigs were also concentrated on and around the site. The temporary villages are built up to two years before the ceremony, and houses remain habitable at least two years afterwards. Many houses built on and within 250m of the ground before 1956 were still occupied in 1958; in 1970, when 77 new houses had been built in readiness for the 1971–2 ceremony, some 200 people were already in residence. Apart from the massive short-lived concentration during the ceremony, there is therefore a significant agglomeration for at least three years in the course of any pig cycle.

There is thus a bipolarity in the distribution of population through the period of a pig cycle. All of Pagl lies within 1,000m of the Mintima ground, and we were once informed that the area, as we saw it in 1958, was first planted for an internal tribal ceremony in 1953, after which it continued in cultivation until after 1960, though with rapidly declining input after 1958. Parts of the area were again being readied in 1970. The value of Pagl is as the 'infield' of Mintima. Together with some other tracts close to the ceremonial ground, it serves to feed the temporary concentration of people and pigs, and thus relieve the pressure on the more permanent 'central' areas.

A large part of the complex story of land-use changes, shifts of residence, and variations in 'tolerable distance' is thus explicable in terms of an internal cycle alone. This cycle may have been retarded due to the coffee innovation, but it is probable that at least equal retardation may have taken place in the past, when it would have been necessary to resolve quarrels and make peace for a sufficient time to plan and mount a ceremony, and this cannot have been achieved easily in a society where resolution of inequalities in population/land relationships was attained through conquest. Within the survey period, it is the persistence and ultimate triumph of the cycle that is important: despite all the disturbing forces that have impinged on the local system, its complex pattern of interrelated internal readjustments through time has not been broken.

People and coffee

We can now re-examine the innovation path of the 1950s and 1960s in a different way from the earlier attempt (Brookfield, 1968b). We noted earlier in this paper the wild swings between hope and disillusionment, correlated to some degree with variations in the coffee price, with the supply of new innovations, and with variations in the management of marketing outlets. It is thus at first sight rather surprising, on examining Fig. 6.2, to observe that the expansion, stabilization and subsequent slight decline in the coffee area has followed a rather smooth curve,* as the initial planting surge weakened until new planting failed to balance losses. This is a cumulative investment curve, not a production curve. There are no data on production by so small an area, and the multiplicity of marketing outlets would make it virtually impossible to obtain adequate data even under continuous field observation, even by sampling, in an area of dispersed settlement. For a short period in 1965, when most marketing was centralized, it was possible to obtain rough data on which yield estimates could be based (Brookfield, 1968b), but this is for only a part of the area. The qualitative impression indicates very clearly that the rate of output has varied much more substantially than the rate of new coffee planting which reflects forward expectations rather than current market perception. But taken as an index of forward expectations, the smoothness of the curve is intriguing. The apparent effect of external innovation and events seems, to put it in the most cautious terms, minimal.

An alternative hypothesis is thus demanded. Can it be argued that willingness to plant coffee and to maintain existing groves in producing condition has been conditioned by the capacity of the existing system? We have observed strains as this capacity was approached, and the recent decline was a direct consequence of renewed emphasis on production of pigs for the internal exchange system. If so, what have been the determinants of this saturation level? Given that massive pig production was to be resumed, has the increasing distance to gardens necessitated a relaxation of inputs either at the centre (coffee) or at the periphery (sweet potatoes and pigs)? Was it beyond the capacity of the system to sustain both? Adequate answers demand data that I do not have, but the question carries us forward into the possibility of a more integrated discussion of trends in relation to cycles.

Pigs and coffee

Fundamental to any interpretation of trends and cycles in Chimbu is the thesis earlier advanced that the highly-elaborated husbandry

* It may be even smoother than it appears. The slight inflexion in 1962 is due to the inferior survey of that year, which was done in a shorter time than the others: it is highly probable that a significant area of young coffee under other growth—such as bananas, or casuarinas—was not seen, and that coffee first appearing on the map for 1963 was in fact already in the ground in 1962.

systems of the central highlanders permit them a freedom of choice in the spatial management and timing of their activities greater than that seemingly enjoyed by fringe groups of simpler technology (Rappaport, 1967; Clarke, 1971). Rappaport indicates that it is the level attained by the pig population, and its burdensome role on the human population, that triggers off the need for a new ceremony. But this is in a small population; such quasi-automatic regulatory mechanisms as Rappaport postulates would hardly be conceivable among the numerous Chimbu with their interlocking cycles. Pig herds are rebuilt to an intermediate level fairly swiftly after a ceremony, and the rebuilding can be accelerated by trade. They are then managed about this level until such time as the need for a ceremony arises from other causes, when they are permitted to increase. Ceremonies are not held primarily to dispose of pigs; they have complex objectives in the maintenance and reinforcement of the whole system of social relationships.*

Naregu could have held a new ceremony in the mid-1960s, and many wished to do so. But at this time adjustment and absorption of the coffee innovation was still in progress. Expansion of area had not ceased; the processing and marketing system was still evolving. In Chimbu, as in surrounding areas, a new form of social differentiation through wealth seemed to be emerging, and with it new patterns of consumption and investment were being explored. By the mid-1960s coffee had advanced as far as was possible without the emergence of specialist coffee-farmers, the evolution of internal trading, the strengthening of individual rights in land, and the emergence of a local proletariat. Such changes were resisted internally, and their possible evolution was weakened by a simultaneous widening of the possible channels for out-migration. Coffee incomes made it possible for Chimbu to pay their own fares to coastal towns, and at the same time opportunities for education and training improved for the young. The more discontented and energetic were

* In Chimbu, the first signal of intent to hold a new pig ceremony is the 'blowing of the flutes'. The quarrel over road work in 1963 was immediately followed by defiant flute-blowing at Mintima. Flutes were again blown several times in the years that followed in attempts to mount support for a new ceremony. The final, and more successful, flute-blowing took place in 1969. The purpose of this signalling device is said to be to halt, or curb, the use of pigs in minor ceremonial occasions so as to build up herds, and at the same time to indicate to all that planning of additional gardens, and of the construction needed on the ceremonial ground, should seriously begin.

155

thus siphoned off. Marketing of foodstuffs increased, but trends toward the evolution of local trading centres aborted as incomes stagnated, and nearby urban retail facilities improved. Widening of opportunity led to diffusion of effort, and incomes came more and more either to be absorbed into the internal system of reciprocal aid and exchange, or else to be used for consumption goods. Productive investment, on the other hand, actually fell away. In short, the marginal propensity to save diminished in opposition to rising marginal propensity to consume. As Griffin (1969) suggests for the wider context of Spanish America, larger external investment may even have contributed to reduced savings.

Table 6.4 Population and land-use trends in the Chimbu study area (ha per head of *de jure* population).
N.B. Values given also in acres for comparability with other data in the literature. Being based on the new map constructed in 1964–5, the values given here replace the lower figures given in Brookfield and Brown (1963), which were based on the original pace-and-compass map.

Year	Estimated de jure population	Open field Ha	(Acs)	All food crops Ha	(Acs)	Coffee Ha	All crops Ha	(Acs)
1958	870	0·11	(0·27)	0·18	(0·44)	0·01	0·19	(0·47)
1959	900	0·14	(0·37)	0·21	(0·52)	0·01	0·23	(0·57)
1962	935	0·15	(0·37)	0·18	(0·44)	0·03	0·21	(0·52)
1963	950	0·15	(0·36)	0·17	(0·42)	0·05	0·22	(0·54)
1965	980	0·15	(0·38)	0·18	(0·44)	0·06	0·23	(0·57)
1967	1,000	0·17	(0·42)	0·18	(0·45)	0·06	0·24	(0·59)

With failure to carry through any real transformation in any fundamental aspect of the local system, with increasing channelling of incomes into consumption of goods and services of external origin, and with inflation of the cash content of internal payments, the development drive offered less and less in terms of a road to wealth and power under local control. Where independence was sought, a greater dependency resulted, and pressures for the demonstrable restatement of the qualities and structures of the internal system through a new pig ceremony were resisted less and less.

The open field and coffee curves in Fig. 6.2 are thus both interrelated and independent. The open field curve, marking the rising demand for cultivated land as pig and human population increased (Table 6.4), demonstrates a continuity of older patterns. Coffee expanded within the system, partly replacing only the labour-intensive mixed gardens that yielded dietary variety now obtainable also by purchase. It reached limits marked out within the system, because the innovation did not succeed in transforming any of the essential variables of the system. The farming system with its pigs, the pattern of settlement, the form of land tenure, the whole complex institutionalized system of reciprocity underlying the structure of society itself—all were basically unchanged. Many of the more innovative left the area to work and live elsewhere, so that population expansion increased the burden of dependency by young and old on those who remained. Once the decision to hold a new ceremony was at last generally accepted, a loss of interest and a diversion of inputs from coffee was an inevitable consequence. Many of the processing innovations, and other investments, of the 1960s were abandoned; the net investment benefit of a large total income, taking account of welfare investments as well as productive investments, is quite remarkably small.

Guessing through longer time

Underlying these changes and cycles is an increase in population, which is certainly now accelerating. Evidence suggests that the rate of growth has not been great since contact, and there may have been some initial loss. Mortality, and especially infant mortality, remain above acceptable levels today. Table 6.4 reveals a substantial increase in *de jure* population, attested by head counts which are now fairly reliable, and a large out-migration has probably not prevented *de facto* population from also increasing. In Fig. 6.5 we leave the realm of probability for that of conjecture, projecting population, open-field and unenclosed land curves backward through time. There is some field evidence to support the contention of a series of forward surges in the area brought within enclosure during the last 40 years, and it is thus implied that successive pig cycles have imposed more and more strain on resources at their peaks. The coffee innovation has complicated the situation during the last cycle, and it is clear that any new surge of innovation must include measures to economize use of land if it is to have much chance of success. This would call for new forms of investment, an area in which experience to date is discouraging in the extreme. The next

157

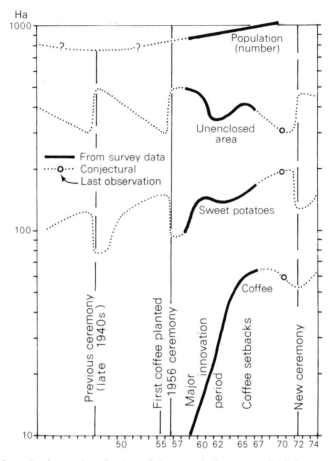

Fig. 6.5 Conjectural projection of the population, open-field (sweet potatoes), unenclosed land and coffee curves beyond the period covered by the surveys

pig cycle, whether or not it is ever completed, will certainly impose greater strain than its predecessors. Structural changes, including land reform and other innovations of a much more far-reaching nature than hitherto contemplated, will be required if the end of this next cycle does not see Chimbu well along the road to becoming a characteristic, dependent rural slum.

CONCLUSION

Fifteen years' intermittent research have been required to correct early mistakes, synthesize spatial with temporal data, and reach some conclusions of rather wider span than previous ones. In terms of a return for input this result would seem to bear comparison with the ultimate benefits of the Chimbu coffee innovation itself, being disappointingly poor, and characterized by a large expenditure of effort and money for small returns. But there are perhaps three more general conclusions that offer some justification.

First, I hope to have demonstrated the major importance of cycles of long duration in the understanding of man–land relationships. It has always been easiest to apply the simple shifting-cultivation model to Chimbu agriculture, as to many others. Several commentators have continued to do this, overriding my own frequently-stated *caveats*. Nothing could be less productive of real understanding, in dealing with a system where intensive application of skills permits a very long cultivation cycle also to support a major pig cycle, which in turn supports a great widening in the scale of social relations and of society itself. The support of the pig cycle in Chimbu entails a complex web of spatial arrangements designed to accommodate the strains of a system which varies its demand on resources through a factor of more than two, each few years. No interpretation of man/land balance, or of spatial organization of activity, can be valid unless it takes account of this repeated expansion and contraction. Long-duration cycles occur in many production systems, and any form of static analysis applied to such systems can be dangerously misleading.

Second, and of wider significance, is the emphasis on the internal system as absorbing and limiting an innovation, and being enabled to do this because the innovation was partial, and not accompanied by other and more comprehensive structural changes. However, the result has not been to leave the internal system unchanged, for it has become attached to a larger system in a dependent relationship that has very deleterious consequences. Such a set of findings need by no means be unique to Chimbu, and similar causes may underly the disappointing results of initially promising innovations in many parts of the world. A well-integrated internal system such as that identified here has very considerable powers of absorption, but it fails to respond adequately to the more subtle forces which whittle

159

down the benefits gained from absorption without transformation. The internal system should never be ignored, and its study becomes a vital part of the total preparation for real change.

But such study is clearly demanding of time and resources, and it has more than once been remarked to the author that the average student is unable to profit from an exercise such as the present except to the extent of feeling that his own short-term efforts are futile. This is not wholly true, for a greater awareness of the need for time depth can also be accommodated by eschewing static models and seeking new sorts of evidence. But it is nonetheless true that more long-continued inquiries are needed, in order to provide a greater range of comparative data. Here, however, a further change that is in progress will be of signal value. The study of the Third World is less and less the monopoly of expatriate researchers. The growing emergence of a body of geographers, anthropologists, economists and others who originate within, are trained within and work within Third World countries is about to transform the nature of this research effort. Locally-based students of society can and will be able to afford more time, and can bring to their work insights and attitudes that are hard for an expatriate to achieve, even if ever wholly possible. In the monitoring of change which is essential to its proper understanding and ultimate guidance, locally-based inquirers will have a key role to play, in the Pacific as elsewhere. Let us hope that they will be less committed to external models than most of us have been, and will make faster progress.

Acknowledgements

Grateful acknowledgement is made to Paula Brown (Glick) for freedom to utilize material which is as much hers as mine, although she bears no responsibility for this interpretation. I am also grateful to Eric Waddell and to Fiona Wilson for critical comments, from very different viewpoints, on late drafts of this chapter. Though they may find their suggestions inadequately regarded, their comments have in each case led to significant changes. I am also grateful to Doreen Hart, David Ley, Larry Springer and Claire Doran for aid in data analysis at various stages, and to Bryan Massam for some technical advice.

160

Perspectives on change

7 Land shortage and population pressure in Tonga

Alaric Maude

The problems of land shortage and population pressure in small islands with only limited resources have been recurrent themes in recent geographical research in the Pacific islands, particularly in island Polynesia where populations are now generally increasing at rates of between 3 and 3·5 per cent annually. This essay is concerned with the chain of islands in western Polynesia which form the Kingdom of Tonga (Fig. 7.1). The 150 islands of the Kingdom, comprising the three main groups of Tongatapu, Ha'apai and Vava'u, and a number of outlying islands, have a total land area of only 663km² and support a population of about 87,000 (1970 estimate). The Kingdom's only natural resources are the soil and the surrounding reefs and seas, and the economy is overwhelmingly agricultural, being based largely on subsistence food cropping and the export of bananas, copra and desiccated coconut. With a limited area of land, a population density in 1970 of about 185/km² of arable land, and a projected annual population growth rate of 3·1 per cent, Tonga faces potential problems of land shortage and population pressure as severe as in any other nation or territory in the Pacific Islands, with the exception of some of the atoll groups.

The focus of this essay is on man/land relationships, for with an essentially agricultural economy these are central to Tonga's population problem. The main objective is a search for, and examination of, possible symptoms of population pressure within the man/environment system. Particular attention is paid to land tenure, which determines how land is allocated amongst the population; the agricultural system, agriculture being by far the most important use of land; and the perception of, and reponse to, population pressure by Tongans. At a more theoretical level, the final part of the essay

163

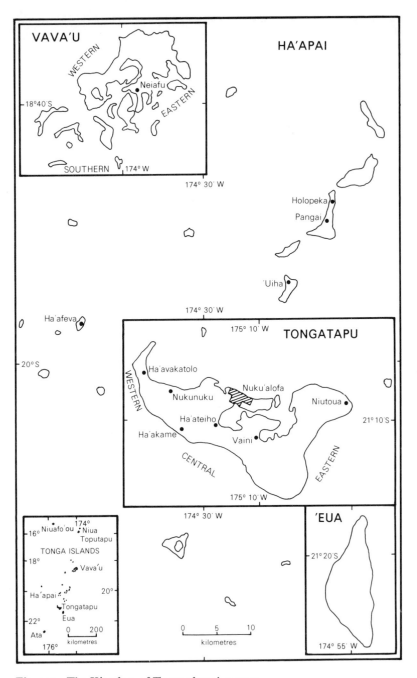

Fig. 7.1 The Kingdom of Tonga: location map

attempts to relate the Tongan material to the general statements of Geertz (1963) and Boserup (1965) on the effect of population growth on man/land relationships.

Varying approaches and methods have been used in this research in an attempt to combine depth of understanding with breadth of coverage. Some aspects of the system of man/land relationships, for instance the uneven population distribution or the pattern of internal migration, can only be understood by analysis at both the national and local levels. Other aspects, such as the functioning of the land-tenure system or the effect of population density on agriculture, require studies of individual gardens, households and villages, and the comparison of areas experiencing differing conditions. Broadly, the material used can be divided into four main types:

(1) Material relating to the whole of Tonga. This includes the reports of the 1956 and 1966 Censuses, the records and maps of the Lands and Survey Department, and official statistics and departmental reports.

(2) Material from detailed surveys at the level of the household and village. This includes a general household questionnaire survey of four villages in Tongatapu, the main island of Tonga, more specialized surveys of land holding (one village in Ha'apai) and food cropping (two villages in Tongatapu and one in Ha'apai), and the results of three previous village studies of land tenure.

(3) Material from reconnaissance surveys, which involved interviews with key informants in a number of other villages throughout Tonga. The object was to determine the extent to which conditions in these villages were similar to, or differed from, conditions in the villages studied in greater detail.

(4) Historical material, obtained through interviews and archival research, and from previous studies in Tonga. Such material, although limited in amount, is valuable in providing a time-dimension to some of the variables involved in man/land relationships.

The bulk of the material is from the detailed surveys, which were made within the framework of the village community. No attempt was made to draw a general random sample of households over the whole of Tonga; instead a small number of villages was selected and either all or a sample of the households in each were studied. At the time field-work was undertaken no suitable frame existed for an overall random sample; but there were also methodological reasons for the choice of an approach through the village. In an unfamiliar culture it is easier to gain an awareness of the less obvious aspects of man/land relationships when all—or a large number of—households from the same village are studied than when individual, widely-scattered households are surveyed largely in isolation from the community of which they form a part. Furthermore, a geographer is frequently interested in comparisons between areas rather than in data aggregated over a wide area, and village communities, each with its own territory, form convenient units for comparison. Consequently, while an overall random sample survey might have produced results with a higher degree of statistical validity when generalized to the whole of Tonga, this would have been at the cost of a lower level of understanding of some of the complexities of man/land relationships.

The main problem in a village approach is the choice of villages. In general, the villages studied were selected in an attempt to determine the effect of one or more variables on other variables in the system of man/land relationships; they were not chosen simply to represent 'typical' Tongan conditions, and therefore the data obtained from them cannot be used to calculate average values for Tonga. In Tongatapu, the four villages surveyed by means of a general household questionnaire were chosen to cover the major variations in population density and land-tenure conditions in the island. The form used included questions on household composition, land, agricultural activities and household income. In Ha'apai the questions on sources of income were dropped, as a hurricane had largely destroyed cash cropping in the group shortly before the time of field research, and more specialized surveys of land holding and food cropping were carried out instead. No detailed surveys were conducted in Vava'u, partly because of the even greater destruction of cash cropping there, and partly because the emphasis in research was on areas of high population density, and in Vava'u population densities are mostly below the national average.

LAND RESOURCES

The three main island groups, Tongatapu, Ha'apai and Vava'u, are all of raised limestone formation. Tongatapu has a flat to gently undulating surface, with only a few small hills rising just above the tops of the coconut palms. The islands of Ha'apai are small, low and scattered, except for the outlying high volcanic peaks of Tofua and

Kao (not shown on the map), while Vava'u is a compact and comparatively hilly group, its surface made up of a series of terraces. The most common soil type on all these islands is a fertile, friable soil, termed *kelefatu* by Tongans, which varies in texture from a loamy sand to a clay. Although almost always underlain by coral limestone, the main parent material of this soil is volcanic ash, which gives it a mineral fertility very much higher than is usual for soils on raised limestone islands. The other main soil type is *tou'one*, a sandy and less fertile soil found at low elevations close to the sea. Although present in all the islands of raised limestone formation it is proportionately most important in Ha'apai, where it may occupy up to half the area of some of the settled islands. It appears to be derived entirely from coral sand or limestone and decayed vegetable matter, with perhaps the addition of small amounts of volcanic ash and pumice.

Rainfall is generally sufficient for good plant growth, with the northern group, Vava'u, having a more humid climate than the islands further south. Mean annual rainfall increases from 1,700mm at Nuku'alofa (Tongatapu) to 1,780mm at Pangai (Ha'apai) and 2,180mm at Neiafu (Vava'u), while the percentage of dry months in the rainfall record, using Mohr's definition of a dry month (Mohr, 1944, 53–8), decreases from 23 per cent and 25 per cent respectively in Tongatapu and Ha'apai to 16 per cent in Vava u. This combination of fertile, volcanically-derived soils, generally adequate but not excessive rainfall, and easy topography provides good conditions for crop production throughout all the main islands of Tonga.

POPULATION DISTRIBUTION AND DENSITY

The total population of Tonga in the 1966 Census was 77,429 persons, distributed as shown in Table 7.1. In the table Tongatapu and Vava'u have each been divided into two districts of contrasting density, and in Tongatapu an attempt has been made to obtain a realistic rural population density figure for the central and eastern district by subtracting both the population of the main town, Nuku'alofa, and the area of agricultural land surrounding the town from the calculation. Areas of high population density are the western tip of Tongatapu, and most of Ha'apai (where individual islands have densities ranging from 121 to 410/km²). Densities are moderate in central and eastern Tongatapu (ranging from 96 to 159/km²) and

167

Table 7.1 Crude population densities by districts and island groups, 1931 and 1966 (Tonga)

District or group	Population 1966	Persons/km² 1931	Persons/km² 1966
Nuku'alofa*	18,686		
Western Tongatapu	2,318	112	210
Central and eastern Tongatapu	26,916	31	126
'Eua	3,391	4	39
Ha'apai	10,591	122	202
Southern and eastern Vava'u	10,668	87	149
Western Vava'u	2,865	32	66
Niuatoputapu and	1,994	37	37

* Includes some of the villages around Nuku'alofa whose lands cannot be separated from those of the town.

in southern and eastern Vava'u, and low in 'Eua and western Vava'u.

Two broad explanations can be offered for this pattern, one static and the other dynamic. As Table 7.1 demonstrates, the contrast between western Tongatapu and Ha'apai, and the rest of Tonga, was much more marked in the past than at present, and it can be shown to date back to at least the nineteenth century. These long-established differences in population density cannot be explained by differences in land quality. Climatic and soil conditions in western Tongatapu and Ha'apai appear to be similar to those in central and eastern Tongatapu, although in Ha'apai the less fertile *tou'one* soil type occupies a higher percentage of the total land area than in Tongatapu. And while there may be some soil differences between western and eastern Vava'u which could help to explain the contrast in population densities there, in the absence of a soil survey there is insufficient evidence with which to test this possibility.* The main

* H. S. Gibbs, in a paper presented to the 1971 Pacific Science Congress in Canberra on the results of a 1967 soil survey, states that the main difference in soil types in Tongatapu is between yellowish-brown sticky clays in the eastern part of the island, and reddish-brown friable clays in the rest of the island. This pattern of soil types does not correlate with the pattern of population densities.

explanation seems to lie in the relationship between settlement and marine resources. In the past, fishing and reef-collecting were important subsistence activities along with food cropping, although in recent years they have declined as canned meat and fish have become more easily obtainable. Settlement therefore tended to concentrate along the most productive shores; in Tongatapu, for instance, over 70 per cent of the villages are located along the low northern shore and around the lagoon, the areas considered to be the most productive in seafoods, while in Ha'apai, which has particularly extensive reefs and fishing grounds, only the very smallest islands or those without *kelefatu* soils have failed to attract settlement. Conversely, in 'Eua the surrounding reef is narrow and sometimes dangerous and the offshore waters deep and unsheltered, and until recently the island, despite its size, had only a tiny population. Population densities were therefore higher where shores and reefs were productive but the land area limited, as in western Tongatapu, Ha'apai and parts of southern and eastern Vava'u, than where productive shores were backed by extensive areas of land, as in central and eastern Tongatapu. The lowest population densities were along unproductive shores, as in 'Eua, western Vava'u and parts of the south coast of Tongatapu.

This subsistence-orientated distribution of population in the past has by now been considerably modified by internal migration, which constitutes the second broad explanation of the present population pattern. Internal migration is largely directed towards Nuku'alofa, the capital, central and eastern Tongatapu and 'Eua, and away from western Tongatapu, Ha'apai, Vava'u and Niuatoputapu. It reflects movement in search of employment, education, land for cash cropping, and the attractions of urban life and is a result of the growing regional inequalities in development and opportunities within Tonga. Further discussion of migration, however, will be left to a later section, where it is examined in the context of the response of Tongans to population pressure. The main effect of internal migration on the earlier pattern of population distribution has been to reduce the contrasts between central and eastern Tongatapu and the long standing areas of high population density, but as migration appears to be continuing at a high rate further changes in population distribution can be expected.

Having outlined the main elements of land resources and population distribution we may now turn to the question of population pressure. As the term is used here, 'population pressure' implies the existence of stress in the man/land system resulting from increases in population density, stress being indicated by a deterioration in some of the variables in the system, such as a decline in the nutrient status of the soil or an increase in land disputes (Farmer, 1954; Lea, 1964, 1965; Street, 1969; Vermeer 1970). The following sections therefore examine three aspects of the man/land system—land tenure, the agricultural system, and the human perception of and reponse to population pressure—to see if there are any indications of stress. Analysis of the effect of population density is mostly through a comparison of areas of different density, chosen so that other independent variables are reasonably constant. For example, study of the effect of population density on the food cropping system is confined to Tongatapu and Ha'apai, for within these two groups climatic and soil conditions are broadly similar, but are different to those in Vava'u.

LAND TENURE

The land-tenure system of Tonga is highly distinctive, differing in a number of respects from the systems found in other parts of the Pacific Islands. Every taxpayer (every male aged 16 years and over) is entitled by law to an allotment of 3·2ha of agricultural land, known as a tax allotment, as well as a small piece of land in a village or town for his house. These allotments are granted to individuals as a lifetime, inheritable leasehold from the Government, if on a Government estate, or from the title-holder on a chiefly estate, and no one may legally hold more than one allotment of each type.

In reality, however, many Tongan men do not have the allotment to which they are entitled. In the 1966 Census only 8,305 or 41·6 per cent of all Tongan males aged 16 and over stated that they had a tax allotment. Although this figure conflicts with the 1966 Report of the Lands and Survey Department, which recorded the total number of tax allotment holders in December 1966 as 12,517 (G. Rogers, 1969, 216), this latter figure is almost certainly incorrect. A more detailed impression of landholding is given in Table 7.2, which presents the results of a number of village studies. The table shows that in only one village, Niutoua, did over half the taxpayers have their legal entitlement, while in most villages a large proportion of taxpayers and households had no land at all. It should be noted

170

LAND SHORTAGE AND POPULATION PRESSURE IN TONGA

Table 7.2   Land distribution: some village surveys, Tonga (*Sources:* Ha'afeva, Ha'avakatolo, Ha'akame and Niutoua, field survey by writer; 'Uiha, Koch (1955), 120—1); Nukunuku, field survey by R. G. Crocombe; Ha'ateiho, Nayacakalou (1959, 104). The figures for Ha'afeva and Niutoua are based on sample surveys.)

Village	Persons/ km²		0 %	0·5–1·4 %	1·5–2·6 %	2·7–3·8 %	3·9–6·2 %	6·3 and over %
			Percentage distribution of households and taxpayers by area of land held (ha)					
Ha'afeva	264	H	43	10	28	12	7	—
1966		T	61	8	29	2	—	—
'Uiha	186	H	9	10	41	24	13	3
1952								
Ha'avakatolo	178	H	18	9	9	27	16	21
1962		T	45	4	9	22	11	9
Ha'akame	150	H	31	—	2	49	4	14
1962		T	55	—	1	37	4	3
Nukunuku	133	H	30	—	1	51	3	
1960		T	51	—	1	44	1	3
Ha'ateiho	110	H	25	—	—	58	—	17
1957								15
Nioutoua	70	H	3	—	—	66	—	31
1962		T	18	—	—	82	—	—

H = percentage of households.
T = percentage of taxpayers.

that a household in Tonga now generally consists of a nuclear family or a nuclear family plus unmarried relatives of the husband or wife, and practically every household has at least one taxpayer, some of them having two or more.

One major reason for this discrepancy between the law and reality in the holding of land is the simple fact that there are now more taxpayers than allotments. The total number of allotments so far marked out is about 12,140, but in 1962,* when four of the village surveys were carried out, there were already about 18,400 taxpayers,

* Based on a count of allotments on the maps of the Lands and Survey Department, with every two blocks of less than 1·6 ha being combined to form one holding, as has been the practice in Ha'apai where many men have their holding split into two sections on different soil types.

and the 1966 Census enumerated 20,003 males aged 16 and over. A second reason is the uneven distribution of population discussed in the previous section. In areas where population densities are about 180/km² and over (i.e. 0·56ha or less, per person, of all land), most holdings have for many years been less than 3ha; when cadastral surveys were first carried out in these areas the population density was already such that holdings were generally about 1 to 2·5ha, and any attempt to stick to the statutory size of allotments would have led to the dispossession of many landholders. Despite the small size of the holdings there are still many more men entitled to land than there are allotments, and the typical pattern of land distribution in these areas is shown in the figures for Ha'afeva and 'Uiha (Ha'apai) and Ha'avakatolo (Tongatapu) in Table 7.2. In Ha'afeva the high level of landlessness is partly a result of the fact that nearly half the persons who held land on the island in 1966 lived elsewhere in Tonga, and this phenomenon of a large number of absentee land-holders is common to many islands in Ha'apai. In areas of moderate population density (around 100 to 150/km²) the pattern of land distribution is as shown in the date for Ha'akame, Nukunuku and Ha'ateiho in central Tongatapu. On these estates almost all allotments are of 3·2ha and consequently a larger proportion of taxpayers and households are generally without land than is the case in villages with higher population densities. Where population density falls to about 80/km² or less the pattern of land distribution is represented by the figures for Niutoua in eastern Tongatapu, where in 1962 only 3 per cent of the households had no land. Landlessness on this Government estate would have been even less had it not been for the fact that one-third of the registered allotments on the estate were held by people who lived in other settlements, mostly either in nearby villages or in Nuku'alofa, a not uncommon feature of Government estates in eastern Tongatapu.

These data on the percentage of households are by themselves of only limited value in an assessment of population pressure. The fact that a man does not hold land, or has only a small allotment, does not necessarily mean that he does not have satisfactory access to land for food production and cash cropping. The borrowing of land from relatives, friends, villagers and estate-holders is common throughout Tonga, and has its basis in the customary, although now weakened, obligations that exist between kinsmen, friends and a chief and his people. It is fairly easy to borrow land for growing short-term subsistence crops, even in densely populated areas, and although many villagers claim that it has become more difficult in recent years it is hard, if not impossible, to find a rural family short of food simply because they cannot borrow enough land for gardening. When land is borrowed from a relative no direct payment is usually made, but in borrowing from others it is customary to give a small part of the crop to the landholder. Although it is illegal, there appear

Table 7.3 Cash-crop income and area of land held by household, Tongatapu, 1961

	Land held by household		
	No land	1 allotment (2·7–3·8 ha)	2 allotments (6·3–7·4 ha)
Number of households	31	59	* 17
Mean cash-crop income ($A)			
per capita	18·4	36·4	36·4
per adult male (aged 16 and over)	69·8	157·6	152·8

to be a growing number of cases in which a cash payment is made for the use of land.

Obtaining the use of land for cash cropping is more difficult. The demand for such land has increased with the growth of the population and the greater commercialization of Tongan agriculture, while in Tongatapu, where the demand is greatest, the amount of spare land has decreased markedly in the last decade as a result of the allocation of allotments in the eastern half of the island, and an increase in banana planting by landholders in response to the improved market in New Zealand. Furthermore, the customary obligation to assist relatives and others, evolved in a society with a subsistence economy, applies less strongly to the rather different conditions of commercial agriculture. Men borrowing land are increasingly having to pay a cash rental. While some of the large-scale banana growers, and market gardeners who can afford to pay such rents and to contribute food crops and pigs to the landholder or estate-holder, still have little difficulty, the ordinary landless

173

villager finds land borrowing for cash production an increasing problem. Land cannot be borrowed for planting coconuts, which rank about equal with bananas as a cash crop, and palms on an allotment are the property of the landholder, regardless of who planted them. A common practice for those without land is to obtain permission to collect one or two cartloads of coconuts for copra-making from the allotment of a relative or close friend, and for this no return is given. Another arrangement found, especially between non-relatives and where the landholder is absent, is for the cash received for the copra to be shared half-and-half.

The effect of landholding on cash-crop incomes is shown in Table 7.3, which presents data from the household survey of four Tongatapu villages mentioned in an earlier section. The inability of the social system and its customary obligations to even out inequalities in landholding is shown in the fact that households without land had only half the income per capita or per adult male of households with a full-sized allotment. On the other hand households with two allotments did not have higher incomes per head than single-allotment households, for although total income was higher these households were larger and had more adult males.*

The main conclusion that can be drawn from this discussion is that the present land-tenure system, although it cannot provide land for every household, is still able to cope with the subsistence needs of the people, but is less able to cope with the rising demand for land for cash cropping. The increasing difficulty of borrowing land for growing cash crops and the trend towards the payment of rentals for land both point to pressure within the system. This pressure, however, is as much the result of the growing commercialization of Tongan agriculture as of population increase alone.

THE AGRICULTURAL SYSTEM

Tongan agriculture is based on a bush fallowing system† for the cultivation of tubers, the main food crops being yams, taro, cassava, sweet potato, bananas and plantains. After clearing and burning, a plot is cropped for two to about five years and then bush fallowed for

---

* The number of households in the survey with allotments smaller than 2·7 ha was too few for useful analysis.

† The term 'bush fallowing' is here used to describe a form of shifting cultivation in which the fallow period is short.

from one to ten or more years, depending on population density. Of the two main cash crops bananas are often incorporated into this bush fallow system, being planted as part of the cropping sequence and yielding for only a couple of years before the land returns to bush; but during the last few years they have increasingly been grown in separate plantations, and chemical fertilizers are now being used both to improve yields and to extend the life of the plot. The other main cash crop, coconuts, is unevenly scattered over all or part of each allotment, with the food-crop gardens being rotated amongst them. The effect of population density on this system will be examined from two perspectives, the ecological and the economic.

An ecological assessment

In Ha'apai, where the agricultural system is under the greatest pressure from high population density, the cropping period is now usually from three to five years, compared with the two or three years common elsewhere, while the fallow period is generally from only one to three or four years compared with three to five years elsewhere. Many farmers in Ha'apai are using shorter fallows than when they began farming, a common change reported amongst older men being a reduction to half the earlier fallow length. The food-crop pattern has also changed with the increase in population density. In areas of high density, cassava has become the staple food crop while yams, the most preferred tuber for eating, are now much less frequently grown. Cassava gives good yields even on heavily-cropped soils and does not require a lengthy fallow, and also yields more per man-hour of labour than the other food crops.

The response of Tongan farmers to population growth has therefore been to reduce fallow periods, lengthen cropping periods and alter the food-crop pattern, and these changes are most pronounced in Ha'apai. There the agricultural system is now fairly intensive by the standards of shifting cultivation, with a cropping period/fallow period ratio of around 1 : 1, and supports population densities of up to about 280/km^2 (cf. Nye and Greenland, 1960, 128). Yet despite the probable doubling in the intensity of cropping over the last 30 to 40 years there has been no change in the bush fallow technique of maintaining soil fertility, and one might therefore expect to find symptoms of ecological stress within the system.

An examination of possible areas of stress, however, suggests the existence of as yet only minor problems. There has been some

175

deterioration in the fallow vegetation, with an increase in the proportion of grasses and other herbaceous plants and the spread of lantana (*Lantana camara*) and guava (*Psidium guajava*), and weeds have become much more of a problem for farmers than in the past. It is also widely believed that soil fertility in Ha'apai has declined over the last few decades. This belief is partially supported by the results of chemical analyses of Tongan soils. Ha'apai soils should be very similar in composition to those of Tongatapu, as parent materials, relief and climate are much the same throughout the two groups, but analysis of a number of soil samples suggests that they have much lower levels of available potassium. Chemical analysis by itself, however, is not a completely reliable guide, and there have been no yield measurements or fertilizer trials which could provide further evidence on soil differences. The comments of farmers, on the other hand, indicate that there has certainly been no serious decline in soil fertility, for satisfactory yields are still obtained despite the intensity of the agricultural system.*

An economic assessment

Assessment of the effect of high population density on the level of living supported by the agricultural system is more difficult, because the level of living is influenced by a large number of variables apart from population density, and data that might be useful in such an assessment are limited. As far as food production is concerned there is no evidence to suggest that people in rural areas of high population density have a diet poorer in quantity or quality than that found elsewhere in Tonga; the worst nutritional problems are in fact in the towns. Production per head appears to have been maintained by the increased frequency of cropping and the change to higher-yield tubers, and any deficiencies which might result from a high consumption of protein-poor cassava are probably balanced by a high consumption of seafoods. Measurement of food gardens in three villages in Ha'apai and Tongatapu showed no relationship between population density and per capita garden area.

Analysis of the *per capita* levels of production of copra and bananas,

* For a fuller discussion see Maude (1970). The only effect of intense cultivation on Tongatapu soils noted by H. S. Gibbs in a paper presented to the 1971 Pacific Science Congress is a possible increase in iron nodules in areas of frequent clean cultivation. Such a change, if present, would tend to lower soil productivity by decreasing the friability of the soil.

on the other hand, suggests that cash-crop incomes tend to be lower in areas of high population density than elsewhere. Data for banana production in rural Tongatapu in 1966, for instance, shows that while there was no relationship between population density and *per capita* production when densities were less than 200/km², in the one area of higher population density production per head fell to 55 per cent of the mean, suggesting that at this level of density land becomes a more important limiting factor in production than labour. A similar analysis of *per capita* copra income within Ha'apai in 1956 (Table 7.4) again suggests some inverse relationship between population density and income per head, but the trend shown is not

Table 7.4 Population density and *per capita* copra income, Ha'apai, 1956 (*Source:* Records of the Tonga Copra Board)

Persons/km²	Copra income per capita ($A)
80–149	58·4
150–229	51·2
230–309	39·6
310–379	45·0

uniform and the co-efficient of correlation between the two variables is only −0·36. For Tongatapu this type of analysis is not possible, as the variables determining the level of copra production are not sufficiently uniform throughout the island, but data from the household survey for three villages which are comparable show a clear inverse relationship between *per capita* income and population density (Table 7.5).

Table 7.5 Population density and *per capita* copra income, three Tongatapu villages. 1961 (*Source:* Records of the Tonga Copra Board)

Village	Persons/km²	Copra income per capita ($A)
Niutoua	70	37·4
Ha'akame	150	29·2
Ha'avakatolo	178	22·0

The above evidence points tentatively to mild symptoms of economic stress in areas of high population density. Land appears to have become a limiting factor in production given the present level of agricultural technology, but at population densities which vary according to the crop; the population density at which *per capita* banana production begins to decline, for instance, is higher than that at which *per capita* copra production is affected, because bananas are a less land-extensive crop. Much more research, including studies of nutrition, is needed before firm conclusions can be drawn.

To what extent are the pressures described in the last two sections consciously felt by Tongans living in areas of high population density? An attempt was made during field-work in western Tongatapu, Ha'apai and eastern Vava'u to ascertain the degree to which people felt hardship as a result of the shortage of land, concentrating in particular on married men without allotments as these were likely to suffer the most. We recall that even in densely-settled areas most men without allotments found it fairly easy to borrow land for cash cropping or collecting coconuts for copra-making. Yet only a small proportion of the men interviewed seemed to feel any hardship, all of these being men with large families to support, and most considered their income sufficient for their essential needs. About 30 men were asked what they would do with $A 1,000 if it were given to them; only one replied that he would spend it on food and other necessities, the rest stating housing or education for their children.

However, the degree to which population pressure is felt is better determined by what men do than by what they say. There are a number of possible reactions to population pressure, but only one of these, migration, is really significant in Tonga. In land tenure, for instance, there has as yet been no trend towards subdivision of allotments, even though this is not prohibited should the legal heir to the land be willing, and land disputes are rare. The only response by those in control of land matters, the Government and the chiefs, to the problems brought by population growth has been a belated effort to complete the survey and allocation of allotments. In agriculture there has been a steady intensification of the system and a shift in food crops, but the use of fertilizers, which represents a basic innovation in the system, is largely confined to cash cropping in Tongatapu and has not been adopted by farmers in more intensively cultivated Ha'apai. Very few farmers see any need to change their traditional techniques.

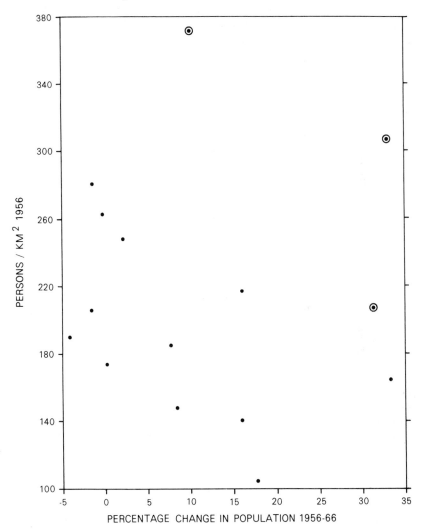

Fig. 7.2   Tonga: scatter diagram showing the relationship of population growth in 1956–66 to the 1956 population density

179

The pattern of internal migration, however, shows more sensitive response to population pressure, particularly in Ha'apai. The basic reason for migration in Tonga is the lack of opportunities to earn money in the outer islands as compared with Tongatapu, but the influence of land shortage is indicated by the fact that, within Ha'apai, population growth between 1956 and 1966 in each island tended to be inversely proportional to the 1956 population density (Fig. 7.2). The three islands which lie furthest from the general trend (circled in Fig. 7.2) all have residents who utilize land on the nearby high island of Tofua, and their effective population densities are therefore lower than those shown. It may be hypothesized that the higher the population density the harder it is for men, particularly those without their own allotments, to achieve a satisfactory cash-crop income, and in Ha'apai this problem is made greater by the fact that until recently cash cropping was largely restricted to coconuts, while opportunities for wage employment in the group have always been very limited. Of 20 cases of migration collected in Holopeka (Ha'apai), for instance, 18 were men without allotments, and 11 of these had left their village at least partly in the hope of obtaining land. That landlessness is not the only reason for migration, however, is shown in the fact noted earlier that those who had left Ha'afeva (Ha'apai) in 1966 included nearly half the men who already held land on the island. Employment following education on the main island, dissatisfaction with village life, a desire to take advantage of the better opportunities to earn money in Tongatapu or to ensure a better education for one's children are all important reasons for movement, while in Vava'u the damage caused to the economy by the 1961 hurricane seems to have been the major determinant of migration from that group in the early 1960s. Nevertheless, the pattern of migration from Ha'apai outlined earlier does demonstrate the significance of land shortage as a factor, and suggests that population pressure is sufficiently felt by many Tongans to stimulate them to leave their home village.

CONCLUSION

In the preceding sections we have examined a number of facets of the man/land system in Tonga. Symptoms of stress or pressure were found in land problems, the fallow vegetation, the nutrient status of the soil, cash-crop incomes and internal migration, and these point to the presence of mild population pressure, particularly in Ha'apai. These problems, however, are as much a result of the failure to adapt the man/land system to cope with rising population densities as of population growth alone. Improvements are possible in land tenure, for instance to ensure that land is only allocated to those who can make good use of it, and in agriculture, through the adoption of new techniques in both food and cash cropping; while changes in the market for cash crops and in the availability and location of non-agricultural employment would also produce changes in the degree of population pressure in Tonga.

To what extent can the material discussed in this case study of Tonga be used in an assessment of the ideas of Boserup and Geertz, both of whom have been concerned with the effect of population growth on traditional agricultural systems? Boserup (1965) argues that the intensification of agriculture, because it involves more labour-intensive techniques and a decrease in mean output per man-hour, only occurs when forced by population pressure. Geertz (1963), on the other hand, in his study of Indonesian economic history, draws a distinction between *sawah* agriculture, a stable system in which increases in population can be easily absorbed by intensification without harm to the environment, and shifting culti-vation, a potentially unstable system highly susceptible to ecological breakdown if intensified in response to population growth. For Boserup agricultural systems of varying intensity from forest-fallow cultivation to multi-cropping lie along the one continuum, while for Geertz shifting cultivation and *sawah* agriculture are unrelated systems with different responses to population pressure.

Taking Geertz's contribution first, it is evident that while there are some signs of mild pressure in Tongan agriculture there is no indication of an impending ecological crisis, despite the doubling in the intensity of cropping over the last 30 to 40 years, and the Tongan system appears much better able to withstand population growth and intensification than the shifting cultivation model described by Geertz. For this there are several possible explanations. Firstly, there are some differences between the Tongan system and the south-east Asian examples on which Geertz's model is based. In south-east Asia the staple crop is rice, whereas the Tongan system is based on tubers, which may help to maintain soil fertility during cropping by pro-viding a better cover for the soil surface, even though the patterns of inter-cropping and crop succession in Tonga are very simple. In

181

addition, the agricultural environment in Tonga is much more favourable for intensive cropping than are the environments in which shifting cultivation is carried on in south-east Asia, for the soils, derived from recent volcanic materials and not subject to heavy leaching, are of high inherent fertility. Although no yield measurements have been made, the decline in yields between the first and second cropping of a plot is certainly nowhere near the 80 per cent drop reported by Geertz (1963, 23) from south Sumatra. Geertz's characterization of shifting cultivation applies to only one type amongst many, and to only one environment amongst the many in which this agricultural system is carried on.

Following from this, I feel that Geertz, perhaps because he has confined his examples to south-east Asia, overestimates the fragility of shifting cultivation and the narrowness of the demographic limits within which it is a stable system. Nye and Greenland (1960, 129), for example, demonstrate that it is possible to crop at varying levels of intensity, and consequently of soil fertility, without catastrophic consequences to the soil. Up to a limit, which varies with the type of shifting cultivation and the environment, decreases in yield as a result of an increase in the intensity of cropping may be more than offset by increases in overall production because of the longer period of cropping. This limit has certainly not been reached in Tonga, where the agricultural system has a greater degree of flexibility in response to population growth than Geertz admits for shifting cultivation systems.

On *prima facie* evidence, Ester Boserup's thesis more closely fits the Tongan situation, and her contention that differences in agricultural intensity are the consequence of differences in population density is supported by the material discussed earlier. However, the intensification of Tongan agriculture in response to population growth has not stimulated any basic improvements in the bush fallow technique of maintaining soil fertility except amongst strongly-commercialized farmers. It is important to an assessment of Boserup's thesis that this lack of change be explained; and two types of explanation are possible.

The first involves a consideration of the conditions under which population growth may fail to stimulate technological advance. Boserup does not claim that intensification will always lead to the adoption of new methods, and suggests several situations where failure is possible, some of which could apply to Tonga at present.

182

Firstly, under conditions of rapid population growth the rate at which the intensity of cropping increases may well be higher than the rate at which farmers are able to change their traditional methods and their accustomed habits of work. The examples drawn on by Boserup to support her thesis are of populations undergoing slower rates of growth than have been recently experienced in Tonga, or in many of the developing countries, and this somewhat reduces the value of her thesis under contemporary conditions. However, observation and questioning in Tonga do not suggest the rate of population growth to be a major reason for the failure to adopt new methods of soil fertility maintenance. Secondly, failure is possible where farmers have no knowledge of the techniques which could be adopted. In Tonga the only new technique known to farmers is the use of chemical fertilizers, which because of their cost have so far been used only with cash crops, whereas many African and Asian shifting cultivators have had a knowledge of other methods or contact with peoples practising more advanced systems of traditional agriculture.*

A third possible situation in which population pressure may fail to produce corresponding technological advances in agriculture is where institutional problems reduce the farmer's incentive, or ability, to undertake improvements. Boserup, for example, in a discussion of investment under landlord tenure, argues that the disorganization of the feudal land-tenure system of India during the colonial period, by slowing down investment in land improvement, especially irrigation facilities, helped to prevent agricultural output from responding to population growth. In Tonga the customs relating to land could produce a similar result. While land is individually held and the security of tenure good, land borrowing, sanctioned by custom, is widespread and requests for land are not necessarily made only to those who have it to spare. Consequently farmers do not have full control over the use of their land, and although field work indicates that this is not yet a reason for the failure to adopt new methods, farmers may in the future be reluctant to make an investment in improved techniques if the benefit of their investment may be gained by someone else.†

* In both these cases the failure to adopt new techniques could lead to the ecological collapse described by Geertz, particularly in drier environments where regeneration of the fallow vegetation is more difficult.

† See also the comments of Waddell (this volume) on the relation of investment in improvements to tenacity of land tenure.

183

While the second of the three situations outlined above is a possible explanation of the failure to improve agricultural techniques in Tonga, another type of explanation—that such improvements are not yet necessary—seems most likely to be correct. As suggested earlier, the soils are of high inherent fertility, and shifting cultivation systems can withstand a good deal of intensification before fundamental changes are essential. The adoption of cassava and dryland varieties of taro, both of which were introduced into Tonga in the nineteenth century, has helped to maintain yields per man-hour as cropping has been intensified, while the adoption of the metal push-hoe has enabled farmers to cope with the changes in the fallow vegetation. Such adaptations in the agricultural system may well be sufficient at the present level of intensity. The symptoms of population pressure are still mild, and the main pressures felt by Tongans, to judge from the material on land problems and migration, are in cash cropping rather than in the food-cropping system. Acceptance of this explanation would thus leave Boserup's thesis in the category of 'not proven', but probable.

However, the fact that the most significant changes in Tongan agriculture, involving such practices as machine preparation of land and the use of chemical fertilizers, have occurred in Tongatapu amongst farmers heavily engaged in cash cropping rather than amongst the less commercialized farmers in more densely-populated Ha'apai, suggests one major qualification to her argument. While land shortage has undoubtedly been a factor in these changes, for they began about the time when land ceased to be easily obtainable in Tongatapu, they indicate that commercialization is also a stimulus to the adoption of improved techniques. Population pressure, as noted above, is felt mostly in cash cropping rather than in food cropping. The income received from cash cropping makes it feasible to purchase industrial inputs such as fertilizers, while changes in cash cropping have repercussions throughout the agricultural system. The increase in the area planted in cash crops, for instance, intensifies the pressure on the bush fallow system, but where food crops are intercultivated with a cash crop like bananas, as is frequently the case, the former benefit from the fertilizer used for the latter, thus making it possible to lengthen the cropping period and reduce the role of the bush fallow. With coconuts, a long-term crop, the need to control bush growth conflicts with the traditional practice of bush fallowing, and the achievement of higher productivity in coconut

184

plantations will thus require changes in food cropping techniques. At present, therefore, commercialization and population pressure would appear to be working together to stimulate agricultural improvements in Tonga, and where one or the other is weak the extent of agricultural advancement is so far limited.

8 A transition in circular mobility
Population movement in the New Hebrides, 1800-1970
Richard Bedford

The growing literature on population questions in the Pacific islands has two foci of concentrated interest, each identifying a particular group of problems facing the region as it emerges from colonial rule. The first is the rapid growth of island populations, with rates of natural increase ranging mostly between 2·5 and 3·5 per cent per annum. The second is a redistribution of population that is simultaneously identified from the censuses, taking the form especially of rapid urbanization: Pacific towns are estimated to be growing at rates between 5 and 12 per cent per annum.*

Much of this growth is due to net immigration from rural areas, but there is abundant evidence to suggest that townward movement in these territories differs significantly from the classic pattern of rural–urban drift. There is no poverty-stricken rural proletariat, or depressed peasantry, in the Pacific territories which can be compared with the massive reservoir of rural poor that is feeding the cities of Asia and Latin America. Migration is not contributing to any substantial creation of a new urban working class which has severed its ties in the villages and outer islands. The migration revealed is part of a complex mobility process in which relocations are often only temporary. In most Pacific territories the rural–urban drift represents rather an increase in the volume of a circular movement—a type of mobility that cannot readily be identified in the existing census tables.

* In ten of the twelve territories of Melanesia, Micronesia and Polynesia (excluding Hawaii), under 30 per cent of indigenous populations were enumerated in urban areas at the most recent census; in seven, under 20 per cent were in towns. Except in French Polynesia and New Caledonia, therefore, levels of urbanization remain generally rather low, so that the present rapid rates of increase still represent only rather small absolute numbers of persons.

Circular migration: definition and general characteristics

In most literature on migration, the type of movement under consideration seems to involve an intention, whether stated or not, to relocate permanently. It is realized that many migrants do not do so. But the implication seems often to be that they have subsequently changed their minds. There is, however, a large class of movements that is not intendedly permanent, even though some such relocations may become longlasting. The intention is to return, within hours, days, months or years, and movements of this initial type have been grouped under the label of 'circulation'. Zelinsky (1971, 225–6) remarks that circulation denotes 'a great variety of movements, usually short-term, repetitive or cyclical in nature, but all having in common the lack of any declared intention of permanent or long-lasting change of residence'.

It is necessary to distinguish between movements within this class if any meaning is to be achieved. Routine daily movements—shopping, the journey to work, to school, visiting—and other movements of short term can collectively be distinguished from movements which will involve a long absence from home. The former may be termed 'oscillation', the latter 'circular migration', and for present purposes an arbitrary time-division of one month's absence from home is employed to make the distinction. An upward limit for 'circular migration' is less easy to establish, since absences on contract work engagements might extend over a number of years. The distinction is essentially one of intention at the time of departure, this intention usually being reflected in the sort of arrangements made either to maintain ongoing home interests, or to wind up affairs at the former residence. Retrospectively, it would be possible to establish a distinction on the basis of some arbitrary time spent away, but this could be applied to only a minority of movers in a dynamic situation.

Circular migration, thus defined, is common in a great many social and economic contexts. Although studied far less than intendedly permanent migration, it is a major form of spatial mobility in the 'modernized' countries with their highly interactive social systems. The peripatetic ways of academics, specialists, many business men, salesmen, students and holidaymakers often involve only temporary absences rather than permanent relocations. In traditional tribal and peasant societies, circulation was probably more common than migration. However, it is in the so-called 'transitional' societies that circular migration has been most intensively studied. Where traditional patterns of living have been disrupted by foreign intrusion, such as colonialism, it is common to find two or more differently structured societies and economies existing side by side within the one whole society. Plural societies and dual economies exist in various forms in most colonial or formerly colonial countries, offering a contrast in ways of life that can be particularly stark. A compromise often adopted by members of the indigenous population is circular migration. Wishing to retain the security of their traditional institutions, generally associated with residence in rural communities, while obtaining some of the benefits of involvement in non-indigenous economic activities, they circulate between village or hamlet and the centres of wage employment—plantations, mining settlements, towns.

Mitchell (1969, 177), who has studied circular migration in a number of African countries, expressed the view that where this form of mobility prevails, there appears to be an appreciation on the part of the migrant of some disparity between the rights and privileges he can claim in his rural community and those he can claim elsewhere. In the rural areas, where there has not been widespread alienation of land to foreigners, customary rights to cultivate land and maintain a house in a village may guarantee a certain degree of economic security, while reciprocal social obligations of kinsmen ensure support in times of stress. In the towns administrative policies or high land values may prevent permanent acquisition of property, or the income derived from full commitment to wage labour may not be considered sufficient compensation by the migrant for abandoning an active interest in rural-based enterprises.

Circular labour migration is generally regarded as a transitional, or compromise, form of mobility associated with an early stage of modernization. With the transition from subsistence to market-exchange economies and the changing aspirations and expectations among people as activities become commercialized, ties to particular localities are weakened. Improvements in transport and communications facilitate mobility and, with increasing diversity of areas and occupations as industrial and urban centres evolve, the necessary conditions are created for more extensive movements involving permanent relocations. Under such circumstances migration is seen as an equilibrating mechanism in a diversifying economy,

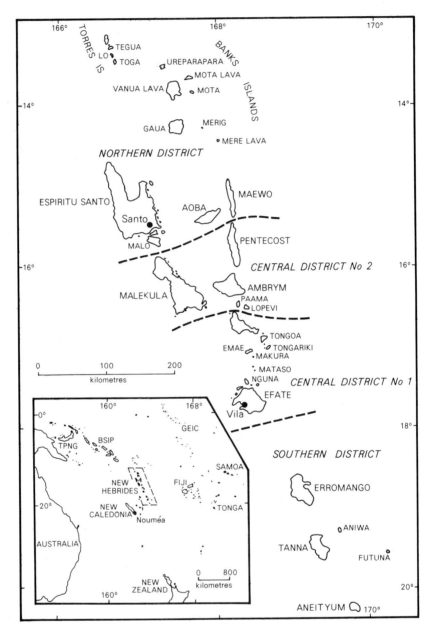

Fig. 8.1 The New Hebrides Condominium: location map

whereby people respond to changing opportunities and redirect the spatial allocation of labour towards an optimum pattern (Rogers, 1968, 73). The process of circular migration acts as a brake on such redistribution, but permanent migration of a considerable proportion of the rural-based population to urban areas is usually seen as inevitable.

In some areas with limited potential for major industrial development, the conomic situation maintained by circular migration has, however, emerged as a relatively stable compromise. This has demonstrated particularly in numerous studies of mobility in colonial or recently independent countries in sub-Saharan Africa (see for example Elkan, 1964, 1967). In the scattered island groups of the south Pacific, with their minuscule parcels of natural resources and small populations, the 'economies of mass' associated with urban-industrial societies are simply not feasible in most areas (Spate, 1965, 259-60), Pacific societies are, as Watters (1970, 137) recently stated, 'societies in search of urbanism—an urbanism that can never be developed in small scale island economies'. In such cases compromises between the traditional social and economic system, and the market-exchange economy introduced by European colonialism over a century ago, have become stable, so that circular migration remains a most significant form of mobility. The intention of this paper is to analyse aspects of this circular migration in a particular island group, the New Hebrides (Fig. 8.1). Two approaches are adopted. In the first place an outline is presented of certain major changes in spatial and temporal characteristics of mobility in the New Hebrides during the colonial period. Following this, contemporary circular migration of islanders living in a selected group of islands is examined in detail to provide a deeper understanding of the reasons for its persistence.*

MOBILITY IN THE NEW HEBRIDES, 1800–1970

Mobility in pre-contact New Hebridean society

From the limited published information referring to patterns of spatial mobility before protracted European intervention in the New Hebrides, it is evident that movement involving permanent relocations was severely constrained by indigenous forms of social, economic, and political organization. New Hebrideans lived in small

* The discussion is based on a more extended treatment in Bedford (1971).

191

Table 8.1 Some pre-contact trading links, New Hebrides

Island/area on island	Areas linked through trading	Goods traded	Goods received	Source
Mota Lava and Rowa	Vanua Lava, Ureparapara, Mota	Shell discs (*Conus ceylanensis Hwass*)	Yams, taro	Rivers (1914. 168)
Mere Lava	Maewo	?	?	Codrington (1891.25)
Torres Islands	Banks Islands and farther south	?	?	Rivers (1912) quoted in Haddon (1937. 38)
Sakau Peninsula (Espiritu Santo)	Gaua, Mere Lava. Mafia, Tutuba, Malo	Hermaphrodite pigs	?	Baker (1928. 117), Harrisson (1937, 400)
Malo	Aoba, Tangoa, north Malekula	Hermaphrodite pigs, mats, turmeric leaves	Pigs, mats, turmeric leaves, shell money	Harrisson (1937, 399–400). Allen (1964. 49)
West coast Espiritu Santo (Wusi)	Inland villages Espiritu Santo. Malekula	Pots and salt	Pigs, yams, taro, other foodstuffs	Harrisson (1936, 249). Shutler (1968. 17)
West Aoba (patrilineal)	East Aoba (matrilineal)	Pigs, mats, 'bustles' (finely woven mats worn hanging down one's back)	Pigs, mats	Allen (1964. 49)
South Pentecost	North Ambrym	Green and blue mineral paints, red mats, money mats, clubs	?	Guiart (1951. 16–17). Lane (1956)
North coast Malekula	North interior Malekula (Big Nambas)	Turmeric leaves (from Tangoa, via Malo)	Tusker pigs	Harrisson (1937: 399–400)

Region	Trading partners	Exports	Imports	References
West and south coast Malekula	Inland tribes	Salt, fish, shellfish	Yams, taro	Deacon (1934, 202–3)
South-west Malekula	East Malekula (Pangkumu)	Greenstone (for pigment for painting)	?	Deacon (1934, 203)
Small islands, north-east Malekula (Vao, Atchin, Wala, Rano)	Malo, Espiritu Santo, Aoba, Pentecost, Ambrym	Pigs, masks, items associated with ceremonial rituals	Turmeric leaves, barks (for belts)	Layard (1942, 253). Layard (1936, 346)
West Ambrym	Port Sandwich region, Malekula, small islands, Epi	Pigs, bar	? Yams, taro, red mineral paints, masks	Guiart (1951, 17–18)
South Ambrym	Paama, Lopevi, Epi	Pigs	Food crops, red mineral paints	Guiart (1951, 17–18)
Shepherd Islands, Emae, Mataso, Makura, Efate and off-shore islands	Same area	Pigs, food crops (ceremonial exchanges)	Pigs, food crops (ceremonial eschanges)	Unpublished papers (Guiart, 1958?). Little written on this group of islands and pre-contact trading patterns not known. Communication was considerable because their unique political system resulted in close inter-village, inter-island cultural and ceremonial links
Erromango	Tanna, Aniwa	Clays for body paint	Shells	Guiart (1961), Robertson (1902, 9)
Tanna	Aniwa, Futuna, Aneityum	? Pigs	Clays for body paint	Guiart (1961)

dispersed settlements, and the rugged terrain of the scattered volcanic islands made communication difficult over long distances. One group of people was separated from another not only by natural barriers, but also by differences in language and customs. As Buxton (1926, 422) argued, a universal fear of sorcery and the magic of strangers was probably the most significant factor in isolating communities. Illness and death were rarely attributed to natural causes: fear of strangers and groups living outside the language area was a considerable force in restricting mobility. Economic activities were largely confined to those associated with basic subsistence gardening, hunting, and fishing. Swidden agriculture was practised in most areas, with varieties of yam (*Diosorea* spp.) as a common staple food. Garden rotation with fallow periods of varying lengths appears to have been widespread and, while cultivation techniques and the range of foods grown varied somewhat with location, an essential characteristic of traditional economies was their lack of diversity. They were subsistence economies and most produce was consumed locally. In such economies, which functioned through a high degree of mutual co-operation and a transaction system based on reciprocity, there was little opportunity for individuals or families to derive a livelihood outside the territorial and social domains of their kin and affines.

Under these circumstances it is hardly surprising that there were few areas to which the New Hebridean would want to migrate. Except for village relocations following natural disasters, warfare, or the search for new garden land, there was little incentive for New Hebrideans to relocate permanently. Migration associated with marriage was widespread, given the principle of exogamy which was usual in both patrilineal and matrilineal descent groups, but the most common forms of spatial mobility were circular. Excluding the oscillatory movements associated with day-to-day living, two aspects of traditional society encouraged quite extensive mobility of small groups of New Hebrideans—the ritual grading ceremonies, and inter-island trade. In most parts of the group, power and prestige were acquired through accumulation and public disposal of tusked pigs. Acquisition of pigs with the requisite tusk size and shape for a major rank-taking ceremony was a lengthy procedure and could necessitate extensive travelling on the part of the candidate. In addition, these ceremonies often involved people from a number of different communities and islands, and temporary movement beyond the spatial domain of kinship groups was not uncommon.

While information on patterns of inter-island trade is very diffuse, it appears that there were quite extensive trading networks for the movement of specialized products which could be acquired only in certain areas. The trading of dyes, clays, barks, pigs, and manufactured articles for use in ceremonies was not uncommon, and some of the networks have been outlined in Table 8.1. However, while New Hebrideans had these connections with people beyond the range of their immediate groups, these were generally tenuous. Mobility in traditional New Hebridean society appears to have been primarily oscillation, and even moves associated with ceremonies and trading voyages rarely involved islanders in lengthy absences from their permanent homes.

Traditional patterns disrupted: sandalwood and the international labour trade

Spatial and temporal characteristics of traditional forms of circulation were transformed by the demand for timber, labour, and crops by European entrepreneurs and settlers. The diffusion of a demand among islanders for non-indigenous material goods stimulated labour migration, since items such as steel tools, calico, paint, and muskets, which rapidly assumed important roles in their social and economic activities, could only be acquired by trading produce or labour. The latter alternative generally meant labouring at the site of a mill or plantation outside the village territory. From its inception this movement rarely involved New Hebrideans in permanent settlement at their destination, and a pattern of circular labour migration evolved.

The discovery of sandalwood in the southern New Hebrides in the 1820s, and the development of a trade in this timber between 1840 and 1860, introduced small groups of New Hebrideans to labour migration, but its impact on mobility patterns was limited to a few islands. Inhabitants of the five southern islands, as well as selected groups from Efate and Espiritu Santo, became familiar with working for Europeans at milling stations, but the great majority of New Hebrideans had no experience of labour migration at this initial stage. Knowledge of the utility of European trade goods was diffused through the traditional trading network to areas not affected by the sandalwood trade, but easy acquisition of this wealth was not possible until the demand for islanders as employees outside their home

195

villages increased considerably. Such a demand arose in the early 1860s, when Europeans sought cheap labour to work their plantations in Australia, Fiji, Samoa, and New Caledonia.

Contract labour migration overseas wrought the first major change in mobility conditions in most parts of the group. Islanders, motivated primarily by a desire to obtain non-indigenous material goods, willingly left their villages for three or more years employment outside the group. The destinations for migrants, distances travelled, and duration of absences from villages during this international labour migration were very different to those in any previous or succeeding period, and mark the first phase in the transitional sequence in New Hebridean mobility patterns. Although precise statistics are unavailable on the numbers of New Hebrideans who left the group during the period (1863–1906) this movement was permitted, it is known they were in excess of 40,000. It is estimated that this number went to Queensland alone (McArthur and Yaxley, 1968, 16). However, the fact that many New Hebrideans went more than once to Queensland, and that this movement cannot be identified in the available statistics, has probably inflated the total of individuals. Movement to Fiji, New Caledonia, and Samoa was much less extensive, but the few available figures suggest that at least 10,000 islanders went to these destinations. Whatever the precise numbers involved in this movement, the impact on traditional society by the demand for labour was profound and widespread.

Initially recruiting was concentrated in the southern islands, where New Hebrideans had some experience of labour migration through the sandalwood trade. The demand for labour was so intense, however, that the focus of recruiting rapidly shifted north; and of the 1,500 islanders taken to Queensland by 1869, over 40 per cent had come from islands where experiences with Europeans had been limited to an occasional visit by a mission or trading vessel (Short, 1870, 56–7). By the 1880s some New Hebrideans from all islands had worked outside the group, and only those people in relatively inaccessible interior locations on the larger islands remained unaffected by the change in mobility patterns. From the point of view of mobility, these first 60 years of protracted contact with Europeans brought three significant changes in New Hebridean society:

(1) an increasing number of places, other than their home villages, where New Hebrideans could reside and derive a living;

(2) a gradual breakdown of linguistic and social barriers with the diffusion of a trade language (pidgin-English), the influence of missionary teachings, and the cultural interchange which accompanied residence at centres of European commercial activity;

(3) changes in the organization of economic and social activities, which dissemination of steel tools and other non-indigenous goods initiated in traditional societies.

The diffusion of information on alternative places where employment could be obtained greatly increased the New Hebrideans' 'action space', or that image of an environment which is relevant to a person's decision-making and spatial behaviour at any time. This cognitive space, which in the pre-contact period appears to have included only a small range of places between which New Hebrideans moved regularly to satisfy economic and social needs, now widened swiftly, and became subject to new forms of discrimination. As knowledge of conditions at the different locations increased in New Hebridean communities, labour recruiters found that islanders became very selective in their choice of destination. Queensland was the favoured destination, especially among coastal people who had considerable recruiting experience by the 1880s. Scarr (1967b, 141) has noted that recruiters seeking labour for plantations in Fiji had to rely increasingly on bushmen from interior locations to meet their quotas. New Caledonia and Samoa only became popular destinations after the governments in Queensland and Fiji banned the supply of guns to islanders in 1884 (Scarr, 1967a, 6–7). By the 1890s it was believed that comparatively few people from coastal villages engaged at all; other alternatives for obtaining the desired goods were becoming available, including the sale of crops to foreign traders or working on plantations which Europeans were establishing within the group. Diversification of the indigenous economy with cash cropping as well as a growing demand for labour within the New Hebrides had further influences on the islanders' mobility patterns.

In addition to transforming New Hebrideans' 'action space' overseas, labour migration greatly increased contact between islanders, and mingling during three years or more of employment outside the home village was of considerable significance in reducing mutual fears and suspicions. Although there was probably not as much mixing of people from different islands on the plantations as might be imagined, islanders worked in groups according to their skills rather than their island of origin (Corris, 1970). On the plantations

197

the emergent leaders were those with greatest experience of colonial conditions rather than the holders of high rank in the traditional hierarchy. While this often caused tensions among labourers, these circumstances introduced many islanders to new concepts of authority and prestige which tested their faith in the traditional order at home. When New Hebrideans who had been strongly influenced by Christian teachings returned to their villages, power struggles within communities often evolved. Disapproving of traditional methods of social advancement and acquisition of power, these converts challenged the authority of customary leaders by proposing a new life founded on Christian principles and, in some areas, cash crop agriculture.

During this period of overseas labour migration, New Hebridean societies were transformed by a technological revolution which made lengthy absences from the home village both possible and desirable. Hours of labour expended in gardening, fishing, hunting, canoe and house construction, and in the preparation of stone and shell implements for this work, were saved through utilization of steel tools and weapons. As Shineberg (1967, 162) has argued, the traditional round of activities was dislocated as there was now more time for local politics and warfare. There was also time to collect coconuts for sale to traders and to work for the Europeans. When political events overseas and in the New Hebrides brought an end to much of the international labour migration, alternatives for economic activity did not diminish. Establishment of the Condominium in 1906, rapid expansion in European settlement and plantation agriculture, the evolution of an administrative and trading centre at Vila, and the diffusion of mission influence throughout the group ensured that the range of options for employment and residence continued to grow.

Contract-labour migration within the New Hebrides

Europeans began establishing plantations in the New Hebrides in the 1860s—initially specializing in cotton but after 1880 growing coconuts, coffee and cocoa in particular. New Hebrideans were needed to work these estates, but competition from overseas recruiters caused acute labour shortages on plantations within the group in the early years. When movement to areas outside the New Hebrides was controlled by legislation in Australia and the Condominium after 1906, the labour situation for planters improved. However, while

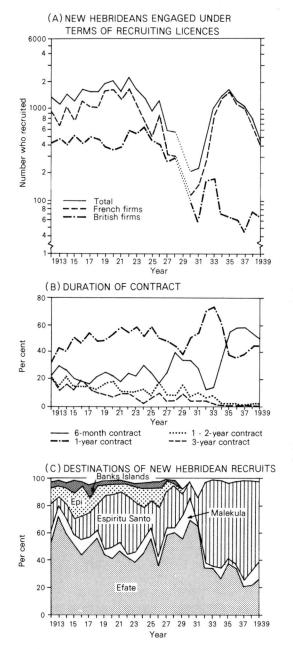

Fig. 8.2 Data on New Hebridean contract workers recruited for plantations within the group, 1912–39

labour migration overseas had involved New Hebrideans in contracts for three or more years, employment on plantations within the group was generally for much shorter periods. Islanders tended to prefer short contracts of twelve months or less, rather than the three-year terms of indenture desired by planters to ensure some continuity and stability in their labour forces.

Between 1912 and 1939 approximately 32,000 contracts were signed involving New Hebrideans in employment on plantations.* Although initially over 1,000 New Hebrideans a year were recruited for such work, the actual number of engagements was generally less than half that permitted under the terms of the recruiting licences. Numbers recruited each year fluctuated between 1,000 and 2,200 until the early 1920s, when there was a steady decline in contracts signed (Fig. 8.2A). This was due initially to increased marketing by New Hebrideans of their own crops, to preference on the part of employers for Vietnamese labour recruited on long-term contract, and later, in the 1930s, to the depression. High prices for copra in the early 1920s encouraged New Hebrideans to sell their coconuts to traders rather than seek employment on plantations, and by 1930 it was estimated that approximately one-sixth of the total copra exported from the Group came from islanders' plots (NHAR, 1931, 10). Throughout the period contracts of twelve months or less were most common, and in the latter half of the 1930s over half were for six months or less—an indication of a growing preference by New Hebrideans for casual employment outside their villages (Fig. 8.2B). By 1932 it was estimated that the proportion of casual or non-contract labourers to New Hebrideans engaged on contracts was two to one on British plantations and four to one on French estates (New Hebrides Annual Report, British National Service, 1932, 10).

Labour recruiting was most successful in those areas where contact with Europeans had been minimal and where continuing intergroup hostilities ensured a steady supply of men seeking weapons. New Hebrideans from the interior of the larger islands (Malekula,

* Bi-annual labour reports containing statistics on the numbers of New Hebrideans recruited by British and French firms were forwarded by the British Resident Commissioner to the High Commissioner of the Western Pacific High Commission. These reports provided the information on which this discussion of contract employment is based—they do not contain a complete record of inter-island labour migration because infringements of the regulations were numerous, and non-contract employment became increasingly popular among New Hebrideans throughout this period.

200

Ambrym, Pentecost) recruited most freely, as it was in these areas that the acquisition of arms was of paramount importance in maintaining the balance of power. Where mission influence was strong, labour recruiting was difficult; consequently the southern islands provided comparatively few labourers for plantations elsewhere in the group. In addition the missions encouraged New Hebrideans to cultivate their own lands and obtain their supplies of imported materials through sale of crops. The increasing range of goods offered by traders in return for copra stimulated this involvement in cash cropping and, in years when the price for copra was high, the numbers seeking contract employment decreased noticeably. Destinations for the recruits were primarily Efate and Espiritu Santo (Fig. 8.2c). Efate, where most plantation activity was concentrated in the nineteenth century, declined slightly in significance with the development of land on other islands. Epi was an important cotton and copra producing area until the late 1920s, when the depression saw the eclipse of the New Hebrides cotton export trade. By this time a second major area of European settlement had evolved in south-east Espiritu Santo and, because there were few New Hebridean communities where the plantations were concentrated, labour had to be brought in from other islands.

By 1940 the pre-contact situation of mobility in restricted spatial domains had vanished from virtually all parts of the group. Patterns of individual movement had undergone sequential change in most areas from traditional oscillation, through a phase of lengthy absences in contract employment overseas and later within the group, to short-term labour mobility associated with casual employment. Improvements in inter-island transport greatly facilitated this transition to short-term circular mobility. Rapid proliferation of plantations, trading stations, mission settlements and administrative outposts in the 1920s demanded an increase in shipping services. With greater freedom of movement, New Hebrideans were not so dependent on employers to return them to their villages. The increasing numbers employed on a casual basis indicated that New Hebrideans were keeping open their various options for economic activity: subsistence gardens, cash crops, and wage employment could all be more readily maintained as viable alternatives with this more intensive circular migration.

Increasing complexity in movement patterns: cash cropping and the movement towards towns

The establishment of military bases on Efate and Espiritu Santo in 1942 was a major event for all New Hebrideans. Construction of camps, airfields, naval bases, and road networks required New Hebridean labour, and thousands of islanders were employed on three-month contracts at the bases. Inter-island migration was channelled towards a new kind of destination, and the plantations could not match either the social or economic attractions of the military bases. The war years were ones of great prosperity for New Hebrideans, but employment outside their village environments was necessary to maximize opportunities. In some areas the exodus of men was so great that preparation and cultivation of gardens suffered. Allen (1964, 28) mentioned that in west Aoba the decline in local food production led to families becoming partially dependent for food and clothing on their relatives employed by the Americans on Espiritu Santo.

Prosperity did not end with the departure of American forces in 1945 and 1946 but, with high prices for copra, New Hebrideans turned increasingly to cash cropping within their rural communities. As early as 1948 it was estimated that about half the total copra exported from the group came from New Hebridean groves, compared with 15 per cent in the mid-1930s (New Hebrides Annual Reports, British National Service, 1948, 25). There was an increase in output from European-owned plantations in this period, but most of the total growth in copra exports was due to New Hebridean production. Increasing New Hebridean involvement in cash cropping has influenced mobility patterns in a number of ways. But while there has been a decline in the significance of the plantation as a source of income relative to returns from cash crops, New Hebridean inter-island mobility has continued to increase in intensity since the war. Throughout the last three decades there has been growing complexity in mobility patterns with the spread of educational and medical facilities through the group, some diversification in the economy in the late 1950s when manganese mining on Efate commenced and a fish-freezing industry was established on Espiritu Santo and, most significantly, with the rapid post-war growth of the two towns, Vila and Santo (Luganville).

Although there has been a legally defined 'town', Vila, in the

Table 8.2 Vila and Santo: population growth, 1955-67 (*Sources:* Bennett (1957, 123); Gauger (1967, 35); McArthur and Yaxley (1968, 31, 109))

Ethnic group	Vila			Santo		
	1955	1965	1967*	1955	1963	1967*
New Hebridean	200	1,312	1,459	170	661	1,534
European	638	578	778	448		303
Asian	452	234	288	746	734†	179
Other Pacific Islanders	50	180	140	20	169	159
Part-Europeans and others	?	312	407	?	?	389
Total	1,340	2,616	3,072	1,384	1,564	2,564

* The legally defined urban areas only.
† Gauger (1967, 35) specified 516 French and British European residents, 102 Vietnamese and Chinese, and 156 'other' ressortissants. Most Vietnamese were repatriated to North Vietnam in 1962–4.

New Hebrides since 1911, the evolution of urban centres where considerable numbers of islanders are employed in non-agricultural activities has been largely a post-World War II development. Santo was a small dispersed plantation settlement with a population of around 400 in 1940 (Ball, 1969, 67), while Vila, the administrative and commercial capital, was estimated to have a population of 1,000 in 1942 (Brookfield and Brown, 1969, iv). The war brought considerable changes to the physical structure of both settlements— wharf facilities were improved, airfields and networks of all-weather roads were constructed, and major housing developments instituted in the form of accommodation for troops and employees. These developments provided the foundation for rapid growth in both settlements which accompanied post-war expansion of administrative services. Since the late 1950s, improvements in education, medical, communications and agricultural services with financial aid from France and Britain have accelerated expansion. Since 1955 the two towns have grown rapidly: Vila's population more than doubled in the 12 years between 1955 and the first national census in 1967, while that of Santo increased by some 80 per cent (Table 8.2). If only the New Hebridean component in the population is considered, the relevant increases are 630 and 820 per cent respectively.*

* Direct comparison between the 1955 and 1967 population figures for urban areas is somewhat risky as the precise areal units which Bennett (1957) considered as defining the towns in 1955 were not stated. However, this comparison gives an indication of the rapid increases in New Hebridean population in these areas in recent years.

Although only 13 per cent of the total New Hebridean population was living in the gazetted towns and their periurban areas in 1967, information on the various social and economic attractions of the two towns has diffused widely, and New Hebrideans from virtually all islands were in temporary or permanent residence in Vila and Santo in 1967 (Fig. 8.3).

Although no question to test the residential intentions of migrants in the towns was asked in the 1967 census, the results of an earlier social census in Vila in 1965 (Brookfield and Brown, 1969) suggested that there was much greater residential stability in the urban migrant population than formerly anticipated. Brookfield and Brown (1969, 44) found the median time in residence to be 5·6 years and over a quarter of the migrants had been living on and off in the urban or periurban areas for more than eight years. The stated number of years resident in Vila should not be considered as implying a period in continuous residence because Brookfield and Brown (1969, 60) requested 'the total number of years lived in Vila, ignoring short breaks as for overseas leave, school, visits to home islands, etc.' Detailed field inquiry into the recent movement behaviour of adult migrants from selected islands resident in three areas in Vila in January 1970 revealed that over half those interviewed had been living in their home villages at some stage in 1969 and only 17 per cent had not been back to these areas for four years (Table 8.3A).* When the proportion of time over these four years which was spent in rural and urban residence was calculated, it was found that, on average, less than half had been spent in the town (Table 8.3B). There were some minor variations in the proportion of time spent in the urban area on the basis of sex and age group, but circulation between village and town, with involvement in social and economic activities in both areas, emerged as the most significant form of spatial mobility. In a similar way the recent revival of New Hebridean migration to New Caledonia is a circular movement.

* As part of a more general inquiry into contemporary circular mobility in the south-central New Hebrides, migration histories of islanders from three islands (Tongoa, Emae, and Makura) who were living in Vila were compiled in January 1970. 'A migration' was defined as a relocation involving the mover in a stay of at least one month's duration at his destination. While the movement behaviour revealed in these histories cannot be considered representative of the total Vila migrant population because of the arbitrary selection of communities of origin and destination, they do provide a useful insight into the nature of New Hebridean rural–urban migration.

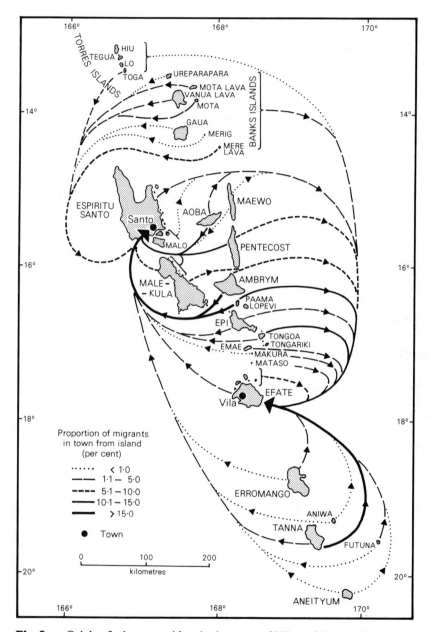

Fig. 8.3 Origin of migrants resident in the towns of Vila and Santo, 1967

Table 8.3 Residence in village and town, 1966–9: (**A**) Year when last spent one month or more in village (per cent); (**B**) Proportion of time, January 1966–December 1969 spent living in town: settlement and age groups (per cent) (*Source:* Migration histories: Tongoans, Emaeans and Makurans in Vila; see footnote p. 204.)

Year	Seaside	Selected areas of Vila Melcofe/ Kofe	Saratokora/ Nakavika	$\bar{M}$	Total F	Total
1969	56·2	60·5	66·7	57·9	58·9	58·5
1968	12·3	6·9	11·1	7·3	12·8	10·2
1967	12·3	4·7	3·7	10·1	7·6	8·8
1966	5·5	4·7	3·7	6·1	4·4	5·3
Earlier than 1966	13·7	23·2	14·8	18·6	16·3	17·2

A

Group	Males $\bar{M}$	S.D.	Females $\bar{M}$	SD	Total $\bar{M}$	SD
Settlement						
Seaside	53·3	33·1	48·5	34·6	52·9	36·5
Melcofe/Kofe	51·3	35·6	45·4	37·5	48·5	41·0
Saratokora/Nakavika	50·0	26·7	38·7	34·2	39·1	32·3
Age						
< 30	42·3	28·5	40·6	34·2	41·8	36·2
30–40	66·0	35·2	58·8	38·1	60·2	39·7
> 40	59·6	32·7	35·6	32·9	37·7	35·4
Total	52·3	32·7	46·3	38·1	41·9	38·9

B

Since 1967 Nouméa has become an important destination for New Hebrideans seeking wage employment because expansion of the New Caledonian economy, consequent on the growth of the nickel industry, generated a demand for labour which could be satisfied locally. New Hebrideans have been attracted to New Caledonia by high wages ($150–$250 per month) and short three to six-month contracts: in 1968 it was estimated that 400 were working there, but by 1971 over 3,000 were believed to be temporarily resident in New Caledonia (Fabre and Kissane, 1971, 3). Nouméa became a more important destination than any within the group for New Hebridean migrants, but the great majority were only temporary residents. Many returned in the depression of 1972.

The circular mobility transition reviewed

This brief survey of the evidence over 150 years does not reveal a transition leading yet to permanent redistribution: it does however reveal a transitional sequence within a particular class of movement behaviour—circulation. Throughout the post-contact period a basic and traditional pattern of inter-island mobility has persisted in which permanent change in place of residence is exceptional. There have been changes in various characteristics of this movement which fall into three major phases—labour migration overseas, contract-labour migration within the group, and a much more complex system where temporary absences from rural communities are associated with casual employment on plantations and in towns, or with moves to schools, hospitals, and mission training centres. These phases in movement behaviour have not progressed simultaneously in all parts of the group but, by the 1960s, the third phase was virtually universal.

It is possible to approach understanding of the circularity characteristic of the first two phases in this transition through reference to a demand for non-indigenous material goods which could only be satisfied by working at locations where, for various reasons, New Hebrideans could not settle permanently. Although islanders who were recruited for employment overseas or on local plantations could re-engage for further terms on completion of their initial contracts, acquisition of their own houses and property was difficult at these destinations. Consequently circular movement between the village and centres of commercial activity was the most common form of spatial mobility. By the third stage of the transition, however, options for satisfying a demand for a cash income had increased. They included cash cropping, which could be met solely by residence in the village, and a principal alternative, wage employment in towns. Permanent settlement was possible in both locations. However, instead of concentrating their time and labour on one or other of these activities, most islanders have chosen to participate in both by means of circular migration. In this way they maintain a range of choices for activity, some associated with their traditional social and economic system and others with the commercial system introduced by Europeans. To understand circular mobility in these circumstances it is necessary to examine the interrelationships between, on the one hand, individual needs and aspirations (which

207

naturally change over a person's life) and, on the other, activities designed to satisfy these. An analysis of previous mobility experiences of New Hebrideans who claimed villages on three islands in the south-central New Hebrides as their permanent homes provided useful insights into the nature of and reasons for continuing circularity in movement behaviour.

CONTEMPORARY CIRCULAR MOBILITY IN THE SOUTH-CENTRAL NEW HEBRIDES

To obtain information on contemporary circular migration required a sample of individuals who were living in places they considered their permanent homes or were in temporary residence elsewhere. As logistic considerations prevented the random sampling of areas throughout the group, a purposive sample was taken of 18 rural and urban communities in the south-central New Hebrides, or that administrative area known as Central District No. 1 (CD1).* New Hebrideans here have a range of residential alternatives, since commercial plantations on certain islands and the town of Vila offer opportunities for employment outside village agriculture (Fig. 8.4). This area also has a number of medical, mission, and educational establishments which can be used as temporary residences by New Hebrideans at different stages of their lives. Fifteen villages on Tongoa, Emae and Makura, and three urban settlements in Vila occupied mainly by migrants from these latter islands, were selected for study. The guiding principle in selecting villages was to obtain a representative sample of all major locational, demographic, and linguistic characteristics of settlements in the south-central New Hebrides which might affect mobility patterns. Although the settlements on all islands are nucleated and have similar customs governing political and economic status, there are differences in site characteristics (interior or coastal locations), population sizes, the availability of land for gardens and cash crops, and the languages and religions of their inhabitants (Table 8.4).†

* The diversity in cultural, linguistic, and locational characteristics of New Hebridean societies, together with a lack of detailed village location maps and limited time and resources for the field inquiry, made it necessary to select a particular group of islands for this analysis.

† Since the 1880s the area has been a stronghold of the Presbyterian Mission, which has boarding schools and hospitals on certain islands. In recent years the

Table 8.4 Villages, New Hebrides: population, location, language and religion, 1969–70

Village	Population M	F	Total	Location	Language group	Religious affiliation
Tongoa						
Lumbukuti[2]	167	160	327	Coastal	*Nakanamanga*	Presbyterian
Panita[3]	55	55	110	,,	,,	,,
Raxenga	30	19	49	,,	,,	Pres./SDA
Lupalea	73	74	147	,,	,,	,,
Puele	91	71	162	Interior	,,	Presbyterian
Worafiu	50	53	103	,,	,,	Pres./SDA
Euta	92	85	177	,,	*Namakura*	Presbyterian
Mangarisu	152	146	298	Coastal	,,	,,
Subtotal	710	663	1,373	—	—	—
Emae						
Sesake	31	37	68	Interior	*Nakanamanga*	Presbyterian
Marae	29	30	59	Coastal	,,	,,
Sangava[4]	75	77	152	,,	*Namakura*	,,
Makatea	45	41	86	,,	,,	,,
Tongamea	31	37	68	,,	5	,,
Finongi[6]	27	31	58	,,	,,	,,
Subtotal	238	253	491	—	—	—
Makura						
Malakoto	37	69	106	Coastal	*Namakura*	Presbyterian
Total	985	985	1,970	—	—	—

[1] Enumerated during field-work surveys.
[2] Including the Presbyterian Mission hospital at Silimauri and school at Napangasale.
[3] Including Saviu and the French school at Lemboroe.
[4] Including the local government station, Wororana, and the small hamlet of Leimbuta.
[5] Inhabitants of these villages also speak a local dialect, *Amuna O Mae*.
[6] Including the population of Ngaone, a section of Finongi, some 200 metres from the main village.

Despite these variations, the migration histories collected from 537 New Hebridean males and females over 15 years of age who belonged to the villages on Tongoa, Emae and Makura, revealed

Seventh Day Adventist Mission has established churches in a number of villages and, because their major educational and medical institutions are on Aoba and Aore to the north, some of the movements of adherents have been beyond the District.

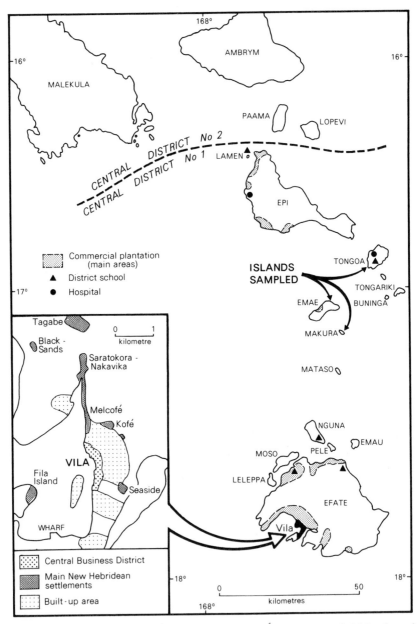

Fig. 8.4 Central District No. 1, New Hebrides: location of sampled islands and of places providing opportunity for temporary residence (*inset:* Vila town area)

that people from these areas had very similar mobility experiences. Inter-island movements involving short absences emerged as being part of the lifestyle of both men and women from all villages studied. The prevailing circularity of mobility was strikingly demonstrated by the fact that the destinations for some 45 per cent of the 3,518 moves were the home villages. To assess the position of the home village as a central node in New Hebridean migration networks a graph-theoretic measure was devised. Using a modified version of Shimbel's (1953) accessibility index, a 'circulation index' was computed on the basis of migration experiences of each respondent.

A measure of circularity in New Hebridean migration networks

Shimbel (1953) defined certain parameters which give some indica-tion of the 'compactness' of a network. Using graph-theoretic techniques he derived an accessibility index which expresses the average topological distance (L) that all nodes (j) in a network (S) are from a particular node (i). By summing all the $L(i,j)$ over j for a given network, S, a measure of the average topological distance separating the various nodes in the network from i is acquired. Shimbel (1953, 502) demonstrated that:

> If the sum is large, then we know that on average the various sites of the network are far removed from site i. If the sum is small, then the various sites of S are readily reached from i. The sum is termed the accessibility of S to i and labelled $A(i,S)$. By definition then:

$$A(i,S) \sum_{j=1}^{n} L(i,j)$$

In the context of migration this index has some potential in giving an overall measure of the structure of an individual's past migration experiences. The places in which he has lived for the prescribed period of time (one month) are the nodes, and the links between them are defined by those nodes which served as the origin and destination points of a particular move. Using the home village as the central node (i), the accessibility of all other nodes (j) to i can be established by using Shimbel's method, and a measure of the extent to which stepwise migration or regular returns to the rural areas has occurred can be derived. If the values of $A(i,S)$ are large, stepwise migration has occurred; if low, the pattern has been one of returns to the rural village before moving to another area. How-

211

ever, where low values for the index are derived, they can also be merely an expression of the small size of the network and not a measure of its internal structure.

To derive a more meaningful measure of circularity in New Hebridean migration networks, Shimbel's accessibility index was modified to give a circulation index, $C(i,S)$:

$$\frac{C(i,S) \sum_{j=1}^{n} L(i,j)}{v - 1}$$

where v is the total number of nodes in the network.

By dividing the summed distance of all nodes (j) from the home village (i) by the number of nodes minus the home village, the actual size of the network (in terms of the number of nodes) becomes irrelevant, and the degree to which circulation in the network has occurred is the significant measure. As there was considerable variation in the size of New Hebridean networks in terms of the number of nodes, an index which measured internal structural characteristics irrespective of size of network was necessary (Fig. 8.5). The circulation index appears to serve this purpose. In cases where the value derived for the index did not exceed 1, all the out-migrations had been initiated from one particular node, and any subsequent moves had been back to this point either directly or via one other alternative place of residence. Movement between different places without any returns to the village resulted in circulation indices exceeding 1, and these indicated that migration had been stepwise rather than circular at certain stages in the individual's migration history.

Of the 537 individuals interviewed two-thirds had circulation indices below 1 and one-third, mainly males, had indices above 1. There were no significant differences between groups aggregated on the basis of age, sex, or home island. High circulation indices (exceeding 2) for males were closely associated with the nature of employment, either past or present. Employment in skilled and semi-skilled occupations (in education, medical services, or local administration) often led to transfers from one school, hospital, or office to another without return to the home village for lengthy periods. With unskilled, casual employment such movement from one locality to another, while still employed in the same job, occurred less frequently. One exception, however, was crewing inter-island

212

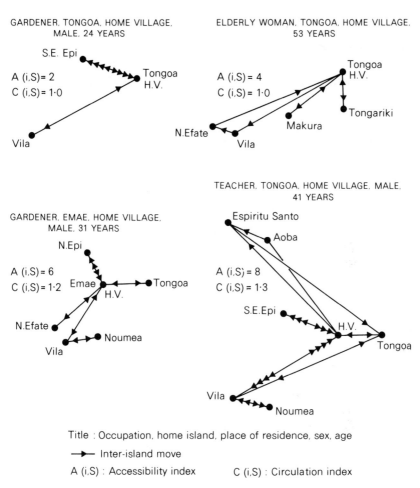

GARDENER, TONGOA, HOME VILLAGE, MALE, 24 YEARS

ELDERLY WOMAN, TONGOA, HOME VILLAGE, 53 YEARS

GARDENER, EMAE, HOME VILLAGE, MALE, 31 YEARS

TEACHER, TONGOA, HOME VILLAGE, MALE, 41 YEARS

Title : Occupation, home island, place of residence, sex, age

→— Inter-island move

A (i,S) : Accessibility index   C (i,S) : Circulation index

Fig. 8.5   Migration networks of four selected New Hebrideans

vessels. As many as 30 per cent of the males interviewed had been employed on ships at some time, and the extent of travel around the group was far greater than the circulation indices implied. However, as stopovers at various islands while an individual was employed as boat's crew rarely involved stays of more than a week, these voyages were not classed as 'migrations'.

The migration behaviour of most New Hebrideans interviewed was thus focused on a particular locality, the home village, which served

213

as the origin point for movement out to alternative residences, and
as a regular destination. When questioned on the reasons for this
circular mobility pattern, New Hebrideans were invariably somewhat confused. The reasons for periodic returns to the rural areas
were, to them anyway, self-evident: movements to alternative places
of residence were never regarded, initially at least, as permanent;
there was thus always the intention to return to the village.

The migration histories revealed that 88 per cent of those interviewed had moved at least once for a period exceeding one month,
the decision being taken either by the mover or by a parent or
guardian. If only those over twenty-five years of age are considered,
97 per cent had moved at least once. Although the information
recorded on reasons for previous moves is of limited value because
of biases caused by *post facto* rationalization, an evaluation of some
factors which influence New Hebrideans' migration decisions is
possible. When reasons for movements were sought, a stereotyped
pattern of responses emerged which reflected something of New
Hebrideans' conception of their basic needs at different stages of
their lives. By relating stated reasons for mobility to the approximate
age of the respondent at the time he claimed to have moved, it was
possible to isolate a sequence of pressures which operate to encourage
movement away from, and back to, villages at different times.
Schematic representation of migration experiences of males and
females, following Mitchell's (1969, 179) paradigm of a Rhodesian
labour migrant's career, could be constructed from the stated reasons
for migration at different ages. As Mitchell has argued, these schema
imply, in sociological terms, that the balance of economic, political,
social, and personal factors favouring the decision to move will vary
consistently with a person's stage in life.

Mobility of New Hebridean men

The 'paradigm' of a male New Hebridean's migratory behaviour
identifies the major stated factors governing movements (Table 8.5).
Over 80 per cent had lived outside their villages for a month or more
at least once before they were 20 years old. Some 20 per cent had
accompanied their parents, a further 20 per cent attended schools
outside their island, while others had made their first moves to visit
friends or relatives, or to seek employment. Turning to adult men,
wage employment dominated the reasons given for migration at all
stages (Table 8.5). Of the males interviewed, 91 per cent had moved

214

at least once to earn a wage income, and this was the reason given for 75 per cent of the moves away from the villages. For unmarried men between 18 and 25 years of age, however, the most common explanations were to experience some of the excitement of living outside the social domain of the village, and to achieve a measure of economic independence from their parents. Young men frequently went 'walk about' (Table 8.5). The close proximity of these islands to Vila, a regular air service between Tongoa and Vila, the presence of kinsmen in the urban area to provide accommodation and the ready availability of unskilled labouring jobs made movement between village and town a relatively secure undertaking. Much of this movement was for very short periods, usually less than a month's duration.

Married men tended to see wage-earning as an easier means of obtaining the capital required to finance various household, agricultural, and social activities, than cutting copra or selling other cash crops. Their responses to questions on the reasons for seeking a cash income outside the village reflected an attitude similar to that found by Finney (1967) in French Polynesia: 'fast money' through weekly pay packets was invariably preferred to 'slow money' or the periodic returns from cash cropping, especially when money was required in quantity for a specific purpose. Opportunities for earning a wage income were very limited on Tongoa, Emae, and Makura: of the 159 interviewed adult males resident in their permanent homes on these islands, only 10 had full-time jobs with regular wage incomes. 30 per cent received irregular cash incomes from entrepreneurial activities (operating a store, taxi-truck, or launch) or from casual employment on a small European-owned plantation on Emae. Assessment of the sources and amounts of income for households over a specified period was part of the research plan, but reluctance among New Hebrideans to reveal this sort of information made this line of inquiry impracticable. Although no adequate reason was given it quickly became apparent that respondents did not wish to provide this information.

New Hebrideans insisted that money derived from copra production, or the local sale of crops, pigs, and bullocks for ceremonial purposes, could not meet their demands for cash. Although copra prices paid by local co-operative societies have been high in recent years ($70 to $103 per ton of smoke-dried copra) returns are often slow in reaching the producer. If money is required quickly in large

215

Table 8.5 Male circular migration, New Hebrides: a schematic representation
(*Source:* Migration histories: Tongoans, Emaeans and Makurans)

Age	Marital and family status	Pressures operating to encourage movement away from village	Pressures operating to encourage returns to the village
< 18	Single, dependent	Largely depends on parent's plans. If seeking education above village level may have to live on another island	If moved with parents will return with them. If attended school outside home island, need to assist in domestic duties and agricultural activities may encourage return
18–25	Single, independent	Money for personal uses, to assist family enterprises, to pay school fees of younger siblings. Wish to participate in 'exciting' town life and visit kin	Obligations to parents, especially if aged. Plans for marriage
25–35	Married, dependents	Finance for wedding, family enterprises, build own house construct wells, fence cattle yards	Assist wife and family in agricultural activities, live with family if remained in village
35–50	Married, adult dependents	Rising cost of maintaining own family, capital to finance business enterprises —store, taxi, launch, plantation	If family remained in village, need to visit them and assist in gardens and plantations. If family with him, costs of maintaining wife and children in town. May take custom title if father dead
> 50	Married/ widowed	Medical treatment. Visit family in town. Finance for business enterprise and customary exchanges	Interest in village politics, need to look after grand-children in village while their parents temporarily absent. Limited employment opportunities for elderly

Reasons given in migration histories for moves			Moves and absences over the four years 1966–9		
Reason	Percentage who moved	Number of moves $\bar{M}$	SD	Months absent $\bar{M}$	SD
With family	22				
Education	20				
Visit family/relatives	18	1·6	1·1	16·6	15·8
'Walk-about'[2]	15				
Seek employment	51				
Acquire money for:					
(i) general personal/family needs[3]	75	2·2	1·3	16·8	13·9
(ii) specific projects[4]	10				
Medical reasons	3				
Acquire money for:					
(i) general personal/family needs	88	1·2	0·9	8·9	9·8
(ii) specific projects	25				
Medical reasons	8				
Employment	16	0·8	1·1	6·0	10·2
Medical reasons	10				
Visit relatives					

[1] Excluding twelve men who have been employed in the same job in Vila for over five years, but who still consider the village their permanent home.
[2] Desire to see the town and experience the 'excitements' of Vila's social life.
[3] General living requirements include clothing, household effects, food.
[4] House construction, purchase of a vehicle, acquisition of bride-price, construction of a village church/school/store.

amounts, alternative means of earning it are invariably sought. There has been a move, particularly in the past decade, to construct sleeping houses from imported materials, to install concrete water tanks, to fence cattle yards, and to improve taxi services within islands and launch transport between them. Hence money in some quantity has been required by most adult men. While a variety of reasons for needing money were stated, only 32 per cent of the men could recall a specific objective for any particular move for employment. It is instructive to consider here Chapman's (1970, 144) findings on reasons for circular mobility in the Solomon Islands where he found that one objective was rarely sufficient to explain a villager's decision to move. Chapman identified 162 'objectives' for moving from the village for a period of 24 hours or more, and 121 underlying reasons to which these could be related. The number of objectives stated at the time of an individual's departure ranged from one to eight. In the light of this evidence, it is obvious that the simple classification of reasons for mobility used in the New Hebridean study greatly oversimplifies the decision process. The problems of *post facto* rationalization of behaviour, and lack of ability to remember motives for earlier decisions, also limit the utility of the data.

A comparison of mobility rates over the four years between January 1966 and December 1969 showed that men under 35 years had been more mobile and spent longer periods in residence outside their villages than older men (Table 8.5). This contrast reflects the differing balance of opportunities in village and town for men in these two age groups. The younger men, still dependent on the holders of customary titles (usually the older men in the community) to obtain access to land, found the economic benefits of wage labour to be much greater than those of cash cropping. Since many of them had been educated to senior primary level they could readily find employment in the town. Older men, particularly those over 45 years, were in a poorer competitive position on the labour market outside the village. Within the village, on the other hand, their economic and social security and prestige were guaranteed through access to land.

Mobility of New Hebridean women

The migratory behaviour of New Hebridean women reflects a somewhat different pattern of pressures, except at younger ages, encouraging movement to and from the village (Table 8.6). As with

218

men, a high proportion (60 per cent) of women interviewed had made their first move before they were 20 years old, and for half parents had directed this move. The two most important factors which emerged from analysis of female mobility were the role played by others (parents, husband) in directing moves, and the need to seek medical attention, especially when pregnant. Except for moves to hospitals or, when single, to seek employment on plantations in south-east Epi or to visit kin in Vila, women offered essentially passive reasons for their moves. Women's Liberation has as yet made little headway in the New Hebrides, and the major economic and social roles of women are to maintain gardens and care for younger siblings or their own children. Movement to other areas for more than one month depends to a large extent on the plans of parents or husbands.

Although 'family migrations' or movements by both husband and wife (with or without their children) are much less frequent in the total of all movements than the relocations of individuals, over half the moves made by New Hebrideans after marriage had been made with their spouses.* 43 per cent of the moves made by men after marriage and 81 per cent of those made by women were 'family migrations' as defined here. In general, moves by a woman for medical treatment led to family migration, and the husband often sought employment in the town to cover the costs involved. Even where the stated reason of movement by men was to seek wage employment, a high proportion of wives either accompanied them or joined them at their destinations soon after their husbands had left the village. Lengthy absences from families are not favoured and respondents argued that if a move was likely to involve residence in other areas for longer than about six months, as in the case of contract employment in administrative or social services, the family would join the husband.

* Definition of 'family migration' as the movement of complete nuclear units (husband, wife, and dependent children) proved unrealistic in the New Hebridean context. Families, as groups, rarely moved together. A man and his wife would move together under certain circumstances, such as if the woman required medical attention, leaving their children in the village with relatives. Other members of the family may subsequently follow, thus completing the group at the destination. In the light of this chain-migration process, a family migration was defined as any movement involving both a husband and his wife either together or in close succession. Of 880 moves recorded for men and women when they were married, 57 per cent had involved both the husband and wife, with or without their children. The remaining 327 migrations had been made by either the husband or his wife.

219

Table 8.6 Female circular migration, New Hebrides: a schematic representation (*Source:* Migration histories: Tongoans, Emaeans, Makurans)

Age	Marital and family status	Pressures operating to encourage movement away from the village	Pressures operating to encourage returns to the village
< 18	Single, dependent	Largely depends on parents plans and a need for post-village education	Depends on parents and, as with males, if moved for education, a need to assist family in village
18–25	Single, independent	Wish to visit town and assist kin in domestic duties there	Obligations to parents, especially if aged. Plans marriage
25–35	Married, young dependents	Medical treatment if pregnant; accompany husband if latter going to town on long-term employment	Children to village school. Aged parents require assistance. Family gardens require attention
35–50	Married, adult dependents	Again largely dependent on husband's activities. Medical treatment if ill. If a member of local church committees short absences at meetings may be necessary	Family demands, especially those of children at school, unless entire family moves to town
> 50	Married/widowed	Dependent on husband unless widowed, when may leave village to live with own children or relatives elsewhere	

Reasons given in migration histories for moves		Moves and absences over the four years 1966–9[1]			
Reason	Percentage who moved	Number of moves $\bar{M}$	SD	Months absent $\bar{M}$	SD
With family	33				
Education	6				
		1·4	1·3	6·4	7·5
Visit family relatives	22				
Seek employment	15				
Acquire money for personal/ family needs	7				
Medical reasons	25	1·1	0·8	9·3	12·1
Accompany husband	48				
Acquire money for personal/ family needs	3				
Medical reasons	31	0·7	0·6	7·2	10·5
Accompany husband	40				
Medical reasons	20				
Visit family	5	0·5	0·8	4·7	9·2
Accompany husband	16				

[1] Excluding eleven women who have been living virtually the entire four years in Vila with their husbands in permanent employment there.

The various activities which characterize the daily lives of men and women on these islands are responses to two basic sets of needs: one associated with food production and the maintenance of a traditional system of reciprocal exchange, and the other concerned with the accumulation and utilization of money. Temporary absences from the village in wage employment have been shown to be an important means of satisfying the latter needs, and it is now necessary to see how circular migration is linked to other cash-producing activities in the village and to the subsistence sector of the economy. Although the two sectors of the village economy are closely interrelated in terms of the allocation of time, labour, and land, it is useful to examine them separately. Absences from the village have different effects on cash-producing activities on the one hand and subsistence gardening on the other.

Circulation migration and cash cropping

Visible evidence of widespread participation in cash cropping in the south-central New Hebrides is given by the extensive areas under tree crops. It was estimated in 1969 that 72 per cent of the land under cultivation on Tongoa and 62 per cent of that on Emae was planted in coconuts (Quantin, 1969, 17). The 100 hectares of cultivable land on Makura was all planted in coconuts and subsistance crops. Tongoans and Makurans, in particular, stressed the problems of maintaining subsistence gardens under the traditional rotation system now that such extensive areas of their land are under tree crops. Attempts to acquire land on nearby islands were in large measure a reflection of the dilemma facing islanders who wish to extend their acreages under coconuts while still participating in subsistence production.

The production of a poor quality smoke-dried copra is the major cash-producing activity in all villages: over 90 per cent of adult males interviewed in such communities gave this as their major occupation. The preparation of smoke-dried copra is essentially a very simple task, not demanding heavy inputs of labour at any particular time of the year. The method produces a low-grade export product, but it has the advantages of simplicity and the fact that there is no special equipment that requires maintenance. It is no inconvenience for the owner to leave his coconut groves for a number of months and work elsewhere—the fallen nuts can be collected by

222

his wife and children, and if they require cash, they can easily prepare the copra themselves.

With the persistence of a market for smoke-dried copra, and the opportunities to obtain wage employment outside the village, few islanders saw advantages in turning their attention to full cash-crop specialization. Employment outside the village was commonly believed to bring higher returns for the time and labour expended* but, if it was considered advisable or desirable to remain in the village, working scattered coconut groves provided the means of sustaining some income. The desire to have a source of cash income in the village was strong, and ownership of a coconut 'plantation' was a universal objective among men in the area.† In addition to its material value, ownership of an extensive area under coconuts carries with it a certain amount of social prestige, even if the productive capacity of the grove is not maximized because the owner devotes his time to other activities.

Competition for land on which to plant coconuts is, consequently, severe and has led to many land disputes within and between villages. While copra production as a cash-earning activity has little influence on the timing of departures from and returns to the village, the need to maintain an active interest in affairs dealing with land and its utilization does play an important role in encouraging islanders to be resident periodically in their villages. Planting coconuts does not necessarily signify ownership of land, but utilization is increasingly being taken into consideration in land disputes. Customary traditions relating to the settlement of these islands, which the chiefs seek to sustain as the basis for proving title to land, are being challenged a by a new concept of ownership through use. It thus pays a man to plant coconuts on land to which he has access, even if he has little intention of devoting much time to cutting, smoking, and selling the copra.

Circular migration and the subsistence sector of the economy

In all the villages surveyed, the production and distribution of

* The catastrophic decline in copra prices that took place in 1971–2 is outside the period of this research. However, it must have confirmed New Hebrideans in the attitudes identified here toward full-time participation in cash-cropping.

† The word 'plantation' is used here in the context of a New Hebridean coconut grove, which in no way resembles a formal plantation. Trees are rarely planted in lines, and the undergrowth is often dense. Fallen nuts are permitted to germinate and self-sown 'plantations' are common.

223

subsistence foods is a major economic activity. All households had access to one or more gardens located at varying distances from the village, and women worked regularly at these sites. A number of crops are grown with varieties of yam (*Dioscorea* spp.), taro (*Colocasia* spp. and *Xanthosoma*), and manioc (*Manihot* spp.) as the major staples. Varieties of sugarcane and cabbage, together with pineapples, tomatoes, watercress, and sweet potato, are also grown along with bananas, mangoes and pawpaw. The only truly seasonal crop is the yam, and the timing of garden preparation is largely governed by its production cycle. In these islands clearing the secondary growth and preparing the yam garden tends to take place between July and August, while planting is usually spread over three or four months (August to December) to provide a run of supplies in the following year. The tubers take between seven and nine months to mature, and harvesting begins in March.*

In studies of circular migration in areas where seasonal cash or subsistence crops are grown, it has been argued that men time their absences from the village to coincide with the period between planting and harvesting.† By returning to the village to assist in preparing gardens or harvesting crops, the men are seen to be maximizing a range of choices for activity in both the subsistence and monetary economies. When questioned on the relevance of these considerations to their circular migration behaviour, New Hebrideans stated that they endeavoured to be in the villages for the yam-planting season. The high proportion (60 per cent) of recorded absences occupying nine or fewer months away from the village suggested that, for many, this may indeed have been the case.‡ When absences in employment over the previous four years were

* Barrau (1956) and Wilson (1966, 159–68) have more detailed accounts of subsistence cultivation in the group.

† Mitchell (1969, 171–6) has evaluated this thesis in the context of circular migration in some African societies.

‡ Precise dating of a person's previous moves was difficult because New Hebrideans, while having some facility for recalling the length of time spent in employment, or hospitals and schools, had little success in establishing how long they had spent in the village between any two moves. As Vansina (1965, 100–2) has argued, the meaning of 'time' in illiterate societies often varies with the type of activity under consideration. For these based in the village, ecological or sociological cycles, rather than calendar time, seemed relevant and it was difficult to get estimates which one could accept with any degree of confidence. It was not possible, therefore, to relate absences in other localities to specific times of the year or to assess, quantitatively, the periodicity in circular migration.

examined, it was found that there was considerable variability in the duration of such moves, indicating that there was no rigid seasonal pattern of movement. The round of subsistence activities seems to adjust quite successfully to temporary absences of men in employment. Reciprocity, the traditional system of exchange, facilitates temporary absences since, as Brookfield (1970, 7) has argued, an individual's responsibilities can readily be spread among others, and he can be reabsorbed easily on return. Absences from the village can therefore be sustained at all times of the year; but periodic returns are essential in order to minimize losses through not utilizing social and economic opportunities in the village. Long-term absences from village-based activities can result in loss of social prestige and maybe even of rights to land.

CIRCULAR MIGRATION: A TRANSITIONAL PHASE?

Analysis of New Hebridean circular migration from the point of view of needs at different times of a person's life has provided fuller understanding of the place of temporary absences in rural social and economic activities. Although the use of stated reasons in this reconstruction makes it difficult to speak with any confidence of causes, it is possible to outline an explanatory generalization. The pattern of behaviour evident in circular migration can clearly be explained within the premise that decisions to move are intendedly rational, although such movement inevitably entails the attainment of suboptimal returns. Only if it is assumed that participation in activities in both the villages and other areas is a necessity can this mobility be said to be operating to maximize returns from inputs of time and labour; clearly such an assumption is no longer valid for a significant proportion of islanders, and a strategy of maximum participation in a range of activities consistent with minimum risk goes far to explain the persistence of circular migration. Brookfield (1970) has argued that in the game against an uncertain world islanders retain the security of the traditional system while making use of opportunities for gaining access to some perceived benefits of the foreign commercial systems. In this way they can minimize risk while utilizing a growing range of options for activity. In the islands, where the 'cultural focus' of society rests on status as landowners, rather than proletarians, the persistent significance of the village as a centre of activity becomes intelligible. While access to land still depends on

225

membership of a social group and continuing interest in village affairs, involvement in rural-based activities remains important for most New Hebrideans. Maintaining this contact may not necessitate lengthy periods of residence in the village, but some circulation between their places of employment and the village is generally considered essential.

The pattern of circular migration, by which this range of options is kept open, continues to change as longer periods are spent in residence outside the village, and a further phase in the circular mobility transition is undoubtedly in its incipient stage. A pattern of circulation based on permanent residence in the town rather than the village is evolving for an, as yet, small number of New Hebrideans. Ward's (1970, 20) statement, in the context of migration to towns in Papua and New Guinea, that 'the evidence suggests that to talk of temporary urban dwellers is largely wishful thinking' will, no doubt, become increasingly relevant in the New Hebrides. But a desire to participate in social and economic activities based in rural as well as urban areas continues, and will continue for some time yet, to influence the mobility patterns of a majority of New Hebrideans. Permanent migration has occurred from certain islands that are isolated from the major centres of economic development, or on which ecological conditions such as volcanic activity or land shortage have made village residence unattractive. In a similar way, some of the small proportion of New Hebrideans (5 per cent of the economically active population in 1967) in professional or administrative occupations have become permanent residents at locations away from their traditional communities. For most islanders, however, rural communities remain their permanent homes to be used as bases from which to participate in a variety of economic activities: subsistence gardening, cash cropping, local business ventures and wage employment.

The fact that most migrants do not regard the town as their permanent home has important policy implications in a territory with a limited potential to absorb or finance a major growth in urban populations. If scarce resources are committed in large part to improving conditions (housing, recreation, public amenities) in towns and thereby creating major disparities in types of accommodation and amenities between town and country, then increasing numbers will obviously want to settle in towns. To a certain extent the process of rural–urban drift is inevitable; but policies designed

226

to encourage this seem pointless if urban unemployment is likely to become a major problem. The complex question of the kinds of policies which will make residence in rural areas as attractive as that in the towns cannot be considered here. But it seems reasonable to assume that village residence could remain acceptable in areas where people have access to land and relatively good contact, through air and shipping services, with the town. In this context the question of the economic and social implications of a continuing high rate of labour circulation, both for the village society and for the employer, should be more closely examined.

There is also an urgent need for more intensive research into the attitudes islanders have towards village life after a lengthy period of residence in the town. In this study emphasis has been on the significance of the village as a place of residence because New Hebrideans have indicated, through their mobility experiences, that it is their permanent home. But attitudes are changing, especially for the young New Hebrideans receiving their education in towns and being trained for employment in an urban environment. A true separation of urban from rural populations has thus far not occurred, because of circular migration. The near future, however, is likely to see both permanent urban and permanent rural populations, with a large bi-local population moving between village and town.

9 Islanders at sea

Change, and the maritime economies of the Pacific

Alastair Couper

At the time of first colonial contact in the Pacific, in the late eighteenth century, the sea-transport systems of the European nations were only beginning to draw significantly ahead of those of many societies that they were about to overwhelm. Especially by their methods of navigation (Lewis, 1964; 1971), the Pacific islanders had evolved great ability to move about freely within their island-strewn ocean. They drew heavily on the natural resources of the sea and, through trade, had access to a range of products from numerous islands in their own archipelagos and beyond. There was a complex spatial component in the economies of the pre-colonial Pacific, demanding considerable planning, extensive geographical knowledge and a relatively high degree of technological skill. These attributes of island culture should have been a basis for successful participation in the maritime trade which arose from the introduced commercial economy. But this happened only partially, and with a record of failures that far outran the successes. Islanders who were demonstrably able to marshal and distribute resources over large areas in the indigenous economy have often failed in their efforts to participate in modern trading systems and in the operation of commercial fisheries. The reasons for this failure have not been adequately examined, and this essay is an attempt to offer some explanations.

THE INDIGENOUS SYSTEM OF MARITIME TRADE

Trade and exchange

In the indigenous trading systems which flourished in the Pacific, goods would move between islands on the basis of trade links between persons. They followed what Hocart (1952) has termed the 'path of feasts and gifts'. Particularly during life crisis occasions such as births, deaths and marriages, exchanges were conducted between island communities related through kin links. Such movements meshed into larger and more formal exchanges, such as the *solevu* transactions of Fiji or the highly formalized 'Kula Ring' of the islands east of Papua (Malinowski, 1922). But at the same time these reciprocal transfers of goods also had an economic function (Brookfield with Hart, 1971); they often evolved on the basis of resource comple-mentarity, so that a dry island might trade yams against the taro of a wet island, or an island people might trade fish against the sago and vegetables of the mainlanders on larger land bodies. They also supported some industrial specialization, most notably in the pottery trade of the Amphlett Islands of eastern Papua, which fed pots into the multifunctional Kula trade. Other islands rich in tall timber might make and trade canoes over long distances. Trade emphasized peace and cohesion in social intercourse, but at the same time it also served utilitarian ends and permitted a fair degree of regional specialization to evolve.

The complementary nature of inter-island trade is well exemplified in many of the exchanges carried out in Fiji. On the high island of Kabara, for example, were to be found carvers of wooden kava bowls and canoe builders, while on some of the low dry islands with poor soils the heavy *nokonoko* wood (*Casuarina equisetifolia*) grew, and was utilized for the making of war clubs. The best matting sails, and other products of pandanus, came from the drier islands. Pottery was made from clays on the volcanic high islands. Salt was made in the tidal mangrove flats along the coastal fringes of some of the main islands. A few of the volcanic islands were renowned as great yam and taro producers. Barkcloth was made in a very great number of islands in Fiji and Tonga, but there were regional specialities of colour and design, and mats also had certain regional characteristics of size, thickness andfunction. Some of the more important links seem to have been between the rich food-growing islands and the less fertile islands whose people specialized in the production of craft goods; between regions inadequately endowed with timber and those which had plenty; and between sea and land peoples every-where (Couper, 1968).

The local specializations which evolved were not simply deter-mined either by the distribution of resources or by kinship ties. Highly-localized village products and crafts appear to have been preserved deliberately in order to give a community the opportunity to enter into trade connections with many places. Communities thereby acquired comparative advantages in the production of particular goods and services, and these gained in value by virtue of their scarcity. There are a few notable studies of these relationships in Fiji. Quain (1948) describes how the village of Nakoroko in Vanua Levu specialized in mat-making at the expense of all else, and would depend on trade to maintain a balanced supply of goods. Hocart (1952) has traced in some detail the complicated flow of goods through the northern areas of Fiji. The people of Vuna, for example, concentrated on the production of lamp-black, trading this for nets made in Taveuni, and in turn exchanging nets for barkcloth from Lau. Thomson (1929) analyses the special trading relationships of the people of Fulaga and Ogea in the southern Lau islands, who obtained much of their food from the richer northern islands through the island of Moce, which acted as an entrepôt at the junction of sea routes. More recently, Sahlins (1962) has brilliantly delineated the interaction in Moala of ecology, kinship and the ethics of inter-island trade. When a community was called upon to trade with another it could not readily refuse, so that islanders were able to exchange their craft products for foodstuffs in distant islands at times of natural catastrophe, such as hurricane and drought. In this way, the quasi-oligopolistic nature of production in particular goods was transformed through the social pressure to conduct trade into a system of mutual support.

Similar trading systems, integrated over wide areas, can be traced in many parts of the Pacific, especially in the New Guinea area* where populations of several hundred thousand were organized into a loose interdependence by institutionalized trade. Strategically-located communities—for example, the Siassi people located in the centre of the Vitiaz Strait between New Guinea and New Britain (Harding, 1967)—could make a living largely by voyaging for trade. Even within a single island there were village specializations. On Bougainville, for example, the village of Malasang traded blackpots over the whole northern half of the island. Commonly, goods would move directly from one village to another with which the first had kinship ties, then onward to a third and a fourth village which had no direct connection with the first. Trade could therefore proceed in the absence of a wide area of peace. The village nodes, and the

* See also Hughes (this volume).

linkages between villages, thus formed complex trading networks (Brookfield with Hart, 1971).

Some trading networks had an 'international' character, linking areas distinct from one another in culture. The Tongans, for example, traded with Fiji and Samoa on a bilateral basis. They brought timber articles to Fiji, obtained scarlet bird plumes and exchanged these with the Samoans for fine mats (Williams, 1870). The people of the low islands of the Tuamotu archipelago voyaged to the high islands of the Society group for stone axes; the Trobriand islanders traded with the people of Muria, north of New Guinea, for axe-heads; the Yap islanders sailed to Palau for calcite discs (Krieger, 1943).

The 'sea people'

While participation in trade was very widespread among the Pacific populations, the greater costs and risks of longer-distance commerce called forth specialists—'sea people' whose activity was voyaging and whose skills in navigation and seamanship were widely valued. Wilkes (1845) noted that the Levukans carried most of the sea-borne trade in the eastern and northern regions of the Fijian archipelago. Women often sailed with the men on long voyages, and it was they who conducted the trade in the villages (Williams, 1870). The navigators who commanded the vessels occupied a special place in the social hierarchies of the islands, as did other men who were renowned for their skill as canoe-builders. Such men took great pride in their craftmanship, as well they might, for many Pacific island vessels engaged in long-distance voyaging reached a considerable size, and some carried more than a hundred seamen. The Fijian *drua*, for example, had on the average greater overall dimensions than Captain Cook's brig *Endeavour*. The building of such ships was a major enterprise, calling on much time and effort, and was accompanied by many rituals and feasts.

The sea thus played a major part in the ecology of Pacific island communities, and extensive voyaging supported a complex system of trading and island or village specialization. With the introduction of European commerce and technology the spatial dimensions of the island economies were changed. At first, when foreign ships voyaged through the islands, the effect may merely have been to support and expand the indigenous trading activity. However, as soon as port towns became established as points of contact between the island economies and international trade, simple and more open radial networks focusing on the ports began quickly to replace the closely-woven island networks. This alteration in spatial relationships reflected the changes which came about in the economic basis of island life. In place of the inter-island kinship and social nexus structuring and containing the utilitarian function of trade, the new radial systems directly expressed the cash nexus forged between commercial centres and the island hinterlands.

Pacific islanders entered the new commercial system and adopted much of the new technology. But even in the fields of transport and fisheries, in which they were particularly experienced, they frequently failed to come to terms with the new pattern of relationships. Their failures were in part due to a lack of understanding of the commercial system and in part to the activities of the expatriate entrepreneurs themselves. But they continued to use the new technology and system of spatial linkages in a traditional way. The failure of many of their shipping enterprises, for example, seems largely to have been due to retention of the concept of a ship as a medium of social contact, rather than as a link in the commercial economy.

ISLANDERS IN THE ISLAND TRADE

The ship in the socio-economic system

For a period after the beginning of colonial development, ship-owning seemed to be emerging as a form of commercial enterprise in which islanders could successfully hold their own. Early in the nineteenth century, the island monarchs Kamehameha I of Hawaii and Pomare II of Tahiti purchased European-style vessels, sailed them under their respective flags, and financed voyages to America, Australia and China; and R. L. Stevenson noted that the notorious King Timinok of Abemama in the Gilbert Islands owned several ships which sailed to New Zealand. His ships invariably returned from foreign voyages in debt owing to the 'world-enveloping dishonesty of the white man' (Stevenson, 1908, 275). Pomare, in particular, was dissatisfied with the terms of trade experienced in dealings with foreign merchants. He sought to monopolize the Tahitian pork trade with Sydney, and later also the arrowroot, coconut oil, sandalwood and pearly trades of his expanding empire. Shipping was a means to empire, to be achieved through the control of the trade resources of the archipelago (Gunson, 1969). Similarly

233

in Hawaii Kamehameha succeded in monopolizing the sandalwood trade within the group, and once even sent a trading expedition to the sandalwood areas in the New Hebrides.

Later in the century, Cook Islanders operated their own schooners for some years on voyages to Tahiti and New Zealand (Moss, 1891–3). However, most of these ships represented prestigious displays of wealth, and were frequently used to carry people and goods between islands with no cash transaction. Since the new ships had to be purchased with cash, much time and effort was expended on crop production for the purpose, and while early despots such as Kamehameha and Pomare could raise forced levies in order to achieve their ends, this ceased to be possible once effective political power had passed into foreign hands. When the dearly-bought vessels were operated uneconomically, the result was the impoverishment of local communities in both cash and subsistence sectors. It was reported from Fiji in the late nineteenth century that:

> oppression is frequently felt and privations endured by communities in providing the price of too large a vessel or of too many vessels. The raising of such monies necessitates the people's abstentions from the use of coconuts as food, and deprives them of the oil and clothes which under ordinary circumstances would be procured by the sale of copra. Growing food is often sold in order to raise money for this purpose. (Colony of Fiji, Commission on . . . native population, 1896, 49)

During the early part of the present century a veritable mania for ship-owning impoverished many communities in Samoa (Smith, 1916). The Cook Island court records contain many references to litigations for debts incurred by local ship-owning societies (House of Representatives, N.Z., Papers, 1888 onward). This history of failure and indebtedness has continued to the present day, even in circumstances in which enterprises are organized under modern Co-operative Society jurisdiction. Typical is the following statement in the 1960 annual report of the Registrar of Cooperative Societies for Fiji:

> Originally purchased to furnish transport for copra and store goods they (the vessels) have since become for all practical purposes the communal property of the related villages which keep them continually in use but seldom contribute adequately toward the expense of upkeep.

Enthusiasm for ships has not been dampened by financial failures, as I witnessed when attending the liquidation of the Tangitang Shipping Union on the island of Abiang in the Gilberts during 1964. Speaking of the Society's only remaining vessel, the Registrar of Co-operatives told the meeting that

> only the *Aritoba* is left and she is unseaworthy. All her timbers are rotten. If the ship is allowed to go to sea it will be at great risk to the people on board. The Society does not have the capital to get the repairs done, and it cannot get a loan as the vessel is too old. My advice is to sell; you could not sell it as a ship, but the parts would fetch some money. (A.D.C., field notes, 1964)

The first response of the meeting was to propose purchase of a new vessel, notwithstanding Abiang experiences of continuous financial failure in shipping enterprises. Ultimately they agreed to sell, and to liquidate the Society. But the sense of loss was palpable. No longer would it be possible to get on the island radio and whistle up the *Aritoba* from a distant part of the group when tobacco stocks were low on the island, or when people wished simply to make a casual trip without having to think too much about profit and loss. A similar fate threatened the *Ninsa* II belonging to the indigeneous New Ireland Transport Association in New Guinea. The Association had purchased the vessel amid great enthusiasm but after thousands of dollars had been lost by her indigenous management and shareholders she was handed over to a Chinese company to be operated under bareboat charter.

The problem is not an inability to master book-keeping. Some books relating to cargoes are in fact scrupulously kept. But these vessels fulfil a dual role: they have to serve the demands of both parts of a dual economy. In island life, a ship has a social as well as an economic function. In carrying cargoes, for example, inordinately small quantities are sometimes accepted for villages with which the master, or the crew, have kinship ties. The purchase of a vessel often involves the financial participation of from a dozen to a hundred people, or even the populace of a whole district; all feel that they have a call on its services, not paid for in a commercial way. During voyages the master and crew may socialize in villages for protracted periods, and the acceptance of such hospitality is an essential element of inter-island relationships.

The relationships between masters and crews on island vessels are themselves complex. A European-type crew structure has been imposed, with division of labour and chains of command that can conflict with social and kinship relations. Crews are sometimes composed of men who are all related to one another; the captain may be in command *de jure*, but the *de facto* authority may belong to the group as a whole. It has often been found by expatriate ship-owners that shipboard work schedules can be maintained only by the imposition of expatriate, or at least non-local captains. We thus have the situation that while many island-owned vessels fail com-mercially, the islanders can often get employment only as seamen or junior officers on expatriate-owned vessels trading among their own islands. When owned and operated by island people, the ship remains almost as much a social institution as it was in the pre-colonial period. Even though the structure of expatriate-owned shipping in inter-island trade is scarcely complex, highly capitalized or efficient when viewed by world standards, there remains a gulf in the funda-mental approach to ship operation which continues to separate the islanders from successful competition in a trade for which their whole history and culture would seem pre-eminently to qualify them.

The persistence of indigenous exchange

Social *mores* have changed far more slowly than has the economic basis of island society. With the growth of port towns, islanders from many parts of each archipelago have settled either temporarily or permanently in urban communities. Suva, for example, contains wage-earning Fijians drawn from every part of Fiji, and both within the town and in the suburban settlements groups have emerged based on the areas of origin of the migrants (Nayacakalou, 1968). These people still have most of their kin in their villages of origin, and may also have kin at other employment centres. Kin groups are thus much more dispersed spatially than in pre-colonial times and the concentration of people into the port towns creates the need for frequent social interaction between town and outer island; inter-action between outer islands, on the other hand, may have diminished.

The modern spatial linkages radiating from the port towns thus serve an extension of traditional exchange, using vessels in regular commercial service. The commodities have changed somewhat, but

Plate 14   The Pacific of dreams: coconut-planted islands in the Solomons, 1969.

Plate 15 (below)   The island Pacific: approach to Lakeba, Fiji, from the south on a fine trade-wind day, June 1973, with cumulus build-up over the island.

Plate 16 Change at sea: a traditional outrigger-dugout in the foreground; moored offshore is a dugout designed to be propelled by an outboard motor. Tikopian migrants at a settlement on plantation land, West Bay, Russell Islands, BSIP.

Plate 17 At the end of the line: loading copra, Solomon Islands, 1969.

Plate 18   Larger inter-island vessels: a group of outer-island ships ranging up to 200 tons at the small-ships wharf in Suva, Fiji, June 1973. Some vessels of this size also trade inter-territorially. They are, however, restricted to comparatively few harbours and reef-passages, and must often lie outside places accessible to smaller ships.

Plate 19   Island trader: the *Adi Lau* at Kabara, Fiji, June 1973. Small passenger-cargo vessels of this type, or even smaller, still provide the main service to many islands. The *Adi Lau* is at present the only vessel serving several outlying islands in the Fiji group on a regular basis.

Plate 20   The new Pacific: the search for new wealth—for someone. Australian workmen on an oil-drilling rig, Papua, 1969.

Plate 21   The new industrial economy: view from the manager's bungalow of labour lines housing male migrant workers—decidedly superior to structures of an earlier date, but basic. Lever's Pacific Timbers, Kolombangara, Solomon Islands, 1969.

Plate 22   Village in the forest, Bougainville, 1969.

Plate 23   The entry of international capital: low-loader about to commence the journey back to the coast from the Rio Tinto-Zinc development site, Panguna, Bougainville, 1969.

Plate 24 Development basic: pulping coffee beans by hand in a 'drum', Chimbu, 1960s.

Plate 25 (*below*) Dis-development: the remains of a hand-built coffee pulpery erected by community effort in 1964. The building and the machines have gone, and have not been replaced, but the fermenting and washing tanks remain useful for laundry purposes. The building in the background is a new medical aid post, built by the government. Taro plants at left. Chimbu, 1970.

Plate 26 The new Pacific is not beautiful. Auki, Malaita, Solomon Islands, in 1965. The market building is in the foreground, beyond it a line of houses and Chinese shops, while in the distance is a pre-urban village, one of a group built on artificial islands in the lagoon. (Telephoto lens.)

Plate 27 (below) Casualty of development. Investment in second-hand vehicles has absorbed large savings in many parts of the Pacific. Maintenance facilities are expensive and scarce; few owners understand the problems, and a majority of these vehicles come to an early end, broken down, cannibalized, and littering the roadsides of the islands.

Plate 28   Modern port-city: the port and central business district of Suva, from the hills north of the city, 1965.

this form of essentially non-commercial trade has become quite significant in Fiji, Tonga and New Guinea; as yet it has not been described elsewhere in the Pacific.

Two examples may illustrate the nature and problems of this adaptation of indigenous exchange to the new transport media. In October 1964 the schooner *Yatu Lau* sailed under charter from Suva to Lakeba island, carrying 49 passengers back to their home island after a visit to relatives employed at the Vatukoula gold mines. At Vatukoula they had presented mats, paper mulberry bark, taro, yams and coconut oil, and had received money in exchange, but as a gift rather than as payment. This money had been used in Suva to buy furniture, kerosene and cloth.

The second example had a tragic end, but it illustrates to rare effect the uneasy blend of old and new (Couper, 1967). In 1963 the church at Waitoga village on Nairai island was in need of repair, and a request was made to a Waitoga woman living in Suva. She contacted other relatives, and it was decided that a party of 28 should visit Nairai, each contributing a sum of money, some kerosene and cloth, and two whale's teeth as a traditional gift. In March 1964, the cutter *Kadavulevu* was charted from its Chinese owner, and the party—which had grown to 90 persons—set off to present an entirely traditional *solevu* to the people of Nairai. They carried kerosene, cloth, furniture and mats, in addition to $800 for the church.

The *Kadavulevu* arrived next day, and the *solevu* was formally presented, followed by feasts and dancing which went on most of the night. The day after, the Waitoga people arranged their return gift in large piles: it comprised 250 mats, two to three tons of yams and more of taro, 800 coconuts, 150 bottles of coconut oil, live pigs and chickens and sundry other goods. The presentation was made and loaded aboard: then feasting and dancing went on through a second night. Next afternoon the *Kadavulevu* sailed with its cargo, stocks of cooked food for consumption on the voyage, and about 100 people. During the night, the overloaded cutter capsized and sank in the Koro Sea: only two women and one boy survived.

In both these examples cash and shop-bought goods moved against traditional articles and foodstuffs. Vessels are quite often chartered for these purposes, but there are probably people travelling to make exchanges on almost every ship engaged in ordinary commercial service. It is difficult to evaluate the effects of this undercurrent of traditional exchange carried on below the mainstream of the

237

commercial flows. It is not easy even to separate the two, for men and women travelling to workplace or to home will use the opportunity to carry goods in either direction. People may bring some goods for gift and others for sale. In February 1965, for example, I recorded that a basketball team on the island of Ha'apai in Tonga was preparing to visit the island of Tongatapu for a competition; each of the Ha'apai visitors were to carry three mats and were expecting to receive in exchange gifts of tapa from the Tongatapu people (Couper, 1967). Similarly, the crewmen on the supply ship sailing from a lumber camp on Santa Isabel in the Solomon Islands to Honiara in March 1969 used the opportunity to carry sixteen live turtles, some for sale in the market, some for gift to their kinsmen at work in town who might in turn sell to others. Tikopians at work on plantations at West Bay in the Russell Islands loaded the regular monthly freighter with copra, then took passage with the ship to Honiara to stay with other Tikopians in town, some to get passage onward to their home island while others planned to return to the Russell Islands with goods bought in town (Brookfield, *pers. comm.*).

The dualism which we saw in ship operation is thus modified to some degree by the adaptation of introduced networks for social purposes, and the use of traditional forms of exchange to integrate the available resources of town and country. It is a costly integration, since goods move in units of bulk that can be handled by individuals; and it is also costly in other ways, since the non-commercial trade itself and the production for it absorb time and 'divert' surpluses into consumption rather than savings. There is undoubtedly pressure on those working and living in the 'modernized' sector of the island economies to accept and make traditional gifts, rather than to save or invest. Time spent in these activities has opportunity cost. But there are also social benefits, and an economic benefit in that participation in traditional exchanges and in the maintenance of kinship linkages provides a very real form of social insurance. No cost/benefit analysis could truly evaluate the balance of advantage to the individual. It would, however, be a mistake to judge this traffic in terms only of its effect on an externally-conceived process of 'development' or 'modernization'. The satisfactions are very tangible, and to the islanders they warrant all the planning, time and marshalling of resources which are necessary, even though these exceed substantially the demands of the ordinary run of commercial trade.

ISLANDERS AND THE MARITIME RESOURCE BASE

The exploitation of sea and reef

The separation of the Pacific islanders from the modern exploitation of the ocean fisheries is even more complete than their separation from the management of overseas trade. Yet here too the islanders had and still have a complex and flexible technology of fishing. Indigenous methods of exploiting the sea for food are many: they vary according to coastal, lagoon and reef conditions, weather and climate, alternative food sources and many local preferences. Netting, the use of weirs and traps, diving, spearing, noosing, rods, hand lines, lampara (lamp and lure) and trolling are all in use throughout the Pacific.

Fishing is rarely an individual matter in the Pacific, and different techniques and resources call forth groups of different composition. The gathering of molluscs and crustaceans on reef flats adjacent to the villages is done by groups of women who walk out over the reefs at low tide. Further out on the flats groups of women will catch fish by encircling them with a net. This inshore gathering of seafood is of immense importance, and a good piece of reef may be a more important resource to a village than its garden land. More distant from the village, canoe fishing by men takes place within the lagoon, along the reef slope on the seaward side and in the open sea. Among the reefs and within the shallow waters of the lagoon marine niches are known and exploited; out at sea there is extensive knowledge of the seasonality of runs of bonito and other species.

In many islands there is clear delimitation of areas of reef and lagoon within which particular communities have rights. Where the lagoons are large, this concept of *mare clausum* diminishes progressively away from the shores toward the centres of the lagoons. The open sea is generally regarded as free to all, and fishing extends seaward to a maximum distance generally determined by the perishability of the fish in hot tropical climates. Only turtles could be kept alive in captivity. The size of vessel and its motive power and the variability of wind and sea conditions thus affect the range, but there is very little indigenous fishing that extends beyond the limits of a day's trip out and home.

Indigenous fishing is therefore seldom a full-time occupation. The crew of a canoe may be made up of closely related people who fish together regularly, but usually they are cultivators as well as

239

fishermen, even on the dry coral islands of the southern Gilberts. Participants are thus seldom isolated from their village communities in the manner in which European fishermen became early habituated to living on their boats, and spending in the aggregate the larger part of their time away from home.

Seafood and shells were a major item in traditional trade, and one of very ancient provenance, for the archaeological record in central New Guinea shows marine shell fragments in material dated as early as 5,000 BC. Being scarce inland from the sea, and obtainable only through trade, shells most nearly of all goods acquired the value of money; even in coastal areas such as the Gazelle peninsula of New Britain, shells of restricted provenance were traded in to serve quite strictly monetary purposes. This use of shell has persisted: Cooper (1971) describes the activities of the Langalanga people of Malaita in the Solomons who still gather shell and produce shell money. He mentions the elaborate rituals and regulated diving seasons which acted to conserve the supply of shells in the indigenous economy. I was interested to note during field-work on Bougainville in 1972 that shell money from Malaita was still valued for special purposes and that it was occasionally brought to southern Bougain-ville by air travellers from the Solomons. Elsewhere in the Pacific, shell was sometimes used rather than stone for adze blades and weapons. As a foodstuff, sea foods could be traded only short dis-tances, but the more durable products of the sea were a resource to areas far removed from the ocean.

Commercialization of marine products

Almost the earliest of the products of the Pacific region to enter commerce was the smoked and dried meat of the *bêche-de-mer* which, together with turtle shell, pearls and a few land products were sought by Macassans and other Indonesians as far east as Torres Strait, and by Chinese on the north coast of West Irian possibly several centuries before the first voyagers entered the area (Hughes, 1971). With the development of European trading with China in the early nineteenth century, *bêche-de-mer* and shell buyers quickly extended their activities eastward into the Pacific, and collection of the large molluscs, trochus and *burgau* (*Turbo marmoratus*), have continued from time to time as commercial products of the reefs. Collected by villagers and sold to traders, these large mother-of-pearl-bearing shells are still exploited in small quantity in the Melanesian islands though the resources are much depleted.

More important were the localized resources of mother-of-pearl-bearing oysters, found especially in the reefs of Torres Strait and in the atoll lagoons of the Tuamotus and northern Cooks. The former have from the first been exploited by outsiders—Indonesians and then Japanese—with minimal local participation, but the latter led to an exploitation in which islanders participated very largely. The pearl and mother-of-pearl trade in the Tuamotus began with great rapacity early in the nineteenth century, and for a period in the 1820s came to be monopolized by a vassal of Pomare (Gunson, 1969). This measure of indigenous management waned, and foreign entre-preneurs took over the control. There was a late burst of activity between 1945 and 1965, when the business was described in detail by Doumenge (1966a). Almost a thousand divers were employed during the 1962 season by some 30 entrepreneurs, mostly Chinese but including a few Tahitians, who sold to ten exporters, all Chinese or European, who also financed the enterprise. Accompanied by their families, divers and their assistants would be taken from their villages to temporary camps where they lived during the season entirely maintained by the entrepreneur. Payments was by results, and a violent and dangerous season would produce sufficient income to live the remainder of the year, either in the home village or in Papeete. From exhaustion of resources the business is now almost dead, and the net result for the Tuamotuans, from a business in which most participated only at the lowest level, hardly shows much credit balance.

This pattern of rapacious commercialization seems now to be paralleled by a massive development of commercial fishing, mainly for tuna and bonito, in which the islanders have almost no share at all.* Most of this large-scale fishery is carried out by Japanese vessels, usually with Korean or Formosan crews. These entered the south Pacific in the early 1950s. At first they used fleets of catchers linked to mother ships, which stored the catches, processed the fish and transported the catch to Japanese and North American markets.

* There was also a much earlier phase of destructive hunting for equatorial whales in the nineteenth century, in which American ships dominated. The islanders provided food to the whalers and clashed with them frequently, but there was no direct participation. The business came to end when the resource was exhausted.

This method proved very costly, and shore bases were sought in the middle 1950s in American Samoa (in association with an American cannery), Fiji, the New Hebrides and New Caledonia. The latter quickly failed because of high labour costs, but the others continued successfully. The scale of the fishery has expanded rapidly since the mid-1960s, so that a new shore base was established in the Solomons in 1970 and in 1972 negotiations were in hand for bases in New Guinea and additional bases in the New Hebrides. In 1971 frozen fish from the New Hebrides base became the principal 'domestic export' by value of that territory, and there are increasing fears that the resource will quickly be overfished if the present rate of expansion is sustained.

The commercial vessels are usually between 100 and 200 tons. They carry 16 to 20 fishermen and fish continuously at sea for four to six weeks before landing their catch at a base, re-storing and returning to sea. The catch is frozen or canned at base, then shipped to overseas markets. The part played by Pacific islanders in all this is minimal. They have no share in the sea business, and only a little employment is generated in and around the freezing plants; most of the skilled work is done by Japanese. If in fact the business turns out to be of short term, as the search for quick profits depletes the reserves of fish, islanders may be fortunate: declining catches will soon lower profit levels and lead to the closure of at least some shore bases. Were the fisheries a significant employer this would result in further problems of unemployment in the port towns.

Attempts have been made to train Pacific islanders for the commercial fishing industry with a view to creation of local fleets. Not only would this provide cash incomes in what is regarded as a traditional way of life, but it would also give the islands a more powerful say in the discussions on the use and conservation of the marine resources of their own region. Moreover, since every Pacific territory is a substantial importer of frozen and canned fish, there would be a tangible benefit from import substitution.

But only very mixed success has attended efforts to develop commercial fishery based on the islands. Superficially at least, the most successful innovation has been the creation of a lagoon and coastal fishery in the Tuamotus to supply the large urban fish market in Papeete. It is organized entirely on a basis of small operating units, some based on Papeete and others in the Tuamotus. But the entrepreneurs are mixed-race and Chinese businessmen in

Papeete: only the fishermen are Polynesians (Doumenge, 1966a). Attempts to train crews for deep-sea fishing have not been productive. Doumenge (1966b) recounts the Samoan experience. A training vessel was bought, and made ten voyages. 160 Samoans were recruited, but 65 of these made only one trip, and only one seaman went out nine times to qualify as a fisherman. Attempts continue along these lines, however. In 1970 Tonga bought a Japanese long-liner to experiment with deep-sea fishing, their previous experiment with the tuna vessel *Teiko* having come to grief when in 1960 the boat was lost with all hands.

Reasons for the failure of many commercial fishing enterprises are not hard to seek. Long-liners range over a wide area and spend several weeks at sea. Conditions on board are hard, and working, sleeping and eating are strictly regulated. Even the Japanese boats cannot get Japanese crewmen to work under these conditions and use mainly Koreans. Islanders, with a reasonable affluence at home, tend to reject the hardships and the social deprivations due to long absences. Other approaches seem more hopeful. In Western Samoa a major attempt is being made to introduce village-based deep-sea fishing using catamarans. In the Cook Islands there is a programme to re-equip locally-based fishing using small powered boats. But the problem of organization and marketing remains, and the French Polynesian experience provides an example of the concentration of entrepreneurship in non-islander hands. Islanders who fish also have gardens, coconut groves and a rich local life. If they wish, they can go away to work for periods, but come home at will. Commercial organization demands specialization, and while it might have been possible to organize an industry which provides centralized services with the participation of the island fishermen, this has not yet been done. It demands a concept of development more closely attuned to the realities of island social life than the imported forms of capitalist enterprise, with a bias toward large-scale operation, that have prevailed in the Pacific in this century. Meanwhile, the oceanic resources are being exploited at an accelerating rate by foreign enterprise, threatening to deprive the islanders of large sources of supply and potential wealth that have been theirs for centuries.

NEW APPROACHES

The state as entrepreneur

Dissatisfaction with a client status toward foreign-owned shipping

243

has grown appreciably in recent years as freight rates have risen sharply, while the continuity of many services has become uncertain. Sea-transport costs represent a major element in the economies of the Pacific islands, but because of the inelasticity of demand for primary products the ocean-freight rates are seldom passed on to buyers of Pacific exports; they tend rather to be deducted from the returns to Pacific producers. On the other hand a proportion of the freight rates on imports to the Pacific is passed on to Pacific island consumers as higher prices. This is one reason why Pacific island territories want their own ships to conduct foreign trade. The introduction of national shipping will not reduce the freight costs but may ensure that payments are made to the domestic economy rather than to overseas companies. Other factors which are encouraging investment in shipping by Pacific governments arise from the fact that foreign shipping companies have been seeking more modern vessels; some companies have withdrawn altogether from the island trade; others have been taken over by large multimodal transport corporations to whom the island trade will not be a major enterprise. Many of the familiar vessels have ceased to operate, and the introduction of new cargo-handling systems has created pressure to concentrate trade into fewer ports. This has given the opportunity, and made necessary, the introduction of Pacific vessels engaged in carrying transhipments. The decision to purchase ships for regional and overseas trade has also been reinforced by the view that national ships can generate trade, represent countervailing power to the conferences, provide an outlet for labour and give prestige to a nation. The value of a national shipping line is, however, difficult to gauge. It could represent a drain on the balance of payments if the ships, their fuels, spare parts and senior officers are drawn from overseas; and docking and repair costs are also incurred there. If for prestige reasons too many Pacific territories purchase vessels this will undoubtedly occur. What is required is renewed territorial specialization with the provision of overseas services by a few territories, the co-ordination of schedules and the concentration of major repair facilities and training at certain places, thereby obtaining the economies of scale required for successful shipping enterprises; in other words a regional plan for Pacific shipping.

As far back as 1956 it was proposed to organize a regional shipping line in the south Pacific, with the sponsorship of governments. Though high-level committees have met to make proposals, no action has been taken, but meanwhile three of the island countries have embarked on shipping enterprises of their own. Tonga first ventured into shipping in the 1950s as a side activity of the Copra Board. Collection of copra was soon supplemented by carriage of other goods and passengers within Tonga, and also to and from Suva in competition with a New Zealand-run service. Finding this successful, the Copra Board then obtained a larger vessel which they operated at first on a quasi-tramp basis, then initiated a regular run from Samoa through Tonga and Fiji to Australia. Other developments have followed, and the Tonga Shipping Line now has some ten ships, operating within the group, to Fiji and internationally. The line is carefully nurtured as a national enterprise and has generated considerable enthusiasm; it is crewed almost wholly by Tongans, though there is still a shortage of qualified officers.

The example has not gone unobserved. The Cook Islands, now an autonomous dependency of New Zealand, have since 1960 been served principally by a New Zealand government vessel following failure to attract an adequate commercial service. In 1970 the Cook Island government began chartering its own vessels to operate the New Zealand service.*

A more significant enterprise for the future, however, is the establishment of the Nauru Pacific Line with four large ocean-going vessels to operate services based on Nauru, but also widely in the Pacific. Recruiting crews in Tonga and elsewhere, this deliberate attempt to diversify the narrow economic base of the newly independent Republic of Nauru is quite specifically put forward in the Pacific as a regional enterprise, worthy of regional support, and in opposition to foreign dominance. It is highly probable that these examples of state entrepreneurship in shipping will be emulated by

* The first charter was of a vessel owned by a New Zealander who successfully set up a small internal shipping line in the New Hebrides in the early 1960s, operating aged vessels within the waters of a territory with no survey requirements. Despite some rather disastrous losses, he was able to branch out in the development of linkages with Fiji, and to widen his business territorially. The vessel chartered to the Cooks government had a Fijian crew: as such it was declared 'black' by New Zealand waterside workers, who demanded replacement with a New Zealand crew and only reluctantly accepted a Cook Island crew instead. This problem of union policy against 'coloured' labour in Australia and New Zealand has bedevilled other attempts to localize the crews of vessels operating between these countries and the Pacific islands, leading to some short-term dislocation of services, and in the longer run encouraging the entry of firms registered abroad, rather than in Australia and New Zealand, into the island trade.

others, for the state, able to call on national pride, and to separate management sufficiently from purely local interests to make possible 'efficient' operation, seems by far the most promising instrument with which to re-establish an island presence in the island trade; but careful planning is required to avoid over-tonnaging and duplication.

CONCLUSION

But it would be folly to suppose that simply because they are working for the state, Pacific islanders will suddenly make the behavioural jump that they have declined to make while working for enterprises under expatriate control or dominance. A ship is a social system, a moving world in miniature that reflects and perhaps exaggerates the larger social system from which it is drawn. The social system of European shipping has evolved through a long period during which the grossest of inequality between commanders and commanded was sustained by harsh discipline, demanding unquestioning obedience to orders on pain of brutal punishment. Reflecting the changes in the wider society, the inequality and discipline have diminished greatly, but the social gulf between 'officers' and 'men' still remains. The Pacific island ship knew nothing of this history; the social gulf was imposed and always resented, and islander officers have never become copies of their European teachers. Mutiny as a crime, though its most famous instance occurred in this ocean, is an alien concept to islander crews. Even in Polynesia, where there was a structure of ranking and hereditary title, the tyranny of power emerged only after European contact. Earlier principles of balance of power, and authority gained through trust, often extended to the degree of sanctioning the slaying or expulsion of an oppressor.

Notwithstanding a very widespread wish to participate in the benefits of the new economy, islanders have been able to retain an attachment to the security of their own social system by possession of a base in what has been called the 'subsistence affluence' of their own well-provided gardens and reefs. From this base they have been ready enough to venture abroad, on labour contracts, as crews, as pearl divers, or simply as speculative migrants. But their view of such ventures has generally been short-term; the long term has remained appropriate only to planning within the known securities of the traditional economy. Selectively, they have adopted many of the innovations into their own way of life, and among these innovations have been new types of ships. But when they have attempted to

246

exploit the adopted technology and political economy in order to gain control of some part of the new system, they have all too often found their path blocked, for control of all the *foci* of power in the new system was already in alien hands. While they have achieved some measure of adaptation to this situation, and even utilized it to advantage, the effect has been that large areas of maritime enterprise have remained open only to foreign entrepreneurs. Attempts are now being made to recapture part of this sector, but it is important that such attempts grow out of the cultural and economic preferences of Pacific islanders and do not slavishly follow external forms of organization.

The assumption that Pacific islanders have failed in commercial shipping and trade because of the complications of such enterprises will not stand up to examination: indigenous trading systems were far more complex, and even large-scale organization—by the standards of the day—was achieved by the early Pacific monarchs before their states were overwhelmed by power from without and undermined by disease, depopulation and despair from within. The islanders are still faced with overwhelming external power, but at least more and more of them are now masters in their own house. From this new base they may be able to regain some control over their maritime environment and its activities, but in order to do this successfully in competition with external operators, they will have to find ways of mobilizing their own social systems into units that are internally viable and externally strong. For the future of these island countries, few areas of enterprise are more important than the maritime sector, for without an effective presence on the sea they are but fragments of land and people in a foreign ocean. As well as developing merchant fleets, islanders must seek measures to safeguard their inshore and offshore environment through suitable regulations and the adoption of types of fishing vessels and gear which are in line with their traditions, and they should critically re-appraise the technology from outside which has allied to it traditions based on a rapacious attitude to maritime resources. It is in turn essential for those who wish to help Pacific island communities, to acknowledge that they will achieve far more by seeking first an understanding of the social organization and social geography of Pacific seafaring than by continuing with policies based on Eurocentric ideas of the sea business, and virtually ignoring the wealth of the maritime heritage of the Pacific islanders.

247

10 Terminal development

From tribalism to peasantry

Diana Howlett

A great surge of writing on the theme of modernization appeared during the 1960s. The concept of modernization is generally postulated as a process of transition from a 'traditional' society toward one characterized by such systemic features as high GNP and *per capita* income, self-sustaining growth, high mass-consumption, and a well-developed and diverse sectoral structure. Notwithstanding some recent criticisms of this approach (e.g. Bernstein, 1971), including some within geography (Connell, 1971; Brookfield, 1973), a belief— or faith—still seems to prevail that, as two-thirds of the world's territory and peoples move out of colonialism and into nationalism, 'modernization' will somehow ensue. This faith is bolstered by evidence derived from growth indicators at the national scale, such as the GNP and *per capita* income, which have improved in many countries—although not always by international achievement—and which can optimistically be seen capable of further advance. However, too little regard has been paid to the condition of the people, especially in rural areas. Where people are seen to have passed from tribalism to peasantry it is widely assumed that this is a transitional phase, and a cause for optimism.

Few have perceived that such a 'transition' might become a permanent state, though Frank (1967) has argued cogently that capitalist development actively creates a condition of underdevelopment, and Geertz (1963) has shown how a development process under external impetus can, under certain conditions, become diverted into the cul-de-sac of 'agricultural involution'. The wider faith which drives most writers on development sweeps aside these objections as either 'leftist' or else peculiarities not capable of generalization: the direction is always forward. But this is not inevitable, as a growing number of writers are now demonstrating—especially from Latin America, rarely yet from the Pacific. I argue here that the condition of peasantry is not always or even often transitional to some higher and more 'developed' state. Peasantries most frequently represent a terminal stage of development.

The faith, and a heresy

What, briefly, is the record of the faith that modernization is universally attainable? One need cite only a few examples, for example Rosenstein-Rodan's 'big push' (1963), Lewis's 'capital formation' (1955), Nurkse's 'balanced growth' (1958), Hirschman's 'unbalanced growth' (1958), Rostow's 'stages of growth' (1960), McClelland's 'n-achievement' (1961), Dix's 'modernization crises' (1967), Tinbergen's 'planned change' (1967), Hunter's 'new path' (1969), among many more. A few, notably Myrdal (1957), recognize the possibility of 'cumulative causation' which has negative as well as positive effects, but the mass of opinion is overwhelmingly optimistic.* Whether proffering approaches or strategies, all believe that progress will come, the backward world can move forward to modernity, and ultimately 'the rich and poor nations' will come closer to parity.

Insufficiently noticed has been another possibility. That is the likelihood that a society in a so-called transitional stage toward modernization may be unable to advance further. Such a society may reach a certain level of growth, but be unable to achieve that additional progress which results in development. In these societies, which are generally identified as peasantries, modernization has been arrested.

No consensus has yet evolved among social scientists in regard to the systemic features of peasant society. Prompted perhaps by Kroeber's (1948) characterization of peasantries as 'part-societies with part-cultures', and Lewis's (1959) concept of 'the culture of poverty', anthropologists and more recently economists have centred much research on specifically cultural attributes and value systems of peasantries. Unfortunately the result has more often amounted to explaining away, rather than explaining, the essential nature of peasant society.†

* These citations are but a few examples of this persistent belief. For an excellent analysis of the outstanding literature, see Ilchman and Uphoff (1969) and Higgins (1968).

† See, for example, Rogers (1969a) and G. Castillo (1969).

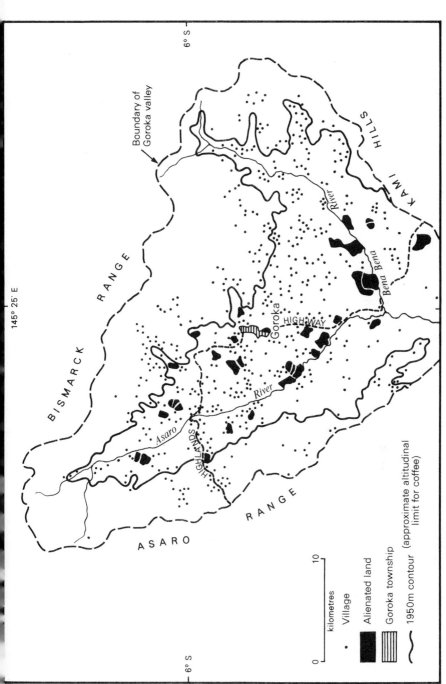

Fig. 10.1 The Goroka Valley, Papua New Guinea, showing villages, alienated land, the bounding watershed, Goroka town and the main road (for location, see Fig. 1.2, p. 23)

Peasant societies may be thought of as situated somewhere along a continuum between the self-subsisting, non-monetized type of economy which is usually termed 'primitive' or 'tribal', and the modern commercial, exchanged-orientated economy (Halpern and Brode, 1967, 65). Thus, whereas tribal socities are essentially self-contained, closed systems, peasant communities are incorporated into larger political units, and as a rule part of their production enters national or international commodity markets. The relative economic equivalence between members of a tribe, or between the components of a tribally-organized population, is replaced by a hierarchical system in which the proto-peasant communities are at the base of the socio-economic pyramid. Certain aspects of peasant society, for example social organization and cultural practice, remain tribal or traditional, while others, such as the monetization of land, labour and produce, reflect the modern system (Dalton, 1967, 156).

Whether one wishes to label peasantries as partial, incomplete, or dual systems is immaterial. What matters is the widely-accepted belief that this condition is transitory. But once a peasantry is established, its structural characteristics tend to remain static. This prospect, it seems to me, will characterize much of the Third World—of which I offer a case.

The Goroka Valley

The traditional social economy of this valley high in the central cordillera of Papua New Guinea was tribal. As such, it displayed the common features of tribal organizations: small communities; their prevailing self-sufficiency; a low level of technology; the rule of custom rather than law; the preoccupation with food supply; the intermeshing of economic activity with social organization; the direct exchange of services and surpluses among groups or their members on the principle of reciprocity; the absence of hiring or selling of land and labour; and a division of labour based on age and sex groups.

Living within the 1,200km² of the valley for unknown generations have been some eighty neolithic tribes, members of three language groups. The total population at first contact by Europeans—white Australians in this context—was perhaps 50,000. Each tribe comprised a cluster of patrilineal clans and their contiguous territories. The political structure was atomistic; no large enduring unions of tribes were ever achieved, although temporary alliances were

252

frequently formed in response to the changing balance of power. These were aggressive people: security, defence and raiding were unremitting concerns.

No class system or hereditary system of leadership developed among the Gorokans. Leadership in the clans and tribes in each generation was achieved through a combination of fighting prowess, outstanding personality, and the accumulation of wealth for its appropriate disposition. As these *desiderata* were ephemeral (except for a few items of wealth, such as shell), so was power itself. In principle, power and status might be attained by any male aspirant. Those who achieved power could only maintain their status by constant competition with clansmen. Thus the valley had a society in which individual enterprise was encouraged, but in which leadership, once established, tended to be all the more forcefully imposed in that its bases were so fragile. As Salisbury (1964, 225) observes, 'although the indigenous ideology was one of democratic equality and competition, the empirical situation . . . was one of serial despotism'.

The Goroka Valley provides a felicitous environment for subsistence cultivation, the main economic activity of the tribes. Lying some 1,500–1,600m above sea-level, and a few degrees south of the equator, the valley has a comfortable, even invigorating, climate of the *tierra templada* type. Looking across the valley from the higher northern ranges, one has an impression of openness, of a wide, undulating plain sloping gently from the foothills to the south. Descent into the valley floor, however, proves the 'plain' to be considerably dissected by streams, gullies and low ridges. Forests remain only at the higher elevations where cultivation is precluded; elsewhere the valley is a patchwork of dark green fields interspersed with wider stretches of fallow land under *Imperata* and other tropical grasses. In the fallow land one may see evidence of past cultivation in the occasional trees, remnant banana groves, and cane-grass hedges. The villages of low circular houses with their conical thatched roofs are rarely visible, but their location is usually indicated by the planted groves of *casuarina* trees and bamboo clumps, and by the radiating networks of narrow paths linking each village to its gardens and to neighbouring villages.

Land was the Gorokans' most permanent and valuable possession, but it is unlikely that it was regarded as such, access to land being a *sine qua non* for all families, and available to all. The hierarchy of land

253

rights was inseparable from the system of social organization. At the tribal level, the only territorial right held in common by all members was the right to graze pigs on uncultivated land. The basic economic rights were vested in the clans, whose male members had a variety of cultivation and use rights as individuals, and sometimes also through their lineages and subclan groups, although no land was 'owned' outright below the clan level. Usufructuary rights were commonly granted to agnates and affinal kin, and reciprocity was implicit.

Few clan territories are so extensive that they cannot be traversed from end to end on foot within an hour or two, yet no real land shortage seems to have developed prior to contact. The first explorers noted that wide tracts in the valley floor were unoccupied and uncultivated. Although the destruction of villages and gardens was a regular concomitant of inter-tribal warfare, it would not seem that such fighting was initiated by actual land shortage. Rather it is likely that disputes over women and pigs, and the real or imputed practice of sorcery, aroused the almost ritual hostilities which broke out every dry season. The acquisition of enemy territory was usually temporary, and the destruction of property largely a matter of prestige. The location of so many villages in the apparently less favourable foothills rather than the valley floor would suggest that considerations of defence were more urgent than land needs.*

The cultivator in a primitive subsistence community must meet three basic objectives: he must produce sufficient food to sustain life for himself and his dependants, provide a maintenance fund to assure continued production, and an additional fund to meet his ceremonial obligations, essential to the participation in social relations (Wolf, 1966). The Gorokans, favoured by local environmental conditions, met these imperatives traditionally with little difficulty.

The elevation of this tropical territory gives the highlanders important advantages over lowland cultivators. Soil deterioration is retarded, weed growth less prolific, insect pests and crop predators

* The freezing of the territorial *status quo* of the tribes as administrative control was established meant that although the less protected tracts of land were made safe, access to them by traditional means was outlawed. Land alienated to Europeans lies largely in the valley floor, often on land which both the Administration and the tribes have regarded as 'no-man's-land'. On the other hand, the desire of villagers to grow cash crops, together with the scarcity of suitable land for this purpose in the hilly regions, has created contemporary problems of land shortage.

fewer. Rainfall, although distinctly seasonal, is adequate to maintain a twelve-month growing season over all but the south-eastern sector of the valley. Land was cultivated with a considerable degree of ecological awareness and skill, although indigenous technology did not include the use of fertilizers, irrigation, or terracing. The agricultural potential of different classes of land was known and cultivation cycles adjusted accordingly, the rotation of field plots varying according to terrain, soil type, drainage conditions and population density within the locality.

Each family was basically an independent production unit within the clan, although major operations such as clearing, fencing and house construction were often occasions for wider co-operation. In addition to the staple, sweet potato, a wide range of secondary crops was grown, some for food, and others for fibres, dyes, building material, decoration, or reputed medicinal or magical qualities. The preparation of good gardens was painstaking, and made more so as only neolithic artifacts were available. All fallow vegetation was completely removed, the earth tilled into loose soil and (for sweet potato) mounded, the plots subdivided by narrow access paths and fenced against inroads by pigs. In these tasks men and women had separate and well-defined roles, with the heavier initial work of clearing falling to the men, and subsequent operations being carried out mainly by women. Women were in fact the main agents of food production, as the men devoted much time to clan and tribal affairs, guard duty, and actual fighting. The production and maintenance of tools and weapons, and the construction and maintenance of houses and fences, was also in the male province. Very little food was obtained by either hunting or gathering, but men hunted small animals and birds in the high forested mountains for decorative fur and plumes. Trade was minimal, confined mainly to salt, certain woods for bows and arrows, and shell, one of the traditional valuables.

All men, many women, and even children owned pigs and valued them highly as the principal item of wealth; but pigs were not husbanded in the sense that land was cultivated. They were commonly allowed free range in the fallow land, occasionally fed or sheltered in the women's houses. Pig distribution, exchange, and consumption were an integral part of ceremonial events, such as bride payments and tribal or intertribal festivals, and thus pigs may be considered as belonging almost exclusively to the Gorokan's ceremonial fund.

Over most of the valley, food shortage and crop failure were virtually unknown. On the contrary, surpluses were readily produced (exigencies of tribal conflict permitting), and, lacking the technical means for their storage, accumulation, or conversion, the greater concern was for the appropriate disposition of such food surpluses. These were transferred also to the ceremonial fund, and their planning, production and distribution not only provided much of the zest of life for clan members, but also an opportunity by which individual as well as clan prestige might be achieved.

The Gorokans, like all highlanders, take pride in display and in manifesting conspicuous consumption. Large festivals between tribes or clans were held every two or three years to honour alliances and commemorate past victories, or to reciprocate former hospitality. Marriages united not only the individuals concerned but also their respective clans and were the occasion for feasts and exchanges. Initiation ceremonies of adolescent boys were corporate activities for clan members, and for individuals there were a number of lesser or personal commitments which made demands on the ceremonial fund.

Development policy and programme in the Goroka Valley

The Goroka tribesmen and many thousands like them within the highlands remained for long unknown to the succession of European colonizers, traders, and missionaries who had been transforming the life of New Guinea's coastal people since the nineteenth century. Not until 1930 were the mountain sanctuaries finally penetrated, initially by Australian gold prospectors, soon after by the Administration's patrol officers and by missionaries.

During World War II the Japanese invasion of Papua New Guinea's north coast brought troops to the highlands but no actual fighting, devastation, or dislocation of the people. For Goroka this was a period of road and airfield construction, and the wider extension of administrative control. Such activity brought a virtual end to overt tribal hostility. By the close of the 1940s conditions in the valley were considered sufficiently peaceful to permit the first Australian settlers to lease land for the development of coffee plantations.

From the perspective of the Australian Administration the years 1930–50 were a preparatory period for the valley, during which a rudimentary infrastructure of administration and communications was established. The period of 'real' economic development is dated from the early 1950s, based on policies formulated at two levels which may be called the 'general' and the 'local', respectively.

The general policy, formulated for the whole territory in the early postwar years, comprised two interlocking aspects (Howlett, 1969). For the indigenous community, the policy was based on the principle of minimal dislocation of the people, both in a geographic and in a cultural sense. Incorporated into the policy until quite recently have been concepts such as 'uniform development' and 'gradualism'.

As economic change, this policy has amounted to modernization via the addition of commercial crops to the traditional base of subsistence foodstuffs. Annual Reports reiterate that

> Economic policy is aimed at developing the resources of the Territory to provide a rising standard of living for the whole population and to create a viable economy. . . . The advancement of indigenous agriculture to improve food supplies, to bring about a more efficient use of village land and increase the production of cash crops, is given a high priority by the Administering Authority. . . . Because of the nature and distribution of the Territory's resources it is clear that, in the short term at least, agriculture must continue to provide the basic income required for the economic advancement of most of the people. (Annual Report, 1967/68, 55–6)

The policy also recognized an obligation to the European settlers in the colony:

> The economic problems involve more than native enterprise. We also encourage European settlement. It is only by European settlement, with the investment, the technical skill and the managerial ability that comes with it, that we will get the rapid results which are essential. . . . Needing Australian settlement we have to recognize that the settler needs security, a fair return for his effort and his customary rights. (Hasluck, 1958, 108)

Within the valley, development was based on this general prescription. Within a few years of European settlement, however, it was further identified by the concept of 'partnership,'* a notion derived

---

* 'Partnership' between Europeans and New Guineans was a concept . . . to justify a seemingly anachronistic attempt to establish a plantation system in the fertile but heavily populated valleys of the Highlands. The settlers were after land . . . and a chance to develop a profitable coffee industry. In return they

257

from central Africa. Given the times and conditions under which contact and development occurred, and certain culture traits of the Gorokans, 'partnership' in the initial years of European settlement was probably appropriate. The postwar years were first brought into plantation production. The Gorokans themselves were eager to have Europeans settle among them. Further, the Goroka Valley has a very much denser population than is characteristic of the lowlands, which meant that the plantation lands could not be alienated in extensive contiguous tracts but perforce had to be scattered in suitable parcels throughout the valley. This circumstance obliged the new settler, before roads were widely constructed through the valley, to maintain good relations with his indigenous neighbours, as he depended on them for many goods and services. Again in contrast to the lowlands, estates around Goroka were small—they were developed by owner-operators, usually undercapitalized, but in any case the optimal size for such holdings is only 40 hectares or so. Thus it would seem that in applying the term 'partnership' to distinguish the course of European development around Goroka, a virtue was made out of necessity.*

In essence, therefore, economic development in the valley was to proceed with the production of commercial crops by both Europeans and the Gorokans, the two races operating on their own lands but co-operating as widely as possible in the provision and exchange of goods and services.

Having briefly summarized the traditional socio-economic structure in the valley, and the relevant aspects of economic development policy, we are now in a position to analyse how these sets of factors have interacted over the last 20 years. This analysis will emphasize the impact of general and local development policies on the indigenous economic structure; but inevitably traditional social and political institutions have been altered also.

For the neolithic tribesmen, the initial years of culture contact, this is, from 1930 to the mid-1940s, were undoubtedly traumatic in many ways. During this period much of the rationale of traditional

---

offered the Highlanders, their 'partners', an opportunity to enter the market economy—as plantation workers, as suppliers of vegetables to plantations, and as coffee growers themselves.' (Finney, 1970, 117).

* Be that as it may, the ideal of partnership between the races seems to have become incorporated into a Territory-wide model by the Minister of Territories towards the end of the 1950s: see Howlett, 1965, 53.

life disintegrated. This was particularly true for the males: with the prohibition of tribal fighting all concomitant political and many social activities were rendered baseless—the planning and strategy of campaigns, negotiations with allied groups, guard duty, manufacture of weapons, victory celebrations. Even adolescent boys were affected, as missionaries attempted to discontinue their initiation ceremonies.

But one aspect of traditional culture survived the early years of contact, and would seem to have been as intimately related to developments in the valley as any of the achievements which the Administration and settlers have claimed. It was observed above that the Gorokans were eager to have Europeans settle among them, and that Gorokans esteemed men in their own society who were able to produce and control the various forms of traditional wealth. In a culture without hereditary chiefs, such entrepreneurs were the 'big men,' the men of power and prestige. The European's range of material goods and his command of resources were thus perceived as indicative of great power. The bearers of the new culture and its manifestations were widely admired and emulated.*

When development proceeds from direct and continuous contact with a new culture, as happened in the valley with the growth of a town and the settlement of a European community, rather than by the indirect diffusion of culture traits, the consequences are both widespread and intense. The introduction of money and its related institutions in particular produces rapid and far-reaching changes in traditional life. The erstwhile tribesman is faced with new demands on his customary production for subsistence, maintenance and ceremonial funds. Now subject to an alien elite, he is obliged to contribute taxes, which must be paid in cash rather than in goods or services, as soon as feasible. The cultivator is thus constrained to devote part of his resources of land and labour or both to produce some commodity for sale. In addition, after exposure to the technology and material goods of the dominant culture, he will inevitably acquire other needs for money, and so hope to provide for what may be termed an 'aspiration fund'.

As the former tribesman is thus incorporated into a new economic system, he must either apply new values to land and labour or exercise a double standard (compounded of the traditional and the new values) in relation to them. Whether he produces agricultural

* See also Newman (1965), and Finney (1970).

commodities for sale on distant markets or becomes a wage labourer outside his village, his control over the factors of production and distribution and the economic rewards for his labours become tenuous, and may be lost altogether. Traditionally, goods and services were exchanged in equivalencies and without intermediaries; but in the new situation exchange ratios are asymmetrical and determined by external authorities and conditions (Wolf, 1966, 9).

The desire to maintain production of a ceremonial fund, the need to meet taxes or other forms of 'rent', and the hope of producing an aspiration fund, have together often placed emerging peasantries in a situation of intolerable conflict. For the Gorokans, however, the potential conflict inherent in this situation was largely, albeit unconsciously, avoided when the new administration outlawed tribal warfare. By this expedient, much of the rationale for the ceremonial fund was simply removed. Further, the burden of maintaining subsistence was greatly eased by the replacement of stone tools with steel implements. Taxes, to be paid in cash, were not immediately imposed by the new authorities, although labour requirements were made for the construction and maintenance of roads. Thus we may deduce that Gorokans readily adopted the new crops and other items from the inventory of European culture not only because, as already observed, they admired the achievement and exercise of all forms of power, but because these innovations also filled the new vacuum in tribal life, at least for the men.

Furthermore, the Goroka people do not conform to the old stereotype which holds that tribal communities are conservative, tradition-bound, wary of change, with a limited time perspective which inhibits future-planning. On the contrary, field-work among them revealed a number of instances involving long-range plans, and a ready acceptance of innovation, characteristics which were as operative before European contact as they have been since. The Gorokans were inherently disposed to many of the behaviour patterns and values by which 'modern economic man' is often characterized.

Commercial agriculture in the valley was begun around 1950 by the first of a community of some 30 European planters. Several years later, in 1953–4, cash cropping for export was introduced in the villages. The active promotion of the new crops by agricultural extension officers, coupled with the demonstration effect of the scattered plantations and the proclivity of the tribesmen toward the new culture, produced an enthusiastic response to the programme.

Inevitably there were problems in the short term, but it is the long-term problems inherent in tropical crop production which are at issue here. Village-grown cash crops are of two kinds: those which can be produced in the short term or in small areas, interfering minimally with traditional patterns of land tenure and use, such as vegetables, groundnuts, passionfruit and tobacco; and coffee, which as a perennial and a tree crop has no counterparts in the traditional complex. Those crops in the first category provide the grower with problems of marketing rather than production; coffee poses problems in both areas; the scale of production is relevant to all cash crops.

The marketing of short-term crops in the 1950s depended totally on the small but growing European community. Lack of organizational and transportation facilities restricted the market for foodstuffs to local outlets such as the town of Goroka or nearby plantations where demand, even for the staple crops produced in the valley, was slow to grow. As late as 1960, stores in Goroka stocked canned sweet potato from the United States, and other vegetables air-freighted from southern Australia. Yet at least 90 per cent of the cultivated land in the valley was under sweet potatoes, and many vegetables were grown in villages bordering the township. Since that time a regular produce market at Goroka has become of considerable size, yet the demand is still local, and very little fruit and vegetable produce reaches consumers outside the valley. Marketing remains of limited economic significance, though the several produce markets held weekly in the valley are important social occasions, widely attended by villagers despite frequent failure to make a rewarding sale.

The other short-term crops, tobacco, groundnuts and passionfruit, require local processing for eventual shipment to distant markets. Although there is a sufficient domestic demand for tobacco, other crops must be disposed of outside Papua New Guinea. Much goes to Australia, where it must compete against local production in protected markets. With no guarantee of outlets or stable prices, the production of these crops has suffered varying fortunes. They rapidly became a relatively minor part of the local economy, although in recent years attempts have been made by agricultural officers to revive them. However, such production requires a considerable investment of time and labour for its uncertain rewards, and tribal values persist to the extent that many of the short-term crops are

261

considered 'women's crops' and as such undignified for male producers.

Coffee is by far the most important of the commercial crops, both by planted area and by value. Gorokans now produce more than 12 per cent of the country's coffee (Finney, 1970, 1,929). Some of the prestige of this crop obviously derives from the fact that the European plantations are almost exclusively devoted to it, and no Europeans have engaged in other crop production except occasionally as a sideline. Village production of coffee is fraught with problems not immediately apparent to the producer, and if apparent, not readily solved. Among them are the long-term commitment of land (up to 30 years for coffee) at the expense of subsistence types of land use; customary patterns of inheritance, with the likelihood of subdivision of plantings among heirs; the difficulty of maintaining quality controls and yields; disposal of the harvests; and price fluctuations on international markets. Such issues affect most tropical smallholders and need not be elaborated. What is critical here is the nature of the local solutions.

Many of the problems of the economic development programme arise from the fact that intrinsically it consisted of a 'once-and-for-all' input of a narrow range of crops. The policy contained no options for additional or alternative crops, and no alternatives to commercial agriculture which could be pursued locally.* With regard to coffee, the initial promotion and extension work were carefully planned and carried out: attention was paid to site selection, planting techniques, the size of coffee groves, and local collection of the crop. When the first planting phase ended in 1955, the local Department of Agriculture stressed the consolidation of existing holdings to bring them up to a minimum size of about 0·2 hectares of some 300 trees. But it was impossible to supervise planting in every village, and enthusiasm for the scheme resulted in much spontaneous planting in small, scattered plots, often on the insecure basis of usufruct. By the end of the 1950s falling prices and the difficulty of marketing the country's coffee obliged agricultural officers to discourage further planting. But they had no alternatives to offer, and the villagers, ignorant of the exigencies of international supply and demand in agricultural commodities, reduced but did not halt their coffee planting.

A watershed in the implementation of the development programme had been reached by about 1960. The decade of the 1950s had been

* See below p. 269.

a period of experimentation, of trial and error in the valley, not only for its villagers but also for those Europeans responsible for introducing a new economic system. By the end of the decade some indication of future trends and disparities was discernible.

A handful of Gorokans had established fairly large coffee plantings by village standards; they were about one-fifth the size of the European operations. These were men who had achieved wealth and power in their clans by traditional means, and such assets as they possessed were converted into access to clan land and to contributions of clan labour. They also had the advantage of association with, or proximity to, local planters from whom they learned husbandry methods. Finally, they benefited from the higher coffee prices of the first harvests, and from a shrewd understanding of the use of money.

However, for most of the villagers living in localities where coffee growing was environmentally feasible, the small size of their coffee groves, inattention to new management methods, the inadvertent problems of land tenure and fluctuating prices meant that coffee production did not provide the anticipated rewards, either financially or socially. For others again, living above the altitudinal limit (approximately 1,950m) for coffee, this crop was uncultivable. No other equivalent cash crops were available, but the scarcity of land restricted any type of commercial agriculture in these more mountainous regions which had previously been refuge areas. It was evident in these communities at least that 'uniform development' based on a single cash crop was out of the question.

In the meantime, the 'local' policy of partnership had undergone fundamental changes by about 1960. As mentioned, circumstances in the valley militated against the acquisition of large areas of land for plantation development or the settlement of a sizeable community of planters. In the early instances of land alienation the prospective settler was known to the villagers from whom he sought land, having been an administrative officer, prospector, pilot, or trader. Negotiations over land acquisition were made on a personal and informal basis, with the anticipation of advantages and rewards for each party, and ratified by the Administration after the fact of the transaction. Most of the estates were acquired in this way; but after 1954, when about 75 per cent of their combined area had been alienated, official policy on land alienation became much more cautious and was applied more formally. Only two further planta-

263

tions, and some minor extensions to existing properties, were made available subsequently.

The foundations for partnership were laid, but not maintained. Most of the estates were operated by men with no previous experience of coffee production—or indeed any form of plantation agriculture—and with inadequate capital to bring their land into full production. The costs of establishing the plantation, the period of several years before a return can be realized, and the later decline in prices meant that a number of the original settlers were unable to continue production. In less than ten years after the first settlement, over a third of the plantations had changed hands, and another five were either on the market or about to be (Howlett 1962, 222). Individual owner-operators were gradually replaced by corporate ownership with hired management, here as elsewhere in the tropics under similar circumstances.

In the process, the ideals of partnership became temporarily defunct. The personal relations which typified the first years of European settlement broke down; the new owners or managers were resented by the villagers who now had less to gain and less to offer. In particular, the improvement of roads allowed the Europeans to be more independent of their Gorokan neighbours. The villagers, as well as their lands, became alienated.

One final aspect of development policy remains to be considered. As stated earlier, the Administration has always subscribed to the policy of fostering European enterprise, a policy which has had many rewards, both for the economy generally and less tangibly as a stimulus to the economic efforts of the indigenous communities. A central provision of official policy in regard to development by Europeans was the assurance of native labour for their enterprises.

Gorokans entered wage employment on a large scale, but for a brief period only, after 1950, when the Highlands Labour Scheme was instituted. After the war a heavy demand emerged for labour to assist in the reconstruction and further development of coastal districts. The recently-pacified highlands contained a potential labour force of many ·thousands of men. The Scheme, with head-quarters in Goroka, regulated the recruitment and conditions of employment of highlanders for plantation labour in other districts.

Initially, the Scheme enjoyed enthusiastic participation by the Gorokans. It is rare to find a clan in the valley from which none of the men has been a migrant labourer. The early momentum was

264

soon lost, however. Disaffection with the regular, monotonous tasks of plantation production and the unaccustomed climate and diet were partly responsible; the newly-created opportunities to grow cash crops on their own lands reinforced the Gorokans' distaste for coastal employment. Even where coffee could not be grown, men rarely engaged for more than one or two terms as migrant labourers. With the beginning of local plantation development, there were employment opportunities within the more congenial and familiar surroundings of the valley.

Such employment opportunities decreased within a few years. The Goroka planters preferred to hire labourers from other parts of the highlands. The reasons for this development are varied, and include the high risk of frequent absenteeism of local labourers to attend clan affairs; the feeling of many planters, whether of the first or second 'generation,' that they would be involved in wider commitments and demands than those usual between employer and employees—for example, that the traditions of reciprocity in the clans would be applied unequally to them; and the fact that men from other parts of the highlands were considered less 'sophisticated' than the Gorokans, and therefore more tractable, and cheaper, as workers.

Thus, by the end of Goroka's first 'development decade', those villagers who were able to do so concentrated their efforts on their own coffee production, other crops being considered inadequate or unacceptable income generators. For those who could not, employment opportunities were basically limited to migrant labour.

Subsequent developments in the valley's economic situation have involved changes of degree and direction, still substantially based on the coffee economy. The new directions were largely unilateral responses by the Gorokans, although a new 'input' of general policy relating to political development had significant economic ramifications, and a new version of the local policy of partnership also influenced Gorokan economic activity in the 1960s.

Rather different conditions applied in the 1960s to those having land on which coffee could be grown, and those others, almost all at higher altitude, who lacked such resources. Expertise in coffee cultivation gradually improved among the former so that their production base became more secure, and at least the periodic low prices did not mean economic catastrophe. Village women continued the traditional subsistence production to assure food supply and the

265

maintenance fund, and gained some income from vegetable marketing. Cash earnings were thus additional to the survival budget, though some cash was now essential at even the most minimal level for the purchase of steel knives and axes. Those unable to grow coffee had to be content with lower aspirations. Their cash-earning opportunities are far more limited, and derive mainly from joining the unskilled workforce, either locally or in coastal regions and towns. Some are able to grow coffee on borrowed land at lower altitudes; however, conflicts often arise over such borrowed land, and its tenancy remains insecure. There has also been a continued drain of absenteeism to the coastal towns.

Perhaps the most apparent difference during the 1960s, compared with the previous decade, was the increasing mobilization of cash resources by the villagers, and the use of cash in new ways. While the estimated *per capita* income of Gorokans is small, it had increased significantly during the 1960s, from about $2·50 early in the decade (Fisk, 1962, 36) to $10 by the mid-1960s and $20 by 1968–9 (Finney, 1969, 14, 21). A large part of the money acquired in the early years was spent on tools, items of processed food, clothing and adornment. The bride price became partially monetized (at highly-inflated rates), and cash entered into transactions involving the exchange of pigs. A number of villages communally purchased small coffee-processing machines, although by 1960 only one Gorokan had been able to buy a motor vehicle and even bicycles were rarely owned. Considerable amounts of money also circulated in gambling games until playing cards were banned throughout the country. However, much money was simply hoarded, buried or hidden in the villages. Some was put into savings accounts in Goroka's two banks.* It must be admitted that the cost of goods in some stores, and the poor quality of goods in others, scarcely encouraged free spending.

During recent years, however, cash resources have been utilized differently and circulated much more widely. Few individuals have the resources to approximate European levels of income, but many village and clan groups do. And almost all Gorokans still aspire to possess European status symbols and to emulate their economic

* For example, in 1960 about 2,900 Gorokans had savings accounts, with deposits totalling almost $80,000. In 1964 one local bank held over $46,000 in more than 1,800 village accounts; the other bank was unable to provide a breakdown for Goroka alone, but for the highlands as a whole held over $300,000 in 9,932 village accounts.

practices. In the achievement of these aspirations, Gorokans have had several 'models', both traditional and modern. First, traditional *mores* have been invoked, in particular the obligations of co-operation and mutual assistance which devolve on kinsmen and the custom of being guided by clan 'big men'. Secondly, an important development was the establishment by the Administration of local government councils throughout the valley between late 1958 and 1962. The primary function of the councils was to broaden the base of political allegiance beyond the tribe and to provide experience in the procedures of democratic administration and organization. However the councils, with the tax revenues they commanded and the guidance of Administration personnel, soon demonstrated the economic power of modern corporate activity. They were able to purchase trucks, tractors and implements to be hired out for passenger service, freight haulage, and land preparation. The councils also contracted periodically for the collection and sale of local produce such as foodstuffs and firewood, thus providing a service which had long been needed by both villagers and Europeans.

The third way was that of partnership, which reappeared in a limited fashion and for a different purpose. With private European guidance and management, and overwhelmingly Gorokan investment, two coffee-buying and processing concerns were established early in the 1960s, and a third in 1965 (Finney, 1969; Fairbairn, 1969).

The indigenous customs of pooling resources—in this case, cash— as needed and of following the leadership of clan 'big men' were successfully applied. Money was contributed in many clans and used to purchase vehicles or to construct and stock small roadside stores. By 1969 Gorokans owned between 70 and 80 vehicles and several hundred small stores (Finney, 1969, 18,42). By these means, the villagers hoped to improve their socio-economic status *vis-à-vis* the European community. The investment by hundreds of small shareholders in the coffee factories was similarly motivated.*

But a great gap intervened between the villagers' aspirations and realization. Gorokans have virtually no knowledge or experience of modern management practice, and few opportunities to acquire any. Lacking awareness of the need for regular maintenance and nonpersonal management in their new ventures, business operations

---

* Finney (1969, 76) reports that the largest factory alone has over 2,000 Gorokan shareholders, and that in the first six weeks almost $50,000 was subscribed.

were jeopardized and have often failed. The upkeep and repair of vehicles were neglected, and the accident rate high; stores have often closed due to non-maintenance of stock and the demands of kinsmen for credit or gifts. The 'partnership' coffee factories, although not managed by Gorokans, have failed to live up to their expectations due to increasing competition from sole-European enterprises, and the dividends have also been lowered by the need for development capital in the initial years (Finney, 1969, 77–8).

Other ventures undertaken by Gorokans, or sponsored by the Administration, have been of minor economic importance so far. They have had either limited potential or insufficient time to make a wide impact; they include small roadside cafés, the Administration attempts to introduce commercial livestock raising of cattle and pigs, and such 'cottage' industries as wool-weaving and brick-making.

Thus the first decade was characterized by the Administration's programme to monetize the primary sector, and in the decade of the 1960s development has been the product of basically indigenous initiative in tertiary-sector enterprises. Throughout the whole period, none of the enterprises has experienced continuous progress; all have been attended by setbacks and uncertain success.

Implications of the development 'system'

Looking at the present situation and only slightly into the future, one may advance the following implications of the installed trends. I hope to demonstrate that the limitations and dilemmas of the existing economic base preclude the attainment of a truly modern society in the Goroka Valley.

Land availability limits the scale of agricultural enterprises. The rate of population growth is now increasing. Former demographic controls such as tribal warfare, female infanticide, and the absence of medical knowledge all kept the pre-contact rate of population growth low. But now these have been removed. Fisk considers that had the former rate of population growth been high, even sub-sistence production could not long have kept pace (Fisk, 1962, 32n.). More certainly, land resources are inadequate to support more than a handful of Gorokans at anything like the contemporary European standard of living. It was observed earlier that land alienation ceased after only 30 leases were made to European settlers; yet there are perhaps 12,000 Gorokan families in the valley. Since 1955, alienation policy has been based in part on a *per capita* land need of 1·3 hectares of arable land for villagers—scarcely adequate for more than smallholder production.

Some opportunity exists for further development in the primary sector, but the greatest potential lies in the improvement of subsistence, not commercial, production.* And the insecure foundation on which primary sector production rests is now jeopardized further by the strong possibility of changes in international marketing arrangements for the country's agricultural exports. In particular, Britain's entry into the European Economic Community might in time compromise many of the market preferences which Papua New Guinea's export commodities now enjoy under Commonwealth agreements; in addition, new tariffs will be imposed on its exports to Britain, which at present takes almost 30 per cent of the country's exports.† In these circumstances the prospect in the highlands for export crops other than coffee will be no better.

Little prospect can be foreseen for the establishment of a significant secondary sector, given the valley's location, an absence of industrial raw materials, and the lack of skilled manpower. At most, potential exists for a few light industries, such as the processing of foodstuffs. Much might still be done to build up the presently embryonic tertiary sector, at least to render current enterprises more balanced and efficient, and to provide a wider range of services.‡

A further dilemma related to land will confront the Gorokans. With the increasing use of money, the role of land as a factor of production will change. The sale of land between Gorokans has rarely occurred, and the formal conversion of land tenure is very recent and thus far minor. So far, no Gorokan is landless. However, a demand for individualization of tenure must be expected to arise and to grow. Without such security, the ownership of perennial crops may be imperilled, and land may not be used as loan collateral. Customary land tenure is widely considered an obstacle to development under Western systems. But it may be anticipated that if land

* For example, much could be done (but little has yet been attempted) to increase subsistence productivity by techniques of irrigation, the use of fertilisers, and perhaps make possible the commercial production of foodstuffs in locations where no other cash crops can be grown.

† Even if Papua New Guinea achieves Associate status with the EEC, there will be some loss of present advantages.

‡ The Second Five-year Plan (1968/9–1972/3) provides for increased manpower training in the Territory; but in Goroka the principal contribution will be made by a Teacher's College. Gorokans will have to go elsewhere for other skills.

269

becomes a commodity by the granting of individual title, some Gorokans will inevitably amass fairly large holdings. Others will become landless. Without skills, these will be obliged to resort to tenancy or migration. I have discussed elsewhere the limited potential for resettlement in the country as a whole (Howlett, 1967, 126ff.); and as most reserve land is in the coastal regions, resettlement there is unlikely to attract many highlanders.

Inherent in the rise of landlord and landless groups is the evolution of a class structure. Any trend toward social stratification in the past was inhibited because wealth and power were largely dissolved with the passage of each generation. But the use of money now provides a means whereby surplus production can be converted into forms which can be stored and accumulated. Wealth and the new forms of power can now be transmitted to succeeding generations. While the possibility of becoming and remaining wealthy holds obvious advantages for some, it also holds the seeds of real poverty, unknown in the past, for at least part of the population.*

There can be no doubt that the Administration's development programme has wrought valuable and positive changes in traditional life, particularly in social and political fields. The Gorokans have been provided with exciting new challenges to replace the fear of sorcery and the barbarism of warfare which were central preoccupations in the past. However, in societies exposed to structural transformation such change cannot be piecemeal or gradual, but must encompass the broadest possible range of inputs from the donor culture on a continuing basis (Mead, 1956; Myrdal, 1957; Dalton, 1967). If the modernization policy is examined in this light, it may be claimed to have been satisfactory only in the initial phases of contact and development. The first Europeans brought a wide range of new political, economic, technological and social innovations and either encouraged or enforced their adoption: the *pax Australiana*, a political hierarchy, new crops and tools, new forms of wealth, Christianity. On the whole these items and institutions were introduced in an atmosphere of good will and benignity.

But, lacking a broad base and important continuing additions, the policy has not proved viable after two decades. Consciously or

* Referring to national development, the former Minister for External Territories has said, 'We don't want an affluence for a few based on mendicancy of the whole. Without substantial economic self-reliance self-government or independence would be a mockery.' (Barnes, 1968a)

otherwise, the villagers have been given unrealistically high expectations of their prospects. They have been served the exemplar of European standards of living, and have been led to believe in the possibility of rapid progress. The policy has not, however, significantly provided for more than the first-contact generation of Gorokans, nor, among this generation, for the whole population. The status of women, for example, has remained virtually unchanged. Current development targets and policy continue to express the intentions and goals of earlier years:

> In Papua and New Guinea agriculture is the key to development of the economy as a whole in terms of export income, in terms of providing the subsistence farmer with the opportunity of entering into the cash economy, and in the achievement in due course of economic self-reliance. (Barnes, 1968b)

This case study has shown the fallacy of such premises. The Second Five-year Plan states that

> The (development) programme is based essentially on the agricultural industries and proposes rapid advances in plantings of slow-maturing tree crops. . . . *In view of marketing problems, no additional plantings of coffee are planned for the programme period.* (Department of External Territories, 1968) (My italics)

By this proviso, Gorokans are in effect excluded from the present development programme.

Avenues of social and political progress will rapidly become cul-de-sacs unless paralleled by economic progress. Gorokans are now reaching a threshold of frustration: they have virtually maximized such opportunities for modernization as were made possible under local conditions by the initial inputs, and have limited scope for further economic advancement. With the restricted local resources, a growing population, inadequacy of the general policy and the failure of the local policy, they will be forced to play an increasingly marginal role within the prevailing system.* Succeeding generations will no doubt bring to their efforts an unwelcome additional dimension, that of disillusionment born of past experience. If it is true, as many anthropologists and economists report, that peasants frequently

* Which, it must be recalled, still includes the Australian economy, not only that of Papua New Guinea.

are suspicious of authority and innovation, fatalistic, conceive of a limited good, lack future orientation, and so on, the Gorokan experience helps explain how such negative traits become established.

The Administration still appears to be sanguine about the achievements in the valley. This region is widely regarded among Europeans as one of the more advanced, progressive and promising districts of the country, its development all the more remarkable in that it proceeded so rapidly. The valley was the first of the highland regions to be opened up, was the testing ground for a number of agricultural innovations, and has held its momentum to maintain an economic lead over the other highland areas. But, as I have argued elsewhere, Australian policy has in no way breached New Guinea's vicious circle of conditions perpetuating underdevelopment (Howlett, 1969). The development policy has been both simplistic and isolationist. Although by no means an original form of development for dependent tropical territories, the defects and hazards of modernization based on a limited range of agricultural export commodities were widely apparent elsewhere in the tropical world by the mid-twentieth century, when the policy was implemented in the highlands. The optimistic official assessment of the Gorokans' progress is based presumably on their rapid adoption of innovation and the comparative prosperity which they now seemingly enjoy. As the foregoing discussion has shown, they have accepted a wide range of new practices and customs and invested their income in many items of production and consumption.

Such indicators are quite superficial and unrealistic measures of socio-economic wellbeing; projections based on them will be meaningless. The preceding analysis has also shown that such 'prosperity' as Gorokans have is not available to all, is based essentially on a single cash crop whose production capabilities have been reached for the present, and provides not only low but also uncertain incomes. There is a ceiling on virtually all factors of production in the valley, and the Gorokans are approaching this ceiling. Even labour, although plentiful, is of limited value while it remains unskilled. Viewed in this way, the events of the past 20 years may be considered as having created a different socio-economic structure, while maintaining an unaltered set of development needs. The population of the valley would seem to be tending toward the evolution of precisely that type of society which is itself such an obstacle to modernization—another peasantry.

272

The infinite pause*

The Territory of Papua New Guinea will soon attain sovereign status. Inevitably, a new nation will join the world community and inevitably also, it will fall among the ranks of those nations now termed underdeveloped. Whatever the political symbols of the new nation, the territory that is now Papua New Guinea will be a peasantry—and quite likely will remain so.

The argument has been developed here that the constraints of the environment, indigenous socio-economic characteristics and development policies do not permit the achievement of a modern society. On the contrary, the inevitable consequence will be the entrenchment of an economically unstable peasantry. In the terminology of outstanding Western commentary, the Goroka Valley (and to that extent, Papua New Guinea) will be for ever 'transitional'. The evidence suggests that this is a terminal stage, modernization arrested. In spite of themselves, the Gorokans will become peasants. An infinite pause will settle on the valley of Goroka.

* I am indebted to Arch Dotson, Professor of Government at Cornell University, for this felicitous phrase.

11   The dilemma of development

William C. Clarke

'. . . a low level of productivity is
the universal economic attribute
of underdevelopment . . .' Robert
Heilbronner (1963), 56

'In most natural ecosystems . . .
there tends to be no net production—in the human context of a
net harvest of materials.' R. O.
Slatyer (1969), 148

Not long ago while in New Guinea I fell into an evening's talk with
a government economist. Having long been a student of the menaces
of environmental over-exploitation and ungoverned population
growth, and having been recently exposed to some of the growing
flood of what seems to be validly alarmist literature on pollution,
I questioned him on the justification of the Australian Administration's explicit goal of raising the level of production in New Guinea
when such an increase would mean, among other things, a movement
of the New Guineans toward the rush to ruin that many believe to
characterize the economic behaviour of Western man. I found his
answers familiar and expected—as he found familiar my gloomy
prophecies. Neither of us gained ground in our continued debate on
the merits of population growth and the likelihood of environmental
impoverishment; but on pollution—about which he seemed to know
little—I felt I was close to convincing him of some potential dangers.
But optimism won the day. 'You must not be able to sleep well,' he
said; 'I couldn't bear to think things are that bad.' Then, cheerfully,
'Goodnight'.

This exchange was the final goad that impelled me to subject the readers of this essay to yet another piece of what a colleague has called 'ecological overkill'. I confess, despite my concern with the subject, that I too sometimes tire of the threats and terminology of the now immense literature and comment on imminent earthly calamities. And understandable are the expressions of hope by officials who belong to institutions whose purpose is to raise the level of production and consumption of peoples in a state of 'low-income equilibrium'. But the optimism of some advocates of development* seems so myopic and their opprobrious use of 'equilibrium' so ironic that one can only preach further on what is, aside from the associated problem of population growth, the most pressing problem in the changing Pacific or in any part of the industrially less-developed world: for all that world's peoples to achieve a standard of living (level of consumption) like that of the presently more industrialized regions is impossible; even to seek it may be suicidal. But the course is set, and many of the helmsmen—represented here by my optimistic economist—believe that to change direction is unthinkable. Obviously, there is no easy, nor perhaps any, solution to this dilemma of development. All I offer here is the distillation of one geographer's thoughts on some aspects of the dilemma in the world as a whole and the way it is manifested locally in Australian New Guinea, particularly the highlands, which have been exposed to western development for only a few decades at the most.

Men who see future glories for mankind are likely to be leaders, for their visions promise gain and give force to their promises. But their understanding can be faulty, as is the comprehension of the physical and biological world by those who advocate continued economic growth on the pattern of the past few centuries. Such a belief in growth has recently been compared with rain-dancing in some other societies (Wagar, 1970, 1,180).

From time to time, the correlation between rainfall and rain dancing must have been good enough to perpetuate the tradition. Similarly, the correlations between exploitation of the environment, growth, and progress were usually excellent in our recent past. So great have been the successes of our economic habits that they have become almost sacrosanct and are not to be challenged.

* I use 'development' in the restricted sense of economic growth.

276

That such works are written, together with the many others in a similar vein, is of course evidence that our economic habits are being challenged. But the reasons for the challenge need to be repeated to the limits of banality if there is a chance that such repetition will move any men, and particularly those in charge of planning and policy, to a new vision of the relations of man and earth. In this conversion, human geographers could and should play a major role, for geography is in part a science of the relations between man and earth—an ecology of man. As such, geographers are heirs to a long tradition of works on the interplay of human life and the land; but they have been curiously timid before the claims of some economists that only economics or economists' techniques of measurement provide the 'sophistication' (another wonderfully ironic word) necessary to interpret or guide the material exchanges between men and the world. In this relationship to economists, ecologically-minded geographers are in a position somewhat similar to that of evolutionary biologists *vis-à-vis* molecular biologists, some of whom have proclaimed themselves as the *real* biologists and scorned other approaches as sterile—a view that George Gaylord Simpson (1969, Chapter 1) has classed as a monomania derived in part from a desire to attain for the science of biology the indefinitely repeatable observations of the physical sciences, which '. . . usually deal with objects and events as invariant types, not as individuals with differing characteristics [and histories]'. That all life from the simplest form to the biosphere is inherently historical and variable does not, of course, make the molecular biologists' work worthless; their models of invariant behaviour at the molecular level are of immense value, but cannot serve to give total understanding of living systems, which enter the hierarchy of complexity at a higher level. To approach such understanding there must be a point of view that encompasses variation in type and change through time of both organism and environment—that is, an evolutionary outlook.

To return to geography and economics, it has been this same lack of a Darwinian framework that has led some economic geographers and economists of development to claim superior understanding from and, even more remarkably, invariant consistency for their models, even though these have to do with change in the world. Ecology, which unlike economics or molecular biology is Darwinian rather than Newtonian in philosophy, can never claim to generate unfailing control or to make predictions of invariant consistency, but

277

it can offer an understanding of the relation between the environment and the past and future trends of human economic systems, an understanding that is vital to what Macfarlane Burnet (1969, 366) has called '. . . the overriding imperative of our scientific age—the development of the Earth as a stable eco-system'. In this effort, present-day economic theory and techniques can be valuable but only subsidiary aids to ecology.

ECOLOGICAL TRUTHS AND ECONOMIC DEVELOPMENT

Having so elevated ecology or geography in its role as an ecology of man, it is in order to set out explicitly the modes of thought that support ecology's superordinate position for understanding and attempting to manage economic development. Such a presentation offers nothing new—simply what is considered a necessary restatement of certain ecological truths. I focus principally on matters of production rather than population, for a permanently-sustained increase in the numbers of people is no longer held to be a desirable goal except by the wilfully unreasonable.

Permanent growth is impossible

Because the goods from the ever expanding factories of the industrially-advanced parts of the world are now so obviously accompanied by what have felicitously been called 'bads', the notion has been forced into the general consciousness of the people of the more affluent nations that something is going wrong. But so far this willy-nilly beginning of what is hopefully a part of 'the impending emergence of ecological thought' (Cole, 1964) has had little effect on official economic policy.* It is true that some national leaders have acknowledged that problems exist, but none yet publicly question the dogma that the benefits of a sustained increase in productivity outweigh its 'disproducts'; we are told instead that we must redirect growth and seek something called 'balanced growth'. Although it is

* Happily, however, the theme is being discussed by some economists, who—much more than is true of biologists unless they be specialists on weapons—are likely to be listened to by political leaders. *The Costs of Economic Growth* by the economist E. J. Mishan (1969) thoroughly criticizes what he calls 'growthmania'. Boulding (1966; 1967) has also argued persuasively on the absurdity of permanently sustained growth, noting in a gentle understatement (1967, 44) that '. . . one has a certain alarming suspicion that a good deal of economic development is a by-product of mild mental ill-health.'

278

THE DILEMMA OF DEVELOPMENT

encouraging to hear expressed any official doubts about the prevailing conventional wisdom of economics, the idea that growth can continue permanently—no matter how balanced—is nonsense. Without bothering with the horror stories that are almost always part of descriptions of anything approaching exponential growth in our world, it is a matter of logic that the growth curve of all living systems must and always does level off (and then frequently even shows a decrease). With regard to human use of the land, the geographer Macinko (1965) has expressed this truth as 'the ecological law of space saturation'. Speaking more broadly, the economist Boulding (1966) and the biologist Cole (1958) have referred to earth as a spaceship or an 'ecosphere'—the master ecosystem that all earthly life, including man, occupies and into which there can be no significant imports other than the energy gained from the sun and the tides. Such a solitary system has limited supplies of materials, energy, and space. Long-sustained increase in numbers or output by any form of life within the system can only be considered as a disease that will somehow be self-limiting, or be slowed by an external restraint, or else lead to a breakdown of the system as such.

However, deluded by the glamour and immediate gain of the short-term growth of north Atlantic and now Japanese economic systems, many economists and political leaders across the world either feel they must evade this logic or else actually believe man to be exempt from physical and biological limits. Shelves and shelves of books have been written to suggest methods whereby the poorer nations can achieve 'take-off' or some less dramatic entry to sustained growth. The inevitably destructive process of positive feedback (a mechanism that accelerates a trend in one direction) that temporarily spurs the economic growth of the richer nations—and it would at present take an active policy of restraint to stop their growth—is praised as a 'self-stimulating spiral' or 'built-in accelerator'. Fortunately, in part because of the otherwise unfortunate increase in population, the poorer countries of today find it hard to start this process into action, and thus the limited supplies and capacity for pollution of spaceship earth are spared an even greater rise in the standard of consumption and excretion.* Still, a mixture of altruism, greed, political competition, search for trade benefits, pride, and need continue to motivate so strong a pressure for eco-

* For instance, the present-day *per capita* energy consumption in the U.S.A. is over four times larger than the world average (Fenner, 1969, 355).

279

nomic development that even to suggest a turn from the ideal meets resistance; but this does not lessen the feeling that the technological euphoria and political 'realism' with which advocates of development often flail their pessimistic opponents are reminiscent of the outlook of the boosters of the *Titanic*.

Man's 'conquest of nature' is not a one-way process

'Biology tells us that the transaction is always circular, always a
mutual feedback.' Paul Shepard
(1969), 1

Because man is part of an organism/environment system, the inter-actionist truth follows that when man acts on the environment, a reaction, not always expected, moves back toward man. Whatever we do to control or direct nature affects us in turn. Further, from an ecological point of view it can be said that economic growth and technical advance do not always give man greater freedom from his environment; instead, they create new environments often more restrictive than before. Consider, for instance, the gradient of technical achievement in means of travel from foot to rocket ship: how free the first, how incredibly hemmed in by requirements and restrictions the last. It is just the unique manipulative ability of man that makes especially significant for him the interplay of influences between organism and environment. Washburn (1960) has extended the ability to our prehuman ancestors, arguing that it was the making and using of tools by man-apes that made man into the creature he is. Oakes Ames (1939, 11) notes for pre-agricultural man, 'Man merely evolved with his food plants and they satisfied his needs because *he had to become adapted to them*' (his italics). Darlington (1969, 75) carries on to neolithic man, observing that the ancestors of our crop plants were '. . . changed into new plants no longer capable of surviving in nature but fitted only to survive under conditions which man had learnt to create for them. They were dependent on the cultivator. And the cultivator, of course, was dependent on them.' For our present age Dubos (1970, 221–2) writes on the same theme with a somewhat different emphasis.

Science enables technology to do almost anything, but there is a painful discrepancy between what man aims for and what he gets. He sprays pesticides to get rid of mosquitoes and weeds, but he thereby kills birds, fishes, and flowering trees. He drives long distances to recapture the purity of nature, but he poisons the air along the way. He eliminates food shortages through scientific agriculture, but creates thereby new patterns of diseases caused by overnutrition. He synthesises drugs to treat many kinds of physical or mental disorders, but finds that new illnesses commonly result from the use of these very drugs. He builds machines to escape from physical work, but the more efficient the machines, the more exacting the constraints they impose on his life.

The whole matter is well summed up with four words from Emerson: 'My cow milks me.'

There are several ways in which this general interactionist truth relates specifically to economic development. To begin with, production means pollution. The industrially-advanced economies not only produce and consume, they excrete. Increased production means increased excretion—that is to say, pollution. The immediate way to reduce aggregate pollution is to reduce production. Thus, even if the problem of the acquisition of unlimited energy and materials were solved, the problem of their dissolution would remain. And yet one of America's leading economists can say: 'We need expansion to fulfill our nation's aspirations. In a fully employed, high-growth economy you have a better chance to free public and private resources to fight the battle of land, air, water and noise pollution than in a low-growth economy.'*

Another way in which economic development is tied to the interconnectivity within the human ecosystem is that all production results in the destruction of something else. Production means impoverishment, the breaking-down and using-up, the spreading-out of previously concentrated materials—technically, the creation of entropy. We cannot live without so creating entropy, but to keep in mind that we are doing so will lessen the pride we feel for our technological executions. Darlington (1969, 673) has written:

> . . . every new source from which man has increased his power on the earth has been used to diminish the prospects of his successors. All his progress has been made at the expense of damage to his environment which he cannot repair and could not foresee. Surely this is the most practical of all the lessons of history.

* The quotation is Walter Heller's, given in *Time*, 2 March 1970. For a more detailed optimistic view, by physical scientists, of energy acquisition and disposal see Weinberg and Hammond (1970).

In his potent effect on his environment and back onto himself, man has been compared (e.g. Fosberg, 1958; Odum, 1969, 269) to pioneer plants, which as they rapidly multiply and 'mine' resources in a newly occupied-site so alter the site that it becomes unsuitable for further occupancy by themselves. Succeeding the pioneers come other species better fitted to the changed conditions. If no external forces intervene, there may eventually develop the mixed aggregation of organisms generally known as the climax community, which can exist for long periods in a seemingly stable condition supported by a cycling of materials—circulated through the organism/environment system with only a slight leakage—and a flowthrough of energy captured from sunlight by the photosynthetic members of the community. A principal cause of the longevity of the climax community is its low or nonexistent net productivity, which means a low backflow of effect to the environment. The energy the community consumes is mostly used for maintenance; the materials are dynamically self-contained. Minimum productivity helps make possible maximum stability.

Although the comparison of human behaviour to stages of plant succession is flimsy, it has value as an illustration of alternative ways of living that have different consequences with regard to long-term survival. Most human communities either do or else want to exist in something like the state of pioneer plants: rapidly expanding in numbers while exponentially expending the environment's accumulated materials. Unlike pioneer plants, however, humans frequently import substances from outside their area of occupancy for use both as materials and as sources of energy. In this way industrial societies and western agricultural systems maintain themselves in a pioneer status with a biologically aberrant negative balance; they consume more energy and materials than they possess. This parasitism on other areas, which is coupled with the pollution of the common terrestrial environment, has been considered good because of a narrow notion of cost in which the earth is seen as a storehouse from which materials that can be acquired cheaply, when measured by money, are considered rightly available and usable. Bring the materials from there to here; increase the local output; return the waste to there or spread it so thinly everywhere that any damage from pollution can be said to be an external cost. Such a provincial operation is economically but not ecologically sensible, for on spaceship earth, there and everywhere are here, and all costs are

282

internal. We are stealing from ourselves and 'trashing' our own and only home.

Diversity is advantageous

If, as is often said, the continuing spread of Western commerce is leading to a worldwide loss of variety in human ways of life and human-dominated ecosystems, man as a species is losing something that may have considerable survival value, for beyond the aesthetic worth of variable landscapes and peoples lie biological advantages. Although the cause-and-effect relationship between diversity an stability is not clear (Odum, 1969, 265), many biologists believe that an ecosystem's stability is enhanced by internal diversity. For instance, both Slatyer (1969, 149) and Schultz (1967, 155) argue that an ecosystem's ability to adapt to invasion or catastrophe or other accidental disturbance is largely a matter of its diversity. If diversity is lacking, the results of disturbance will reverberate through the whole system. To give a simple and well-known example, attempts at economic development of agriculture often lead, at the scale of orchard, field, or garden, to a move from polyculture to monoculture. Development economists talk of the benefits of 'diversification', but they refer to the regional or national scale and are concerned to create a buffer against economic over-specialization, not to protect against the outbreaks of insects and disease that result from the local monoculture considered efficient in a cost-motivated world.

At a more abstract level, a value for the preservation of diversity in landscapes (specifically, undeveloped wilderness) comes from Luten (1967), who pictures the environment as a guide that keeps organisms or, more complexly, ecosystems on course during their evolution. If the evolving entity is to avoid becoming extinct, it must stay within certain environmental constraints. But what sort of guidance is possible? For humans, Luten suggests a reference point — 'an immutable Polaris'—in the form of the natural scene, an unimpaired wilderness. Disclaiming either sentimentality or aesthetics, he writes (1967, 34) that wilderness '. . . is a resource, perhaps the most important of all resources, . . . because it is essential for the long-range welfare of man. Nature is the final helmsman; no other reference point can be imagined.'

Also, evolution occurs through the operation of selection on variation. The future evolution of man's body as well as his social

283

and material behaviour requires diversity for selection to take place—even if the selection is not all 'natural'. For Darlington (1969 679) this diversity is so important that he concludes his long work *The Evolution of Man and Society* with a plea for the preservation of

> the diverse habitats which diverse peoples need for their survival. To be sure, the restricted and specialized habitats of civilization give the greatest opportunities for what we . . . are pleased to call intelligence. But we have now learnt that intelligence is of many kinds. It has to be measured not on one scale but on many. And its diversity, if lost, cannot easily be recovered. We have therefore to preserve these diverse habitats, along with their diverse inhabitants, from damage which civilization has so far wantonly wrought upon them.

THE DILEMMA IN NEW GUINEA

As Tuan (1970) has recently noted, the temptation is strong for Westerners to romanticize the people of technically simple cultures, to presume that they are 'in harmony with nature', that their animism provides them with an ethic that safeguards their habitat. Such is seldom the case. Although they may be skilled environmental managers, and although they may be close to nature in the senses that the materials they use undergo little transformation from the natural state and (unlike some Western city dwellers) they know they gain their sustenance from plants and animals, their innate human capacity and desire to manipulate and change their environment is as great as that of technologically-advanced peoples. All they lack is the power to do it on the same scale. In New Guinea, even when their only tools were fire, stone axes and adzes, and wooden spades and dibbles, the highland horticulturalists converted thousands upon thousands of hectares from forest to grassland, a transformation that can be argued (Clarke, 1966) to be an impoverishment of the environment. In some of the densely-populated areas, the neolithic agricultural activities almost undoubtedly resulted in accelerated sheet erosion and even gullying.* And I have seen wholly pagan men

---

* For instance, in the Chimbu area Europeans on first-contact patrols in the early 1930s report the presence of check barriers constructed to prevent accelerated erosion (Ian Hughes, *pers. comm.*, 1970), which is still readily evident today in the upper Chimbu valley, as noted by Brookfield and Brown (1963, 28) and Street (1969, 105).

284

in the recently-contacted Jimi valley happily felling half a sacred grove of primary-forest trees that they firmly believed to be the homes of their ancestors, whose anger at being disturbed was appeased by killing a pig and sprinkling the blood about the tree trunks. Thus, it cannot be argued that the intrusion of white men into New Guinea introduced environmental change or deterioration into previously wholly stable, harmonious ecosystems. Nor have the highland New Guineans before or after European contact desired the local self-sufficiency so dear to ecologists. There is little they enjoy more than buying and selling, trading, importing, exporting; they are eager to be part of the modern economic system or at least to possess the products and benefits associated with it. The truth is that if a poll could be taken, the New Guineans—along with most of the world's peoples—would side with the development economist, not with the worried ecologist, thus adding force to the cry 'You can't just leave them as they are' that is often the ultimate argument against the view that many forms of deterioration could be avoided by slowing down development or directing energy to other endeavours.

To present some aspects of this development dilemma as it is now present in New Guinea, I will outline 'pressures' toward development and potential deterioration and then discuss 'openings' toward environmental preservation and man-environment stability.

Pressures

Beyond the enjoyment, benefit, and intrinsic fascination of the new artifacts and services, the indigenous New Guineans want modernization for reasons of self-esteem and, perhaps, because of a lack of knowledge of the alternatives to and the full implications of the modernization. Like all humans, the New Guineans want their 'shred of dignity', they want to feel at least as respected as other men whom they see to be of equivalent position. Thus, a Papuan politician has recently made political capital out of a supposed disparity in the Australian Administration's distribution of development capital between Papua and the Trust Territory of New Guinea. Of course a far greater and more real disparity exists in the distribution of wealth between the expatriate residents and all the indigenous peoples of Australian New Guinea as a whole. During and for a time after initial contact, the many remarkable possessions and powers of the newly-arrived outsiders were accepted as a natural attribute.

285

Now, with the spread of education, the increasing knowledge of a shared humanness with the outsiders, and the disproportionate profit gained by the outsiders when both groups engage in common economic enterprises, the New Guineans are coming more and more to question the 'seemingly unearned affluence' (Reay, 1969, 65) of the expatriates. In other words, they are coming to experience what sociologists call relative deprivation, which (Coser, 1968, 74)'. . . arises not so much from the absolute amount of frustration as from the experienced discrepancy between one's lot and that of other persons or groups which serve as standards of reference'.

In highland New Guinea, then, as in all regions of rising expectations, much of the goad for further economic development will come from sought relief from relative deprivation. Naturally, the ecological implications of development will scarcely be considered, for concern with the ecological truths outlined earlier in this essay is a function of affluence. Nor is ecological preaching by academic or other visitors likely to be considered legitimate behaviour by affluent expatriate residents who are in New Guinea either for personal gain or as agents of change. And as is evidenced by the recent series of comments and replies on the Australian government's five-year plan for the economic development of Papua New Guinea (Territory of Papua and New Guinea, 1968), there is little questioning even by scholars of the aggregate benefit of development—only a dispute over the propriety of differing proportions of expatriate and indigenous participation in the development (Crocombe, 1968; Arndt, Shand, and Fisk, 1969; Crocombe, 1969; Epstein, 1969; Reay, 1969). In short, almost the entire weight of opinion, external and internal, official and unofficial, favours economic development. Almost all New Guineans want it, at least to some degree; the United Nations Trusteeship Council urges it; the Australian Administration plans and tries to stimulate it; and the patrol officers work for it at the community level, directing the building of roads, encouraging the planting of cash crops, and eulogizing the coming of companies prospecting for minerals. No idea of an alternative good is easily available. Cultural ethnocentrism is implicitly accepted. As Spencer (1960, 37–7) queried in his paper on 'underdevelopment' in Malaya:

> Is all 'underdevelopness', as defined in Occidental terms, bad for the residents of the region in question, or is it so for the residents of the developed region at some far distance? Why is it so urgent that the dense jungle of some distant rural region be reduced to a

'developed' state of deforestation? . . . For whom is the life of the quiet riverine rural village bad? For whom is the substitution of factories in the forest essentially good? . . . A New Guinea native might well look at certain sub-tropical parts of the United States and exclaim how 'undeveloped' are certain aspects of American economy today in terms of his concept of the development of area potentials. . . .

To continue, with specific regard to New Guinea, the argument that development is a multi-faceted process—not all beneficial—I will here deliberately take a dark view and outline some of the detriments. Obviously, the introduction of cash cropping and the increase in population, which results from the *Pax Australiana* and the spread of medical services, mean increased use of agricultural land, which in turn means a shortening of the fallow period and probable deterioration of the soil under systems of simple shifting cultivation and an intensification of labour input in the more complex agricultural systems. Associated with increasing intensity of land use is a deterioration of diet as the zones accessible for hunting and collecting diminish and a horticultural specialization in the highest-yielding tubers increases. Studies need to be made as to whether or not the spreading use of imported rice and canned fish means a further nutritional deterioration, but such has commonly been the case for comparable changes elsewhere.* It certainly seems likely that for many highland New Guineans the amount of protein now gained by eating an occasional bit of canned fish is less than the protein that was obtained by eating protein-rich young leaves (Pirie, 1969), whose previously important place in the diet has lessened with increasing urbanization† and commercialization.

Increasing commercialization also means a new dependence on external sources of supplies for goods such as fertilizer, machinery, clothing, tobacco, tools, flashlights, kerosene, and so forth. The new roads, usually seen as proud and concrete symbols of advance, can also be viewed as means not only of increasing administrative control and centralization but also as mechanisms whereby the New Guineans are subordinately linked ever more tightly into the Western com-

* See Finney (1965) for a discussion of economic change and dietary consequences in another part of the changing Pacific.

† I cannot here otherwise treat the many physical and psychological benefits and detriments that are associated with the urbanization taking place in New Guinea. Marion Ward (1970) provides a discussion of the matter.

287

mercial system as the produceable wealth of New Guinea, agricultural or mineral, is drawn off to the outside world. Beyond such new dependencies and the likelihood of the physical impoverishment of land and diet is the increased perception that comes with development: the expatriate simply by his presence makes the New Guinean poor. By being introduced to the external world, the New Guineans are changed from members of integral and what were most amply-fed communities to a 'backward' or 'underdeveloped' people. To assuage this new condition missionaries and government officials urge the New Guineans to abandon their traditional sporadic employments and entertainments—some lethal but still exciting—for the pleasures of unremitting toil, the result of which for many New Guineans is likely to be a still greater sense of deprivation. That a few men are relatively successful in the increasing individualization of economic activity that accompanies development means the growth of inequalities of wealth in what were in pre-contact times more egalitarian economic systems.*

Finally, development means a lessened diversity both within New Guinea and in the mosaic of the world's regions. As Western influences spread through New Guinea, the previously varied ways of life and sustenance all merge into what seems in part to be a single trashy fringe of Western civilization. On the worldwide scale, the last great, self-sufficient reservoir of subsistence agricultural systems is increasingly penetrated and standardized by the ecologically unsound ideas of commercial production.

Openings

As already implied, to resist development is in many senses unrealistic—this truth is at the core of the dilemma of development. Certainly, I have few expectations that anything approaching a starry-eyed ecologist's utopia can emerge in New Guinea. But if the expatriate manipulators of New Guinea are serious about granting future free choice to the new nation's people, the openings toward ecosystem stability should at least be presented as alternatives to the present course of becoming an impoverished reflection of the temporarily affluent Western world. When argued now, the case for development—'but that's what the people want'—is unethical, for

* See Brookfield (1968b) for specific details of this process and of other consequences of the introduction of cash cropping within the Chimbu region of New Guinea.

it is certainly not the obligation of a government to acknowledge and encourage the desire for development while not informing of the consequences of that development. Of course people want things, but they should know what they will have to pay for them; then the choice they make can be free.

An important first opening is that although the New Guineans may feel that they are not keeping up, or catching up, with the locally perceivable Joneses, they nonetheless maintain themselves in a state of what the economist E. K. Fisk (1966; 1971) has called primitive affluence or subsistence affluence, in which, relative to many peoples elsewhere in the world, the New Guineans are '. . . able to produce in abundance the essentials of a relatively comfortable life with the expenditure of only a small proportion of the labour and land resources available to them'. In other words, they already have what many of the world's people are seeking. Of course, as Fisk further points out, the New Guineans' subsistence economies and associated political fragmentation cannot be successfully organized into an economically-developing nation. But because, as I argue, such development is a mixed blessing, the New Guineans might feel favoured that they have no immediate physical need for increased production, that they are still free to take other roads—for instance, the road that Aldous Huxley describes in his visionary novel *Island* (1964, 218–19),

. . . the road of applied biology, the road of fertility control and the limited production and selective industrialization which fertility control makes possible, the road that leads towards happiness from the inside out, through health, through awareness, through a change in one's attitude towards the world; not towards the mirage of happiness from the outside in, through toys and pills and non-stop distractions.

Another case for not immediately trying to catch up with the technologically-advanced nations is made by the anthropologist Service (1960). In a world evolving as rapidly as ours, backward nations have the capacity and the privilege to leapfrog over whole stages of technological development. But once committed to certain specialized techniques, the productive system becomes partially frozen and new advances (or steps in other directions) become difficult to make. Evolutionary potential is sacrificed.

Aside from the freedom of future choice latent in their usually low population densities and unelaborated technologies, the New Guineans might also treasure their large areas of only slightly-used forests, the low flow of industrial pollutants (including commercial fertilizer) into their environment, and the efficiency of production of their agriculture. The forests could be kept as reservoirs of wilderness; in this effort the New Guineans might learn from the history of over-exploitation in other parts of the tropical world and contain the next few decades' inevitable growth of population and agriculture in the already developed areas, rather than seeing further road-building and forest-clearing as signs of progress.* With regard to pollutants, the New Guineans could profit from the knowledge now present in the more industrialized world; unlike the process of pollution that has occurred there, the dangers can now be anticipated before a threshold evident to all is reached—by which time the induced condition is often almost beyond remedying. With regard to their agriculture, the New Guineans could take pride in its high productivity relative to the total input of energy and materials. Although the value productivity may be low compared with Western, commercial agriculture, there is no doubt that the mixed plantings and quasi-natural, tiered arrangement of many New Guinean gardens give a fuller utilization of sunlight and a higher net energy production. In fact, as noted already—given the input of energy in the form of fuel, machinery, fertilizer, and other chemicals— the net energy production of the most highly-industrialized Western agriculture must frequently be negative. Lastly, despite their materialism and quest for new goods, many New Guineans still view land in the traditional way as a community possession that must provide sustenance for the sons as well as the fathers, a means of permanent support for all, not a source of maximum present profit for some. This attitude, which in some of its manifestations has been condemned as a hindrance to economic development, is worthy of preservation; but official policy with regard both to agricultural resettlement projects (R. G. Ward, 1969, 14) and to payment for land purchases (Crocombe, 1968, 62) favours the prejudice toward individualism and profit.

STEPS TOWARD SOLUTIONS

It may seem quixotic to associate New Guinea, with its small and

* Some steps are being made in these directions through initial planning for the establishment of national parks.

mostly agricultural population and its broad stretches of nearly empty land, with the environmental crises now part of the daily life of industrially-advanced regions. But because all parts of the world are contained within spaceship earth, all are subject with greater or lesser impact to the effects of further economic development—effects that connect directly to the unified terrestrial environment as well as acting indirectly through the stimulating mechanism of relative deprivation. In both ways the aggregate problem is common to all human beings. What steps toward solutions can be found?

In his widely-cited paper 'The Tragedy of the Commons', the biologist Garrett Hardin (1968, 1,244) describes the remorseless deterioration faced by our finite but crowding world if there is no change from our present course. 'Ruin is the destination toward which all men rush, each pursuing his own best interest in a society that believes in the freedom of the commons. Freedom in a commons brings ruin to all.' For this impending ruin, Hardin sees no technical solution; instead, there must be, he argues (1968, 1,247), a moral or political solution, '. . . mutual coercion, mutually agreed upon by the majority of the people affected'. The political scientist Crowe (1969) in a critique of Hardin's paper agrees that there is no technical solution—and adds that he sees no political solution either. Certainly the dilemma of development that I have tried to pose has no easy technical, political, or moral solutions. Specific harmful effects can be prevented or minimized by careful study and planning, but some environmental disruption is an unavoidable concomitant of development (Carter, 1969). And even though the potential for damaging disruption is now widely recognized,* it is hard to picture many leaders of the third world giving up political opportunities in order to abandon unwise development plans or to moralize on ecology while their nations' gross national products diminish, relatively or absolutely. To cite Boulding (1966, 234): 'This is a grim note to sound, but it is, I think, the peculiar business of ecologists to be pessimistic. In these days ecology may well take the mantle of doom and the name of "the dismal science" from economics.'

But perhaps despair and recognition of crisis is the only place from

---

* Witness, for instance, the United Nations conference on the human environment convened in 1972, a meeting that was in large part concerned with ecological problems arising from various forms of development, and other interference. The proceedings of this conference do not inspire much hope for the approach advocated here, but at least there is growing awareness of the problem.

which a start can be made. We can see that our unilinear cause–effect modes of thought have moved us toward the possibility of extinction; it has further become clear (Simpson, 1953, 295) that the case of extinction '. . . is neither in the organisms nor in their environment but in the relationship between the two'. Such perceptions have brought a turn to an ecological (systematic, interactionist, cybernetic, . . .) mode of thought. 'Finally,' as Schultz writes (1969, 78), 'we realize that nature is not as piecemeal as science is', and, further (Schultz, 1967; 1969), that 'in the concept of the ecosystem we have a tool that allows us to look at big chunks of nature as integrated systems, as space-time units that are not abstracted categories like underdeveloped economies'. Because ecosystems are real, there can be an intelligent approach to their management if the managers operate from an ecological rather than an economic viewpoint. Economists' techniques are necessary aids to choosing rationally among certain alternative allocations of resources; but economists and their bizarre theories of growth must be pried from the places of power. The poet Gary Snyder (1968, 127) put it well. 'Ecology: "eco" (*oikos*) meaning "house" (cf. "ecumenical"): Housekeeping on Earth. Economics, which is merely the housekeeping of various social orders—taking out more than it puts back—must learn the rules of the greater realm.'

Several obstacles to the implementation of this ecological viewpoint have already been implied or stated; these can only be reiterated briefly together with the mention of a few others. I deliberately confine myself to the largely psychological obstacles that function in the industrial countries and in primitively affluent countries like New Guinea. Obviously, in overpopulated countries with truly impoverished peoples and environments there is another set of obstacles. To begin with, there will always be a lag between the recognition of a need for change and the act of change. Old and once successful ways are not easily abandoned, nor is it easy to believe them harmful. The aspect of our nature as *Homo Faber*, Man the Maker, also weighs against quick adoption of the ecological viewpoint. The tools and artifacts that may account for our intelligence also fascinate us; we have had a millennia-long love affair with things. Economic growth promises ever more things for ever more people, with the problems of continuing expansion to be countered by inventions and discoveries—an expectation we might call the *El Dorado* complex, the latest expression of which is the 'green

292

revolution' of dwarf cereals, a revolution whose apparent benefits some believe to be illusory or in the long run calamitous (e.g. Paddock, 1970). But past successes in agriculture and other forms of environmental manipulation have broken down whatever mechanisms paleolithic man may have possessed to balance population with resources (Wynne-Edwards, 1966). In fact, with the coming of the neolithic, an increase in productivity and population became adaptive for social groups—a heritage that may act against the re-establishment of necessary controls. Particularly unyielding obstacles to ecological management are relative deprivation and political competition. If the gap between rich' and 'poor' cannot be lessened, deliberate efforts to slow or limit expansion of production appear impossible. Underlying regional, national, or international prestige is the personal pride of professional planners and instigators of the glamourous activity of development. Such technical intelligentsia, 'the new Mandarins' as Chomsky (1969, 25) calls them, must use their skills or lose their self-esteem. Professionally pompous, they may be incapable of adjusting to new directions or relinquishing power. Summing up, economic development seems something like drug addiction. Consumption of energy and materials in ever larger amounts gives even lessening pleasure and health, but the industrial world—like a drug addict—spreads the gospel of the lift of economic 'take-off,' partly for political reasons, partly out of generosity, and partly (one cannot help suspecting) in order to ease the opening of new sections of storehouse earth to overexploitation and to bring other peoples into conformity with industrially commercial life so that the industrial world will have more companions—mostly willing companions—in their addition. It is widely felt to be only right that 'Development is the faithful imitation of the developed' (Galbraith, 1965, 3).

A few possible approaches to help overcome the many obstacles to ecological vision may be suggested. First, education. The idea of the ecosystem is simple, as is the logic of most ecological truths. The appeal of formal ecological thinking is now obvious in the affluent world; further teaching can only implant the ideas more firmly. But resistance to ecological imperatives will continue, if not through ignorance then for the sake of short-term profit. To counteract this motive, attempts to arouse fear may be added to more reasoned education. Crowe (1969) suggests that it is up to scientists to strive to maintain a 'dis-assurance' with regard to the environment so that

293

political pressure for amelioration is generated and sustained. With regard to what may be our innate drives to expand and manipulate, we could turn to ethologists for insights into our basic motives and their expression so that we might then learn, as Murnet (1969, 367) suggests, to twist our environmentally destructive patterns of behaviour, to trick ourselves, toward rational action; to substitute new forms of cultural behaviour for missing natural control; mechanisms, as we already do with restriction of land use, which functions as an analogue of 'territoriality' (Odum, 1969, 269). The comparison of economic development to drug addiction suggests that a psychic restructuring is necessary to dissolve the one-sidedness of our attention and desires. We can now only grope towards the means to accomplish such restructuring, but clearly there must be devised new gratifications, new 'pay-offs', that are harmless to the physical world but stimulating enough physically to lessen our predatory hunger for energy and materials. Mishan (1969, 206–13), Mumford (e.g. 1967), and many others believe that some such gratifications have been present but have been diminished or lost— for example, the gratification gained from skilled workmanship has declined with increasing mechanization so that the decline and the mechanization have worked hand in hand to encourage quantity at the expense of quality, consumption at the expense of appreciation To extend attention beyond quantity and consumption I can only suggest that ecology must encompass ideas such as Jung's regarding the individuation process and Gregory Mateson's (unpub. MS.) regarding the relevance of aesthetic judgment to ecosystem management. A way around the ominous obstacle of relative deprivation and the stated commitment of the affluent world to lessen that deprivation seems even further from hand. Furthermore, how can the affluent world even suggest a change in goal from development toward stability?

> The underdeveloped nations, so-called, . . . have a perfervid belief in our technology. And were we to try to explain that we were not quite so sure of our cleverness, that we have made some deplorable mistakes, it would be interpreted as one more example of the West wanting to deny the benefits of technology to the rest of the world. We in the West are in a cleft stick. . . . (Darling, 1970, 56).

The only escape from the cleft is for the affluent to drag their feet

294

against further increases in production for themselves, to say: 'We have too much of a good thing; from now on we are going to become richer by reducing our desires.' The enclaves of deliberate poverty that have recently grown up within the affluent world may be taken as a hopeful sign that eutrophication (the process of overfeeding) is recognized as an illness of the whole system of the affluent world, not just of lakes. Further spread of knowledge of the mechanisms of relative deprivation might militate against the argument that lack of economic advance means revolution; instead, it is more likely that small advances, which indicate the potential while limiting the fact of greater advance, create revolt. If the economically superordinate group was seen to be descending, the goad of relative deprivation would diminish. In the aggregate the approaches toward ecological vision imply the necessity of ways by which the felt boundaries between groups of men can be blurred by the spreading knowledge that all men share the life-support system of spaceship earth and that co-ordinated we have a chance to do what we cannot do as competitively-expanding groups—design a style of sustenance wherein energy and materials are mostly used not for growth but for maintenance, so that human evolution can continue permanently among diverse groups of people with diverse styles of living in diverse parts of the world.

I have already noted that human geography or its field of study by any other name is particularly fitted to attempt much toward the solution of the dilemma of development, for more than any other scientists human geographers observe men as cultural beings that live in a physical landscape. Geographers have always seen a connection between man and environment, even if they have sometimes seen the flow of influence as going only one way. However, with a few exceptions, geographers' studies have been of scholarly interest only. What practical contributions could they make to the measurement and amelioration of the present-day pathology of the socio-economic system? Taking New Guinea as the specific site for work, several possibilities can be outlined.

Following Brookfield's studies and theoretical discussions (e.g. 1962; 1968a; 1968b), I suggest that the study of areas below the regional scale, '. . . at the level meaningful to the local people' (1962, 242), gives the most exact knowledge of the interactions between man and environment. Of course, as has often been said, even a small ecosystem contains an enormously complex set of

295

interrelations, but one can through close familiarity gain a holistic comprehension of the mode of functioning of such a 'chunk of space-time' and a feeling for its trend (direction of evolution) without having or needing a total mastery of its internal intricacy. In agricultural ecosystems such as those of New Guinea certain techniques are useful in this study. One of the most readily available of these is examination of the uncultivated plant cover, for many data on land use and the physical characteristics of the ecosystem are automatically integrated and indicated by the ecosystem's spontaneous vegetation. Particularly where shifting cultivation is being practised, the state of the fallow vegetation (species present, stage, diversity, physiognomy, etc.) goes far toward indicating the intensity of land use, the fertility of the soil, and more abstractly the system's 'health', trend, and entropy content. Collection of data on soil, erosion, and crop yields provides further and long-utilized means of assessment. Techniques of remote sensing—for instance, the measurement of percentage of bare ground by infra-red photography—are newer and valuable techniques, as are the use of radioactive tracers to decipher the nutrient budget or follow the movement of materials through ecosystems. If the skill, facilities, and confidence that what has been measured is sufficiently meaningful are available, high-speed computers can be used to simulate the results of alternative interactions among a large aggregate of environmental components.* Other simpler techniques that can be used by the geographer in the field include observations on the people's health, their land-use system and their attitudes toward, and satisfaction with, local man/land relations (perhaps utilizing a self-anchoring scale such as that described by Cantril, 1965). Ratios of agricultural inputs to outputs and of numbers of people to unit of land may also be calculated for useful comparative purposes, as may the 'carrying capacity', with the provision (Street, 1969) that the presence of a population size below the calculated capacity not be considered by itself an indicator of lack of deterioration. Finally, knowledge of past conditions within a system is an invaluable supple-

* On the topic of soil and fallow vegetation, Nye and Greenland (1960) provide the best general treatment; Kellman's (1969) is an example of the analysis of soil and vegetation in relation to shifting cultivation in a specific site in the montane tropics. Schultz (1967) and Fosberg (1965) provide further discussion and bibliography on many techniques of assessing environmental potential and monitoring environmental conditions.

ment to knowledge of the present, for the system is evolving, has direction. Knowledge of the past gives increased perception of this direction and of the significance of present changes, such as the modification among the Tiv of Nigeria of a traditional pattern of crop rotation—the sort of change that in this specific case and perhaps in other cases '. . . may be keen sensors of unstable agricultural systems and may be predictive of significant societal alterations . . . and warn of possible systemic breakdown . . .' (Vermeer, 1970, 314).

Beyond giving understanding of specific local processes, the knowledge gained from intense study of small ecosystems gives a firm basis for comparative understanding of larger regions, as Brookfield (1962; 1968a) and Waddell (1968) have argued as well as exemplified through their studies of highland New Guinean agricultural systems. A fairly deep understanding of the functioning of one system serves as a model by which to discern similarities and variations in other systems. By using both objective criteria and the valuable capabilities of subjective judgment, 'families' of ecosystems can be perceived and regional patterns emerge—as, for instance, the clear distinction between the highland core and highland fringe of montane New Guinea. Within each family—which of course possess, together with the component ecosystems, defined but not impermeable boundaries—*loci* of ecological malfunctioning will show up (and dis-assurance be generated) by comparison with healthier members of the family. The nature of the malfunctioning may also become apparent through comparative analysis, and particular rearrangements of some of the system's parts be seen as possible cures.

I can envision—even if quixotically—that within New Guinea's government an environmental management authority could be established to operate a programme of monitoring and design along ecological lines and also be empowered to examine and stop (through the ability to deny funds) development projects. Lack of popular motivation and support make failure likely; on the other hand, there would be certain odds in favour of such an authority in a region like New Guinea, for it is relatively underpopulated and undespoiled and contains only a few well-organized pressure groups. A venture by a soon-to-be-independent country in the direction of this sort of ecological management would give a striking opportunity to be a leader in relieving and preventing ecological distress, in 'acting like gods' to take hold of 'a runaway world' (Leach, 1968).

297

To continue and conclue the dream, where might such a venture lead? Toward development that is not morbid growth but another sort of expansion in ways of living? Toward men giving up their vain attempts to control nature directly and beginning instead to try to design their functions within a man/nature system so that neither is diminished? Toward a rearrangement of human behaviour so that '. . . the pressure to maximize productivity is relaxed and the pressure to maintain ecological stability is increased' (Slatyer, 1969, 152)? Toward a 'strategy of ecosystem development' (Odum, 1969) that includes a division of the environment into compartments enough of which would be 'protective' or 'compromise' to maintain a viable ecosphere? Toward a move from anthropocentrism and economic ethnocentrism to ecocentrism? All of these potentialities imply the image of man related to an earth that is not a separate storehouse but a conveyance that evolves together with all life— stable but not without transition. The image requires, therefore, a paradoxical coupling of the idea of evolution with a sense of here and now, an attentiveness to completion in the immediate world, that civilized man—perhaps because of his ideas of lineal time and progress—lacks (Diamond, 1964). Until they learn of the 'paradise of production', some not-long-contacted New Guineans do seem to have a sense of cyclic time and of completion and continuity in and with their land. With them, could we not all

. . . find in comforts of the sun,
In pungent fruit and bright, green wings, or else
In any balm or beauty of the earth,
Things to be cherished like the thought of heaven?*

* Wallace Stevens, 'Sunday Morning', *The Collected Poems of Wallace Stevens* (London, Faber and Faber, 1955).

12 Geography and geographers in the changing Pacific

An islander's view

Isireli Lasaqa

No essay on the role of geography and geographers in the changing Pacific can hope to do justice to the entire field and its numerous practitioners. Only a limited range of topics can be considered. Two lines of thought are paramount. Geography attempts to analyse the spatial realities of the real world, basing its analysis on varied themes. But its aim is to contribute to understanding of the world and man's place in it. The aim of Pacific geography is to understand the Pacific and man's place in the region. Taking this as my starting-point, I will try broadly to assess how a selection of geographers have analysed and interpreted certain human characteristics of the region. Almost all the geographers of the Pacific islands have until now been expatriates, and I will therefore attempt specifically to throw some light on the question: how adequate is the expatriate geographers' view of the islands, and of the inner workings of their diverse systems?

This essay, then, is a general personal assessment of how geographers have addressed themselves to certain features, problems and needs of the islands. This is not an easy task for a Melanesian who is committed to, and a participant in, the process of development in the region. To undertake it may appear to some presumptuous. However, the time is now ripe for such an exposition, particularly as geographers are increasingly applying derived concepts gleaned from other disciplines, and from remote and very different regions. Also the territories are now moving rapidly away from their colonial status through internal self-government to political autonomy, and now is the time for an island geographer who is also an islander to speak his mind. I begin with a review of my own experience of island research, which will help explain my reactions to the work of others.

299

From Dawasamu to Tadhimboko: a personal experience of Pacific geography

My first contact with serious academic geography was in 1961 at the University of Auckland Graduate School of Geography headed by Professor K. B. Cumberland. The most permanent impression gained then was that all geographical study must be based on the land and how man interacts with his land. Although the idea of areal differentiation, following mainly Hartshorne's viewpoint, was regarded as the central theme of all geographical inquiry, I considered that the interaction of man and land was a more fundamental starting point of geographical investigation: differences from place to place would then automatically emerge. Thus the way man used his land was the major focus of my interest in geography in this early period. This led to my investigation of the features and problems of land use in Dawasamu, a small part of north-east Viti Levu, Fiji, my own country (Lasaqa, 1962). The field-work necessary for that study involved four months' residence in two villages in the locality. The contemporary land-use pattern was observed and mapped in the field, thus using a traditional geographical methodology. The villagers' gardens were visited and examined in detail. The village hinterland was also visited. Interviews and discussions were held with every adult male in the villages and with groups of them. These interviews and group discussions were aimed at getting the villagers to express their opinions on a variety of subjects which ranged through land-utilization techniques, the availability of finance to village economic enterprises, the effectiveness of official agencies, social organization and traditional customs, marketing of produce, and national politics. To supplement the interviews and discussions with the villagers, a number of individuals were requested to keep diaries of their daily activities and the amount of food and cash crops planted and harvested during the period of field-work. The village headmen were also asked to keep an account of the activities of the village, especially village clearing, house building and other communal work. The available literature supplemented field data.

This early investigation had two basic objectives. The first was to examine and analyse some of the many-faceted and interrelated obstacles which at present make difficult, if not impossible, a more effective and more intensive utilization of land in Dawasamu. These obstacles were conveniently grouped into physical and human categories. To understand the first category required an examination of the inherent physical characteristics of the land insofar as these effectively inhibit full use of land. The second category derive from the people and their institutions. The starting-point of this investigation was an understanding of the contemporary land-use pattern. This demanded not only a description of the pattern of land use, tracing also the course of its development; in addition it required an analysis of both the physical and cultural factors which underlie the present land-use pattern. These factors were also analysed in terms of the obstacles and handicaps they may provide for future successful land development. Such an approach to land-use study is deemed to be basic to the successful development of efficient land-use plans and to the evolution of successful indigenous economies which in Dawasamu, even in the 1970s, are still characterized to a considerable extent by subsistence agriculture.

The second objective was to test the validity of the thesis that in this part of Fiji, human obstacles and handicaps—social, economic and political—were more important than physical obstacles in preventing the most effective and most intensive utilization of land. With the removal of these human obstacles, agricultural production for both local consumption and export could be increased substantially.

The field investigation revealed that land resources were not used to the full. In Dawasamu high-quality land requiring no improvement is limited. It is therefore necessary fully to utilize the available first-class land. Such a situation is accentuated further by the prevalence of a dry period during the mid-year months. And yet extensive stretches of high-quality lowland lay idle throughout the year of field-work. This lends sufficient support to the above thesis that the inherent physical characteristics of the land do not provide the most important obstacles to the most effective and most intensive utilization of land. Therefore, one had to look to the relevant aspects of the human geography of the area for a more adequate explanation of the low level of its land use. Among the relevant aspects of the area's human geography, those which have their roots deeply founded in Fijian culture are the most important. These include the present village social organization and its traditional customs and obligations, particularly as they apply to the land, customary land tenure, outmoded agricultural techniques and a primitive technology. All these facets of Fijian society are complexly interrelated, and together they constitute what may be called the prevailing

301

traditional social milieu of Dawasamu, within which subsistence agriculture operates. Transport and marketing facilities at the time of field-work were hopelessly inadequate. These proved to be powerful disincentives to increased agricultural production. They too are part of the human geography of the area.

One of the most important results of the approach adopted in this study was the demonstration of the necessity to understand clearly the inner workings of the society and its complex relationships in order to appreciate the nature of its land use. This is vital to any geographical investigation in Fiji, and the Pacific islands generally, dealing with the use of land resources.

The value of understanding clearly the inner workings of society in any study of land use and other aspects of life in any part of the Pacific islands was more than amply demonstrated when I later investigated the problems of choice and participation in the cash economy among the Tadhimboko of northern Guadalcanal, British Solomon Islands (Lasaqa 1969; 1972). There, as in Dawasamu, the Tadhimboko's land-use pattern was and still is fundamental to the investigation of choices effectively open to him to enter and participate meaningfully in the commercial economy.

In order to gain a balanced picture of the Tadhimboko situation, it was necessary to conduct an in-depth analysis of the area in both its temporal and spatial aspects. The history of contact, as it applies to entry into the cash economy, was traced and the major themes highlighted, while Melanesian reactions to contact were noted. The physical environment too was examined in some detail. Rapport was quickly established, largely because of my own origin and because the Tadhimboko felt sure that their contact experience was really no different from those experienced elsewhere in the Pacific, including those of my own country Fiji. This is fundamentally true. It is also true that throughout the Pacific contact with the white man involved also fraudulent transactions in land. In Tadhimboko and the Solomons generally, this particular aspect of contact was a bitter one and the bitterness persists into the 1970s.

Fundamentally, the approach adopted in the Tadhimboko study involved analysis of Melanesian participation in the market economy. This was done within the context of the people's traditional economy, including factors of production such as access to land, labour, capital and technology. It was necessary to elucidate the opportunities and limitations of each of the available openings to a cash economy, and to clarify the range of effective choices available, and how these vary areally and temporally. An underlying theme in this approach is that freedom of choice is exercised within a framework of competing preferences, resource allocation priorities, varying degrees of return to labour, and the producer's status in the social milieu.

But despite what appeared to be an overall approach to the subject, the Tadhimboko regarded the question of land as fundamental, and the one that ought to receive closest attention in official quarters. This view applied especially to their not unreasonable contention that past land deals involving them with Europeans had been unfair, as European land-buyers had taken advantage of their innocence and purely subsistence concept of land worth. Too often geographers readily dismiss such views as naïve and unreasonable, without examining closely the nature of the relationships existing between islanders and their land.

Geographers and land matters

Nearly all geographers who have worked in the Pacific islands have commented on the relationship between the traditional land tenure system and economic development. For Fiji, Spate (1959, 11) noted that 'the essential disadvantage of *matagali* (clan) holding is that there is no rational relation at all between the numbers of cultivators in any one unit and the amount of land available to them'. This disparity also applies to 'unearned' income obtained through leasing. Spate (1959, 13) notes also that land 'matters must be put on a business footing: some security of tenure must be given and some return made in rent'. Cumberland (1961, 322) has said that 'the absence of provision for individual use and development of land is a formidable check to production . . . under the impact of a money economy the most serious disadvantage of communal tenure of land is that land can never be pledged as security for advances of money for the development of land. . .'. R. G. Ward (1965) and Watters (1969) take basically the same position.

All of this is true enough. However, there seems to be little sensitivity to the entire involvement of such groups as the *aiga* in western Samoa and the *matagali* in Fiji, as cohesive social units, in anything pertaining to native land tenure and ownership. Few of the later writers appear to realize fully, as Spate (1959, 10) did, the full and wide-ranging implications: 'the land is the people; break up the land you break up the people.' Writers like Cumberland,

Ward and Watters appear to give the impression that it is only the islanders' system of land holding and associated rights and obligations that must change, and where change is needed most; there is nothing wrong with the introduced commercial and legal systems. These need not be adapted to suit the phase of change the islanders have reached at a particular point in time. Take for example this statement by Watters (1969, xiv): 'For it is with deep regret that I have concluded that the evidence points to the necessity of change, of jettisoning the old when it conflicts with the new.' The implication, and it may border on arrogance, is that the new is perfect; it need not be modified and there is no room for give-and-take. The point and plea that must be made here is that external observers must attempt at least to analyse the situation also through the eyes of the local inhabitants. Only in this way can they claim to attain a balanced understanding of the islander's position in a situation of flux.

Clearly, change and development cannot be a one-way process. New and introduced concepts need to be continually modified too to suit the stages of advancement reached by the people who are to benefit from them. It is quite clear to me that this approach is vital in many if not all development efforts in the Pacific today, more particularly in the relatively underdeveloped islands of westen Melanesia. There the people's experience of Europeans and government is not a happy one. And, generally speaking, much of the difficulties could have been avoided had the 'agents of civilization' attempted to view the land position through the prism of the islander's mind. Distortions there will inevitably be—and what society is without conceptual distortion? But to ignore the local perception of the local situation is to invite valid methodological criticism, and to reach false conclusions.

Researchers and researched

There can be little doubt that one of the causal factors in the somewhat 'unfavourable reaction' recently shown towards outside researchers by Fiji is the point just outlined above. Too often expatriate researchers take little account of the internal viewpoint on problems of far greater concern to the researched than to the researcher. For the first time, perhaps, the local establishment has questioned the value of much of the external research conducted into local situations, especially that falling within the field of the social sciences, in an attempt to formulate a policy on and towards outside researchers. The novelty of the act has taken outsiders perhaps by surprise; some may have regarded the local attitude as hostile to researchers in general. This is not so. The attempt is merely to ensure formally that any piece of research will be of value to the country and that some useful results will be forthcoming eventually. Surely this is better than leaving the situation a free-for-all and open-ended one with no formal obligation on the approved researcher to produce results pertinent to the welfare of the local people.

Other factors too have been important. A particular piece of research is bound to have policy implications. While welcoming constructive criticism, research reports which tend to overlook the practical implications of their recommendations are not usually enthusiastically received. Such reports display a lack of appreciation of the local context into which recommendations must fit and operate, if implemented. This situation is aggravated by the fact that the researcher is not readily available for discussion when his report becomes available.

It is true that research results are primarily for external purposes; they *may* be of value to the local people and their decision-makers. This fact is appreciated to varying degrees throughout the islands. A general awareness of what research is and what benefits it can bring tends to encourage the acceptance of external researchers by the local establishment.

Understanding development

The literature on development and modernization has tended to emphasize both explicitly and implicitly the need to exploit physical resources and to improve technologies. In general, social considerations have played a secondary role in the drive for economic advancement. All this is seen in the push to increase productivity, the drive to increase the production of goods for sale, and the various measures to stimulate still further production for the commerical exchange mechanism. Note for example the frequent use of income *per capita* and the gross national product as indices not only of increasing wealth but also of development among writers on the Third World, including the Pacific islands. The emphasis, then, seem to be on increased productivity in monetary and quantifiable terms. And so analysis of the development situation is often focused on aspects which can be measured statistically. In these terms, then, development means more bread, more tinned fish, more transistor

305

radios, more houses built of imported materials, more motor cars, and so on. I do not say that the acquisition of these goods is a bad thing and should therefore be discouraged. The basic point is the extent to which these goods ought to be acquired and how far should they become the goals of all our efforts to improve the living conditions of the Pacific islanders.

The acquisition of goods is important; and a minimum quantity of new goods and services is essential. But it is the quality of our lives rather than the mere quantity of goods we have and consume that is of greater importance. This concept should receive the attention of students of development and change in the Pacific islands and in the Third World generally far more than it has in the past. In terms of approach this means that we ought to be planning for the kinds of lives we want to lead. It is the attainment of the 'particular kind and quality of life' we desire to achieve that must be the objective of development in any situation. The technologies and economies must be regarded as tools for achieving this objective. Leading on from this is the determination of the kind and nature of society that Pacific islanders want to create in the region. Of course, there will be variations from territory to territory, but recognition of this fact does not obviate the need to clarify our thinking on the subject, and particularly on the internal configuration of each component social group and how these relate with one another. What modifications, by how much, how fast, and when, for example, are necessary in Fijian society today if the Fijians are to lead a more satisfying way of life in the future? These indicate the sort of question that needs to be asked and analysed in any development planning in the Pacific islands today. They are basic to our comprehension of the development process in the region now and in the future.

What are the objectives of social change?

Many students of Pacific geography have stated or implied in their publications that the major problems facing the peoples of the Pacific today arise from their position in the process of social change. This is more obvious than useful, for it does not locate precisely the point at which such societies may be found in relation to the two ends of the change continuum. Further, the end result seems vaguely perceived. Watters (1969, 2) has said that the Fijians can solve many of their current problems if they 'adapt their culture to the needs of modern times'. This could be said of numerous other societies in the Pacific. Again this statement is not new; neither is it difficult to say. However, it is much more difficult to spell out its implications in detail, especially as it affects group and interpersonal relations, social structure and value systems, use of time and resources, local leadership, and the people's view of themselves and the external world around them.

Writing in 1959 Spate (1959, 9) declared 'that for the Fijian countryside the objective should be a community of independent farmers, living or working on holdings heritable, and alienable at least between Fijians, but retaining in each village or old *Tikina* area a common centre—church, school, guesthouse, parish hall, chiefly residence—where the old dignity which the *koro* is so rapidly losing might be recaptured'. Ten years later Watters (1969, 265) arrived at essentially the same conclusions. The implications of this objective are many and varied; they are also complex. It means a drastic change in the traditional tenure and settlement systems throughout Fiji which could alter the basis of the *mataqali* as a cohesive social unit and change its very *raison d'être*. Not only would modification of certain of their aspects change the nature of traditional customs: at the same time their meaning and symbolic significance to their adherents would alter. Perhaps they would cease to be practised altogether, because their symbolic significance had been eroded and nothing socially and ceremonially satisfying had emerged to replace them. These are only some of the possible consequences of the particular objective of change advocated above by Spate. A close study is required in order that those likely to be affected by their adoption can see the possible ultimate consequences of their choice. In essence then, the Fijians of the future, adopting the course recommended by Spate and endorsed by Watters, may not be recognizable by the present generations. Put another way, it is the nature of the Fijian people of the future that should first be broadly determined, in order that the appropriate courses of action may be taken in good time and not rushed into when the position is almost lost. This requires a thorough analysis of the consequences and implications of a particular direction of social change. Geographical research could do much to clarify the implications of particular choices, and the nature of the alternatives available. Watters (1969) does this for four sample villages: more detailed studies of that sort are needed.

The search for understanding of development and change

Many attempts have been made to describe and understand the nature of development and change in the Third World in the last decade. For the Pacific, the most recent and most comprehensive of these is by Brookfield and Hart: *Melanesia: A Geographical Interpretation of an Island World* (1971). The first part of this book is more traditionally geographical than the second. It discusses the nature of the Melanesian environment and evaluates it in terms of population and population change and the subsistence economy of old Melanesia. Modern agricultural developments are also examined, together with timber and mineral exploitation in the region. All this provides the platform for jumping into a more sophisticated academic approach that seeks to enhance our understanding of the Melanesian real world in a situation of flux, the conditions of which appear to be externally determined to a considerable extent. The second part of the book adopts a very useful and realistic approach: the transport systems are analysed in relation to production and trade; the peasant and plantation systems are studied independently and in their interconnections; the central places and the periphery are seen to be competing locations for activity now and in the future.

In reviewing *Melanesia* for the *New Zealand Geographer* in 1972, I have said that the authors demonstrate a sympathetic understanding of how the traditional inhabitants of this island world perceive the process of development in their homeland. I think they have honestly tried to understand the Melanesian viewpoint on development issues and on change, given the level of resolution and generalization on the data available. However, in this regard I think the book succeeds only as far as it goes. For example, the concept of Von Thünen rings is applied skilfully and with accuracy to a model of Melanesian trade; market instabilities for the few export crops are examined with clarity; the dilemma of governments presented by the drive for export and the extension of social services is exposed; and the keen awareness of the islanders of the importance to them of their land and its resources now and in the future is captured. The book points out that it is in the New Hebrides that feeling among the Melanesians about the unfair alienation of their land is strongest (p. 219). However, the depth of this feeling and its likelihood of becoming permanent and determining the external outlook of the New Hebrideans in the future are not indicated.

308

To the New Hebrideans, and the supporters of the *Na Griamel* movement in particular, the land is tied up with both political and economic power, not to mention traditional social links. They see that much of the high-quality land on Santo is well developed and in foreign control. They believe that many of the transactions over this land were either fraudulent or inequitable. But they have been and are powerless to redress the situation. They see the Administration as supporting and perpetuating the existence of the large expatriate landholders who in their eyes control the commercial economy of the territory. Only a change in the legal framework can change the legal position of large landholdings in the New Hebrides, assuming that *Na Griamel* will not seek a more effective resolution of their land grievances outside the law. That supporters of *Na Griamel* are prepared to go to prison for whatever act committed in the name of the movement which the law prohibits indicates the strength and depth of support they have for the cause. Many of them would be prepared to give their lives in the name of the movement. Unless the Administration acts sufficiently early and satisfies their wants regarding land in an adequate fashion, the generally anti-government attitude of the supporters of the movement may strengthen and is likely to persist for a long time.

Like the Tadhimboko, members of *Na Griamel* clearly believe that their strength lies in unity and a united front against the expatriate government. This outlook is born of the belief that individually, as small peasants or as poor subsistence cultivators, they stand mute in the face of a formidable and intelligent foe, who not only knows all the 'rules of the game' but can change and interpret the rules to suit his purposes. This is one reason why Melanesians at various times and places have fallen back to a search for and revival of what they considered their traditional customs, mixing these in their forms of organization with certain introduced ideas, to provide some spiritual and practical support to them individually and collectively in their opposition to the dominance of resident alien power.

The feeling associated with a colonial status is particularly applicable to parts of western Melanesia. It is a feeling of minuteness in the face of what appears to be the excessive affluence and power of the expatriate and his government. Associated with this feeling is a measure of pride in the knowledge that the expatriate cannot really grasp the inner workings and nuances of indigenous societies. This leads in many cases to a patterned and artificial set of behaviour by many Melanesians in the presence of most expatriates, in contrast to the more casual and more real responses in the company of familiar local people. This is not dishonest behaviour; it is simply a natural reaction to a colonial status which contains little that encourages and preserves self-respect among islanders. This is the sort of feeling and situation that is not likely to be immediately apparent to expatriate observers, thus missing study and analysis. Such attitudes are important in that they affect Melanesian behaviour and are certain to have spatial implications, including the use of resources.

However, in this new situation of change and development, where the islanders are being encouraged to enter fully into the commercial system as part of the process of modernization, many of them seem to be unaware of the development of a new colonialism within their newly-won political autonomy. This is the colonialism imposed by a market economy, and largely emanating from external sources. Local primary producers are dependent on overseas markets and prices, and must produce goods acceptable to the overseas buyer, both in quality and in volume. Some islanders already see this and probably accept that it is inevitable, and that other meaningful and acceptable alternatives are not in sight—at least in the short-term. The effect could be worse and more demoralizing than the old form of colonialism, since the basic decision affecting the state of the people's belly, especially those in the wage economy, might very well be made all the time outside the country.

This essay does not advocate that we take a fundamentally different view of the processes we are studying in the field of change and development in the Pacific, and that we see them only from the point of view of the islanders themselves. This would be a one-way approach that will lead to futility. What I think is needed is a clear analysis of the islander's position and his own viewpoint in the context of the external world and its hard realities. This is the only way we can hope to achieve a full understanding of the islander's milieu. Such an approach will throw up the points at which, on both sides, value adaptation and compromise can be made. It will also clear up the mutual incomprehension of motives and objectives that dominates the difficulties between the people and the Government in many parts of the Pacific islands.

The future

A deeper analysis of the viewpoint of the local people set against the realities of the modern world is obviously a line of inquiry that should be developed further in the future. This is just beginning, but more could be done to the advantage of the researcher and the researched. Pacific island geographers should be able to do this effectively. One of the areas in which this approach could fruitfuly be adopted now is the islander's attitude towards his homeland. For example, how do the Solomon Islanders regard the Solomons as their homeland? Do they regard it exclusively as theirs? Must they be regarded as having prior claim to the group as the first inhabitants and therefore accorded due right in all spheres of activity and decision-making? If so, how does this affect their behaviour and their view of resources, especially of land? And so on. Similar questions could be asked about other Pacific islands and the results could be very interesting and revealing. Data on these sorts of issues are useful for understanding the processes of development and change throughout this island world.

The above raises the issue about the way islanders ought to view their homeland. The islanders cannot shut themselves off from outside influences and thus attempt to control their effects. However, they must realize that their homeland is part of a constantly-changing world, and that change will itself alter a changed situation. The elucidation of the processes of change by future Pacific island geographers, especially by highlighting the kind of life islanders want for themselves, should lead to a better understanding of the region and yield useful data for planning. I doubt if all this will lead to the production of a new sort of Pacific island geography altogether. But it should enrich our knowledge and understanding of our homelands.

References

Allan, W. (1949): 'Studies in African land usage in Northern Rhodesia', *Rhodes-Livingstone Papers* **15** (Lusaka).
(1965): *The African husbandman* (Edinburgh).
Allen M. R. (1964): *The Nduindui: a study in the social structure of a New Hebridean community* (Ph.D. Thesis, Australian National University, Canberra; unpublished).
(1968): 'The establishment of Christianity and cash-cropping in a New Hebridean community', *Journal of Pacific History* **3**, 25–46.
Ames, O. (1939): *Economic annuals and human culture* (Cambridge, Mass.).
Arndt, H. R., Shand, R. and Fisk, E. K. (1969): 'An answer to Crocombe', *New Guinea and Australia* **4**, 54–71.
Aufenanger, H. (1966): 'Friendship in the highlands of New Guinea', *Anthropos* **61**, 305–6.
Bailey, K. V. (1963): 'Nutrition in New Guinea', *Food and Nutrition Notes and Reviews* **20**, 3–11.
Bailey, N. T. J. (1959): *Statistical methods in biology* (London).
Baker, J. R. (1928): 'Notes on New Hebridean customs with special reference to the intersex pig', *Man* **81**, 113–18.
Ball, D. (1969): *Vila and Santo: development plans, 1970–1990* (Vila; unpublished).
Barnes, C. E. (1968a): 'An Australian policy for New Guinea', *Australian External Territories* **8**, 9–15.
(1968b): 'Development of Papua and New Guinea', *Australian External Territories* **8**, 20–21.
Barrau, J. (1956): 'L'agriculture vivrière indigène aux Nouvelles Hébrides', *Journal de la Société des Océanistes* **12**, 181–215.
Bedford, R. D. (1971): *Mobility in transition: an analysis of population movement in the New Hebrides* (Ph.D. Thesis, Australian National University, Canberra; unpublished).
Bennett, J. M. (1957): 'Vila and Santo: New Hebridean towns', *Geographical Studies* **4**, 116–28.
Bernstein, H. (1971): 'Modernization theory and the sociological study of development', *Journal of Development Studies* **7**, 141–60.
Berry, B. J. L. (1965): 'Identification of declining regions: an empirical study of

the dimensions of rural poverty', in R. S. Thoman and W. D. Wood, eds., *Areas of economic stress in Canada* (Kingston), 22–66.

Berry, B. J. L. and Marble, D. F. (1968): *Spatial analysis: a reader in statistical geography* (Englewood Cliffs, N.J.).

Borger, R. and Cioffi, F., eds. (1970): *Explanation in the behavioural sciences* (Cambridge).

Boserup, E. (1965): *The conditions of agricultural growth: the economics of agrarian change under population pressure* (London).

Boulding, K. (1966): 'Economics and ecology', in F. F. Darling and J. P. Milton, eds., *Future environments of North America* (New York), 225–34.

— (1967): 'The prospects of economic abundance', in J. D. Roslansky, ed., *The control of environment* (Amsterdam), 41–57.

Brookfield, H. C. (1960): 'Population distribution and labour migration in New Guinea', *Australian Geographer* **7**, 233–42.

— (1962): 'Local study and comparative method: an example from central New Guinea', *Annals of the Association of American Geographers* **52**, 242–54.

— (1964): 'The ecology of highland settlement: some suggestions', *American Anthropologist* **66**, 20–38.

— (1968a): 'New directions in the study of agricultural systems in tropical areas', in E. T. Drake, ed., *Evolution and environment* (New Haven), 413–39.

— (1968b): 'The money that grows on trees: the consequences of an innovation within a man-environment system', *Australian Geographical Studies* **6**, 97–119.

— (1969): 'The environment as perceived', *Progress in Geography* **1**, 52–80.

— (1970): *Dualism and the geography of developing countries* (Presidential address to section 21, A.N.Z.A.A.S. (Port Moresby; unpublished).

— (1973): 'On one geography and a third world', *Transactions of the Institute of British Geographers* **58**, 1–20.

Brookfield, H. C. and Brown, P. (1963): *Struggle for land: agriculture and group territories among the Chimbu of the New Guinea Highlands* (Melbourne).

— (1969): *The people of Vila* (Canberra).

Brookfield, H. C. with Hart, D. (1971): *Melanesia: a geographical interpretation of an island world* (London).

Brown, P. and Brookfield, H. C. (1967): 'Chimbu settlement and residence: a study of patterns, trends and idiosyncracy', *Pacific Viewpoint* **8**, 119–51.

Burnet, F. M. (1969): 'Life's complexities: misgivings about models', *Australasian Annals of Medicine* **18**, 363–7.

Buxton, P. A. (1926): 'The depopulation of the New Hebrides and other parts of Melanesia', *Transactions of the Royal Society of Tropical Medicine and Hygiene* **19**, 419–58.

Cantril, H. (1965): *The pattern of human concerns* (New Brunswick, N.J.).

Carniero, R. (1960): 'Slash and burn agriculture', in *5th International Congress of Anthropological and Ethnological Sciences* (Philadelphia).

Carter, L. J. (1969): 'Development in the poor nations: how to avoid fouling the nest', *Science* **163**, 1046–48.

Castillo, G. (1969): 'A critical view of a subculture of peasantry', in C. R. Wharton, Jr., ed., *Subsistence agriculture and economic development* (Chicago), 136–42.

Chang, Jen-hu (1968): *Climate and agriculture: an ecological survey* (Chicago).

Chapman, M. (1970): *Population movement in tribal society: the case of Duidui and Pichahila, British Solomon Islands* (Ph.D. Thesis, University of Washington, Seattle; unpublished).

Chayanov, A. V. (1966): *The theory of peasant economy*, ed. B. Thorner, B. Kerblay and R. E. F. Smith (Homewood, Ill.).

Chomsky, N. (1969): *American power and the new mandarins* (Harmondsworth).

Clarke, W. C. (1966): 'From extensive to intensive shifting cultivation: a succession from New Guinea', *Ethnology* 5, 347–59.

(1968): *The Bomagai-Angoiang of New Guinea: the world's most efficient farmers?* (paper read to Association of American Geographers, Washington; unpublished).

(1971): *Place and people: an ecology of a New Guinean community* (Berkeley).

Codrington, R. H. (1891): *The Melanesians, studies of their anthropology and folklore* (Oxford).

Cole, L. (1958): 'The ecosphere', *Scientific American* 198, 83–92.

(1964): 'The impending emergence of ecological thought', *Bio-Science* 14, 30–2.

Commission on Native Population (1896): *Report of the Commission appointed to enquire into the decrease of the native population* (Suva).

Commonwealth of Australia, Territory of New Guinea: *Annual reports* (Canberra).

Connell, J. (1971): 'The geography of development', *Area* 3, 259–65.

Cooper, Matthew (1971): 'Economic Context of Shell Money Production', *Oceania* 41, 266–75.

Corris, P. (1970): 'Pacific Island labour migrants in Queensland', *Journal of Pacific History* 5, 43–64.

Coser, L. A. (1968): 'Violence and the social structure', in S. Endleman, ed., *Violence in the streets* (Chicago), 71–84.

Couper, A. D. (1967): *The Island trade: an analysis of the environment and operation of seaborne trade among three island groups in the Pacific* (Ph.D. Thesis, Australian National University, Canberra; unpublished).

(1968): 'Indigenous trading in Fiji and Tonga: a study of changing patterns', *New Zealand Geographer* 24, 50–60.

Crocombe, R. G. (1968): 'That five year plan', *New Guinea and Australia* 3, 57–70.

(1969): 'Crocombe to his critics', *New Guinea and Australia* 4, 49–58.

Crowe, B. L. (1969): 'The tragedy of the commons revisited', *Science* 166, 1103–7.

Cumberland, K. B. and Fox, J. (1961): *Western Samoa: Land and Livelihood in tropical Polynesia* (Christchurch, N.Z.).

Dalton, G. (1967): 'The development of subsistence and peasant economies in Africa', in G. Dalton, ed., *Tribal and peasant economies: readings in economic anthropology* (New York), 155–68.

Darling, F. F. (1970): *Wilderness and plenty* (London).

Darlington, C. D. (1969): *The evolution of man and society* (London).

Davies, O. L., ed. (1956): *The design and analysis of industrial experiments* (Edinburgh).

Deacon, A. B. (1934): *Malekula: a vanishing people in the New Hebrides* (London).

Department of External Territories (Australia) (1968): 'Papua and New Guinea development programme', *Australian External Territories* 8, 37–8.

Derrick, R. A. (1950): *A history of Fiji* (Suva).

Diamond, S. (1964): 'Introduction: the uses of the primitive', in S. Diamond, ed., *Primitive views of the world* (New York), 5–29.

315

Dix, R. (1967): *Colombia: the political dimensions of change* (New Haven).

Djilas, M. (1969): *The unperfect society: beyond the new class*, trans. D. Cooke (New York).

Doumenge, F. (1966a): *L'Homme dans le Pacifique Sud; étude géographique* (Paris).

(1966b): *The social and economic effects of tuna fishing in the South Pacific* (Nouméa).

Dubis, R. (1970): 'The biology of civilisation, with emphasis on perinatal influences', in S. V. Boyden, ed., *The impact of civilisation on the biology of man* (Canberra), 219–29.

Elkan, W. (1964): 'Some social policy implications of industrial development in East Africa', *International Social Science Journal* **16**, 390–9.

(1967): 'Circular migration and the growth of tourism in East Africa', *International Labour Review* **96**, 581–9.

Epstein, S. (1969): 'The plan and its assumptions', *New Guinea and Australia* **4**, 59–63.

Fabre, J. and Kissane, M. F. (1971): *Report on mission to Nouméa, to the British and French Commissioners of the New Hebrides* (Vila; unpublished).

Fairbairn, I. J. (1969): 'Namasu: New Guinea's largest indigenous-owned company', *New Guinea Research Bulletin* **28**, 1–90.

Farmer, B. H. (1954): 'Problems of land use in the dry zone of Ceylon', *Geographical Journal* **120**, 21–31.

Fenner, F. (1969): 'Brahma, Shiva and Vishnu: three faces of science', *Australasian Annals of Medicine* **18**, 351–60.

Fiefia, F. N. (1968): *Report on the results of the 1966 census* (Nuku'alofa).

Finney, B. R. (1965): 'Economic change and dietary consequences among the Tahitians', *Micronesica* **2**, 1–14.

(1967): 'Money work, fast money and prize money: aspects of Tahitian labour commitment', *Human Organization* **26**, 195–9.

(1969): 'New Guinean entrepreneurs', *New Guinea Research Bulletin* **27**, 1–83.

(1970): ' "Partnership" in developing the New Guinea highlands, 1948–1968', *Journal of Pacific History* **5**, 117–34.

Fisk, E. K. (1962): 'Planning in a primitive economy', *Economic Record* **38**, 462–78.

(1962): 'The economy of Papua-New Guinea', in D. G. Bettison, ed., *The independence of Papua-New Guinea: what are the prerequisites?* (Sydney), 25–43.

(1966): 'The economic structure', in E. K. Fisk, ed., *New Guinea on the threshold: aspects of social, political and economic development* (London), 23–43.

(1971): 'The significance of non-monetary economic activity for development planning', *Journal of Development Planning*.

Fitzpatrick, E. A. (1965): 'Climate of the Wabag-Tari area', in *General report on lands of the Wabag-Tari area, Territory of Papua and New Guinea, 1960–61* (Melbourne), 56–69.

Foote, D. C. (1967): *The East Coast of Baffin Island, N.W.T. An area economic survey* (Ottawa).

Foote, D. C. and Greer-Wootten, B. L. (1966): *Man–environment interactions in an Eskimo hunting system* (paper prepared for 'Man–animal linked cultural subsystems' symposium at 133rd annual meeting of American Association for Advancement of Science; unpublished).

1968, 'An approach to systems analysis in cultural geography', *Professional Geographer* **20**, 86–91.

Fosberg, F. R. (1958): 'The preservation of man's environment', in *Proceedings of the Ninth Pacific Science Congress* (Bangkok), 159–61.

(1965a): 'The entropy concept in ecology', in *Symposium on ecological research in humid tropics vegetation* (Djakarta), 157–63.

ed. (1965b): *Man's place in the island ecosystem: a symposium* (Honolulu).

France, P. (1968): 'The founding of an orthodoxy; Sir Arthur Gordon and the doctrine of the Fijian way of life', *Journal of the Polynesian Society* **77**, 6–32.

Frank, A. G. (1967): *Capitalism and underdevelopment in Latin America: historical studies of Chile and Brazil* (New York).

Frazer, R. M. (1961): *Land use and population in Ra Province, Fiji* (Ph.D. Thesis, Australian National University, Canberra; unpublished).

(1964): 'Changing Fijian agriculture', *Australian Geographer* **9**, 148–55.

(1968a): 'A social and economic history of Ra Province', *Transactions and Proceedings of the Fiji Society* **9**, 93–112.

(1968b): *A Fiji-Indian rural community* (Wellington).

(1969): *An analysis of interprovincial migration of Fijians using a technique of age-cohort analysis* (paper presented to the Association of Pacific Coast Geographers, Northridge, California; unpublished).

Friedmann, J. (1966): *Regional development policy: a case study of Venezuela* (Cambridge, Mass.).

Galbraith, J. K. (1965): *Economic development* (Cambridge, Mass.).

Gauger, R. (1967): 'The urban zone of Santo on the island of Espiritu Santo', *South Pacific Commission Technical Paper* **152**, 34–7.

Geertz, C. (1963): *Agricultural involution: the process of ecological change in Indonesia* (Berkeley).

Gleave, M. B. and White, H. P. (1969): 'Population density and agricultural systems in West Africa', in M. F. Thomas and G. W. Whittington, eds., *Environment and land use in Africa* (London), 273–300.

Gordon Cumming, C. F. (1885): *At home in Fiji* (Edinburgh).

Gourou, P. (1969): *Les Pays Tropicaux: principes d'une géographie humaine et économique* (Paris, 5th edition).

Griffin, K. (1969): *Underdevelopment in Spanish America: an interpretation* (London).

Guelke, L. (1971): 'Problems of scientific explanation in geography', *Canadian Geographer* **15**, 38–53.

Guiart, J. (1951): 'Société rituelle et mythes du Nord Ambrym (Nouvelles Hébrides)', *Journal de la Société des Océanistes* **7**, 5–103.

(1961): 'The social anthropology of Aniwa, southern New Hebrides', *Oceania* **32**, 34–53.

Gunson, N. (1969): 'Pomare II of Tahiti and Polynesian imperialism', *Journal of Pacific History* **4**, 65–82.

Haddon, A. C. (1937): *The canoes of Melanesia, Queensland and New Guinea*, Vol. 2 of A. C. Haddon and J. Hornell, *Canoes of Oceania* (Honolulu).

Haggett, P. (1964): 'Regional and local components in the distribution of forested areas in southeast Brazil: a multivariate approach', *Geographical Journal* **130**, 365–77.

(1965): *Locational Analysis in Human Geography* (London).

Hall, E. T. (1968): 'Proxemics', *Current Anthropology* **9**, 83–108.

Halpern, J. M. and Brode, J. (1967): 'Peasant society: economic changes and revolutionary transformation', *Bienneial review of anthropology* **5**, 46–139.
Hardin, G. (1968): 'The tragedy of the commons', *Science* **162**, 1,243–8.
Harding, T. G. (1967): *Voyagers of the Vitiaz Strait: a study of a New Guinea trade system* (Seattle).
Harris, M. (1968): *The rise of anthropological theory* (New York).
Harris, C. (1971): 'Theory and synthesis in historical geography', *Canadian Geographer* **15**, 157–72.
Harrisson, T. H. (1936): 'Living in Espiritu Santo', *Geographical Journal* **88**, 243–61.
(1937): *Savage civilisation* (London).
Harvey, D. (1969) *Explanation in geography* (London).
Hasluck, P. (1958): 'Present tasks and policies', in J. Wilkes, ed., *New Guinea and Australia* (Sydney).
Heider, K. G. (1967): 'Speculative functionalism: archaic elements in New Guinea Dani culture', *Anthropos* **62**, 833–40.
Heilbronner, R. L. (1963): *The great ascent: the struggle for economic development in our time* (New York).
Higgins, B. (1968): *Economic development: problems, principles and policies* (New York).
Hirschman, A. O. (1958): *The strategy of economic development* (New Haven).
H.M.S.O.: *New Hebrides Annual Report* (London).
Hoagland, H. (1968): 'Cybernetics of population control', in J. B. Bresler, ed., *Human ecology: collected readings* (London), 351–9.
Hocart, A. M. (1952): *The Northern States of Fiji* (London).
Howlett, D. (1962): *A decade of change in the Goroka Valley, New Guinea: land use and development in the 1950s* (Ph.D. Thesis, Australian National University, Canberra; unpublished).
(1965): 'The European land settlement scheme at Popondetta', *New Guinea Research Unit Bulletin* **6**, 1–73.
(1967): *A geography of Papua and New Guinea* (Melbourne).
(1969): 'Australia in New Guinea: none so blind', in F. Gale and G. H. Lawton, eds., *Settlement and encounter: geographical studies presented to Sir Grenfell Price* (Melbourne), 185–211.
Hughes, I. M. (1969): *Some aspects of traditional trade in the New Guinea central highlands* (paper to A.N.Z.A.A.S. congress, Adelaide; unpublished).
(1971): *Recent neolithic trade in New Guinea: the ecological basis of traffic in goods among stone-age subsistence farmers* (Ph.D. Thesis, Australian National University, Canberra; unpublished).
Humphreys, C. B. (1962): *The Southern New Hebrides: an ethnological record* (Cambridge).
Hunter, G. (1969): *Modernizing peasant societies: a comparative study in Asia and Africa* (London).
Hunter, J. M. (1966): 'Ascertaining population carrying capacity under traditional systems of agriculture in developing countries: notes on a method employed in Ghana', *Professional Geographer* **18**, 151–4.
Huxley, A. (1964): *Island* (Harmondsworth).
Ilchman, W. F. and Uphoff, N. T. (1969): *The political economy of change* (Berkeley).

Jackson, J. A., ed. (1969): *Migration* (Cambridge).

Kaberry, P. M. (1941): 'The Abelam tribe, Sepik District, New Guinea. A preliminary report', *Oceania* 11, 233–58 and 345–67.

(1942): 'Law and political organization in the Abelam tribe, New Guinea', *Oceania* 12, 79–95; 209–25 and 331–63.

(1965): 'Political organization among the Northern Abelam', *Anthropological Forum* 1, 334–72.

Kellman, M. C. (1969): 'Some environmental components of shifting cultivation in upland Mindanao', *Journal of Tropical Geography* 28, 40–56.

Kelly, R. C. (1968): 'Demographic pressure and descent group structure in the New Guinea highlands', *Oceania* 39, 360–63.

Kemp, W. B. (1971): 'The flow of energy in a hunting society', *Scientific American* 224, 104–15.

Koch, G. (1955): *Sudsee-gestern und heute; der kulterwandel bei den Tonganern und der versuch einer deutung dieser entwicklung* (Braunschweig).

Krieger, H. W. (1943): *Island peoples of the Western Pacific Micronesia and Melanesia* (Washington).

Kroeber, A. L. (1948): *Anthropology* (New York).

Lane, R. B. (1956): 'The heathen communities of southeast Pentecost', *Journal de la Société des Océanistes* 12, 139–80.

Lasaqa, I. Q. (1962): *Dawasamu-Bure, N. E. Viti Levu, Fiji: a geographical analysis of economic problems and potentialities* (M.A. Thesis, Uuiversity of Auckland; unpublished).

(1969): 'Honiara market and the suppliers from Tasimboko West', in H. C. Brookfield, ed., *Pacific Market-places* (Canberra).

(1972): 'Melanesians' Choice: Tadhimboko participation in the Solomon Islands' cash economy', *New Guinea Research Bulletin* 46.

Lawrence, P. (1964): *Road belong cargo* (Melbourne).

Lawrence, P. and Meggitt, M. J. (1965): *Gods, ghosts and men in Melanesia: some religions of Australian New Guinea and the New Hebrides* (Melbourne).

Layard, J. (1936): 'Atchin twenty years', *Geographical Journal* 88, 342–51.

(1942): *Stone men of Malekula: Vao* (London).

Lea, D. A. M. (1964): *Abelam land and sustenance* (Ph.D. Thesis, Australian National University, Canberra; unpublished).

(1965): 'The Abelam: a study of local differentiations', *Pacific Viewpoint* 6, 191–214.

(1969): 'Some non-nutrition functions of food in New Guinea', in F. Gale and G. H. Lawton, eds., *Settlement and encounter: geographical studies presented to Sir Grenfell Price* (Melbourne).

(1972): 'Indigenous horticulture in Melanesia: some recent changes', in R. G. Ward, ed., *Man and landscape in the Pacific islands* (London).

Lea, D. A. M. and Weinand, H. C. (1971): 'Population growth and some consequences in an area of high population density: the Wosera, East Sepik District', *New Guinea Research Unit Bulletin* 42.

Leach, E. (1968): *A runaway world?* (London).

Lee, R. B. (1969): '!Kung bushman subsistence: an input–output analysis', in A. P. Vayda, ed., *Environment and cultural behaviour: ecological studies in cultural anthropology* (New York), 47–79.

Lewis, D. (1964): 'Polynesian navigational methods', *Journal of the Polynesian Society* **73**.

(1971): ' "Expanding" the target in indigenous navigation', *Journal of Pacific History* **6**, 83–95.

Lewis, O. (1959) *Five families: Mexican case studies in the culture of poverty* (New York).

Lewis, W. A. (1955): *The theory of economic growth* (London).

Luten, D. (1967): 'Resource quality and value of the landscape', in S. V. Ciriacy-Wantrup and J. J. Parsons, eds., *Natural resources: quality and quantity* (Berkeley), 19–34.

Mauss, M. (1967): *The gift*, trans. I. Cunnison (London).

McArthur, M. (1967): 'Analysis of the genealogy of a Mae-Enga clan', *Oceania* **37**, 281-5.

McArthur, N. and Yaxley, J. F. (1968): *Condominium of the New Hebrides: a report on the first census of the population 1967* (Sydney).

McClelland, D. C. (1961): *The achieving society* (Princeton, N.J.).

McLoughlin, J. B. (1969): *Urban and regional planning: a systems approach* (London).

Macinko, G. (1965): 'Saturation: a problem evaded in planning land use', *Science* **149**, 516–21.

Malinowski, B. (1922): *Argonauts of the Western Pacific: an account of native enterprise and adventure in the archipelagoes of Melanesia and New Guinea* (London).

Maude, A. M. (1970): 'Shifting cultivation and population growth in Tonga', *Journal of Tropical Geography* **31**, 57–64.

Mead, M. (1956): *New lives for old: cultural transformation, Manus, 1928–1953* (New York).

Meggitt, M. J. (1958): 'The Enga of the New Guinea highlands: some preliminary observations', *Oceania* **28**, 253–330.

(1965): *The lineage system of the Mae-Enga of New Guinea* (Edinburgh).

(in press): 'From tribesmen to peasants: the case of the Mae Enga of New Guinea', in L. R. Hiatt and C. Jayawardena, eds., *Essays in oceanic anthropology* (Sydney).

Mishan, E. J. (1969): *The costs of economic growth* (Harmondsworth).

Mitchell, J. C. (1969): 'Structural plurality, urbanization and labour circulation in Southern Rhodesia', in J. A. Jackson, ed., *Migration* (Cambridge), 156–80.

Mohr, E. C. J. (1944): *The soils of equatorial regions, with special reference to the Netherlands East Indies*, trans. R. L. Pendleton (Ann Arbor).

Morrill, R. L. (1969): 'Geographical aspects of poverty in the United States', *Proceedings of the Association of American Geographers* **1**, 117–21.

Morris, D. (1968): *The naked ape* (London).

Moss, F. J. (1891–3): 'Appendices', *Journal of the House of Representatives of New Zealand*.

Moss, R. P. (1968): 'Land use, vegetation and soil factors in South-West Nigeria: a new approach', *Pacific Viewpoint* **9**, 107–27.

(1969): 'The ecological background to land-use studies in tropical Africa, with special reference to the West', in M. F. Thomas and G. W. Whittington, eds., *Environment and land use in Africa* (London), 193–238.

(1969): 'The appraisal of land resources in tropical Africa: a critique of some concepts', *Pacific Viewpoint* **10**, 18–27.

Moss, R. P. and Morgan, W. P. (1967): 'The concept of the community: some applications in geographical research', *Transactions of the Institute of British Geographers* **4**, 21–31.

Mumford, L. (1967): 'Quality in control of quantity', in S. V. Ciriacy-Wantrup and J. J. Parsons, eds., *Natural resources: quality and quantity* (Berkeley), 7–18.

Myrdal, G. (1957): *Economic theory and underdeveloped regions* (London).

Native Lands Commission (1927): *Final report by chairman on the provinces of Lomaiviti, Ra, and Tailevu (South)*.

Nayacakalou, R. R. (1959): 'Land tenure and social organization in Tonga', *Journal of the Polynesian Society* **68**, 93–114.

(1968): 'Urban Fijians in Suva', in A. Spoehr, ed., *Pacific port towns and cities* (Honolulu).

Nelson, R. R. (1956): 'A theory of low-level equilibrium trap', *American Economic Journal* **46**, 894–908.

Newman, P. L. (1965): *Knowing the Gururumba* (New York).

Nilles, J. (1943–4): 'Natives of the Bismarck Mountains, New Guinea', *Oceania* **14**, 104–23 and **15**, 1–19.

Nurkse, R. (1958): *Problems of capital formation in underdeveloped countries* (Oxford).

Nye, P. H. and Greenland, D. J. (1960): *The soil under shifting cultivation* (Harpenden).

Odum, E. P. (1969): 'The strategy of ecosystem development', *Science* **164**, 262–70.

Paddock, W. C. (1970): 'How green is the green revolution?', *Bio-Science* **20**, 897–902.

Panoff, M. (1970): 'Marcel Mauss's The Gift revisited', *Man* **5**, 60–70.

Pirie, N. W. (1969): *Food resources: conventional and novel* (Harmondsworth).

Porter, P. W. (1969): *Environments and economics in East Africa* (Berkeley).

(1970): 'The concept of environmental potential as exemplified by tropical African research', in W. Zelinsky, L. A. Kozinski and R. M. Prothero, eds., *Geography and a crowding world: a symposium on population pressures upon physical and social resources in the developing lands* (New York).

Prince, H. C. and Smith, D. M. (1971): 'America! America!: views on a pot melting', *Area* **3**, 150–7.

Quain, B. (1948): *Fijian village* (Chicago).

Quantin, P. (1969): *Notice explicative de la carte pédologique de reconnaissance au 1/50,000 d'Epi et des iles Shepherd (Nouvelles Hébrides)* (O.R.S.T.O.M. Nouméa; unpublished).

Rappaport, R. A. (1967): *Pigs for the ancestors: ritual in the ecology of a New Guinea people* (New Haven).

(1971): 'The flow of energy in an agricultural society', *Scientific American* **224**, 116–32.

Reay, M. (1959): *The Kuma* (Melbourne).

(1969): 'But whose estates?', *New Guinea and Australia* **4**, 64–8.

Rivers, W. H. R. (1914): *The history of Melanesian society* Vol. 1 (Cambridge).

Robertson, H. A. (1902): *Erromanga: the martyr isle* (London).

Rogers, A. (1968): *Matrix analysis of inter-regional population growth and distribution* (Berkeley).

Rogers, E. M. (1969a): 'Motivations, values and attitudes of subsistence farmers: toward a subculture of peasantry', in C. R. Wharton Jr., ed., *Subsistence agriculture and economic development* (Chicago), 111–35.

Rogers, G. (1969b): 'Some comments on the 'Report on the results of the 1966 census, Kingdom of Tonga, 1968', *Journal of the Polynesian Society* **78**, 212–22.

Rosenberg, G. (1968): 'High population densities in relation to social behaviour', *Ekistics* **25**, 425–7.

Rosenstein-Rodan, P. N. (1963): 'Problems of industrialization of Eastern and Southeastern Europe', in A. N. Agarwala and S. P. Singh, eds., *The economics of underdevelopment* (Bombay), 245–55.

Rostow, W. W. (1960): *The stages of economic growth: a non-communist manifesto* (London).

Saarinen, T. F. (1966): *Perception of the drought hazard on the great plains* (Chicago).

Sahlins, M. D. (1962): *Moala: culture and environment on a Fijian island* (Ann Arbor).

Salisbury, R. F. (1956): 'Asymmetrical marriage systems', *American Anthropologist* **58**, 639–55.

(1962): *From stone to steel: economic consequences of a technological change in New Guinea* (Melbourne).

(1964): 'Despotism and Australian administration in the New Guinea highlands', *American Anthropologist* **66**, 225–39.

Sanders, W. T. and Price, B. J. (1968): *Mesoamerica: the evolution of a civilization* (New York).

Scarr, D. (1967a): 'Recruits and recruiters: a portrait of the Pacific Islands labour trade', *Journal of Pacific History* **2**, 5–24.

(1967b): *Fragments of Empire: A history of the Western Pacific High Commission 1877–1914* (Canberra).

Schofield, F. D. (1963): *Health and nutritional status of the peoples of the Wosera Report* (Port Moresby; unpublished).

Schultz, A. M. (1967): 'The ecosystem as a conceptual tool in the management of natural resources', in S. V. Ciriacy-Wantrup and J. J. Parsons, eds., *Natural resources: quality and quantity* (Berkeley), 139–61.

(1969): 'A study of an ecosystem: the arctic tundra', in G. M. van Dyne, ed., *The ecosystem concept in natural resources management* (New York, 77–93.

Schwartz, T. (1963): 'Systems of areal integration', *Anthropological Forum* **1**, 56–97.

Seemann, B. C. (1862): *A mission to Viti or Viti: an account of a government mission to the Vitian or Fijian Islands, in the years 1860–1861* (Cambridge).

Service, E. R. (1960): 'The law of evolutionary potential', in M. D. Sahlins and E. R. Service, eds., *Evolution and culture* (Ann Arbor), 93–122.

Shepard, P. (1969): 'Introduction: ecology and man—a viewpoint', in P. Shepard and D. McKinley, eds., *The subversive science: essays towards an ecology of man* (Boston), 1–10.

Shimbel, A. (1953): 'Structural parameters of communications networks', *Bulletin of Mathematical Biophysics* **15**, 129–46.

Shineberg, D. (1966): 'The sandalwood trade in Melanesian economics, 1841–1845', *Journal of Pacific History* **1**, 129–46.

(1967): *They came for sandalwood: a study of the sandalwood trade in the south-west Pacific 1830–1865* (Melbourne).

Short, R. (1870): *The slave trade in the Pacific* (London).

Simpson, G. G. (1953): *The major features of evolution* (New York).

Simpson, G. G. (1969): *Biology and man* (New York).

Slatyer, R. O. (1969): 'Man's use of the environment—the need for ecological guidelines', *Australian Journal of Science* **32**, 146–53.

Smith, C. P. (1916): *Six months in the Pacific* (Auckland).

Smith, D. M. (1968): 'Identifying the "grey" areas—a multivariate approach', *Regional Studies* **2**, 183–93.

Snyder, G. (1968): *Earth household* (New York).

Sorre, M. (1947): *Les fondements biologiques*, Vol. 1 of *Les fondements de la géographie humaine* (Paris).

Spate, O. H. K. (1959): *The Fijian people: economic problems and prospects* (Suva).

(1965): 'Islands and men', in F. R. Fosberg, ed., *Man's place in the island ecosystem: a symposium* (Honolulu).

Spencer, J. (1960): 'The cultural factor in "underdevelopment": the case of Malaya', in N. Ginsburg, ed., *Essays on geography and economic development* (Chicago), 35–48.

Steel, R. W. (1970): 'Problems of population pressure in tropical Africa', *Transactions of the Institute of British Geographers* **49**, 1–14.

Stevenson, R. L. (1908): *In the South Seas* (London).

Stewart, G. A. (1968): *Land evaluation* (Melbourne).

Stoddart, D. R. (1967): 'Organism and ecosystem as geographical models', in R. J. Chorley and P. Haggett, eds., *Models in geography* (London), 511–48.

Street, J. M. (1969): 'An evaluation of the concept of carrying capacity', *Professional Geographer* **21**, 104–7.

Territory of Papua and New Guinea (1968): *Programmes and policies for the economic development of Papua and New Guinea* (Port Moresby).

Thomson, L. M. (1929): *Southern Lau: an ethnography* (Honolulu).

Thurnwald, R. (1914): 'Von mittleren Sepik zur Nordwestkuste von Kaiser Wilhelmsland', *Mitt. Aus. den Deutschen Schutzgebieten* **27**, 81–4.

Tinbergen, J. (1967): *Development planning* (New York).

Townsend, G. W. L. (1968): *District officer* (Sydney).

Tuan, Y. F. (1970): 'Our treatment of the environment in ideal and reality', *American Scientist* **58**, 244–9.

Vansina, J. (1965): *Oral tradition: a study in historical methodology*, trans. H. M. Wright (Chicago).

Vayda, A. P., Leeds, A. and Smith, D. B. (1961): 'The place of pigs in Melanesian subsistence', in *Proceedings of the 1961 annual spring meeting of the American Ethnological Society* (Seattle), 69–77.

Vermeer, D. E. (1970): 'Population pressure and crop rotational changes among the Tiv of Nigeria', *Annals of the Association of American Geographers* **60**, 299–314.

Vickers, G. (1968): 'The concept of stress in relation to the disorganization of human behavior', in W. Buckley, ed., *Modern systems research for the behavioural scientist* (Chicago).

Waddell, E. (1968): *The dynamics of a New Guinea highlands agricultural system* (Ph.D. Thesis, Australian National University, Canberra; unpublished).

(1972a): *The mound builders: agricultural practices, environment and society in the central highlands of New Guinea* (Seattle).

323

(1972b): 'Agricultural evolution in the New Guinea highlands', *Pacific Viewpoint* **13**.

Waddell, E. and Krinks, P. A. (1968): 'The organization of production and distribution among the Orokaiva', *New Guinea Research Bulletin* **24**.

Wagar, J. A. (1970): 'Growth versus the quality of life', *Science* **168**, 1179–84.

Wagner, P. L. (1965): *On explanation: an explanation* (paper presented at a special session on cultural geography at the 61st annual meeting of the Association of American Geographers; unpublished).

Ward, M. (1970): 'Urbanisation—threat or promise?', *New Guinea and Australia* **5**, 57–62.

Ward, R. G. (1965): *Land use and population in Fiji: a geographical study* (London).
(1969): 'Reshaping New Guinea's geography', *Bulletin of the Geographical Society of New South Wales* **1**, 9–15.
(1970): 'Distribution and density of population', in R. G. Ward and D. A. M. Lea, eds., *An atlas of Papua and New Guinea* (London).
(1970): *Internal migration and urbanisation in Papua and New Guinea* (Port Moresby; unpublished).

Washburn, S. L. (1960): 'Tools and human evolution', *Scientific American* **203**, 62–75.

Watson, J. B. (1965): 'From hunting to horticulture in the New Guinea highlands', *Ethnology* **4**, 295–309.

Watson, J. B. (1970): 'Society as organized flow: the Tairora case', *Southwestern Journal of Anthropology* **26**, 107–24.

Watt, K. E. (1968): *Ecology and resource management: a quantitative approach* (New York).

Watters, R. F. (1969): *Koro: economic development and social change in Fiji* (Oxford).
(1970): 'The economic response of South Pacific societies', *Pacific Viewpoint* **11**, 120–44.

Weinberg, A. M. and Hammond, R. P. (1970): 'Limits to the use of energy', *American Scientist* **58**, 412–18.

Wilkes, C. (1845): *Narrative of the United States Exploring Expedition* (London).

Williams, T. (1870): *Fiji and the Fijians* (London).

Wilson, J. S. G. (1966): *Economic survey of the New Hebrides* (London).

Wolf, E. R. (1966): *Peasants* (Englewood Cliffs, N.J.).

Wolpert, J. (1966): 'Migration as an adjustment to environmental stress', *Journal of Social Issues* **22**, 92–102.

Wynne-Edwards, V. C. (1966): 'Regulation in animal societies and populations', in H. Kalmus, ed., *Regulation and control in living systems* (London), 397–421.

Zelinsky, W. (1971): 'The hypothesis of the mobility transition', *Geographical Review* **61**, 219–49.

Index

Europeans: and distribution of goods, 114; as employers, 194–5, 207; contact with, 252, 256, 260, 270, 302–4; in New Hebrides, 191, 197–8

Fabre, J. and Kissane, M. F., 206
Fairbairn, I. J., 267
Farmer, B. H., 170
female migration: *see under* migration
fencing, 218
fibres, 101, 109, 111
Fiji, 10; and future development, 17; fisheries, 242; inter-island transport, 230–32, 234, 237, 245; land use and social change in, 300–07; New Hebridean labour in, 196–7; provincial administration in, 81–2; shipping lines, 245; social groups in, 236; the village in, 13, 75–95 *passim*
Finisterre Ranges, New Guinea, 109
Finney, B. R., 215, 258 n., 262, 266–8
fish and fishing; imported canned, 242; in Tonga, 169; industry, 202, 241–243; inter-island trade in, 230, 239; methods, 239
Fisk, E. J., 266, 268, 289
Fitzpatrick, E. A., 145–6
Five-Year Plans, 269 n., 271
flute-blowing, 155 n.
Foote, D. C. and Greer-Wootten, B. L., 59, 60
Fosberg, F. R., 25, 282
Foraba clan, New Guinea, 110
Formosans, 241
France, P., 80, 85
Frank, A. G., 249
Frazer, Roger, 10, 13, 17, 77, 81, 83, 87, 88, 94
Friedmann, J., 70
frost, 35, 45, 47
Fulaga, 231

galala movement (independent farmers), 76, 88–92, 94
Galbraith, J. K., 293
Ganz River, New Guinea, 123–4
Gawanga district, New Guinea, 66
Gazelle Peninsula, New Guinea, 63, 240
Geertz, C., 57, 165, 181–2, 183, 183 n., 249
Gende clan, 101, 108–10, 115
geography: microgeographic method, 10–12, 21–2; 'new geography', 3; quantitative methods in geography, 3–5; regional geography, 10; social relevance in geography, 22
Gibbs, H. S., 168 n., 176 n.
gifts, exchange, 237, 238; *see also* prestation
Giglmuno, New Guinea, 144

Gilbert Islands, 233, 239
gold, 237
Gordon, Sir Arthur (*later* Lord Stanmore), 81, 85
Gordon Cumming, C. F., 80
Goroka Valley, New Guinea: cash crops, 261–3; economic development in, 256–66; land tenure and use, 254 n., 261, 263, 264, 266, 268–70; population, 258, 268, 271; tribal life and economy, 251–6, 267; wage employment in, 264–6
Gouron, P., 57
government: as development force, 19–20, 70–71, 137, 256–68, 271–2, 297, 308; as entrepreneur, 243–6; as law-making pacifying agency, 94–5, 309
gravity model tests, 5
'green revolution', 292–3
Greenland, D. J.: *see under* Nye, P. H.
Greer-Wootten, B. L: *see under* Foote, D. C.
Griffin, K., 156
Gross National Product (GNP), 249, 305
groundnuts, 261
Guadalcanal, 302
Guelke, 5 n.
Gumine speakers, 108
guns, 197
Gunson, N., 233, 241
Guyana, 6

Ha'afeva, Ha'apai, 172, 180
Ha'akame, Tongatapu, 172
Ha'apai, 165–70, 171 n., 175–80, 184, 238
Ha'ateiho, Tongatapu, 172
Ha'avakatolo, Tongatapu, 172
Hagen, Mt, New Guinea, 115 n.
Haggett, P., 146
Hall, E. T., 74
Halpern, J. M. and Brode, J., 252
Harbour, Lake, Baffin Island, 14 n.
Hardin, Garrett, 291
Harding, T. G., 121, 231
Harris, M., 5 n., 25
Hartshorne, R., 4, 300
Harvey, David, 4, 5, 8, 9 n., 127, 139
Hasluck, P., 257
Hawaii, 187 n., 233
Heilbroner, Robert, 275
Heller, Walter, 281 n.
Hettner, A., 4
Highlands Labour Scheme, 264
Hill, Polly, 8
Hirschmann, A. O., 56, 250
Hoagland, H., 57
Hocart, A. M., 229, 231
Holopeka, Ha'apai, 180
Honiara, 238

THE PACIFIC IN TRANSITION

plantation work, 195, 197, 200
plumes: see birds and bird-plumage
political organization in New Guinea highlands, 39–41
pollution: as result of production, 281–3; in New Guinea, 275, 290
Pomare II of Tahiti, 233–4, 241
population density, 19; in New Guinea, 27–8, 55; among Chimbu, 136–7, 157; among Wosera, 64–7; and agriculture in New Guinea highlands, 37, 45, 49–50; and areas of stress, 58, 62, 137, 178; in Fiji, 80, 83–4; in Tonga, 163–85; in New Hebrides urban areas, 203–4, 226; see also morality rate
Poru Plateau, New Guinea, 100, 104, 108
pottery, 99–101, 230
prestation, 117, 123

Quain, B., 231
Queensland, Australia, 196–7

Ra Province, Fiji, 76–95
Rai Coast, New Guinea, 109
Raiapu Enga clan, 13, 29–53
rain dancing, 276
rainfall, in Tonga, 167
Ramu region, New Guinea, 100–01, 110, 112, 115
Rappaport, R. A., 13, 25–6, 58, 123–5, 135, 155
Reay, M., 134, 286
reef, resources of, 239–40
Rhodesia, 214
rice, 181
Rogers, 170, 191
Roko Tui, 81, 84, 89
Rosenberg, G., 56
Rosenstein-Rodan, P. N., 250
Rostow, W. W., 6, 250
Russell Islands, 238

Saarinen, T. F., 74
sago, 100, 230
Sahlins, M. D., 231
Salisbury, R. F., 123 n., 253
salt, trade in, 99–101, 104–5, 111–13, 115, 118–19, 124–5, 230, 255
Samberigi people, New Guinea, 121
Samoa: fisheries, 242–3; inter-island trade, 232, 234, 245; land use in Western S., 303; New Hebridean labour in, 196–7
sandalwood: in New Hebrides, 195; trade in, 233–4
Santa Isabel, 238
Santiago, Chile, 20
Santo, New Hebrides, 202–4, 309
savings, 266

Scarr, D., 197
Schofield, F., 67 n.
Schultz, A. M., 283, 292
Schwartz, T., 117 n., 122
sea, exploitation of, 239–47
sea-shells: as valuables, 240, 253, 255; in manufacture, 240; trade in, 99, 101, 104–5, 109, 114, 118–19, 122, 125, 240
Seemann, B. C., 80
Service, E. R., 289
setaria palmaefolia, 29–30
settlement patterns, among Chimbu, 129, 144, 146, 150–53; changes in, 81, 83, 87
settlers (European), 256–9, 264
shells: see sea-shells
Shephard, Paul, 280
Shimbel, A., 211–12
Shineberg, D., 198
ships and shipping: associations, 234–5; crewing, 236, 245–6; freight rates, 244; local investment in, 243–7; inter-island trade, 232–4, 238
Short, R., 196
Siane clan, 50
Siassi people, 121, 231
Simbai Valley, New Guinea, 101, 123–4
Simpson, G. G., 277, 292
Singganigl Valley, New Guinea, 115
Slatyer, R. O., 275, 283, 298
Smith, C. P., 234
Smith, D. M., 57
Snyder, Gary, 292
Society Islands, 232
soil, composition in New Guinea, 34, 37, 45–6; erosion, 254, 284; in Tonga, 167–8, 175–6, 182
solevu, 220, 237
Solomon Islands: circular mobility in, 218; fisheries, 242; inter-island trade, 238; land use, 302; natives' view of, 311; shell-money, 240
sorcery: in New Guinea, 108, 110–11; in New Hebrides, 194
Sorre, M., 25
Spate, O. H. K., 80, 86, 89, 92, 191, 303, 307
Spencer, J., 286
steel tools: in New Guinea, 114; in New Hebrides, 195, 197
Stevens, Wallace, 298 n.
Stevenson, Robert Louis, 233
stone tools, 99, 101, 104–5, 109, 111, 113–15, 117–19, 122, 124–5, 232
Stoddart, D. R., 25
Street, J. M., 58, 170, 296
sugarcane, 29, 90, 130, 224
Sumatra, 182
Suva, 86, 236, 237